The History on Film Reader

Historical film studies is a burgeoning field, with a large and ever growing number of publications from across the globe. *The History on Film Reader* distils this mass of work, offering readers an introduction to just under 30 of the most critical and representative writings on the relationship between film and history. Films discussed include: *Gladiator, Forrest Gump, Pan's Labyrinth, Titanic,* and *Life is Beautiful.*

Thematically structured, this book offers an overview of the varying ways in which scholars see film as contributing to our understanding of history, from film's relationship with written histories, to each one's particular characteristics and also their role in education, indoctrination, and entertainment. It draws together the contributions of scholars from a variety of fields, such as Pierre Sorlin, Natalie Zemon Davis, Robert Rosenstone, Marcia Landy, Hayden White, Jean Baudrillard, Roland Barthes, Philip Rosen, Roy Rosenzweig, and David Thelen. Together, these writings represent a novel combination of insights from film theory, cultural studies, historiography, the history of cinema, and film promotion and reception.

Including an introduction which describes the field of historical film studies, section introductions which contextualise the chapters and a filmography, this is an essential collection for all those interested in the relationship between history and film.

Marnie Hughes-Warrington is Associate Professor in Modern History at Macquarie University. She is the author of *'How Good an Historian Shall I Be?'* (2003), *History Goes to the Movies* (2007) and *Fifty Key Thinkers on History* (2008), and is the editor of *Palgrave Advances in World Histories* (2005).

Routledge Readers in History

The Decolonization Reader
Edited by James Le Sueur

The Enlightenment: A Sourcebook and Reader
Edited by Olga Gomez, Francesca Greensides and Paul Hyland

The European Women's History Reader
Edited by Christine Collette and Fiona Montgomery

The Fascism Reader
Edited by Aristotle A. Kallis

The Feminist History Reader
Edited by Sue Morgan

The Global History Reader
Edited by Bruce Mazlish and Akira Iriye

The History and Narrative Reader
Edited by Geoffrey Roberts

The History on Film Reader
Edited by Marnie Hughes-Warrington

The Irish Women's History Reader
Edited by Alan Hayes and Diane Urquhart

The Modern Historiography Reader
Edited by Adam Budd

The Nature of History Reader
Edited by Keith Jenkins and Alun Munslow

The Oral History Reader
Edited by Robert Perks and Alistair Thomson

The Postmodern History Reader
Edited by Keith Jenkins

The Postmodernism Reader: Foundational Texts
Edited by Michael Drolet

Renaissance Thought: A Reader
Edited by Robert Black

The Slavery Reader
Edited by Gad Heuman and James Walvin

The Terrorism Reader
Edited by David J. Whittaker

The Victorian Studies Reader
Edited by Kelly Boyd and Rohan McWilliam

The Witchcraft Reader
Edited by Darren Oldridge

The World War Two Reader
Edited by Gordon Martel

The History on Film Reader

Edited by

Marnie Hughes-Warrington

Routledge
Taylor & Francis Group
LONDON AND NEW YORK

First published 2009 by Routledge
2 Park Square, Milton Park, Abingdon, Oxon OX14 4RN

Simultaneously published in the USA and Canada
by Routledge
270 Madison Ave, New York NY 10016

Routledge is an imprint of the Taylor & Francis Group, an informa business

Typeset in Perpetua and Bell Gothic by
Florence Production Ltd, Stoodleigh, Devon
Printed and bound in Great Britain by
TJ International Ltd, Padstow, Cornwall

British Library Cataloguing in Publication Data
A catalogue record for this book is available from the British Library

Library of Congress Cataloging in Publication Data
History on film reader/Marnie Hughes-Warrington, [editor].
p. cm. – (Routledge readers in history)
Includes index.
1. Motion pictures and history. 2. Historical films – History and criticism. 3. History in motion pictures. I. Hughes-Warrington, Marnie.
PN1995.2.H57 2009
791.43′658 – dc22 2008047364

ISBN10: 0–415–46220–7 (hbk)
ISBN10: 0–415–46219–3 (pbk)

ISBN13: 978–0–415–46220–4 (hbk)
ISBN13: 978–0–415–46219–8 (pbk)

Contents

Acknowledgements

I WOULD LIKE TO THANK Victoria Peters, Eve Setch and Elizabeth Clifford at Routledge for their support throughout this project. I am also grateful to Matthew Bailey for scanning and performing OCR work on a number of the readings, and to Julene Knox for seeking permissions.

I would also like to acknowledge the ongoing support of Macquarie University, particularly the document supply staff in the library, the many students who have engaged with these readings and others in HIST243/366: History on Film since 2000, colleagues in the Centre for Media History and the Head of Modern History, Mary Spongberg. Finally, thanks, as always, to Bruce and Alice and to the Hughes and Warrington families.

I gratefully acknowledge permissions provided by the following copyright holders and authors.

Pierre Sorlin, excerpts from *The Film in History*, Oxford: Blackwell, 1980, pp. 19–22. Reproduced by permission of Wiley-Blackwell Publishing and the author.

Natalie Zemon Davis, 'Any Resemblance to Persons Living or Dead', *Yale Review*, 1987, vol. 76(4), pp. 452–82. Reproduced by permission of Wiley-Blackwell Publishing and the author.

Robert A. Rosenstone, 'History in Images/History in Words' reprinted by permission of the author and publisher from *Visions of the Past: The Challenge of Film to our Idea of History* by Robert A. Rosenstone, pp. 19–44, Cambridge, MA: Harvard University Press, Copyright © 1995 by the President and Fellows of Harvard College. First appeared in *American Historical Review*, vol. 93(5), pp. 1173–85.

Marcia Landy (ed.), *The Historical Film: History and Memory in Media.* Copyright © 2001 by Rutgers, The State University. Reprinted by permission of Rutgers University Press.

Hayden White, 'Historiography and Historiophoty', *American Historical Review,* 1988, vol. 93(5), pp. 1193–9. Reproduced by kind permission of the author.

Jean-Louis Comolli, 'Historical Fiction: A Body Too Much?', trans. B. Brewster, *Screen,* 1978, vol. 19(2), pp. 41–53. © 1978, Society for Education in Film and Television, London. Reproduced by kind permission of the author and Oxford University Press.

Mary Ann Doane, 'The Representability of Time' reprinted by permission of the publisher from *The Emergence of Cinematic Time: Modernity, Contingency, the Archive* by Mary Ann Doane, pp. 1–32, Cambridge, MA: Harvard University Press, Copyright © 2002 by the President and Fellows of Harvard College.

Maureen Turim, Introduction from *Flashbacks in Film: Memory and History,* New York: Routledge, 1989, reprinted by kind permission of the author.

Gilles Deleuze, *Cinema 2: The Time-Image,* trans. H. Tomlinson and R. Galeta, London: Athlone, 1989/University of Minnesota Press, 1991, pp. 270–9. © 1985, first published in France as *Cinema 2: L'Image-Temp, Les Editions de Minuit.* Reproduced by permission of the publishers.

Sander L. Gilman, 'Is Life Beautiful? Can the Shoah be Funny? Some Thoughts on Recent and Older Films', *Critical Inquiry,* 2000, vol. 26(2), pp. 279–308. Copyright © 2002, Wenner-Gren Foundation for Anthropological Research. Reproduced by kind permission of The University of Chicago Press.

Lawrence Baron, 'Serious Humor: Laughter as Lamentation' from *Projecting the Holocaust into the Present,* New York: Rowman and Littlefield Publishers, Inc., 2005. Reprinted by permission of the publisher.

Robert Burgoyne, 'Prosthetic Memory/Traumatic Memory: *Forrest Gump* (1994)', *Screening the Past,* 1999, no. 6. Reproduced by kind permission of the journal and author.

D. Desser and G. Studlar, 'Never Having to Say You're Sorry: Rambo's Rewriting of the Vietnam War', *Film Quarterly,* 1988, vol. 42(1), pp. 9–16. Copyright 1988 by University of California Press Journals. Reproduced with permission of University of California Press – Journals in the format Textbook via Copyright Clearance Center.

Marilyn B. Young, 'In the Combat Zone', *Radical History Review,* vol. 85, pp. 253–64. Copyright, 2003, MARHO: The Radical Historian Organization, Inc. All rights reserved. Used by permission of the publisher, Duke University Press.

Susan Aronstein, 'Revisiting the Round Table: Arthur's American Dream', in *Arthurian Knights: Cinema and the Politics of Nostalgia,* Basingstoke: Palgrave Macmillan, 2005, pp. 191–213, 245–6. Reproduced by kind permission of the author and publisher.

Monica Silveira Cyrino, 'Gladiator (2000)', in *Big Screen Rome,* Oxford: Blackwell, 2005, pp. 238–56. Reproduced by permission of Wiley-Blackwell Publishing and the author.

Jean Baudrillard, *History: A Retro Scenario,* in M. Poster (ed.), *Simulacra and Simulations,* Stanford: Stanford University Press, 1998, pp. 43–8.

Copyright © 1983 by Semiotext(e). Used by permission of the publisher: www.semiotexte.com.

Philip Rosen, 'Detail and Historicity in Mainstream Cinema: Reality and Indexicality from Bazin to Barthes', in *Change Mummified: Cinema, Historicity, Theory*, Minneapolis: University of Minnesota Press, 2001, pp. 166–99. © 2001, by the Regents of the University of Minnesota. Reproduced by permission of the publisher.

Roland Barthes, *The Romans in Films*, from *Mythologies* by Roland Barthes, published by Jonathan Cape. Reprinted by permission of The Random House Group Ltd.

Michelle Pierson, 'A Production Designer's Cinema: Historical Authenticity in Popular Films Set in the Past', in G. King (ed.), *Spectacle and the Real*, Bristol: Intellect, 2005, pp. 145–55. Reproduced by kind permission of the publisher.

Linda Williams, 'Mirrors without Memories: Truth, History, and the New Documentary', in B. Henderson and A. Martin with L. Amazonas (eds), *Film Quarterly: Forty Years, a Selection*. Copyright 1999 by University of California Press – Books. Reproduced with permission of the author and University California Press – Books in the format Textbook via Copyright Clearance Center.

H. A. Giroux, 'Memory and Pedagogy in the "Wonderful World of Disney": Beyond the Politics of Innocence', in E. Bell, L. Haas and L. Sells (eds), *From Mouse to Mermaid: The Politics of Film, Gender and Culture*, Bloomington, IN: University of Indiana Press, 1995, pp. 43–61. Reproduced by kind permission of the publisher.

Roy Rosenzweig and David Thelen, *The Presence of the Past: Popular Uses of History in American Life*, New York: Columbia University Press, 1998, Introduction. Reproduced by permission of the publisher.

Linda Hutcheon, 'Irony, Nostalgia, and the Postmodern', from www.library.utoronto.ca/utel/criticism/hutchinp.html. Reproduced by kind permission of the author.

Charles Eckert, 'The Carole Lombard in Macy's Window', in J. Gaines and C. Herzog (eds), *Fabrications: Costume and the Female Body*, London: Routledge, 1990. Originally from *Quarterly Review of Film Studies* now *Quarterly Review of Film and Video* (Taylor & Francis Ltd, www.informaworld.com, reprinted by permission of the publisher).

Jeff Smith, 'Selling My Heart: Music and Cross-Promotion in Titanic', from Kevin Sandler and Gaylyn Studlar (eds), *Titanic: Anatomy of a Blockbuster*. Copyright © 1999 by Rutgers, The State University. Reprinted by permission of Rutgers University Press.

Richard Maltby, 'On the Prospect of Writing Cinema History from Below', *Tijdschrift voor Mediagescheidenis*, 2006, vol. 9(2), pp. 74–96. Reproduced by kind permission of the author.

Introduction

History on film: theory, production, reception

MARNIE HUGHES-WARRINGTON

IN FEBRUARY 2006, Robert Schneider announced a temporary suspension of film reviews in the *American Historical Review.* The decision, he explained, reflected widening dissatisfaction with how the journal had engaged with an 'important and influential medium'.[1] Three months later he elaborated further, explaining that it was difficult for scholars – many of whom lacked film studies training – to engage with works that 'do not always contribute to an analytical, sophisticated understanding of history'.[2] The American Historical Association's struggle to accommodate film in scholarly discussions is not unusual. As Dana Polan has noted, film studies scholars have long been torn between the imperatives of recognising film as a distinctive form of art and questioning its ability to inform, educate and even empower viewers.[3]

Ours is a world in which films rank second only to photographs as the means by which people claim to connect with the past (reading 23). For all their contact with films, however, people appear to be sceptical about what they see. Why films are treated with such suspicion is yet to be adequately explained, but preliminary responses suggest that viewers see them as prone to ideological and commercial manipulation.[4] Some scholars who have written on history and film are similarly sceptical, as with Frank Sanello's assessment that:

> Commercial imperatives most often fuel cinematic rewrites of history. Complex economic and social issues are puréed into easily digestible bits of information intended for consumption by Hollywood's most sought-after demographic: the lowest common denominator.[5]

That scepticism is also expressed in the conventional comparison of historical films with written historical scholarship.

It is as if, Robert Rosenstone has argued, written history is the standard by which other forms of history making are to be judged (reading 3).[6] Written histories are assumed to be more ideal, showing through direct citations of evidence and other scholarship, for instance, that they offer a more considered and nuanced account of past phenomena than that on offer through films.[7] For over forty years, a small but growing number of scholars have called the hierarchical arrangement of written histories over filmic ones into question. They have made their case in specialist journals – beginning with *Film and History* in 1971 and followed by the *Historical Journal of Film, Radio and Television* and *Screening the Past* – books on pedagogy such as *Image as Artefact* (edited by John O'Connor in 1990) and *Celluloid Blackboard* (edited by Alan S. Marcus in 2006), works of advice for those who want to undertake productions (Barbara Abrash and Janet Sternberg, *Historians and Filmmakers*, 1983; and William Guynn, *Writing History in Film*, 2006), general theoretical works by writers such as Marc Ferro (*Cinéma et histoire*, translated as *Cinema and History*, [1977] 1988), Pierre Sorlin (*The Film in History*, 1980), Marcia Landy (*Cinematic Uses of the Past*, 1996), Robert Toplin (*Reel History*, 2002), Philip Rosen (*Change Mummified*, 2001) and Robert Rosenstone (*Visions of the Past*, 1995; and *History on Film/Film on History*, 2006), edited collections of film analyses such as those by Robert Rosenstone (*Revisioning History*, 1995), Mark Carnes (*Past Imperfect*, 1995), Marcia Landy (*The Historical Film*, 2001) and analyses of particular kinds of historical films, as with Jon Solomon's survey of films set in the ancient world (*The Ancient World in the Cinema*, 2001), Jeanine Basinger's analysis of combat films (*The World War II Combat Film*, 1986) or George Custen's account of biographical pictures or biopics (*Bio/Pics*, 1992).

Current contributors to the field, along with the editorial teams of *American Historical Review*, *Film and History*, the *Historical Journal of Film, Radio and Television* and *Screening the Past*, continue to insist that the criticisms made about historical films often reflect a lack of understanding.[8] History educators such as Peter Seixas see film as playing a role in the development of young people's historical consciousness, but school and university syllabuses are still heavily focused on the handling of written texts.[9] There also appear to be few examples where historians have played a major role in film production, and even fewer where they have communicated about their experiences in a positive way.[10] Additionally, there is a clear need for more filmmakers to communicate about their experiences in researching, making and designing history, as Errol Morris and Alec Morgan have done for their award-winning documentaries.[11]

Responses to the purported lack of understanding of historical film – as distinct from individual productions – conventionally take the form of theoretical reflections on its nature and purposes. Those reflections, communicated in many different languages, and drawing on different intellectual traditions, stress at least three key points. The first is that film is a distinct form of history. Marc Ferro, for instance, describes film as 'a new form of expression' for history; Richard White sees film as a distinct variety of historical narrative; David Herlihy, O'Connor and Robert Brent Toplin talk of 'history in images' as unlike 'history in words'; and Natalie Zemon Davis holds that when we understand the differences between film and prose, 'we can take film seriously as a source of valuable and even innovative historical vision' (reading 2).[12] That understanding will also entail, Hayden White has advanced, recognising that the study of various visions of the nature and purposes of historical film – historical film theory – is not best served by the term 'historiography', but by a new one: 'historiophoty' (reading 5).

Second, such scholarship not only distinguishes filmic from written histories, but also 'historical films' from other kinds of film. Fredric Jameson, for example, asks us not to confuse the historical film with the 'nostalgia film', arguing that in the latter 'the surface sheen of a period' is transformed into a commodity as 'compensation for the enfeeblement of historicity in our own time'. Historical films, on the other hand, have 'holes' or are 'perforated', leaving us to navigate through gaps and to work at meaning making.[13] In *Visions of the Past,* Rosenstone suggests a distinction along similar lines, separating 'mainstream' or 'standard' films from 'serious', 'experimental' or 'postmodern' historical films on the grounds that the former 'deliver the past in a highly developed, polished form that serves to suppress rather than raise questions', whereas the latter are 'intellectually dense' and use:

> the unique capabilities of the media to create multiple meanings . . . raising questions about the very evidence on which our knowledge of the past depends, creatively interacting with its traces . . . they are forays, explorations, provocations, insights.[14]

Standard films affirm what we already know about an event or person; at best they advance understanding by 'personalising, and emotionalising the past'. He makes it clear, though, that this does not mean the use of the medium at its best: that can only come from opposition to 'mainstream' conventions of realism and narrative that privilege the use of antique furnishings and happy endings over serious engagement with the past (reading 3). In *Revisioning History* and *History on Film/Film on History,* Rosenstone's preference for 'serious historical' films is reasserted, but he also elaborates that 'standard' films are equivalent to 'costume dramas' and 'typical documentaries', which make use of the past 'solely as a setting for romance and adventure' or simply blend archival footage and stills with talking-head interviews. Neither of these qualifies as 'new' historical film, for they are made to entertain and make profits and cannot represent the past with any density or complexity.[15]

Pierre Sorlin (reading 1) and Leger Grindon also suggest a twofold classification of films – historical and costume – and delineate them by suggesting that the makers of costume films are more enamoured by the look of the past than by the social and political issues favoured by the makers of historical films. Historical fiction films may include and foreground the activities of particular historical agents or fictional characters, but there is always some link to wider political concerns.[16] The 'melodramatic' films that Marcia Landy describes (reading 4) also lack a political dimension, but she goes further than Sorlin and Grindon in arguing that they use emotional appeals, the valorisation of individuals and the familiar to help viewers to manage and even avoid the challenges of present-day life. Melodramatic history, she concludes, hinders the process of socialisation because it preserves ideal past worlds instead of creating new ones: that is, it renders viewers socially and politically inactive.[17] Charles Tashiro also connects melodrama with affect, but, unlike Landy, sees it as only holding sway over viewers when the actions and values of those on screen approximate our own, as with the masculinity of Maximus in *Gladiator* (2000).[18]

'Faction' is how Brent Toplin describes the fusion of fictional characters with historical settings in films like *Gladiator*. Faction is not necessarily 'good cinematic history' because the creators of faction tend to focus on the actions of individuals at the expense of major historical events, avoid conflicting perspectives and suggest that people in the past were motivated by values and beliefs like our own. They do so, in Toplin's view, because they believe that they will be held less to account over matters of veracity or accuracy than the makers of 'good' or 'more historically oriented films'.[19] 'Heritage' film, as Andrew Higson labels it, also denotes an absence of political engagement. In heritage, the past is no more than a look or style, or a mass of material artefacts. This offers the viewer escape from the problematic expansion and rearticulation of British identity that was prompted by immigration from past and present parts of the Empire and now the Commonwealth.[20] Where faction is 'other' to history because of its blend with fiction, and heritage because of its evasion of the political, 'period' film is characterised more by happenstance. Period films are not historical films, Brian McFarlane and Stephen Crofts insist, because they just happen to be set in the past: the personal narratives they advance could just as well be set in the present or another time. Here we gain the sense of a wasted opportunity to reconstruct and interpret historical events and even to upset viewer understandings of the present.[21]

Time and again, non-historical films are defined by their lack of attention to affairs of state and international relations. Further, they are characterised by their lack of historiographical complexity, as measured by their presentation of a seamless and linear comedic or romantic narrative that ends on a happy note. They are, as Deleuze would describe them, films of the 'movement image' rather than the 'time image' (reading 9). Historical films, on the contrary, seem to be akin to 'independent' cinema or 'new documentary' (reading 21), which Geoff King sees as operating at a geographical, financial and stylistic distance from mainstream 'blockbuster' cinema.[22] The edited collection *Revisioning History*, for example, features reviews of *Distant Voices, Still Lives* (Britain), *Ghare Baire* (*The Home and the World* [India]), *Eijanaika* (Japan), *Hiroshima mon amour* (France), *Radio Bikini* (USA) and *Hitler, a Film from Germany* (Germany), none of which feature in the higher ranks of international box office receipt charts.

Box office performance and historiographical complexity need not be mutually exclusive. The use of tinting, desaturated colour and the process of 'crushing' colours to intensify contrast, for example, alerts viewers to the constructed comic book status of *300* (2006); and in *Titanic* (1997), 1990s teen idol Leonardo DiCaprio 'punctures' the story of Jack and the 1912 disaster. All historical films, like written histories, are constructions, and none of them are stylistically or temporally seamless. By using the word 'construction', I do not want to suggest that films are entirely fictional, or so idiosyncratic that no comparison is possible. On the contrary, films communicate history in no small part through the use of editing devices such as 'flashback' or 'jump cuts' (readings 7 and 8), the inclusion of objects or actions that act as 'icons' or 'shorthand' designations for a period (readings 18 and 20), like the 'insistent Roman fringe' of Roland Barthes's essay (reading 19), and patterns of action, as with physical comedy conventions in particular Holocaust films (readings 10 and 11). Indeed sometimes conventions are 'quoted' by filmmakers to draw connections with, pay homage to or even undercut the authority of earlier films. Todd Haynes's *Far from Heaven* (2002), for instance, reinterprets 1950s melodramas such as Douglas Sirk's *All that Heaven Allows* (1955) and *Imitation of Life* (1959) and Mel Brooks's otherwise uninspiring *History of the World: Part I* (1981) lampoons the 'insistent Roman fringe', as well as many of the other features we expect to see in 'swords and sandals' films set in the ancient world.

Nor have the makers of 'blockbusters' avoided issues in national and international politics: for example, World War II and the Vietnam War are among the most popular topics in late twentieth-century films. So why are independent films and new documentaries consistently favoured in historical film theory? The answer to this question brings us to the third point emphasised in historical film scholarship, that historical films are distinguished not only by their content, but also by their expected or purported effect on viewers. Is it the case that viewers need happy or hopeful endings to cope with or even atone for a bleak past and present, as the key character in *Atonement* (2007) insists, and that that happiness or hope comes at the price of historical understanding and political engagement? Are viewers lured away from political engagement by the 'better than life' images of films (reading 17) and towards a nostalgia-laden stupor (reading 24)? Are their actions like those of a compulsive gambler who cannot refrain from 'playing the game' (reading 6)?

We are only now beginning to appreciate that historical films are historical not just by virtue of what they represent on-screen (their 'diegetic' worlds), but also because historical agents watch them in different times and places (reading 27). The study of film viewers is labelled variously 'audience history', 'reception history' and 'film culture' research. Film viewer history is difficult to research, because contemporary primary evidence such as memoirs, letters, diaries, fanzines, photographs or film-inspired outfits are not often preserved or lodged in publicly accessible archives. It also has to be acknowledged that few of the people who watch a particular film leave some tangible record of that experience. As Melvyn Stokes summarises:

> The history of the audience remains the most elusive aspect of cinema history, since audiences form only the most temporary of communities, and leave few traces of their presence.[23]

Such a claim, though, has to be weighed against a small but growing number of oral histories that show that some people and groups maintain memories of films and filmgoing over their lives. Many of the elderly subjects interviewed by Annette Kuhn, for example, show how memories of moviegoing might function to secure memories of family, friends and local and global events.[24] These examples are important, for they suggest that one of the principle functions of filmgoing – like producing and looking and home movies and photographs – has been to 'solemnise', 'consecrate' and 'immortalise' the integration of the family or social group.[25] That is, watching a historical film allows viewers the opportunity to place themselves in family and friendship networks, and perhaps also to destabilise those networks. Such findings might help us to begin to understand why photographs and film and television programmes play such a prominent role in sociological studies of where the past is present for people other than professional historians (reading 23).

'Reception' is perhaps not the best description for film-watching activities, for viewers are not simply the receivers or consumers of films, but agents who draw films into their lives and use them to their own ends. Robert Burgoyne (reading 12), echoing Alison Landsberg, prefers to talk of film-viewer activities under the label of 'prosthetic memory', because films allow viewers to take on the experiences represented in films much as amputees wear artificial limbs.[26] Although this suggests a more active role for viewers than the term 'reception', it is nonetheless a problematic analogy because it implies that memories belong to, or are even private to, particular individuals and cannot be shared by other individuals in anything other than an artificial or mediated sense. The idea of memories being private to individuals or even being encoded or decoded by them[27] makes no sense, because if they are unintelligible to others, then they would also be unintelligible to their originators. This is because they would be so idiosyncratic as to be unrepeatable to them. If I recall the image of the spider web on the window of my office, for instance, and then respond to a knock at the door, and then think of the spider web, is it the same memory? Is it not conventional to talk of 'returning' to the same memory, or thinking 'again' of the spider web? Here the meaning of the word 'same' is quite important: it means identity in conceptual meaning, not temporal, numerical and spatial identity. When I recall the spider web, I may be in different times and places, yet I still talk about it as the same memory, not two or more distinct memories. If we do not grant these points, then those who first express a memory are also the wearers of 'prosthetic' memories on subsequent occasions. If we do grant these points, and understand that sharing the 'same memory' means conceptual identity – and not temporal, spatial and numerical identity – then it is possible for different people to share the same memory or thought, or pain. This explains how sharing thoughts through re-enactment is possible, as R. G. Collingwood argues with great force:

> If the objector says that *no* kind of re-enactment is possible, merely because nothing can happen twice, we shall treat his objection with less courtesy: pointing out that he would himself not hesitate to speak of dining twice in the same inn, or bathing twice in the same river, or reading twice out of the same book, or hearing the same symphony twice. Is the binomial theorem as known to him, we should ask, the same theorem that Newton invented, or not? If he says yes, he has admitted all we want. If he says no, we can easily convict him of self-contradiction: for he is assuming that in our mutual discourse we have ideas in common, and this is inconsistent with his thesis.[28]

Common language furnishes us with the criteria by which to judge the identity of memories and thoughts. And common language also provides us with the means to share thoughts and memories.

It is for these reasons that I prefer to think of viewers not as receiving films, or wearing film experiences as prostheses, but as sharing in films or as active participants in film culture as they share in history and are active participants in historical culture. This does not commit all viewers to sharing the same response to a film, as Landsberg notes:

> commodities and commodified images are not capsules of meaning that spectators swallow wholesale but are the grounds on which social meanings are negotiated, contested, and sometimes constructed. Two people watching a film may each develop a prosthetic memory, but their prosthetic memories may not be identical. For each, the memories are inflected by the specificities of his or her other experiences and place in the world.[29]

Landsberg's point is borne out not simply by the activities of movie viewers in purchasing, adapting and creating film objects or by their efforts in generating sequel or parallel plots more amenable to their views of what is 'canon' or historically and socially plausible or desirable (readings 25 and 26).[30] It is also seen in varying interpretations of the same film (readings 10 and 11) and in cases where critics and scholars see the same present-day issues in films with diverse historical settings (readings 13–16).

Historical – rather than hypothetical – examples of film culture highlight the difficulty of drawing general conclusions about the purported effects of films. It is not evident that the producers, promoters or critics of films hold sway over audiences (reading 22). Nor is it clear that audiences control the meaning of films. The relationship between the producers, promoters and viewers of films may be, at turns, cohesive and conflicting. This is an instructive point, for it might lead us to a more nuanced view of historical film theory. If the relationship between the makers, circulators and audiences of films is not fixed, then it is also worth thinking about whether the relationship between written and filmic histories is fixed. While it might have been useful for scholars in the past to emphasise the distinct features of historical films against those of written histories, a continuing focus on differences may lead scholars to miss opportunities to identify common insights into the nature and purposes of histories. Much would be gained, for instance, in thinking about how those who make histories shape time. Are there written equivalents of the editing devices that Mary Ann Doane examines in her account of the shaping of cinematic time, or of Gilles Deleuze's 'movement' and 'time' image? Conversely, do films like Todd Haynes's *I'm Not There* (2007) – which casts seven women and men in the part of Bob Dylan – give us a sense of the 'positioned' or 'decentred' self that is of interest to postmodern historiographers? Further, it is not clear that the boundaries that scholars have constructed to divide historical films from other films can or even should survive scrutiny. To date, for instance, musicals, comedies and animated films have been neglected in historical film studies. The marginalisation of these filmic forms – like the marginalisation of film studies in historiography *per se* – should at least alert us to the need to think about the presuppositions that shape historians' understandings of the nature and purposes of history. Understanding historical film entails understanding what history is and can be, and any difficulties that might be expressed at present about understanding film should be understood as difficulties about understanding history.

The primary aim of this *Reader* is to foster discussion on films as history and on the premises and methods of historical research and communication that currently privilege the written word over the image. It does so by drawing together a sample of readings from a very large and scattered body of print and electronic literature. It differs from other edited collections on historical films in that it is not a collection of reviews or analyses of particular films. Rather, the texts have been selected both because they provide an introduction to the major ideas and issues that have shaped historical film scholarship in the past thirty years, and because they provide an opportunity for readers to make connections with wider historiographical debates. As I have stressed above, thinking about historical films also means thinking about the nature and purposes of history. In order to foster reflection on the connections between historical film scholarship and contemporary historiography, I have arranged the readings in five parts and offered a brief introduction to each.

Part 1 brings together readings on the nature and purposes of historical films. It highlights the interest of historical film scholars – alongside other historiographers – in discussing the virtues of various mediated accounts of past phenomena, the extent to which representations of the past are statements about the present, the varying reasons why histories are made and the ways in which representations might be compared or even judged. Part 2 extends the discussion commenced in Part 1 by exploring the idea that histories offer not only mediated but also 'textualised' accounts of past phenomena. The readings drawn together explore the fictive acts of filmmakers, not only in decisions of casting and costuming, but also in the use of editing conventions and narrative structures. In Part 3, the emphasis of the *Reader* shifts towards an analysis of the purposes and uses of historical films. Four examples are offered of the ways in which historical films are read for evidence of present-day concerns, assumptions and aspirations, and these are connected to an account of the idea of 'prosthetic memory', which was introduced above. Part 4 unpacks the claims that are made about the role of historical films in fostering political disengagement, exploring how the medium is framed as a commodity designed to render viewers as consumers, and asks whether documentary and children's films represent 'high-' and 'low-water' marks in a spectrum of works that encourage viewer empowerment. Finally, in Part 5, the focus of the *Reader* comes to rest upon the promoters and audiences of historical films, questioning blanket conclusions about the latter that present them as either agents of resistance or as passive consumers. It returns to the question 'what are histories, and what are they for?' and offers some advice on historicising research on historical films. As with any Reader, the assembled extracts provide a starting point for further discussion and research.

I believe, however, that the ideas collected in this book will provide a rich resource for anyone interested in the nature and purposes of history.

Further reading

Abrash, B., and Sternberg, J. (eds), *Historians and Filmmakers: Toward Collaboration*, New York: Institute for Research in History, 1983.

Basinger, J., *The World War II Combat Film*, New York: Columbia University Press, 1986.

Cannadine, D. (ed.), *History and the Media*, Basingstoke: Palgrave Macmillan, 2004.

Carnes, M. (ed.), *Past Imperfect: History According to the Movies*, New York: Henry Holt, 1995.

Cartmell, D., Hunter, I. Q., and Whelehan, I. (eds), *Retrovisions: Reinventing the Past in Fiction and Film*, London: Pluto, 2001.

Cook, P., *Screening the Past: Memory and Nostalgia in Cinema*, London: Routledge, 2005.

Custen, G., *Bio/Pics: How Hollywood Constructed Public History*, New Brunswick, NJ: Rutgers University Press, 1992.

Davis, N. Z., *Slaves on Screen: Film and Historical Vision*, Cambridge, MA: Harvard University Press, 2000.

Ferro, M., *Cinema and History*, trans. N. Greene, Detroit, MI: Wayne State University Press, 1988.

Film and History, vol. 1, 1971–.

Grindon, L., *Shadows on the Past: Studies in the Historical Fiction Film*, Philadelphia, PA: Temple University Press, 1994.

Guerin, F., and Hallas, R. (eds), *The Image and the Witness: Trauma, Memory and Visual Culture*, London: Wallflower, 2007.

Guynn, W., *Writing History in Film*, New York: Routledge, 2006.

Hamilton, P., and Ashton, P., 'At Home with the Past: Initial Findings from the Survey', *Australian Cultural History*, 2003, no. 23, pp. 5–30.

Historical Journal of Film, Radio and Television, vol. 1, 1980–.

Hughes-Warrington, M., *History Goes to the Movies: Studying History on Film*, London: Routledge, 2007.

Landsberg, A., *Prosthetic Memory: The Transformation of American Remembrance in the Age of Mass Culture*, New York: Columbia University Press, 2004.

Landy, M. (ed.), *The Historical Film: History and Memory in Media*, New Brunswick, NJ: Rutgers University Press, 2001.

Landy, M., *Cinematic Uses of the Past*, Minneapolis, MN: University of Minnesota Press, 1996.

Marcus, A. S. (ed.), *Celluloid Blackboard: Teaching History with Film*, Charlotte, NC: Information Age, 2006.

Morris-Susuki, T., *The Past within Us: Media, Memory, History*, London: Verso, 2005.

O'Connor, J. E. (ed.), *Image as Artefact: The Historical Analysis of Film and Television*, Malabar, FL: Krieger, 1990.

Rosen, P., *Change Mummified: Cinema, Historicity, Theory*, Minneapolis, MN: University of Minnesota Press, 2001.

Rosenstone, R., *History on Film/Film on History*, London: Longman, 2006.

Rosenstone, R., *Revisioning History: Film and the Construction of a New Past*, Princeton, NJ: Princeton University Press, 1995.

Rosenstone, R., *Visions of the Past: The Challenge of Film to our Idea of History*, Cambridge, MA: Harvard University Press, 1995.

Sanello, F., *Reel v. Real: How Hollywood Turns Fact into Fiction*, Lanham, MD: Taylor Trade, 2003.

Screening the Past, no. 1, 1997, online at: www.latrobe.edu.au/screeningthepast (accessed 15 May 2008).

Solomon, J., *The Ancient World in the Cinema*, New Haven, CT: Yale University Press, 2001.

Tashiro, C. S., *Pretty Pictures: Production Design and the History Film*, Austin, TX: University of Texas Press, 1998.

Taves, B., *The Romance of Adventure: The Genre of Historical Action Movies*, Jackson, MS: University Press of Mississippi, 1993.

Toplin, R. B., *History by Hollywood: The Use and Abuse of the American Past*, Urbana, IL: University of Illinois Press, 1996.

Toplin, R. B., *Reel History: In Defense of Hollywood*, Lawrence, KS: Kansas University Press, 2002.

Warren-Findley, J., 'History in New Worlds: Surveys and Results in the United States and Australia', *Australian Cultural History*, 2003, no. 23, pp. 43–52.

Notes

1 Robert A. Schneider, 'In This Issue', *American Historical Review*, 2006, vol. 111(1), p. xvii.

2 Robert A. Schneider, 'On Film Reviews in the *AHR*', *Perspectives*, May 2006, online at: www.historians.org/perspectives/issues/2006/0605/0605aha2.cfm (accessed 23 April 2008).

3 Dana Polan, *Scenes of Instruction: The Beginnings of the US Study of Film*, Berkeley, CA: University of California Press, 2007, pp. 14, 25.

4 R. Rosenzweig and D. Thelen, *The Presence of the Past: Popular Uses of History in American Life*, New York: Columbia University Press, 1998; and P. Ashton and P. Hamilton, 'At Home with the Past: Background and Initial Findings from the National Survey', *Australian Cultural History*, 2003, no. 23, pp. 5–30. See also J. Warren-Findley, 'History in New Worlds: Surveys and Results in the United States and Australia', *Australian Cultural History*, 2003, no. 23, pp. 43–52.

5 F. Sanello, *Reel v. Real: How Hollywood Turns Fact into Fiction*, Lanham, MD: Taylor Trade, 2003, pp. xi–xii.

6 See also R. Rosenstone, *Visions of the Past*, Cambridge, MA: Harvard University Press, 1995, p. 49.

7 See for example I. C. Jarvie, 'Seeing Through the Movies', *Philosophy of the Social Sciences*, 1978, vol. 8, p. 378; and M. Cousins, 'Why the Film So Rarely Beats a Good Book', *Australian Financial Review*, 28 February 2003, p. R11.

8 S. Schama, 'Television and the Trouble with History', in D. Cannadine, (ed.), *History and the Media*, Basingstoke: Palgrave Macmillan, 2004, p. 24; and 'The Historians Film Committee', *The Historians Film Committee Newsletter* [now *Film and History*], vol. 1(1), 1971, p. 1.

9 P. Seixas, 'Popular Film and Young People's Understanding of the History of Native American–White Relations', in A. S. Marcus (ed.), *Celluloid Blackboard: Teaching History with Film*, Greenwich, CT: Information Age Publishing, 2006, pp. 99–120.

10 B. Gammage, 'Working on Gallipoli', *Australian Film and Television School Conference 2*, North Ryde, Sydney: Australian Film and Television School, 1984, pp. 67–72; J. Jeffrey, '*Amistad* (1997): Steven Spielberg's 'true story''', *Historical Journal of Film, Radio and Television*, 2001, vol. 21(1), p. 4; and N. Z. Davis, *The Return of Martin Guerre*, Cambridge, MA: Harvard University Press, 1983, p. viii.

11 A. Morgan, 'Re-designing the Past Imperfect: The Making of *Hunt Angels*', *Senses of Cinema*, 2006, no. 41, online at: www.sensesofcinema.com/contents/06/41/hunt-angels.html

(accessed 15 May 2008); and T. Ryan and E. Morris, 'Making History: Errol Morris, Robert McNamara and *The Fog of War*', *Senses of Cinema*, 2004, no. 31, online at: www.sensesofcinema.com/contents/06/41/hunt-angels.html (accessed 15 May 2008).

12 M. Ferro, 'Does a Filmic Writing of History Exist?', *Film and History*, 1987, vol. 17(4), p. 82; R. White, 'History, *The Rugrats*, and World Championship Wrestling', *Perspectives*, April 1999, online at: www.historians.org/Perspectives/Issues/1999/9904/index.cfm (accessed 12 October 2007); D. Herlihy, 'Am I a Camera? Other Reflections on Film and History', *American Historical Review*, 1988, vol. 93(5), pp. 1186–92; J. E. O'Connor, 'History in Images/History in Words: Reflections on the Importance of Film and Television Study for an Understanding of the Past', *American Historical Review*, 1988, vol. 93(5), pp. 1200–9; R. B. Toplin, 'The Filmmaker as Historian', *American Historical Review*, 1988, vol. 93(5), pp. 1210–27; and N. Z. Davis, *Slaves on Screen: Film and Historical Vision*, Cambridge, MA: Harvard University Press, 2000, p. 15.

13 F. Jameson, *Signatures of the Visible*, London: Routledge, 1992, pp. 179–80.

14 Rosenstone, *Visions of the Past*, pp. 11, 12, 44.

15 R. Rosenstone, *Revisioning History: Film and the Construction of a New Past*, Princeton, NJ: Princeton University Press, 1995, pp. 3–5; and id., *History on Film/Film on History*, London: Longman, 2006.

16 P. Sorlin, *The Film in History*, Oxford: Blackwell, 1980, pp. 116, 144, 208; and L. Grindon, *Shadows on the Past: Studies in the Historical Fiction Film*, Philadelphia, PA: Temple University Press, 1994, pp. 2, 9, 10, 11, 223.

17 M. Landy, *Cinematic Uses of the Past*, Minneapolis, MN: University of Minnesota Press, 1996, pp. 17–24, 36, 161.

18 C. S. Tashiro, *Pretty Pictures: Production Design and the History Film*, Austin, TX: University of Texas Press, 1998, p. 66.

19 R. B. Toplin, *Reel History: In Defense of Hollywood*, Lawrence, KS: Kansas University Press, 2002, pp. 92, 94, 103, 114, 118, 131.

20 A. Higson, *Waving the Flag: Constructing a National Cinema in Britain*, Oxford: Oxford University Press, 1995, p. 113.

21 Brian McFarlane, *Australian Cinema 1970–1985*, London: Secker and Warburg, 1987; and S. Crofts, 'Shifting Paradigms in the Australian Historical Film', *East–West Film Journal*, 1991, vol. 5(2), p. 6.

22 G. King, *American Independent Cinema*, London: I. B. Tauris, 2005, p. 2.

23 M. Stokes, 'Introduction: Reconstructing American Cinema's Audiences', in *American Movie Audiences: From the Turn of the Century to the Early Sound Era*, London: British Film Institute, 1999, p. 9.

24 A. Kuhn, *An Everyday Magic: Cinema and Cultural Memory*, London: I. B. Tauris, 2002. Published in the USA as *Dreaming of Fred and Ginger: Cinema and Cultural Memory*, New York: New York University Press, 2002.

25 P. Bourdieu, *Photography: A Middle-Brow Art*, trans. S. Whiteside, Cambridge: Polity, 1990, pp. 20, 29, 36, 40. See also G. Westwell, 'The Domestic Vision of *Vietnam Home Movies*', in F. Guerin and R. Hallas (eds), *The Image and the Witness: Trauma, Memory and Visual Culture*, London: Wallflower, 2007, pp. 145–55; and M. Citron, *Home Movies and other Fictions*, Minneapolis, MN: University of Minnesota Press, 1999.

26 A. Landsberg, *Prosthetic Memory: The Transformation of American Remembrance in the Age of Mass Culture*, New York: Columbia University Press, 2004, p. 20.

27 James Berger promotes an encoding/decoding reading of prosthetic memory in 'Which Prosthetic?: Mass Media, Empathy and Progressive Politics', *Rethinking History*, 2007, vol. 11(4), pp. 597–612.

28 R. G. Collingwood, 'Outlines of a Philosophy of History', in W. J. Van Der Dussen (ed.), *The Idea of History*, rev. edn, Oxford: Oxford University Press, 1994, p. 446.

29 Landsberg, *Prosthetic Memory*, p. 21.

30 On the concept of 'canon' in film viewing, see M. Hughes-Warrington, *History Goes to the Movies: Studying History on Film*, London: Routledge, 2007, ch. 8.

PART 1

Introducing historical film

REVIEWS OF INDIVIDUAL FILMS ASIDE, much of the scholarship on historical films focuses on the relationship between film and history and film and the past, and on the relationship between filmic and written histories. Like other historiographers – scholars of histories – historical film scholars offer varied accounts of these relationships, and thus varied definitions of history. Some, for instance, see histories as firmly anchored 'realist' reconstructions of the past, others see them as mediated representations that are shaped by the assumptions, values and aspirations of individuals and groups, and others conclude that they are fictive constructions that reflect only the assumptions, values and aspirations of their creators' presents. As representative of this range of scholarship, I have selected five readings, all of which have been cited repeatedly by historical film scholars.

In an early contribution to the field of historical film studies, Pierre Sorlin argues that rather than comparing films with 'real history', we should recognise their 'documentary value' as records of attitudes at the time of production. Historical films – as distinct from 'the work of the historian' – offer superficial and part fictional accounts of the relationship between facts from the past, but rich indications of a society's 'historical capital', or the dates, individuals and events that are used to foster the integration of a group or its distinction from other groups. Natalie Zemon Davis is also of the opinion that historical films do not measure up to written histories, particularly when it comes to suggesting multiple explanations for past phenomena, indicating their status as representations and acknowledging their sources. This judgement no doubt reflects her experiences in working as a historical consultant to the critically acclaimed film *Le retour de Martin Guerre* (1982), which are documented in the preface to her book *The Return of Martin Guerre*. Nevertheless, she acknowledges that the makers of historical films can achieve 'authenticity' when they move beyond presenting the 'look of the past' in props, costumes, locations and local casts and convey the distinct values, relations and concerns of people from the past. Authenticity may be found, she suggests, in the compressed and stylised account of the trial of Joan of Arc in *La passion de Jeanne d'Arc*, as it might be in Guillermo del Toro's 'fairy-tale' account of the civil ruptures in Spain in 1944 in *Pan's Labyrinth* (2006).

While Davis's use of the word 'authenticity', like Sorlin's use of the phrase 'real history', is suggestive of a 'realist' view of history, she also recognises the skill of some filmmakers in helping viewers to understand that histories are representations. Such a view is even more pronounced in the writings of Marcia Landy and Robert Rosenstone. Marcia Landy agrees with Sorlin that historical films 'are a barometer of the social and cultural life of the last decades of the twentieth century', but she also looks to the writings of Nietzsche, Gramsci and Foucault to distinguish at least two kinds of films. First, there are films which, through the use of emotional representations (affect) and continuity editing, glue inconsistent, illogical and discrete discourses together and render a past that is worthy of unquestioned respect, imitation and preservation. This 'Monumental' form of history is for Landy socially crippling, for it 'knows only how to preserve life, not how to engender it; it always undervalues that which is becoming . . . it hinders any resolve to attempt something new'. 'Critical' historical films, on the other hand, employ discontinuous editing and fragmented narration to draw attention to the uses of history to shore up prevailing and desired 'mythical' notions of the nation-state. Rosenstone also distinguishes two groups along similar lines, but is insistent that only discontinuous and self-reflexive films should be described as 'historical'. 'Mainstream' or 'Hollywood' films involve 'trade-offs' such as the use of 'tidy' endings or affect, which are designed to keep viewers entertained.

Landy and Rosenstone share an interest in comparing the nature and purported social effects of different kinds of films, not in comparing written and filmic histories. This is because – at least in the case of Rosenstone – he is clear that written histories do not provide an unquestioned and unproblematic standard for history making. Indeed films have the potential to show us new notions of history, and thus to think about what history can and should be. On this point, he reflects Hayden White's assertion that visual evidence needs to be read with 'a lexicon, grammar, and syntax' that is 'quite different' from that used for written evidence. Films differ from written histories both in nature and in purpose. Following that point through, White calls for the recognition of the term 'historiophoty' – the study of visual histories – and for the training of historians in the use and analysis of visual materials. What Part 1 documents therefore is the rise of the now prevalent view that the historical film is a distinct form of history that needs to be understood on its own terms.

Reading 1

Pierre Sorlin

THE FILM IN HISTORY

The Film in History: Restaging the Past, Oxford: Blackwell, 1980, pp. 19–22.

WHEN WE WANT TO CHARACTERIZE a film briefly, we try to isolate the features it has in common with other films, so that it can be classified as a type. Most of the types that we are familiar with – westerns, thrillers, comedies, science fiction, horror – developed within the world of the cinema, despite their literary origins, and they no longer exist except as cinematic types. The peculiarity of historical films is that they are defined according to a discipline that is completely outside the cinema; in fact there is no special term to describe them, and when we speak of them we refer both to the cinema and to history. This is a point that should be of interest to historians: it would seem that audiences recognize the existence of a system of knowledge that is already clearly defined – historical knowledge, from which film-makers take their material.

A spectator watching an unfamiliar film can typecast it within minutes. In the case of the historical film, what are the signs by which it can be recognized as such? There must be details, not necessarily many of them, to set the action in a period which the audience unhesitatingly places in the past – not a vague past but a past considered as historical. The cultural heritage of every country and every community includes dates, events and characters known to all members of that community. This common basis is what we might call the group's 'historical capital', and it is enough to select a few details from this for the audience to know that it is watching an historical film and to place it, at least approximately. When the period is less well known, or does not belong to the common heritage, then the film must clearly stress the historical nature of the events.

A well known American film, *Intolerance*, illustrates both these processes. The film consists of four stories, three of them taking place in the past and one in the present, which are shown alternately rather than in chronological sequence. Two episodes, the life of Christ and the religious wars of the sixteenth century, are easily recognizable: they can be identified by the costumes, the attitudes, famous scenes and occasionally portraits. But one of the episodes is set in ancient Babylon, a period virtually unknown to audiences, so the film provides abundant detail to establish the period, informing the audience that a certain object was found during excavations, that a particular custom is described in Greek or Babylonian texts. By compensating for the gaps in the audience's knowledge, it emphasizes the historical nature of what is shown.

What I think is important in both cases is the understanding that is formed, with no difficulty, between the film-makers and the audience: for both, something real and unquestionable exists, something which definitely happened and which is history. The contingent aspect of the historical tradition, with which historians are deeply concerned, is completely ignored by the producers of historical films. It must be said that this type of film is not an historical work: even if it appears to show the truth, it in no way claims to reproduce the past accurately. So I think that when professional historians wonder about the mistakes made in an historical film, they are worrying about a meaningless question. They would do better to concentrate on other problems.

We have noted some of the methods by which a film identifies itself as historical and allows the audience to find its bearings. In this way every historical film is an indicator of a country's basic historical culture, its historical capital. Which characters do not even have to be introduced, which have at least to be named and which need to have some details given about them? What scenes, meetings and events are recognized unhesitatingly? When, and on what points, do explanations have to be given? Behind the common knowledge, we can detect what is much more important, the underlying logic of history. What facts does the film select? How does it develop them? What connections does it show between them? The historical film is a dissertation about history which does not question its subject – here it differs from the work of the historian – but which establishes relationships between facts and offers a more or less superficial view of them. The understanding of historical mechanisms as developed in the cinema is another field for our research.

Historical films are all fictional. By this I mean that even if they are based on records, they have to reconstruct in a purely imaginary way the greater part of what they show. Scenery and costumes similar to those of the period represented can be based on text and pictures, but the actors alone are responsible for the gestures, expressions and intonations. Most historical films (though not all – this does not apply to *October*) combine actual events and completely fictitious individual episodes. It is very seldom that a film does not pass from the general to the particular, and arouse interest by concentrating on personal cases; this is one of the most direct forms of the appeal to identification, an appeal which is in fact not specific to the cinema. Fiction and history react constantly on one another, and it is impossible to study the second if the first is ignored. The same type of analysis can be applied to an historical film as to any feature film.

Natalie Zemon Davis

'ANY RESEMBLANCE TO PERSONS LIVING OR DEAD'

Film and the challenge of authenticity

'Any Resemblance to Persons Living or Dead': Film and the Challenge of Authenticity, *Yale Review*, 1987, vol. 76(4), pp. 461–82. Text and discursive note edited.

A RECENT ESSAY BY NOEL CARROLL argues that 'the power of movies' comes neither from anything intrinsic to the medium of film nor from the audience's confusion of the image and its referent, but from a set of Hollywood-like choices about framing, cutting, and narrative order that lead to 'easily graspable clarity,' to 'the spectator perceiving exactly what she should be perceiving at the precise moment she should be perceiving it.' My sense of movie audiences is that they are a tougher bunch to tame – hooting, laughing, or sober in unexpected parts even of Hollywood movies, arguing with each other about the film as they leave the theatre or turn off the VCR. But insofar as Carroll's argument is valid, it leaves open a field of cinematic choices where complexity and ambiguity, as well as distinctions between image and 'reality,' are possible for the historian or for the filmmaker endowed with a historian's eye.

How, then, is historical authenticity conceived in the common parlance of the film world? Most frequently it is a matter of the 'look' of the past, or rather 'the period look,' 'period props,' and 'period costume.' 'The period look of the film . . . is authentic, with lush colors and a vivid evocation of the clothing, furnishings, art and architecture of the time,' says an otherwise lukewarm *New York Times* review of a film set in mid-nineteenth century Italy. 'Period props are everywhere,' says a favorable review of a film set in Brooklyn in the 1930s, 'and yet they aren't unduly conspicuous. The film's look is simply inviting and believable, the perfect backdrop [for the action].' For the historical eye, the flaw in a period look would not just be the obtrusiveness or staginess of the props and costumes. Worse, an overdone period look is static. It ignores the mixture of goods, clothes, and buildings found in documents from the past: the old and the hand-me-down along with the new, the archaic with the fashionable, the inherited with the purchased, a dynamic mixture expressive of central processes in a society. Nor, for the historical eye, would visual authenticity rest on the evocation of a period independent of contemporary actors and events. Objects, apparel – the world of things – are important for what they meant to the people of the time, for the way things were used to shape space, time, and body, and for the way they make statements about social relations. The farm machines in Roman Polanski's *Tess* lend reality and credibility through their connection with nineteenth-century work rhythms. Even the Dundee marmalade jar placed on the newly dug grave of Tess's baby – a Roland Barthes reality effect par excellence – calls forth the hand of a poor woman improvising a vase.

The use of paintings from the past is another element in the common discourse about film authenticity. From the early days of silent film, paintings have been, of course, a major source for motifs, gestures, clothing, and customs of earlier periods. In 1934, Jacques Feyder's *Kermesse héroïque* promised viewers that 'the characters seem to step out of the frames of famous Flemish paintings to live again for your pleasure.' His re-creations from Brueghel and other painters worked superbly here, for the film itself was a Renaissance genre, a women-on-top carnival from start to finish. The current habit of quotation from painting, however, goes well beyond this: colors, light, and composition drawn from paintings now represent the 'realities' of their time. Certainly this enhances the beauty of the film and allows the audience the pleasure of recognition, but how does quotation contribute to historical 'genuineness'? The painter is a privileged witness, yet his or her vision is but one cultural artifact among many. Authenticity can be obtained only when it is derived from such an understanding. This means using painting to suggest rather than prescribe a period's ways of seeing, and it means playing off one painter's visual construction against another's and against other quite different sources for the way people have perceived their world – even using them to subvert each other. (Similar queries and recommendations could be made about the use of period music.) *The Return of Martin Guerre* was informed not only by the Flemish Brueghel and the seventeenth-century La Tour, but also by popular woodcuts, documentary sources about favorite colors in the sixteenth-century Pyrenees, and the director Daniel Vigne's experienced eye for traditional French agriculture. *Barry Lyndon* was informed not only by Gainsborough and Watteau, but also by the painterly eye of its cinematographer, John Alcott, who was aided by fast lenses that could register dimly lighted gaming tables, and by the concern of the director, Stanley Kubrick, who scoured Europe for regions and atmospheres suitable to Thackeray's novel.

Kubrick's countrysides bring us to another common conception of authenticity: it is believed to emerge from filming in the right historical location rather than in the studio and from casting local inhabitants rather than actors. Listen to Ermanno Olmi, director of the superb *Tree of Wooden Clogs* (a film set in rural Lombardy at the opening of the twentieth century):

> [I prefer] a relationship with reality, not reconstructed in a studio . . . The real tree is continually creative; the artificial tree isn't . . . Thus with the actor. Maybe there exists an extraordinary actor, but really, I have always felt in them a bit of cardboard in respect to the great palpitating authenticity of the real character . . . In a film about peasants I choose the actors from the peasant world . . . [They] bring to the film a weight, really a constitution of truth that, provoked by the situations in which the characters find themselves, creates . . . vibrations so right, so real, and therefore not repeatable.

Olmi concludes that the camera must capture the light on the real tree, the expression on the real peasant, before they slip away.

Historians are surely responsive to such a view. The physical traces of the past in a contemporary building, the faces long particular to a region, the hands familiar with a craft – all seem a good start toward authenticity. Yet the past is also separate and different. Present-day peasants do not necessarily carry with them a memory of that difference, and even on a 'real' location, there must be artful reconstruction. The credibility of the film emerges, then, from the relation of the 'real' actors to knowledge of the retold past. The work of René Allio on *Moi, Pierre Rivière* suggests one way that this knowledge may be acquired. The scenario and dialogue of the film are closely linked to the account of the young Norman, Pierre Rivière, who tells why and how he murdered his mother and sisters in 1835. (His written recital was published by Michel Foucault and his students in 1973.) Allio lived in a Norman village for weeks before he cast Pierre and his family (only the outsiders – the legal and medical personnel – were played by professional actors). Every Friday a large local assembly saw and discussed the rushes and the next week's filming. The issues of marriage and property raised in the film still had resonance for them. Thus 'history' in the film was created out of a three-way exchange among local actors, filmmakers, and an authentic text.

On the other hand, a similar exchange can be set up with professional actors amid the greater artifice of the studio, as we will see in a moment when we examine the films of Carl Dreyer. Everything here depends on the extent to which the participants are informed of and take seriously the strangeness as well as the familiarity of the past. Some have argued that the use of professional actors helps viewers remember that a history film is not literally a depiction of the bygone age, but an interpretation, a representation whose accuracy must always be questioned. There may be something to this, so long as the actor's persona bends itself to the historical persona rather than dominates it. (One thinks, for example, of how effectively Charles Laughton lent himself to the re-creation of Henry VIII and Rembrandt, however limited the other historical merits of Alexander Korda's films on these figures may have been.)

About each of the usual marks of historical authenticity in films – period props, paintings, location, and local people – I have expressed similar reservations. They add to the credibility and genuine historicity of the film only insofar as they are connected to the values and habits of a period and are used with some discernment about their truth status. This means that there is no automatic privileging of the 'realistic' or naturalistic film as the mode for representing the past. The symbolic or evidently constructed mode – Bazin's image film – has its role to play, too, and even a few advantages for showing how past societies work. This also means that there are more ways in which film can establish authenticity than is usually thought – some tried and unrecognized, some yet to be discovered.

To explore these claims, I want now to consider three important films. The first two were directed by Carl Theodor Dreyer, in which the deep qualities of the fifteenth and seventeenth centuries are established through relatively non-naturalistic means through 'simplification,' to use Dreyer's word, through intensity, slow pacing, symbolism. The third was directed by René Allio, in which the socioreligious conflicts and political dynamics of early eighteenth-century France are given effective expression through a more 'naturalistic' mode, abundant detail, and narrative richness.

Dreyer's *La Passion de Jeanne d'Arc* and his *Day of Wrath* figure prominently in film criticism for their cinematic novelty, but are little discussed for the historical achievement which was so much a part of Dreyer's avowed purpose. The silent film on La Pucelle was made in 1927 for the Société Générale des Films, but the Danish filmmaker had already begun to read about Jeanne shortly after her canonization in 1920, eventually getting to a new edition of the 1431 trial records. As he put it:

> The more familiar I became with the historical material, the more anxious I became to attempt to re-create the important periods of the virgin's life in the form of a film. Even beforehand, I was aware that this project made specific demands. Handling the theme on the level of a costume film would probably have permitted a portrayal of the cultural epoch of the fifteenth century, but would have merely resulted in a comparison with other epochs. What counted was getting the spectator absorbed in the past; the means were multifarious and new.
>
> A thorough study of the documents from the rehabilitation process was necessary: I did not study the clothes of the time, and things like that [though in fact, when he was later rebuked by critics for the steel helmets on his soldiers and the horn-rimmed glasses on a monk, he insisted he had fifteenth-century sources in his support]. The year of the event seemed as inessential to me as its distance from the present. I wanted to interpret a hymn to the triumph of the soul over life. What streams out to the possibly moved spectator in strange close-ups is not accidentally chosen. All these pictures express the character of the person they show and the spirit of that time.

The resulting film compresses the several months of the trial and its major turning points into an indeterminate time span, and puts all its force into the mysticism and agony of the village girl who dresses as a man and into the reactions of her learned inquisitors, her mocking jailers, and the people of Rouen who watched her execution. Through close-ups and a few carefully selected images, episodes, and captions, the film gives an arresting and plausible portrait of the religious and political visionary and of the simplicity and craftiness, the terror and certainty that resonate from her answers at the trial. Face, gesture, and movement (the men circle around Jeanne; Jeanne's eye circles around them) suggest the yawning gap between most fifteenth-century doctors of theology and law and this illiterate village woman, the clerics' incomprehension and suspicion when confronted with Jeanne's religious understandings, experience, and claims. The absorption and tears – and finally, the rioting – of the spectators at her death show how popular sainthood is born.

Dreyer's style is spare and concentrated. The way a vision comes is suggested by the cross that forms on the floor of Jeanne's cell, made by the shadow of the window grate, which she reads as a message from God. The straw crown she plaits and with which she is ridiculed by the soldiers makes the analogy with Christ's passion, or to use the fifteenth-century phrase, makes of her end an Imitation of Christ. The fear behind her short-lived abjuration is evoked by a skull turned up by a gravedigger in the churchyard, which Jeanne sees as she is threatened with death unless she signs the document prepared by her inquisitors; the hope she feels as she later awaits the flames is evoked by a mother offering her breast to her infant in the crowd.

Historical authenticity in *La Passion de Jeanne d'Arc* rests not so much on the instruments of judicial torture with which Jeanne is threatened or on the people of Rouen amusing themselves with acrobats and pipers while Jeanne's head is shorn, as on the personalities and relationships that are in most instances informed by fifteenth-century values and sensibilities – what the Danish filmmaker called 'the soul' of a period. The visual embodiment of this 'soul' was shaped by the film's connection with the trial records, whose editor, the learned Pierre Champion, served as Dreyer's historical consultant. *La Passion de Jeanne d'Arc* opens with a hand slowly turning pages of the Bibliothèque Nationale's transcript of the trial. The film has the rhythm and movement of an inquisition. The 'technique [of the trial] is what I tried to transpose to the film,' said Dreyer. 'There were questions, there were answers . . . Each called for a close-up.'

But the visual expression was also shaped by Dreyer's belief in 'simplification' and 'abstraction' and by his critique of the excessive concern in American films for multiple realistic detail. Writing in 1920, he said of them:

> The greatest care was exercised to make each of the film's smallest details believable . . . All of it was so real and so correct and so believable, and yet one did not believe it . . . A devil whispered in one's ear: 'Is it not all technique?' It was soul that was lacking!

In *La Passion de Jeanne d'Arc* settings and costumes are simple. Only certain details are highlighted – and never so as to detract from the faces, free of makeup – 'in order to give the truth.' The huge (and costly) cement castle that was constructed for the outdoor scenes is hardly present in the film; its main role was to make the actors, all professionals, believe in the historicity of their tale. The film was shot in the order of events, not in the order of sets.

And the illusion worked. The actors continued to play their roles after the cameras stopped, and the crew became involved in the trial. As the costume designer recalled:

> [It was] particularly moving the day when [Renée] Falconetti's hair was cropped close to her skull in the wan light of the execution morning and in the total silence on the set. We were as touched as if the mark of

> infamy were truly being applied . . . The electricians, the mechanics held their breaths and their eyes were full of tears. [Falconetti herself cried.] Then the director slowly walked towards the heroine, caught some of her tears in his finger and touched them to his lips.

Dreyer thought that he had found in the boulevard actress whom he directed as Jeanne (it was her only cinematic role) 'the martyr's reincarnation.' The association lasted long after the French Right of Dreyer's day had made Jeanne a national symbol. In 1973, when the Librairie Gallimard brought out extracts from the trial edited by Professor Georges Duby of the Collège de France, it was not one of the fifteenth-century miniatures of the Maid of Orleans which was on the cover, but Dreyer's Falconetti.

If *La Passion de Jeanne d'Arc* is a distillation of historical experience, *Day of Wrath* (*Vredens Dag*) is a gradual revelation about one of the darkest and most overdetermined phenomena in sixteenth- and seventeenth-century Europe: witchcraft and its prosecution. *Day of Wrath* was adapted from a Norwegian play written in 1908, which Dreyer had seen in 1920. By the time he and two fellow countrymen produced a script in 1942, he had a folder full of research notes on the subject. The black-and-white sound film that premiered in Nazi-occupied Copenhagen in 1943 presents what was then a minority view but would now be a central view in scholarship about sorcery: that witchcraft was not simply a fantasy projected by judges on old women who confessed under torture, but was part of a shared cultural system about the occult which could be manipulated by the women themselves. ('In *Day of Wrath*,' Dreyer said later, 'Christians show their intolerance for those who are attached to remnants of ancient religions.' Perhaps Michelet's *La Sorcière* was on his bookshelf.) The historical accomplishment of the film is to situate magical practice and diabolic accusation in the intimacy of everyday healing, harming, desire, and jealousy rather than in the spectacles of Sabbath and possession.

The film opens with the *Dies Irae* (Day of Wrath) hymn for the dead that tells of the Last Things and the Last Judgment; we hear it and we also see it on a scroll printed in Gothic type and decorated with archaic woodcuts. It then moves to one of the several documents from the year 1623 that will determine the fate of the old woman, Herlof's Marte – court orders, a sentence, a journal entry – the kinds of documents from which the history of witchcraft prosecution is established, but which social historians go beyond, as does Dreyer's camera, to discover the 'inner secrets,' the actual beliefs and practices of a period. Herlof's Marte is a neighborhood healer dispensing gallows herbs when we first see her, but she later proves to be capable of prophesying evil and promising revenge against those who will not help her. As she escapes from the crowd coming to arrest her for witchcraft, the scene fades to the vicarage that will be the setting for much of the film. Absalon, the aging Lutheran pastor who lives there, had several years before married a second wife, Anne, who was much younger than himself – a 'scandal' in the eyes of his old mother Merete, who also fears what will happen when her grandson Martin returns from his sojourn abroad. There, the still-vigorous Merete dominates and humiliates Anne, jealously trying to maintain control of her son's household and loyalty. And there Absalon, his sexuality slipping away, treats Anne with affection but not with passion, and has given her no child.

Dreyer introduces this situation with his usual economy of means; then he brings back Martin, and the beautiful stepmother and the handsome son immediately begin to fall in love. Now the story of Herlof's Marte intersects with the family at the vicarage, as the terrified woman beseeches Anne to hide her, telling her she had once saved Anne's dead mother from prosecution as a 'hex.' Herlof's Marte is found, tried, tortured to produce a confession, and burned alive. Along the way Anne overhears Marte remind Absalon that he had protected Anne's mother so that young Anne could be his wife. And the audience overhears Absalon intoning prayers to drown out Marte's threat to denounce Anne as a witch's daughter.

The rest of *Day of Wrath* fulfills the predictions of old Merete and Herlof's Marte. Absalon, guilty because he has 'lied to God,' allows Merete to develop suspicions about Anne and confesses to his wife that her mother had the power to summon the living and the dead and to wish someone to die. Anne 'summons' Martin, and he enters her room just afterward. They become lovers in the summer woods. Anne, her passion fully awakened, dreams of a life together and a child; Martin is torn between suicidal guilt and desire. Absalon, by now ill, returns through a night storm, preoccupied with his death and seeking his wife's forgiveness for having married her without her love. In anger, Anne says that she has often wished him dead and then reveals her affair with Martin; her husband shouts 'Martin' and falls lifeless. At the funeral – an extraordinary scene where the camera moves slowly across the singing choir and the black-clad clergy and finally lights on Anne, who is dressed all in white – Martin speaks agitatedly but frees Anne from any blame in his father's death. Whereupon old Merete rises up and denounces Anne as a witch who has beguiled Martin and murdered Absalon with the help of the Evil One. Everything now falls into place for Martin; he retreats from Anne to his grandmother's side. Abandoned, Anne makes a confession to Absalon on his bier: 'Yes, I did murder you with the Evil One's help . . . and with the Evil One's help I have lured your son into my power. Now you know.' The film ends with the *Dies Irae* – which foretells the Last Judgment, but in an image (the printed scroll) specific to the early modern period – and then a witch's cross foreshadows Anne's burning.

There may be no precise sorcery case involving one Anne Pedersdotter, but the historical power of *Day of Wrath* rests on the centrally important family issues embedded in the film and on the typology of magical practice it offers. (Dreyer's historical consultant, Kaj Uldall, was probably of little help here, for his speciality was folk art and furniture.) A somewhat cluttered play by Hans Wiers-Jenssen was the story's source, and Dreyer's process of simplification – 'of purifying the motif,' 'purging it of trivial details' – gave clarity to the historical forms. The second marriage with gross disparity in age was a source for charivari in early modern Europe, precisely because of its dangers for sexuality and fertility. Merete was right when she called it a scandal. And as a Lutheran pastor, Absalon would have much on his conscience, since he married Anne without her consent, presumably to salvage his lost desire, and then covered his failure by disparaging conjugal sexuality. Anne was right when she rebuked him for taking away her joy. (Modern critics misread this film as equating Christianity with hostility to all sexuality. One aspect of the Lutheran Reformation was its defense of married sexuality, and whatever Dreyer's personal beliefs about religion, *Day of Wrath* is consistent with that view. Absalon owed his wife her pleasure.) The other quarrel in the film – that between widowed mother-in-law and daughter-in-law – was another feature of the extended household in early modern Europe, especially when the daughter-in-law was a second wife. The more common accusation made against the daughter-in-law was that she was a whore, but the circumstances at the vicarage make the charge of witchcraft understandable.

Witchcraft emerges in the film, as it does in recent scholarship, as a complex phenomenon that merges folk belief and clerical doctrine and is concerned with such daily matters as health and sexuality. Herlof's Marte is a typical practitioner, using her gallows herbs to help a neighbor one day (as the film shows), and on another day using herbs and charms to allow a neighbor to get revenge. Marte admits to making an accord with the devil and renouncing Christ only when it is proposed to her under torture; Dreyer leaves it uncertain whether she really believes this or is just an old eccentric 'not afraid,' as she says to Absalon, 'of Heaven or Hell, only afraid of dying.' Anne can understand herself as a practitioner because of the widely held view that occult powers are hereditary. In her case the power in question is necromancy, that is, communication with the dead – for instance, with the dead Absalon, to whom Anne is talking at the end of the film. The aid of the Evil One she admits only when deserted by Martin and powerless. The genius of *Day of Wrath*, noted by many critics, is its unfolding of a story that can be interpreted at every step in either natural or supernatural terms – not only by today's viewers but also by the men and women of the seventeenth century. Why does Martin come to Anne? Why does Absalon die? Why does Anne cast the devil as her helper? The intersection between wish, despair, and cultural belief is given remarkable narrative and visual expression.

As with *La Passion de Jeanne d'Arc*, historical authenticity comes first and foremost from the film's credible connection with 'the spirit of a period' – in its large forms and sometimes in its small details. Anne's eyes are a test for understanding her (Absalon sees them as pure and clear; Martin as mysterious and with a flame of passion; Merete as burning with witchcraft). They change before the camera as she herself changes: they gaze with curiosity and terror at the start of Marte's burning; they enchant Martin; they rebel against Merete; they show Absalon her angry resentment. This narrative link fits a time that believed in and feared the 'evil eye' and read faces for character. The costumes seem inspired by Rembrandt, as do some of the beards, but the more important influence may be facial expression. The sets and props are characteristically simple, focusing only on what is important for the action (Anne's embroidery frame, the linen closet). Nor was Dreyer bothered by a chest with the carving 'anno 1639' – a date years after the action – which can readily be seen standing between Martin and Merete after she tells him he must find a wife.

Finally, as in *La Passion de Jeanne d'Arc*, certain cinematic techniques assist the historical telling. The film shifts from sharp whites (collars, coifs) and sharp blacks to soft and misty grays, a shift suggesting movement from clarity to ambiguity. The slow pace and the lingering camera, which Bazin and other critics found boring or self-indulgent, give the viewer time to explore what is happening, to make up her mind – perhaps even to reflect, despite Dreyer's denial of any political intent, on what the words of the *Dies Irae* could have meant to the Copenhagen audience in November 1943, six weeks after the roundup of Jews had begun. Dreyer summoned the living and the dead in his film and allowed viewers to judge their actions. But, magician though he was, he could not escape the Nazi forces and had to flee to Sweden with his reels.

With René Allio's *Les Camisards*, a film which was made three decades later and which was a pioneer in the revival of the historical film in France, we are in a world of color, fast pacing, and detailed reconstitution. Allio tries overall for 'realistic' representation, but in that process he does not lose the sense of basic social forms and establishes a constant play between the alien features of the past and the more recognizable look and categories of the present.

Les Camisards is an account of several months in the Protestant rural uprising in the Cévennes region of south central France, an uprising which was a response to forcible conversion by Catholic missionaries. After the credits a rather long caption explains to viewers that 'In 1685, Louis XIV outlawed Protestantism by revoking the Edict of Nantes.' It goes on to mention the razing of Reformed churches, the exiling of pastors, and the punishment of rebels; it concludes with a description of the first violent resistance in the Cévennes in 1702, in which an important abbot, several priests, and the inhabitants of a chateau were slain. The film's action then starts. A silent and hostile congregation of 'converts' gets news from its priest of the capture and punishment of the assassins by the local Catholic authorities. Some of the peasants go off to a clandestine assembly, first to hear the Word of God from one of their own and then from the prophetic young preacher, Abraham Mazel, who moves through the countryside crying, 'Repent, repent, leave Babylon, renounce idolatry.' Out of the listeners is formed a band of armed resisters – young men and even a few women – led by the former blacksmith, Laporte, with the inspired Mazel at his side.

It is this band we track through the film, first as they manage to combine resistance with their farm work, harvesting under the eyes of Catholic soldiers, and then as they become guerrillas – their numbers growing, receiving food from sympathetic villagers, and advancing unseen through the hills they know. Then they burn a church used for the Mass; they kill soldiers and a government official; and, aided by the celebrated roving leader, Jean Cavalier, and his men, they put to rout a large but indifferent army from the occupying Catholic garrison. Interspersed with the Protestant action, we see Catholic maneuvers at the chateau: one aristocratic captain seeks the hand of the propertied widow of the slain royal official, while the other courts the daughter of the local seigneur. This noble father has himself returned to the Mass, but is still taking out the Protestant Bible from his coffer and even breaking bread with the rebels. The film ends with a defeat in battle for the Protestants (Laporte and many others are slain) and a marriage for the Catholics (the seigneur's daughter makes her aristocratic match under her father's tolerating eye). A new and tough royal official is in place, but the Protestant resistance has only begun: a woman survivor of the battle carries the cry 'Repent, mercy, pardon' to the villagers, and as the men walk by the displayed head of Laporte, a last overvoice says, 'It was about this time that people began to call us Camisards.'

René Allio made *Les Camisards* in 1970, in part (as he put it) 'in the spirit of historical reflection that followed May 1968' and in part to enjoy himself in the fields of the Cévennes, where he grew up. In addition, the film represents an early collaboration between a director and the new school of French social history, embodied in the work and person of Philippe Joutard, a specialist in the historical ethnography and collective memory of the Camisard revolt. Here was a chance for Allio to find a way 'to represent the popular classes,' to break, as he said, with the hero and star so dear to the usual financers of the feature film. Here was a chance for Joutard, whose edition of Camisard journals had first inspired Allio, to insist during the filming on the distinct spiritual and prophetic features of the movement, as against, say, peasant resistance to taxes. The results are not only the 'authenticity' of local names and real personages (Mazel, Laporte, Cavalier) and cinematic events which are a reasonable composite of historical events, but also the establishment of two distinct cultural styles. The simplicity of Protestant dress and hairstyle is opposed to the ornate garb of the well-off and well-born Catholics (even the ex-Protestant seigneur does not yet wear a wig); the ordered authority of the Catholic priest is opposed to the ecstasy – even the fits – of the prophetic Mazel; the royal troops entering battle with drumbeats are opposed to the Protestant peasants and artisans singing their Psalms of David.

Even more important is the presence of a Camisard voice in the film. A young man is shown going to join Laporte's band while an overvoice speaks in the first person, identifying him as the woolseller Jean-Jacques Combassous, a Protestant full of shame for having married in the Catholic rite: 'I heard of some who had taken up arms to defend our faith. I resolved to go and join their troops and examine their conduct, and if I was edified, to stay with them, and if not, to go back home.' The film is not thenceforth told from his vantage point, but every once in a while he is heard in overvoice, interpreting the action by the lights of Camisard sensibility and also offering the last statement of the film. The audience never knows, however, where Combassous's words come from: Are they a text from the time? Or are they the director's device for giving personality and stance to one of the mass of resisters?

If *Les Camisards* makes little effort to reflect on its own truth status – of which more later – René Allio himself thought much about the filmmaker's relation to history. He had not 'resurrected' the past, he said, but had tried 'to reinvent it' in all its strangeness. We sense that strangeness at several points: the quiet Protestant meals eaten from wooden bowls, with the tiniest gesture suggesting a courtship; the Protestants' mocking laughter at the love letter sent by the aristocratic captain to the widow, which they read aloud from a seized mail packet; the Camisard who beats a royal officer to death while the victim shouts, 'Thou shalt not kill, thou shalt not kill.' In retrospect, Allio says that he would have preferred to have used local peasants rather than actors (this he did only later in *Moi, Pierre Rivière*) and to have had them speaking the local language of Occitan. (Here Philippe Joutard demurred: the Camisards were perfectly bilingual in French and Occitan; French was the language of Protestant worship and of Camisard journals. Using French ensured both historical authenticity and a broad audience for the film.) At least he filmed amid the nineteenth-century houses and decayed villages of the Cévennes, where there were physical and memory traces of a more prosperous past. Here was a landscape that would yield the muted colors suitable to Protestant sobriety, a landscape he could interpret according to the lessons of seventeenth- and eighteenth-century painting.

In particular, Christine Laurent's costumes experimented with how to create genuine authenticity rather than static period accuracy – that is, how to find a visual language and vestimentary signs which would suggest the way clothing looked and was worn in the Cévennes. Laurent put them together on a small budget from seventeenth-century sources, secondhand stores, and theatre trunks. The shirts or camisoles which the film's Protestants wear were inspired by shirts from the nineteenth-century American West – an important choice, since it was said that from such garments came their sobriquet, 'Camisards.'

Reality and credibility are the components of authenticity, best achieved (so I have been suggesting) when films represent values, relations, and issues in a period; when they animate props and locations by their connections with historical people, and when they let the past have its distinctiveness before remaking it to resemble the present. The three films we have been considering, whether in their 'simplified' or in their 'naturalistic' features, help us in a central way to visualize and think about events in Europe from the fifteenth to the eighteenth centuries.

But whatever their contribution, there are two allied historical tasks they do less well, or not at all: suggesting the possibility that there may be a very different way of reporting what happened, and giving some indication of their own truth status, an indication of where knowledge of the past comes from and our relation to it. What do I mean by a different way of reporting what happened? All three films concern discordant situations: the inquisitors versus the Maid, Catholics versus Protestants, and the like. Dreyer intended his judges to be understood not as wicked men, but as persons who took seriously the dangers of sorcery and of challenges to clerical control. Nonetheless, the camera is positioned in *Jeanne d'Arc* to tell only *one* story, however balanced it tries to be in creating believable historical judgments. The same is true of the frankly partisan *Camisards*. Only *Day of Wrath*, with its wondrous ambiguity, experiments with telling two stories at once and showing multiple ways in which the same event could be interpreted.

Let us expand our examples by considering *The Mission*, a film which, while well-intentioned and visually impressive, is somewhat tenuously related to events and persons that were documentable as the Spanish and Portuguese monarchs redrew their borders in Paraguay in the 1750s. In this film, Joffé, his scenarist Robert Bolt, and theological advisor Daniel Berrigan give ample treatment to the conflicting views and interests of Jesuits, of Portuguese and Spanish estate owners and their governments, and of the papacy on the issue of the destiny of the Guarani Indians. We hear Jesuit and Spaniard arguing about whether the Guarani are enslaved on the estates or whether they are held in stricter subjection on the Jesuit missions. We see Jesuit argue with Jesuit about whether a member of a religious order should bear the sword to stand with his flock or hold to the pacifism of Jesus. At the end of the film, the pope's legate looks out at us questioningly, evoking the doubts he has expressed throughout his entire mission: is the saving of the entire Jesuit order worth the price of local destruction and Indian uprooting and enslavement? But these contrary views are all told within the frame of a single Jesuit story, and the independent voice of the Guarani is heard only once – when the Guarani chief, speaking in his own tongue and translated by Father Gabriel, tells the legate that he too is a king and that he does not think the pope has interpreted God's plans aright. The Indians are pastoralized in *The Mission*; how they themselves might have accounted for events is lost in this 'true' representation.

'What's so bad about a partisan history film?' you may be asking. Nothing necessarily, so long as one indicates to the audience what one is doing. 'Why should Allio have to give equal voice to the Catholics in his excellent film?' you also may be asking. He needn't, but think how visually and intellectually interesting might be a brief scene from a Cévenol Catholic village, where one living peasant culture could be confronted with another. 'Don't historians also tell a single story?' you finally may be asking. They do, but at least their footnotes should suggest other accounts of what happened, and the best current historical practice tries to flag other tellings to readers and to be at least briefly reflexive about its own stance.

Film has countless possibilities for showing more than one story at once and for indicating in a concise and arresting way the existence of other interpretations. Before going on to suggest what they might be, let me clarify what I mean by the truth status problem in the three films I have been considering. None, of course, uses the 'any resemblance to actual events is coincidental' disclaimer, but only Dreyer's *Jeanne d'Arc* does anything to complicate a truth claim. *Les Camisards* opens with its anonymous caption 'In 1685 . . .' and the overvoiced artisan's commentary floats without a reality status. (I tracked it down at the library; it is mostly taken from the Camisard journal of the woolseller Jean Bonbonnoux, written in Geneva long after the events, with some sentences added from the memoirs of the preacher, Mazel.) What if, at the end of the film, the words 'It was after this that people began to call us Camisards' were said by a post-story Bonbonnoux, who turns to the theater audience and says that he's left them a journal? At least this would be a start toward portraying history as an encounter between us and sources from the past.

La Passion de Jeanne d'Arc begins with such a source, the slowly turned pages of the Bibliothèque Nationale manuscript, which then flows into the cinematic representation of the text. Present-day scholars may grumble that this opening depicts archival sources as too transparent to the historian, and present-day filmmakers may grumble that this is now a visual cliché. Nonetheless, at the time it was devised in 1927, it told viewers that knowledge of the past is constructed, and provided an image of the film's narrative source.

Let me conclude with a set of ideas drawn from existing films to inspire us to expand the repertory of cinematic techniques for good telling about the past. Some have simple Brechtian distancing functions; some evoke multiple tellings or controversy; some locate the film in relation to historical knowledge; some do all three at once.

Reminding viewers of the distance between past and present: the opening of Federico Fellini's *And The Ship Sails On*, where a silent film gradually and comically moves into sound and color until the action begins, a brief history of film suggesting the decades that lie between the viewer's present and the present of the film, which is set before World War I; the moment toward the end of *La Nuit de Varennes*, when a central figure, Restif de la Bretonne, steps out of his revolutionary France into the streets of contemporary Paris; the diagrammatic maps used in *The Story of Adèle H.* to indicate narrative, period style, and geographical movement.

Especially suggestive are the techniques used by Bertrand Tavernier in *Que la Fête Commence* (*Let Joy Reign Supreme*), a film set in 1719–20 during the regency of Philippe d'Orleans over young Louis XV, and intertwining the hopeless efforts of a group of backwoods nobles to establish an independent republic of Brittany with the plots and festivities of the regent and his minister, the abbot Guillaume Dubois. Tavernier positions spectators surprisingly close to the past – 'filming as if we are contemporaries of the events,' he called it, 'cracking the historical varnish' – and then distances them by various cinematic comments. The former means habituating the audience to the ambiance of the past by long extended shots (a peddler running along a Breton shore), while omitting from the film any captions or conversations intended solely to explain to modern viewers what is going on (we learn of John Law's new bank notes only as much as the Breton conspirators learn). Distancing is accomplished by making us laugh at, rather than with, the characters (Dubois tells a prostitute his political troubles while her feet are on his shoulders) and by having us listen to music which is in ironic tension with the action (the regent's own stately composition plays as a peasant girl sets fire to his coach). And through sudden freezes the camera links its subjects with past and future histories of resistance: the face of the Breton leader before his execution, the face of the peasant girl watching the burning coach.

Suggesting multiple tellings: Kurosawa's great *Rashomon*, of course, with its three accounts of a sexual and violent encounter; *Last Year at Marienbad*, with its repeats, sudden shifts, dissolves, and mixed clues about memory; *Blow-up*, with its unreadable photograph on which the evidence of murder depends; *Reds*, with its witnesses commenting on the action and characters (a device much better in its conception than in its realization, as the scenarist Trevor Griffiths and the historical consultant Robert Rosenstone both pointed out).

Ways of showing where knowledge of the past comes from: the opening of Welles's *Citizen Kane*, with its newsreels, journalist's inquiries, and final mystery, unravelled only to the theatre audience and not to the reporter; the opening of *Mueda: Memorial and Massacre* – the remarkable film from Mozambique about the yearly reenactment of an event in the struggle for independence – in which a predominantly dark opening sequence gradually lightens to an expansive open field where the white director Ruy Guerra discusses plans with the black players about what difference the film will make to their ritual. And in *The French Lieutenant's Woman*, the film within a film allows a constant interplay between twentieth-century actors and nineteenth-century lovers; the street scene of nineteenth-century whores is prepared for by a bedroom scene in which the actress is reading a history of London prostitution and commenting on it to her leading man.

One could multiply such ideas at length, thinking of ways that overimages, overvoices, slowing down and speeding up of film, moving from color to black and white, and juxtaposed images and angles could play the role of the historian's 'perhaps,' 'maybe,' 'this is controversial,' or 'this is how we think we know.' One could generate ideas about better openings or end credits: why not acknowledge a historical source if one can acknowledge villages, chateaux, foundations, and suppliers of hats and food? Why not find the visual equivalent of a preface and say what the film intends?

Robert A. Rosenstone

HISTORY IN IMAGES/ HISTORY IN WORDS

'History in Images/History in Words: Reflections on the Possibility of Really Putting History onto Film', *American Historical Review*, 1988, vol. 93(5), pp. 1173–85. Text edited.

FOR AN ACADEMIC HISTORIAN to become involved in the world of pictures is at once an exhilarating and disturbing experience. Exhilarating for all the obvious reasons: the power of the visual media; the opportunity to emerge from the lonely depths of the library to join with other human beings in a common enterprise; the delicious thought of a potentially large audience for the fruits of one's research, analysis, and writing. Disturbing for equally obvious reasons: no matter how serious or honest the filmmakers, and no matter how deeply committed they are to rendering the subject faithfully, the history that finally appears on the screen can never fully satisfy the historian as historian (although it may satisfy the historian as filmgoer). Inevitably, something happens on the way from the page to the screen that changes the meaning of the past as it is understood by those of us who work in words.

The disturbance caused by working on a film lingers long after the exhilaration has vanished. Like all such disturbances, this one can provoke a search for ideas to help restore one's sense of intellectual equilibrium. In my case, the search may have been particularly intense because I had a double dose of this experience: two of my major written works have been put onto film, and both times I have been to some extent involved in the process.

The two films were almost as different as films can be. One was a dramatic feature and the other a documentary; one was a fifty-million-dollar Hollywood project and the other a quarter-million-dollar work funded largely with public money; one was pitched at the largest of mass audiences and the other at the more elite audience of public television and art houses. Despite these differences, vast and similar changes happened to the history in each production, changes that have led me to a new appreciation of the problems of putting history onto film. After these experiences, I no longer find it possible to blame the shortcomings of historical films either on the evils of Hollywood or the woeful effects of low budgets, on the limits of the dramatic genre or those of the documentary format. The most serious problems the historian has with the past on the screen arise out of the nature and demands of the visual medium itself.

The two films are *Reds* (1981), the story of the last five years in the life of American poet, journalist, and revolutionary, John Reed; and *The Good Fight* (1984), a chronicle of the Abraham Lincoln Brigade, the American volunteers who took part in the Spanish Civil War. Each is a well-made, emotion-filled work that has exposed a vast number of people to an important but long-buried historical subject, one previously known largely to specialists or to old leftists. Each brings to the screen a wealth of authentic historical detail. Each humanises the past, turning long-suspect radicals into admirable human beings. Each proposes – if a bit indirectly – an interpretation of its subject, seeing political commitment as both a personal and historical category. Each connects past to present by suggesting that the health of the body politic and, indeed, the world depends on such recurrent commitments.

Despite their very real virtues, their evocations of the past through powerful images, colourful characters, and moving words, neither of these motion pictures can fulfil many of the basic demands for truth and verifiability used by all historians. *Reds* indulges in overt fiction – to give just two examples – by putting John Reed in places where he never was or having him make an impossible train journey from France to Petrograd in 1917.[1] *The Good Fight* – like many recent documentaries – equates memory with history; it allows veterans of the Spanish war to speak of events more than four decades in the past without calling their misremembrances, mistakes, or outright fabrications into question.[2] And yet neither fictionalisation nor unchecked testimony is the major reason that these films violate my notion of history. Far more unsettling is the way each compresses the past to a closed world by telling a single, linear story with, essentially, a single interpretation. Such a narrative strategy obviously denies historical alternatives, does away with complexities of motivation or causation, and banishes all subtlety from the world of history.

This sort of criticism of history on film might be of no importance if we did not live in a world deluged with images, one in which people increasingly receive their ideas about the past from motion pictures and television, from feature films, docudramas, mini-series, and network documentaries. Today, the chief source of historical knowledge for the majority of the population – outside of the much-despised textbook – must surely be the visual media, a set of institutions that lie almost wholly outside the control of those of us who devote our lives to history.[3] Any reasonable extrapolation suggests that trend will continue. Certainly, it is not farfetched to foresee a time (are we almost there?) when written history will be a kind of esoteric pursuit and when historians will be viewed as the priests of a mysterious religion, commentators on sacred texts and performers of rituals for a populace little interested in their meaning but indulgent enough (let us hope) to pay for them to continue.

To think of the ever-growing power of the visual media is to raise the disturbing thought that perhaps history is dead in the way God is dead. Or, at the most, alive only to believers – that is, to those of us who pursue it as a profession. Surely, I am not the only one to wonder if those we teach or the population at large truly know or care about history, the kind of history that we do. Or to wonder if our history – scholarly, scientific, measured – fulfils the need for that larger History, that web of connections to the past that holds a culture together, that tells us not only where we have been but also suggests where we are going. Or to worry if our history actually relates us to our own cultural sources, tells us what we need to know about other traditions, and provides enough understanding of what it is to be human.

Perhaps it seems odd to raise such questions at this time, after two decades of repeated methodological breakthroughs in history, innovations that have taught us to look at the past in so many new ways and have generated so much new information. The widespread influence of the Annales school, the new social history, quantification and social science history, women's history, psychohistory, anthropological history, the first inroads of Continental theory into a reviving intellectual history – all these developments indicate that history as a discipline is flourishing. But – and it is a big BUT, a BUT that can be insisted on despite the much discussed 'revival of narrative' – it is clear that at the same time there is a rapidly shrinking general audience for the information we have to deliver and the sort of stories we have to tell. Despite the success of our new methodologies, I fear that as a profession we know less and less how to tell stories that situate us meaningfully in a value-laden world. Stories that matter to people outside our profession. Stories that matter to people inside the profession. Stories that matter at all.

Enter film: the great temptation. Film, the contemporary medium still capable of both dealing with the past and holding a large audience. How can we not suspect that this is the medium to use to create narrative histories that will touch large numbers of people. Yet is this dream possible? Can one really put history onto film, history that will satisfy those of us who devote our lives to understanding, analysing, and recreating the past in words? Or does the use of film necessitate a change in what we mean by history, and would we be willing to make such a change? The issue comes down to this: is it possible to tell historical stories on film and not lose our professional or intellectual souls?

Thirty years ago, Siegfried Kracauer, a theoretician of both film and history, dismissed the historical feature as stagy and theatrical, in part because modern actors looked unconvincing in period costumes, but in larger measure because everyone knew – he argued – that what was on the screen was not the past but only an imitation of it.[4] If he neglected to deal with the equally obvious shortcoming of written history, or to explain why we so easily accept the convention that words on a page are adequate to the task of showing us the past, Kracauer at least took a stab at the theoretical problems of history on film. This is more than one can say of recent scholars. Despite a great deal of professional activity concerning history and the visual media – the articles and monographs, the panels at major conventions, the symposiums sponsored by the American Historical Association, New York University, and the California Historical Society – I have encountered but two discussions of what seems a most basic question: whether our written discourse can be turned into a visual one.[5]

R. J. Raack, a historian who has been involved in the production of several documentaries, is a strong advocate of putting history onto film. Indeed, in his view, film is possibly a more appropriate medium for history than the written word. 'Traditional written history,' he argued, is too linear and too narrow in focus to render the fullness of the complex, multi-dimensional world in which humans live. Only film, with its ability to juxtapose images and sounds, with its 'quick cuts to new sequences, dissolves, fades, speed-ups, [and] slow motion,' can ever hope to approximate real life, the daily experience of 'ideas, words, images, preoccupations, distractions, sensory deceptions, conscious and unconscious motives and emotions.' Only film can provide an adequate 'empathetic reconstruction to convey how historical people witnessed, understood, and lived their lives.' Only film can 'recover all the past's liveliness.'[6]

Philosopher Ian Jarvie, the author of two books on motion pictures and society, took an entirely opposite view. The moving image carries such a 'poor information load' and suffers from such 'discursive weakness' that there is no way to do meaningful history on film. History, he explained, does not consist primarily of 'a descriptive narrative of what actually happened.' It consists mostly of 'debates between historians about just what exactly did happen, why it happened and what would be an adequate account of its significance.' While it is true that a 'historian could embody his view in a film, just as he could embody it in a play,' the real question is this: 'How could he defend it, footnote it, rebut objections and criticise the opposition?'[7]

Clearly, history is a different creature for each of these two scholars. Raack saw history as a way of gaining personal knowledge. Through the experience of people's lives in other times and places, one can achieve a kind of 'psychological prophylaxis.' History lets us feel less peculiar and isolated; by showing that there are others like us, it helps to relieve our 'loneliness and alienation.'[8] This is hardly the traditional academic view of the subject, but if one looks at history as a personal, experiential way of knowing, then Raack's arguments seem to make sense. He is certainly right that, more easily than the written word, the motion picture seems to let us stare through a window directly at past events, to experience people and places as if we were there. The huge images on the screen and the wraparound sounds overwhelm us, swamp our senses, and destroy attempts to remain aloof, distanced, critical. In the movie theatre, we are, for a time, prisoners of history.

That, for Jarvie, is just the problem: a world that moves at an unrelenting twenty-four frames a second provides no time or space for reflection, verification, or debate. One may be able to tell 'interesting, enlightening, and plausible' historical stories on the screen, but it is not possible to provide the all-important critical elements of historical discourse: evaluation of sources, logical argument, or systematic weighing of evidence. With those elements missing, one has history that is 'no more serious than Shakespeare's Tudor-inspired travesties.' This means that virtually all filmed history has been 'a joke,' and a dangerous one at that. A motion picture may provide a 'vivid portrayal' of the past, but its inaccuracies and simplifications are practically impossible for the serious scholar 'to correct.'[9]

If most academic historians are likely to feel closer to Jarvie than to Raack, it is still necessary to ask to what extent his arguments are true. Take the notion that the 'information load' of film is impoverished. Surely, this depends on what one means by 'information,' for in its own way film carries an enormously rich load of data. Some scholars claim not only that an image of a scene contains much more information than the written description of the same scene but also that this information has a much higher degree of detail and specificity.[10] One does not need to be an expert to discover this – all one need do is attempt to render into words everything that might appear in a single shot from a movie like *Reds*. Such an assignment could easily fill many pages, and if this is the case with a single shot, how much more space would be needed to describe what goes on in a sequence of images? The question thus becomes not whether film can carry enough information but whether that information can be absorbed from quickly moving images, is worth knowing, and can add up to 'history.'

What about Jarvie's assertion that history is mainly 'debates between historians'? Scholars do continually disagree over how to understand and interpret the data of the past, and their debates are important for the progress of the discipline – one might even say that debates help to set the agenda for research by raising new issues, defining fields, refining questions, and forcing historians to check each other's accuracy and logic. And it is true that each and every work of history takes its place in a discourse that consists of preexisting debates, and the very meaning of any new work is in part created by those debates, even if they are not acknowledged within the work itself.

The question for history on film, however, is not whether historians always, or usually, or even sometimes, debate issues, or whether works take their place in a context of ongoing debates, the question is whether each individual work of history is, or must be, involved in such debates and involved so overtly that the debate becomes part of the substance of the historical work. To this, the answer is no. We can all think of works that represent the past without ever pointing to the field of debates in which they are situated; we all know many excellent narrative histories and biographies that mute (or even moot) debates by ignoring them, or relegating them to appendices, or burying them deep within the storyline. If written texts can do this and still be considered history, surely an inability to 'debate' issues cannot rule out the possibilities of history on film.

When historians think of history on film, what probably comes to mind is what we might call the Hollywood historical drama like *Reds*, or its European counterpart, *The Return of Martin Guerre* (1982) – the big-budget production in which costumes, 'authentic' sets and locations, and well-known actors take precedence over attempts at historical accuracy. Such works in truth fall into a genre that one might label 'historical romance.' Like all genres, this one locks both filmmaker and audience into a series of conventions whose demands – for a love interest, physical action, personal confrontation, movement toward a climax and denouement – are almost guaranteed to leave the historian of the period crying foul.

Yet this need not be so. In principle, there is no reason why one cannot make a dramatic feature set in the past about all kinds of historical topics – individual lives, community conflicts, social movements, the rise of a king to power, revolutions, or warfare – that will stay within the bounds of historical accuracy, at least to the extent that one need not resort to invented characters or incidents. If, by its very nature, the dramatic film will include human conflict and will shape its material in accordance with some conventions of storytelling, this does not entirely differentiate it from much written history. One may argue that film tends to highlight individuals rather than movements or the impersonal processes that are often the subject of written history, yet we must not forget that it is possible to make films that avoid the glorification of the individual and present the group as protagonist. This was certainly one of the aims and accomplishments of Soviet filmmakers in the 1920s in their search for non-bourgeois modes of representation. If the best known of their works – Sergei Eisenstein's *Battleship Potemkin* (1925) and *October* (1928) – are for political reasons skewed as history, they certainly provide useful models for ways to present collective historical moments.

To represent history in a dramatic feature rather than a written text does involve some important trade-offs. The amount of traditional data that can be presented on the screen in a two-hour film (or even an eight-hour mini-series) will always be so skimpy compared to a written version covering the same ground that the professional historian may feel intellectually starved. Yet the inevitable thinning of data on the screen does not of itself make for poor history. On many topics, one can find short and long and longer works, for the amount of detail used in a historical argument partakes of the arbitrary or is at least dependent on the aims of one's project. Jean-Denis Bredin's recent book, *L'Affaire* (1983), although four times as long, is no more 'historical' than Nicholas Halasz's earlier *Captain Dreyfus* (1955), and Leon Edel's one-volume biography of *Henry James* (1985) no less 'accurate' than his full five-volume version.

If short on traditional data, film does easily capture elements of life that we might wish to designate as another kind of data. Film lets us see landscapes, hear sounds, witness strong emotions as they are expressed with body and face, or view physical conflict between individuals and groups. Without denigrating the power of the written word, one can claim for each medium unique powers of representation. It seems, indeed, no exaggeration to insist that for a mass audience (and I suspect for an academic elite as well) film can most directly render the look and feel of all sorts of historical particulars and situations – farm workers dwarfed by immense western prairies and mountains, or miners struggling in the darkness of their pits, or millworkers moving to the rhythms of their machines, or civilians sitting hopelessly in the bombed-out streets of cities.[11] Film can plunge us into the drama of confrontations in courtroom or legislature, the simultaneous, overlapping realities of war and revolution, the intense confusion of men in battle. Yet, in doing all this, in favouring the visual and emotional data while simultaneously playing down the analytical, the motion picture is subtly – and in ways we do not yet know how to measure or describe – altering our very sense of the past.

The other major type of history on film comes under the label of documentary. Whether it is the film compiled of old footage and narrated by an omniscient voice (the voice of History) or a film that centres on 'talking heads' (survivors remembering events, experts analysing them, or some combination of the two), the historical documentary, just like the dramatic feature, tends to focus on heroic individuals and, more important, to make sense of its material in terms of a story that moves from a beginning through a conflict to a dramatic resolution. This point cannot be too strongly emphasised. All too often, historians who scorn dramatisations are willing to accept the documentary film as a more accurate way of representing the past, as if somehow the images appear on the screen unmediated. Yet the documentary is never a direct reflection of an outside reality but a work consciously shaped into a narrative that – whether dealing with past or present – creates the meaning of the material being conveyed.

That the 'truths' of a documentary are not reflected but created is easy to demonstrate. Take, for example, John Huston's famed *Battle of San Pietro* (1945), shot during the Italian campaign in 1944 with a single cameraman. In this film, as in any war documentary, when we see an image of an artillery piece firing followed by a shell exploding, we are viewing a reality created only by a film editor. This is not to say that the shell fired by the gun that we saw did not explode somewhere or that the explosion did not look like the one that we saw on the screen. But, since no camera could follow the trajectory of a shell from gun to explosion, what we have in fact seen are images of two different events spliced together by an editor to create a single historical moment. And if this happens with such a simple scene, how much more does it mark complicated events shown to us?

As a form capable of conveying history, the documentary has other limits as well. Some of them are highlighted by my experience with *The Good Fight*. In writing narration for this film, I was frustrated by the directors in my attempt to include the issue of possible Stalinist 'terrorism' in the ranks. Their objections were as follows: they could find no visual images to illustrate the issue and were adamant that the film not become static or talky; the topic was too complex to handle quickly, and the film – as all films – had so much good footage that it was already in danger of running too long. This decision to sacrifice complexity to action, one that virtually every documentarist would accept, underlines a convention of the genre: the documentary bows to a double tyranny – which is to say, an ideology – of the necessary image and perpetual movement. And woe to those aspects of history that can neither be illustrated nor quickly summarised.

The apparent glory of the documentary lies in its ability to open a direct window onto the past, allowing us to see the cities, factories, landscapes, battlefields, and leaders of an earlier time. But this ability also constitutes its chief danger. However often film uses actual footage (or still photos, or artifacts) from a particular time and place to create a 'realistic' sense of the historical moment, we must remember that on the screen we see not the events themselves, and not the events as experienced or even as witnessed by participants, but selected images of those events carefully arranged into sequences to tell a story or to make an argument.

Historians can easily see how such film conventions of both the dramatic feature and the documentary shape or distort the past, in part because we have written work by which the piece of visual history can be judged. What we too easily ignore, however, is the extent to which written history, and especially narrative history, is also shaped by conventions of genre and language. This needs to be underscored. So many scholars have dealt with questions of narrative in recent years that 'narratology' has become a separate field of study. Here I only wish to call to mind a few of their insights that seem relevant to history on film. First, neither people nor nations live historical 'stories'; narratives, that is, coherent stories with beginnings, middles, and endings, are constructed by historians as part of their attempts to make sense of the past. Second, the narratives that historians write are in fact 'verbal fictions'; written history is a representation of the past, not the past itself. Third, the nature of the historical world in a narrative is in part governed by the genre or mode (shared with forms of fiction) in which the historian has decided to cast the story – ironic, tragic, heroic, or romantic. And, fourth, language is not transparent and cannot mirror the past as it really was; rather than reflecting it, language creates and structures history and imbues it with meaning.[12] If written history is shaped by the conventions of genre and language, the same will obviously be true of visual history, even though in this case the conventions will be those of visual genres and visual language. To the extent that written narratives are 'verbal fictions,' then visual narratives will be 'visual fictions' – that is, not mirrors of the past but representations of it. This is not to argue that history and fiction are the same thing or to excuse the kind of outright fabrication that marks Hollywood historical features. History on film must be held accountable to certain standards, but these standards must be consonant with the possibilities of the medium. It is impossible to judge history on film solely by the standards of written history, for each medium has its own kind of necessarily fictive elements.

Consider the following: in any dramatic feature, actors assume the roles of historical characters and provide them with gestures, movements, and voice sounds that create meaning. Sometimes, film must provide a face for the faceless, such as that South African railway conductor, undescribed in Gandhi's autobiography, who pushed the young Indian out of a train compartment for whites and started him on the road to activism. In such cases, certain 'facts' about individuals must be created. Clearly, this is an act of fictionalising, yet surely no real violence is done to history by such an addition to the written record, at least not so long as the 'meaning' that the 'impersonators' create somehow carries forth the larger 'meaning' of the historical character whom they represent.

To begin to think about history on film not simply in comparison with written history but in terms of its own is not an easy task. Current theories of cinema – structuralist, semiotic, feminist, or Marxist – all seem too self-contained and hermetic, too uninterested in the flesh-and-blood content of the past, the lives and struggles of individuals and groups, to be directly useful to the historian. Still, the insights of theoreticians do offer valuable lessons about the problems and potentialities of the medium; they also point toward some of the important differences between the way words on the page and images on the screen create versions of 'reality,' differences that must be taken into account in any serious attempt to evaluate history on film.[13] At the very least, historians who wish to give the visual media a chance will have to realise that, because of the way the camera works and the kinds of data that it privileges, history on film will of necessity include all sorts of elements unknown to written history.

Although the big Hollywood feature and the standard documentary are currently the most common forms of history on film, it would be a mistake to regard them as the only possible forms. In recent years, directors from a variety of countries have begun to make movies that convey some of the intellectual density that we associate with the written word, films that propose imaginative new ways of dealing with historical material. Resisting traditional genres, these filmmakers have moved toward new forms of cinema capable of exploring serious social and political issues.

The best of these films present the possibility of more than one interpretation of events; they render the world as multiple, complex, and indeterminate, rather than as a series of self-enclosed, neat, linear stories . . .

For the historian interested in the possibility of complex ideas being delivered by film, the most interesting and provocative of such works may be the feature-length *Sans Soleil* (1982). This best-known work of Chris Marker, an American who lives in Paris, is a complex and personal visual and verbal essay on the meaning of contemporary history. The film juxtaposes images of Guinea-Bissau and the Cape Verde Islands with those of Japan in order to understand what the filmmaker calls 'the poles of existence' in the late twentieth-century world. It can also be seen as an oblique investigation of Marker's contention (made in the narrative) that the great question of the twentieth century has been 'the coexistence of different concepts of time.'[14]

Far from Poland (1985) made by Jill Godmilow is another good example of how film can render historical complexity. An American who had spent some time in Poland, Godmilow was unable to get a visa to go there to make a 'standard' documentary on the Solidarity labour movement. Staying in New York, she made a film anyway, a self-reflexive, multi-level work, one that utilises a variety of visual sources to create a highly unusual 'history' of Solidarity – it includes actual footage smuggled out of Poland, images from American television newscasts, 'acted' interviews from original texts that appeared in the Polish press, 'real' interviews with Polish exiles in the United States, a domestic drama in which the filmmaker (read 'historian') raises the issue of what it means to make a film about events in a distant land, and voice-over dialogues of the filmmaker with a fictional Fidel Castro, who speaks for the possibility of contemporary revolution and the problems of the artist within the socialist state. Provocative visually, verbally, historically, and intellectually, *Far from Poland* tells us much about Solidarity and even more, perhaps, about how Americans reacted to and used the news from Poland for their own purposes. Not only does the film raise the issue of how to represent history on film, it also provides a variety of perspectives on the events it covers, thus both reflecting and entering the arena of debates surrounding the meaning of Solidarity.

The topics of both Marker and Godmilow may be contemporary, but the presentational modes of their films are applicable to subjects set more deeply in the past. Nor are documentarists the only filmmakers who have been seeking new ways of putting history onto the screen. All historians who feel a need to resist the empathic story told in Hollywood films, with its 'romantic' approach and its satisfying sense of emotional closure, will find themselves at one with many Western radical and Third World filmmakers who have had to struggle against Hollywood codes of representation in order to depict their own social and historical realities.[15] In some recent Third World historical films, one can find parallels to Bertolt Brecht's 'epic' theatre, with its distancing devices (such as direct speeches or chapter headings for each section of a work) that are supposed to make the audience think about rather than feel social problems and human relationships. Although the filmmakers are no doubt working from a native sense of history and aesthetics, this distancing is what seems to happen in such works as Ousmane Sembène's *Ceddo* (1977) and Carlos Diegues's *Quilombo* (1984), both of which present historical figures with whom it is almost impossible to identify emotionally. Made in Senegal, *Ceddo* portrays the political and religious struggle for dominance that occurred in various parts of Black Africa during the eighteenth and nineteenth centuries, when a militant Islam attempted to oust both the original native religion and the political power structure. The Brazilian film, *Quilombo*, presents a history of Palmares, a remote, long-lived, seventeenth-century community created by runaway slaves that for many decades was able to hold off all attempts of the Portuguese to crush its independence. Each film delivers its history within a framework of interpretation – *Ceddo* upholds the pre-Islamic values of Black Africa, and *Quilombo* glorifies the rich tribal life of a culture freed of the burden of Christian civilisation.[16]

For anyone interested in history on film, the chief importance of these works may lie less in their accuracy of detail (I have been unable to find commentaries on them by specialists in their fields) than in the way they choose to represent the past. Because both films are overtly theatrical in costuming and highly stylised in acting, they resist all the usual common-sense notions of 'realism' that we expect in movies like *Reds*. Clearly, the camera in these films does not serve as a window onto a world that once existed; clearly, it represents something about the events of the past without pretending to 'show' those events accurately. Just as clearly, each of these films is a work of history that tells us a great deal about specific periods and issues of the past.

In their unusual forms, *Ceddo* and *Quilombo* work to subvert a major convention of history on film – its 'realism.' At the same time, they also highlight, and call into question, a parallel convention of written history – the 'realism' of our narratives, a realism based, as Hayden White showed two decades ago, on the model of the nineteenth-century novel. It is possible, in fact, to see these works as examples (in a different medium) of what White was calling for when he wrote that, if history were to continue as an 'art,' then to remain relevant to the issues of our time historians would have to move beyond the artistic models of the nineteenth century. *Ceddo* and *Quilombo* may be products of Third World nations, but they point the way toward the narrative forms of the twentieth century, toward the necessity for modernism (expressionism, surrealism) in its many varieties, or even post-modernism, as modes of representation for dramatising the significance of historical data.[17]

Almost a century after the birth of the motion picture, film presents historians with a challenge still unseized, a challenge to begin to think of how to use the medium to its full capability for carrying information, juxtaposing images and words, providing startling and contrastive mixtures of sight and sound, and (perhaps) creating analytic structures that include visual elements. Because the conventions of the visual media are strong and, to the historian, initially startling. They also serve to highlight the conventions and limitations of written history. Film thus suggests new possibilities for representing the past, possibilities that could allow narrative history to recapture the power it once had when it was more deeply rooted in the literary imagination.[18]

The visual media present the same challenge to history that they have to anthropology, a field in which the ethnographic documentary, invented to illustrate the 'scientific' findings of written texts, has in recent years cut loose from its verbal base to seek what one scholar calls 'a new paradigm, a new way of seeing, not necessarily incompatible with written anthropology, but at least governed by a distinct set of criteria.'[19] Now it seems time for such a 'shift in perspective,' one occasioned by the opportunity to represent the world in images and words rather than in words alone, to touch history. Doing so will open us to new notions of the past, make us ask once more the questions about what history can or cannot be. About what history is for. About why we want to know about the past and what we will do with that knowledge. About possible new modes of historical representation, both filmed and written – about history as self-reflexive inquiry, as self-conscious theatre, as a mixed form of drama and analysis.

The challenge of film to history, of the visual culture to the written culture, may be like the challenge of written history to the oral tradition, of Herodotus and Thucydides to the tellers of historical tales. Before Herodotus, there was myth, which was a perfectly adequate way of dealing with the past of a tribe, city, or people, adequate in terms of providing a meaningful world in which to live and relate to one's past. In a post-literate world, it is possible that visual culture will once again change the nature of our relationship to the past. This does not mean giving up on attempts at truth but somehow recognising that there may be more than one sort of historical truth, or that the truths conveyed in the visual may be different from, but not necessarily in conflict with, truths conveyed in words.

History does not exist until it is created. And we create it in terms of our underlying values. Our kind of rigorous, 'scientific' history is in fact a product of history, our special history that includes a particular relationship to the written word, a rationalised economy, notions of individual rights, and the nation-state. Many cultures have done quite well without this sort of history, which is only to say that there are – as we all know but rarely acknowledge – many ways to represent and relate to the past. Film, with its unique powers of representation, now struggles for a place within a cultural tradition that has long privileged the written word. Its challenge is great, for it may be that to acknowledge the authenticity of the visual is to accept a new relationship to the word itself. We would do well to recall Plato's assertion that, when the mode of the music changes, the walls of the city shake. It seems that to our time is given this vital question to ponder: if the mode of representation changes, what then may begin to shake?

Notes

1 A fuller discussion of the historical shortcomings of *Reds* can be found in my '*Reds* as History,' *Reviews in American History*, 1982, vol. 10, pp. 297–310.

2 A fuller discussion of the historical shortcomings of *The Good Fight* is in my paper, 'Memory, Documentary: "The Good Fight" Fifty Years After,' delivered at a symposium entitled 'The Abraham Lincoln Brigade and the Spanish Civil War: History, Memory and the Politics and Culture of the 1930s,' National Museum of American History, Smithsonian Institution, Washington, DC, December 5, 1986.

3 A few historians such as Daniel Walkowitz, Robert Brent Toplin, and R. J. Raack have become deeply involved in filmmaking projects. For an interesting insight into some of the problems of the historian as filmmaker, see Daniel Walkowitz, 'Visual History: The Craft of the Historian-Filmmaker,' *Public Historian*, 1985, vol. 7, pp. 53–64.

4 Siegfried Kracauer, *Theory of Film*, Princeton, NJ: Princeton University Press, 1960, pp. 77–9.

5 By now, any list of articles, books, and panels on film would be very long. Perhaps the most important symposiums were the ones at New York University on October

30, 1982, and in Washington, DC, in April–May 1985, sponsored by the AHA. The former resulted in Barbara Abrash and Janet Sternberg, eds., *Historians and Filmmakers: Toward Collaboration*, New York: Institute for Research in History, 1983; and the latter in John O'Connor, ed., *Image as Artifact: The Historical Analysis of Film and Television*, Malabar, FL: Krieger, 1990.

6 R. J. Raack, 'Historiography as Cinematography: A Prolegomenon to Film Work for Historians,' *Journal of Contemporary History*, 1983, 18 July, pp. 416, 418.

7 I. C. Jarvie, 'Seeing through Movies,' *Philosophy of the Social Sciences*, 1978, vol. 8, p. 378.

8 Raack, 'Historiography as Cinematography,' p. 416.

9 Jarvie, 'Seeing through Movies,' p. 378.

10 Seymour Chatman, 'What Novels Can Do That Films Can't (and Vice Versa),' *Critical Inquiry*, 1980, vol. 7, pp. 125–6.

11 Pierre Sorlin argued the value of film in giving a feeling of certain kinds of settings in 'Historical Films as Tools for Historians,' in O'Connor, *Image as Artifact*.

12 Hayden White has made this point in a number of works, including *Metahistory: The Historical Imagination in Nineteenth-Century Europe*, Baltimore, MD: Johns Hopkins University Press, 1973; and in various articles in *Tropics of Discourse: Essays in Cultural Criticism*, Baltimore, MD: Johns Hopkins University Press, 1978.

13 A good survey of recent film theory is Dudley Andrew, *Concepts in Film Theory*, New York: Galaxy Books, 1984.

14 Quotations are from the narration of *Sans Soleil*. A longer discussion of the film as a work of history is contained in my lecture on *Sans Soleil*, delivered at the Neighborhood Film Project, Philadelphia, April 3, 1987. An interesting article on it is Janine Marchessault, 'Sans Soleil,' *CineAction!* 1986, vol. 5, pp. 2–6.

15 See Teshome H. Gabriel, *Third Cinema in the Third World: The Aesthetics of Liberation*, Ann Arbor, MN: University of Michigan Press, 1982; and Roy Ames, *Third World Filmmaking and the West*, Berkeley, CA: University of California Press, 1987, especially pp. 87–100.

16 For a full discussion of *Ceddo*, see Gabriel, *Third Cinema in the Third World*, pp. 86–9; and Ames, *Third World Filmmaking*, pp. 290–1. For *Quilombo*, see Coco Fusco, 'Choosing between Legend and History: An Interview with Carlos Diegues,' and Robert Starn, '*Quilombo*,' both in *Cineaste*, 1986, vol. 15, pp. 12–14, 42–4. For the history of Palmares, see R. K. Kent, 'Palmares: An African State in Brazil,' *Journal of African History*, 1965, vol. 6, pp. 161–75; and Arthur Ramos, 'The Negro Republic of Palmares,' in *The Negro in Brazil*, Washington, DC: Associated Publishers, 1939, pp. 42–53.

17 Hayden White, 'The Burden of History,' *History and Theory*, 1966, vol. 5, pp. 110–34; especially pp. 126–7. This article is also reprinted in White, *Tropics of Discourse*, pp. 27–50.

18 Hayden White has made this argument in a number of articles. See, for example, 'Historical Text as Literary Artifact,' and 'Historicism, History, and the Figurative Imagination,' both in *Tropics of Discourse*, pp. 81–120.

19 Bill Nichols, *Ideology and the Image*, Bloomington, IN: University of Indiana Press, 1981, p. 243.

Reading 4

Marcia Landy

THE HISTORICAL FILM

History and memory in media

'Introduction', in M. Landy (ed.), *The Historical Film: History and Memory in Media*, New Brunswick, NJ: Rutgers University Press, 2001, pp. 2–12.

THERE IS BY NO MEANS unanimous agreement about the nature, role, or forms of historicizing. A brief overview of the controversies surrounding the means and ends of historical representation offers a sense of what is at stake in reexamining the past. For example, at one extreme there are such writers as Francis Fukuyama who have propounded the notion of 'an end to history,' seeing the new era as one which is self-regulating, and in which there is no need to have recourse to the past to determine the present.[1] But there are other writers – Walter Benjamin, Michel Foucault, Gilles Deleuze, and Felix Guattari – with different and more complex views on the motives of traditional historiography; these critics resist monolithic views and especially the penchant for teleology.[2] They do not forsake history; rather, they urge the abandonment of monolithic, messianic and deterministic views toward the past, suggesting instead that the material of history takes many forms and, moreover, that these forms are not innocent nor purely 'objective.' These writers are suspicious that too often existing forms of history are disseminated by the victor and therefore deserve to be challenged as well as reexamined so that different conceptions of social and cultural change may be developed.

Historicizing has played a key role in consolidating notions of national, gendered, ethnic and racial identities, presenting deterministic and essentialist conceptions of time and human action. In the words of Etienne Balibar:

> The history of nations . . . is always already presented to us in the form of a narrative that attributes to these entities the continuity of a subject. The formation of the nation thus appears as the fulfillment of a 'project' stretching over centuries, in which there are different stages and moments of coming to self-awareness, which the prejudices of historians will portray as more or less decisive.[3]

This quotation is a reminder that national boundaries (geographical and cultural), the nature of the 'citizen-subject,' the forms of education, and conceptions of rights and duties are all dependent on constructed versions of the past. Versions of history thus play a powerful role in determining how individuals and groups inherit and understand their social and cultural milieu. History and memory have also played a part in destabilizing conceptions of the nation.

In twentieth century debates over representations of history, the work of the philosopher Friedrich Nietzsche has been extremely influential, especially for dissecting forms of historicizing and their relations to knowledge and power. In particular, his essay 'On the Uses and Disadvantages of History for Life' is an examination of modes of treating the past. Here, Nietzsche argues for the necessity of remembering the past, but he is critical of what he considers the excesses of attachments to the past. He invites his readers to contemplate that 'the unhistorical and historical are necessary in equal measure for the health of an individual, of a people and of a culture.'[4] Nietzsche outlines three dominant forms of historical construction – the monumental, the antiquarian, and the critical – arguing that to a degree each of these is necessary for regarding the past.

Monumental history is 'an engagement with the classic and rare of earlier times . . . the greatness that once existed.'[5] However, according to Nietzsche, too great an attachment to the monumental past is destructive:

> As long as the past has to be described as worthy of imitation, as imitable and possible for a second time, it of course incurs the danger of becoming somewhat distorted, beautified . . . incapable of distinguishing between a monumentalized past and a mythical fiction.[6]

Monumental history as purveyed in the cinema has certain defining characteristics. In its uses of narrative it relies on a vision of the past during moments of crisis and heroic conflict, and it reveals a penchant for the actions of heroic figures, such as Napoleon, Elizabeth I, Rembrandt, and Louis Pasteur. These figures come to define an age, and their actions are considered as models to be emulated. While unique, they are not isolated from the moral and social climate of their times; to the contrary, they are inseparably integrated into their era. In this view of history, there is often an implied contrast between the greatness of that past and the decadence of the present. However, monumental history may become rigidified and prescriptive, and, in its too-great attachment to, and veneration of, the past, thus block new conceptions.

Antiquarian history takes a different, though related, direction. The positive contributions of this type of history reside in its preservation of and reverence for 'ancestral goods.' In its portrayal of the past, it focuses on the artifacts of the past in minute detail; it probably has a greater claim to 'objectivity' than monumental history. But this form of history can also be insidious for, like monumental history, it 'knows only how to preserve life, not how to engender it; it always undervalues that which is becoming; . . . it hinders any resolve to attempt something new.'[7] Thus, what might be a necessary means for understanding uses of the past is in danger of becoming a destructive enterprise.

Critical history attempts to 'break up and dissolve a part of the past,'[8] concerned with what is deemed to be a necessary reexamination of the methods and values that have animated historians; but this form of history can also be excessive. In challenging the past without a regard for what is to be maintained and what is to be forgotten, the historian employing this method can end up disillusioned, completely denying the past, and refusing to understand and accept imperfection and injustice.[9]

From Nietzsche's comments, it is possible to draw several caveats about how history is understood, and how this understanding is acted out in practice; the conception and handling of history inevitably have an impact on how history is represented. First of all, in the cannibalizing of monuments and antiquities, any sense of critical comprehension of the relation between past and present is obliterated. The monumentalization of people and events can 'inspire the courageous to foolhardiness, and the inspired to fanaticism.'[10] Second, the antiquarian's veneration of historical objects destroys the critical discrimination necessary to enter into any assessment of what deserves remembering. Moreover, these objects take on a life of their own, completely disconnected from past or present. The cynicism that attends critical history lends itself to judgment and litigation rather than critical insight; on the positive side, this form of history can challenge prevailing and restrictive assessments of good and evil; on the negative side, when excessive, it inhibits alternative ways of thinking about the past.

Nietzsche's ideas on history are seminal for an understanding of how history continues to be represented and how critical challenges to traditional investments in the past can be expressed. Given the cataclysmic events of the twentieth century – two world wars, the rise of Fascism, and the Holocaust – and given the role of media in disseminating reductive and non-analytic monumental and antiquarian renditions of these events, philosophers and historians have been compelled to ask questions not only about the presentation of these events, but, even more, to ask, 'What is history?'

Following Nietzsche, the writings of Michel Foucault have been instrumental in rethinking the relations of forms of historicizing to the creation, legitimization, and exercise of power through western cultural institutions. In exploring the past, Foucault sought to avoid the excesses of history in contemporary culture and politics. In his essay 'Uses and Disadvantages of History for the Present Time' in Logic, Counter-Memory, and Practice, Foucault rehearses the three major lines of argument outlined in Nietzsche's Untimely Meditations; Foucault focuses finally on the importance of counterhistory as 'effective history.'[11]

According to Foucault, following Marx's *The Eighteenth Brumaire of Louis Bonaparte*, history repeats itself, first as tragedy, then as farce. In Foucault's terms, counterhistory is 'farcical.' Related to Nietzsche's conception of critical history, farcical history serves to undermine existing views of history as linear, as tending toward a purposive end (teleology), and as progressive. In the Nietzschean vein, counterhistory relinquishes its absolute claims to truth about the meaning and direction of history.[12]

Instead, counterhistory offers questions about the role of history as myth contributing to the consolidation of the nation-form, the State, and citizenship.

Foucault's analysis of historicizing has occasioned much commentary in the critical literature and in representations of history in literature and film. His work (and, in a different vein, the writings of the Annales historians in France and the New Historians in the United States) has fueled many of the current debates on history. The proliferation of historical monuments and museums has been concomitant with the phenomenal increase of historical texts – academic, literary, biographical, cinematic, and televisual.

Nietzsche's conceptions of the three modes of drawing on the past are often replicated in the styles of filmmaking as they draw on past modes of thinking about the past to dramatize that past. However, changing aspects of social and cultural life are revealed in the media's making of history now.

In this respect, the work of Jacques Derrida has been a major critical force in the reevaluation of historical thought. From *Of Grammatology* to *Archive Fever*, Derrida's writings have been influential in challenging received notions of representation and have had important philosophic implications for rethinking questions of language, history, memory, and the impact of electronic media in altering how we think about the past.[13] His deconstructive process, with its complex attention to the indeterminacies of language in speech and writing, is an assault on unitary and totalizing thought that have characterized Western narratives and especially history-writing, obscuring its multiple voices and reducing history to repetition and sameness. In the deconstructive focus on the multiple and ironic play of language, 'what Derrida offers as history,' writes Paul Bové, 'is repetition and trace.'[14] Unfortunately, Derrida's writing against history has, in the name of textuality, often been appropriated in such a way as to obscure the 'materiality of the very discourses it claims to deconstruct,' and thus 'fails to understand the realities of power.'[15] In the hands of many imitators, the deconstructive process can become another institutionalized academic mode of formal textual analysis shorn of any conceptual grappling with the nature or importance of understanding the political and cultural objectives in confronting the uses and abuses of the past. In this moment of postmodernity and globality, the assault on classic storytelling and 'master narratives' instead can also serve opportunism, relativism, and cynicism, fueling the sense that meaning, and hence cultural transformation, is not only impossible but superfluous. However, in another direction, Derrida's work has been productive for French and American feminists and for writers on postcoloniality in their quarrels with received history as they reveal gaps and misunderstandings, but also traces of other submerged, forgotten, and unexamined truths concerning gender, sexuality, and race.

Not only are conceptions of the past being revised, but histories of both film and television have had to be rewritten in the light of reexamined and altered conceptions of social development and change. New forms of media history have challenged reductive notions of historical development, especially the idea that historical change is linear, moving from the simple to the complex, and from the primitive to the technologically advanced. The films themselves – as well as the criticism of them – have played an increasingly important role in reshaping representations of history. Rather than reflecting history through verisimilitude, films reflect our received notions of the past and offer, either reflexively or obliquely, an understanding of how cinematic history is constituted in monumental, antiquarian, and critical fashion as well as in ways that counter the excesses of these modes.

One of the most challenging theoretical discussions of the changing aspects of cinema from its beginnings to the present can be found in Gilles Deleuze's two-volume study, *Cinema 1: The Movement-Image* and *Cinema 2: The Time-Image*. Drawing on Nietzsche's theories of history, Deleuze provides a map for charting how cinema capitalizes on its uses of the past and present. In the first volume, the reader is introduced to the various ways in which pre-World War II cinema was attached to an 'organic' form of narration in which the image of time was indirect. In this form of narration, the emphasis is on action and on a narrative whose parts are related to the whole. Examples can be found in the works of Abel Gance, Jean Renoir, Sergei Eisenstein, and Fritz Lang, who relied on sameness, repetition, and self-identity; in their creation of character and milieu, they emphasized affective forms of perception, not thought.

From the standpoint of early commercial cinema, the historical film – a staple of most cinemas – resembles the monumental and antiquarian forms described by Nietzsche.[16] As Deleuze frames it: 'The American cinema constantly shoots and reshoots a single fundamental film, which is the birth of a nation-civilisation.'[17] The decay of the movement-image is nowhere so blatantly exhibited as in the Nazi cinema where the past has been atrophied, where 'the revolutionary courtship of the movement-image and an art of the masses become subject was broken off.'[18]

Deleuze gives us a new conception of the uses of the past and present, indicating how the work of filmmakers such as Alfred Hitchcock and neorealists such as Roberto Rossellini opened the way to new conceptions of the image and its relation to the passage of real time and to objects and empty spaces. Instead of indirection, these filmmakers provided a sense of the everyday, of fantasy, or of a dream: the image takes on a sense of indeterminacy where the boundaries between the real and the imaginary blur. Instead of the monumental hero, the protagonists have become falsifiers, counterfeiters, somnambulists, and even children. Instead of the images of 'truth,' the audience is given images of the 'false,' in a 'crystalline' narration, a surface that reflects many layers and many discrete perspectives.[19] Moreover, instead of the unifying dimensions of action and affect, there is a new kind of narration, one that is discontinuous and fragmenting, rather than connected and unified. Both the characters in the film and the external audience become observers acutely aware of seeing and of recognizing images differently. In his analysis of the later films of Italian director Roberto Rossellini, Deleuze writes:

> Whether it is in Socrates, Christ, Augustine, Louis XIV, Pascal, or Descartes, the speech-act is torn away from the old style, at the same time as space forms a new layer which tends to cover the old: everywhere a struggle marking the itinerary of the difficult birth of a new world, under the double forceps of words and things.[20]

In short, if one is to follow Deleuze, one learns not only that the cinema is a major source for learning about the various forms that history has taken in the twentieth century, but also that particular cinematic styles signal important cultural changes closely tied to pedagogical conceptions of the nation or its critique.

I find that the contributions of Italian philosopher Antonio Gramsci are particularly helpful in understanding the powerful hold of the past on the present. Although most of the essays contained in this volume do not invoke the particular figure of Gramsci, his work has been central to many British critics in their attempts to understand historical representation. Such writers as Stuart Hall were responsible for a reintroduction in the 1970s of Gramsci's writings to the English-speaking world. Gramsci's work has been useful (especially for work of the Birmingham Centre for the Study of Contemporary Culture) in delineating new methods for rethinking the nature of popular and mass culture in relation to the uses of the past.[21]

The aspects of Gramsci's thought that appealed most to the Birmingham school stressed the workings of 'common sense as folklore' as an instrument for forging consensus.[22] In this view, the past is not inherited in a consistent, logical, and unified fashion. Rather, history is circulated in a form that is often clichéd, based on legalistic forms, oratory, and aphorisms. Gramsci's examination of common sense exposed the various ways in which movement toward consensus is dependent on these contradictory and fragmented forms of knowledge derived from the past. The shards of the past are embedded in these inconsistent, illogical, and disunified forms of common sense. Most important is that the cement for these fragments is affective, for the investment in the past is melodramatic. This component of Gramscian analysis is useful in identifying the persistence of certain models and formulas. Whether or not critics allude specifically to the notion of 'common sense as folklore,' I contend that they are eager to rethink the ways in which folklore is being understood and even combated by historical films.

From earliest embodiments in the cinema, the penchant for documenting the past has been evident. Early cinema focused on novelties, spectacles, funerals, marriages, sports, military exercises, and the activities of the rich and famous. A demand for 'veracity' and 'facticity' was raised early, especially around staged events on film purported to be 'authentic.' With the appearance of longer films and with genre differentiation in the teens and twenties, as well as the distinction between 'fiction' and 'nonfiction,' historical and fantasy (or escapist) films became common. Given the scrutiny of any cinematic work according to these standards of factuality and nonfictionality, it is not surprising that the 'historical film' was seldom considered to be a conduit for any believable and legitimate sense of history.

The major genres that rely on images of the past are historical films and costume dramas, and the tendency to describe these films as unhistorical, escapist, and unrealistic has been a dominant trend of film and historical criticism until recent decades. Film criticism has begun to rethink the cinematic representations of political events that occurred during the twentieth century. In particular, concomitant with the criticism that has sought to understand the historical preoccupation with nation formation, the academic study of cinema has focused on relations between cinema and nation as attempts have been made to describe and analyze what is meant by a 'national cinema.'

The sound films of the 1930s and 1940s – the biographical film ('biopic'), the costume spectacle, and the historical film – depicted significant individuals and events associated mainly with traditional and watershed moments of a country's past. Historical films employed major stars and celebrated significant events in the forging of national identity. These films frequently served as a form of collective morality as well as source of morale. They were often produced on a grand scale in the mode of 'monumental history,' and they have been instrumental in establishing conventions about the commercial cinema's uses of spectacle in its treatment of the past.

The genre of the historical film often reveals the excesses of monumental history and its fascination with both the spectacle and the heroic figure – embodied in stars who assumed the roles of the rich, famous, and powerful. This kind of historical film flourished up to (and to a lesser extent during) the World War II years; examples include *Queen Christina* (1934), *The Scarlet Empress* (1934), *The Grand Illusion* (1937), *Young Mr. Lincoln* (1939), *Ivan the Terrible* (1942–1946), and *Young Mr. Pitt* (1942). Their uses of folklore and legend temporarily waned in the late 1940s and 1950s in the aftermath of World War II and during the Cold War. The cinematic 'epic' of ancient Rome and Greece was resurrected beginning in the 1950s, characterized by such films as *Spartacus* (1960) and by Italian spectacles involving Hercules in particular.

The post-World War II years witnessed the rise of neorealism in cinema, expressed in such films as *Rome, Open City* (1945), *Paisan* (1946), and *The Bicycle Thief* (1948). In its wake, filmmakers reacted negatively to genre films, such as costume dramas and historical films, advocating a focus on the present and a rejection of monumental and antiquarian forms of filmmaking. Emphasizing a 'new realism,' these filmmakers sought to convey a different sense of the social milieu. Not only did notions of acting change (extending even to the use of nonprofessional actors), but there was also a reaction against the conventional melodramatic distinctions between hero and villain. By implication, not only was history on trial, so was the history of the classic cinema.

Significantly, in the occupied and 'defeated' countries of Japan and Germany, the occupying governments established limits, if not prohibitions, on the historical film as a 'precautionary' measure against films that exalted militarism. In Eastern Europe only in the late 1950s and 1960s was there a reemergence of historical films (such as the films of Andrej Wajda). These films focus specifically on World War II and raise the question of the uses of that historical event in relation to current events in 'communist' countries such as Poland and Hungary.

More recently, the historic political convulsions in Europe in 1968 had an impact on how history was to be represented generally and on the cinema in particular. Throughout the sixties and early seventies, films identified as 'New Wave' played a key role in the further globalization of cinema. Their impact was felt from Hong Kong to Hollywood and they were instrumental in the styles of both experimental and popular films. New Wave filmmakers, like François Truffaut, Jean-Luc Godard, and Pier Paolo Pasolini, were engaged in forms of criticism and filmmaking that would alter the course of cinema and conceptions of the time-image and, hence, of history. These filmmakers, first of all, took a fresh look at Hollywood cinema; they developed a critical terminology, in journal essays and on film, designed to rescue cinema – and particularly commercial and mass cinema – from its stigma of escapism and unreality. Moreover, in the ways that they employed cinematic language, these filmmakers broke down the classic realist cinema's structures of continuity editing: their narratives were episodic and fragmented. They employed star images and genre forms reflexively, increasingly calling critical attention to how the commercial cinema, identified with Hollywood, had forged its mythology.

Following the precedent of the neorealists, in these films the protagonists are no longer the 'heroes' found in earlier cinema, but instead are either flawed or pasteboard figures. The earlier emphasis on action-oriented narratives gave way to a paralysis on the part of the characters, who are seen as observers like their audience. These films are multilayered and intertextual, emphasizing the role of looking and hearing instead of action and transformation of the social milieu. In these ways, the spectator is enlisted to view and to rethink the uses of time and of the past. These New Wave films had a profound impact in several ways: they initiated new forms of narration; they produced new relations to the actor/stars; and they offered a 'pedagogy' of spectatorship and of film history in such films as the Antoine Doinel cycle, *Breathless* (1960) and *Alphaville* (1965).

In the 1970s and 1980s, a new generation of German filmmakers (Rainer Werner Fassbinder, Volker Schlöndorff, Hans-Jürgen Syberberg, and Helma Sanders-Brahms, to name a few – all influenced especially by Jean-Luc Godard), were eager to challenge their elders' silence about the Nazi past. They experimented with cinematic methods, seeking to develop a language that would be able to communicate their understanding of Germany's suppressed history. At the same time, film and television became a major source for portraits of historical events; examples include the television series *Holocaust* and the film *Heimat*. An important precursor of, and model for, treatments of the Holocaust on film had been Resnais's *Night and Fog* (1955), considered by most critics of historical films to be a 'truthful' and unsentimental examination of that event. The Holocaust continues to be a subject of interest to filmmakers. In France, during the 1980s, two documentary films – Claude Lanzmann's *Shoah* (1985) and Marcel Ophuls's *Hotel Terminus* (1988) – examined the history of the Holocaust by means of interviews with both former Nazis and Holocaust survivors. Films employing a fictional format, such as *Au revoir les enfants* (1988), have sought to address the ravages of the Nazi past, using melodrama in ways that can create an affective relation to events, re-animating a sense of a past that is becoming increasingly remote in time. Commercial cinema and television have not been far behind in their productions of Nazism and the Holocaust; both media have triggered debates about the uses of history in film and television. The vehement discussions of the film *Schindler's List* (1993) are a case in point. Most recently, the war between documentation and 'fiction' film continues in the assessment of Roberto Benigni's *Life Is Beautiful* (1998). Both of these commercial films are considered, by and large, to falsify events, to attempt to put into pictures what is inherently inexpressible, and thereby to display disrespect for victims of the Holocaust.

The production of history has proved popular and profitable. Since the late 1970s, Britain has experimented with what Andrew Higson has termed the 'heritage film.' In this form of filmmaking, 'the evocation of pastness is accomplished by a look, a style, the loving re-creation of period details,' producing 'a fascinating but self-enclosed world.'[23] The heritage film is exemplified by such diverse texts as *Chariots of Fire* (1981), *Another Country* (1984), *Scandal* (1984), *Dance with a Stranger* (1985), *Maurice* (1987), and *Carrington* (1995). Unlike these heritage films, a number of critical films on Ireland – such as *Four Days in July* (1984), *In the Name of the Father* (1993), *Michael Collins* (1996), and *The Butcher Boy* (1997) – are less preoccupied with a detailed representation of a period in the Irish national past than they are with offering unsettling versions of familiar national conflicts through their revision of history. In the United States, the blockbuster historical film continues into the 1990s with Hollywood films that have been concerned with revisiting the past cinematically; examples include *Malcolm X* (1992), *Forrest Gump* (1994), *Panther* (1995), *Amistad* (1997), and *Titanic* (1998).

The historical film and documentary filmmaking are also experiencing a revival in the cinemas of Asia, Africa, and Latin America. In the wake of postcoloniality and its preoccupation with memory instead of with official history, African cinema has sought to create a counterhistory of colonialism and imperialism; examples may be found in such films as Kwah Ansah's *Heritage Africa* (1988) and Ousmane Sembène's *The Camp at Thiaroye* (1989). In contrast to the action cinema of Hong Kong, the mainland Chinese cinema has contributed to the rethinking of the past in such films as *Raise the Red Lantern* (1991) and *Farewell My Concubine* (1993). Diaspora films, including *Mississippi Masala* (1992) and *The Joy Luck Club* (1993), also play a part in rethinking histories of the nation and conceptions of national identity. The questions raised by these films, and others coming from Asia, Africa, and Latin America, are closely tied to the redefinition of contemporary culture as 'postmodern.' For many who write on the 'postmodern condition,' history is regarded as an assemblage of images, as part of the world of information commodities, endlessly recyclable and transformable, repeatable and devoid of meaning.

Television also constitutes a major venue for the dissemination of historical images. As cable stations proliferate, we have growing numbers of channels devoted to biography and history, offering miniseries that replay different moments in history – especially the ones that have captured the national imagination, such as the Civil War. World War II has been a perennial source of new programming and reruns of older programs. Periodically, historically interesting events of shorter duration and narrower scope – such as the 'disasters' (as they are termed on television) of John F. Kennedy's assassination and more recently the events surrounding the death, mourning, and funeral of Princess Diana enlist the devices of historical memory.[24] What are the effects of this proliferation of history on television?

Umberto Eco offers a disturbing answer to this question: 'It doesn't matter what you say via the channels of mass communication . . . The important thing is the gradual uniform bombardment of information, where the different contents are leveled and lose their difference.'[25] Anton Kaes, too, in writing about the proliferation of films and television programs dealing with the Holocaust, has questioned the effects of repetition, whether this 'bombardment' dulls the thinking and makes it impossible to see or understand the very events that are purportedly under examination.[26] Has the ability to discriminate been eradicated? In place of discrimination, is the spectator treated to discrete and indigestible bits of 'information,' an endless procession of substitutable disaster? If so, history becomes tabloid, catastrophe, and scandal; or, at its worst, historical representation appears as 'opinion' in a world of conflicting opinions, where there is no way of arriving at unassailable 'truth.'

In one sense, this complaint about film and television has been around a long time, focusing always on mass and popular culture. These negative views are especially relevant to any attempts to assess the uses of history in media. How is it possible to understand the inevitably changing aspects of history? And what is to be made of the impossibility of irrevocably 'fixing' attitudes toward and judgments about the past? Is there a methodology that will help to deliver us from the vicissitudes of relativism? It is obvious that a 'belief' in the possibility of reconstructing the past with absolute objectivity 'as it was' already founders on one of the Nietzschean caveats about the effects of an excess of history. Moreover, the nature of investments in the past – whose investments and toward what end – can be revealing of another excess: namely, a belief in the possibility of total objectivity, absolute truth, and complete veracity.

From another side, the attack on media history is launched in terms of its sentiment. When a critic seeks to attack popular history, the pejorative term usually directed at the 'fiction' is that it is 'melodramatic,' which implies that this type of representation is unhistorical. In this view, popular history relies on clichés, on wisdom inherited from the past, and on an emotional investment in the past. This folklore inheres in melodrama, which seeks to make sense of the past, but does so in formulaic terms. In recent decades, critics have taken a serious look at melodrama in an effort to understand its language and cultural basis in the context of modernity. Taken seriously, melodrama 'becomes the principal mode for uncovering, demonstrating and making operative the essential moral universe in a postsacred era.'[27]

I have argued, in a discussion of films on the Italian Resistance and on the Holocaust, that the presence of melodrama is important in the enterprise of understanding popular forms of historicizing.[28] In films employing melodrama, the investment in reliving the past through flashback, somnambulism, or fetishism of certain objects is evident. Forms of religiosity and legality are also central to melodrama; they play key roles in attempts to expose the criminality often at the heart of the historical event. Inherent in the 'melodramatic imagination is the imperative of judgment that attends the preoccupation with the past. The quest for assigning responsibility is common to both high and mass culture. Melodrama is thus not ahistorical but central to the folklore that inheres in popular history.'[29]

Historically, the study of film is a relative latecomer to cultural analysis. From the 1970s onward, the field of film studies has derived intellectual sustenance from, and sought to accommodate, various philosophical positions. It has sought to establish a critical and political language for cinematic analysis examining the history of the medium, its development within certain national contexts, its relation to the other arts, and, more recently, its relation to other disciplines, such as philosophy and history. The emphasis has begun to shift from the necessary initial accumulation of data about film, from interpretations of individual texts, and from the exclusive attention to individual auteurs, to addressing questions of the cultural impact and reception of film and television. The appearance of a number of books on the topic – such as Rosenstone's *Revisioning History*, Pierre Sorlin's *The Film in History*, Vivian Sobchack's collection of essays, *The Persistence of History*, and my *Cinematic Uses of the Past* – testify to the rethinking of the relationship of media to historical representation.

Notes

1 Francis Fukuyama, *The End of History and the Last Man*, New York: Maxwell Macmillan, 1992.

2 Walter Benjamin, 'Theses on the Philosophy of History' in *Illuminations*, ed. Hannah Arendt, trans. Harry Zohn, New York: Schocken Books, 1976, pp. 251–64.

3 Etienne Balibar, 'The Nation Form: History and Ideology' in *Race, Nation, Class: Ambiguous Identities*, London: Verso, 1995, p. 86.
4 Friedrich Nietzsche, 'The Uses and Disadvantages of History for Life' in *Untimely Meditations*, ed. J. O. Stern. and trans. R. J. Hollingdale, Cambridge: Cambridge University Press, 1991, p. 63.
5 Ibid., p. 69.
6 Ibid., p. 70.
7 Ibid., p. 75.
8 Ibid., p. 73.
9 Ibid., p. 76.
10 Ibid., p. 73.
11 Michel Foucault, 'Nietzsche, Genealogy, History' in *Logic, Counter-Memory, Practice: Selected Essays and Interviews,* ed. Donald F. Bouchard, Ithaca, NY: Cornell University Press, 1988, pp. 139–65.
12 Ibid., pp. 160–3.
13 Jacques Derrida, *Of Grammatology*, trans. and ed. Gayatri Chakravorty Spivak, Baltimore, MD: Johns Hopkins University Press, 1976; *Archive Fever: A Freudian Impression*, trans. Eric Prenowitz, Chicago, IL: University of Chicago Press, 1996.
14 Paul Bové, *Mastering Discourse: The Politics of Intellectual Culture*, Durham, NC: Duke University Press, 1992, p. 74.
15 Ibid., p. 75.
16 Gilles Deleuze, *Cinema 1: The Movement-Image*, trans. Hugh Tomlinson and Barbara Habberjam, Minneapolis, MN: University of Minnesota Press, 1986, p. 150.
17 Ibid., p. 148.
18 Deleuze, *Cinema 2: The Time-Image*, trans. Hugh Tomlinson and Roberta Galeta, Minneapolis, MN: University of Minnesota Press, 1989, p. 64.
19 Ibid., pp. 126–31.
20 Ibid., p. 248.
21 Stuart Hall, *The Hard Road to Renewal: Thatcherism and the Crisis of the Left*, London: Verso, 1984.
22 Antonio Gramsci, *Selections from the Prison Notebooks*, ed. and trans. Quintin Hoare and Geoffrey Nowell Smith, New York: International Publishers, 1978, pp. 323–3, 419–25.
23 Andrew Higson, *Waving the Flag: Constructing a National Cinema in Britain*, Oxford: Oxford University Press, 1995, p. 113.
24 Wheeler Winston Dixon, *Disaster and Memory*, New York: Columbia University Press, 1999.
25 Umberto Eco, *Travels in Hyperreality: Essays*, trans. William Weaver, San Diego, CA: Harcourt Brace Jovanovich, 1986.
26 Anton Kaes, *From Hitler to Heimat: The Return of History as Film*, Cambridge, MA: Harvard University Press, 1989, p. 198.
27 Peter Brooks, *The Melodramatic Imagination: Balzac, Henry James, Melodrama, and the Mode of Excess*, New York: Columbia University Press, 1985, p. 15.
28 Marcia Landy, 'History on Trial: The Case of *Porzus*' in *Screening the Past*, Arthur Lindeman and Anthony Guneratne, Latrobe University (April, 1999), www.latrobe.edu: np.
29 Marcia Landy, 'Cinematic History, Hollywood, and the Holocaust,' in *Humanity at the Limit: The Impact of the Holocaust on Christians and Jews,* Bloomington, IN: Indiana University Press, 2000.

Reading 5

Hayden White

HISTORIOGRAPHY AND HISTORIOPHOTY

'Historiography and Historiophoty', *American Historical Review*, 1988, vol. 93(5), pp. 1193–9.

ROBERT ROSENSTONE'S ESSAY [reading 3] raises at least two questions that should be of eminent concern to professional historians. The first is that of the relative adequacy of what we might call 'historio*photy*' (the representation of history and our thought about it in visual images and filmic discourse) to the criteria of truth and accuracy presumed to govern the professional practice of historio*graphy* (the representation of history in verbal images and written discourse). Here the issue is whether it is possible to 'translate' a given written account of history into a visual-auditory equivalent without significant loss of content. The second question has to do with what Rosenstone calls the 'challenge' presented by historiophoty to historiography. It is obvious that cinema (and video) are better suited than written discourse to the actual representation of certain kinds of historical phenomena – landscape, scene, atmosphere, complex events such as wars, battles, crowds, and emotions. But, Rosenstone asks, can historiophoty adequately convey the complex, qualified, and critical dimensions of historical thinking about events, which, according to Ian Jarvie, at least, is what makes any given representation of the past a distinctly 'historical' account?

In many ways, the second question is more radical than the first in its implications for the way we might conceptualize the tasks of professional historiography in our age. The historical evidence produced by our epoch is often as much visual as it is oral and written in nature. Also, the communicative conventions of the human sciences are increasingly as much pictorial as verbal in their predominant modes of representation. Modern historians ought to be aware that the analysis of visual images requires a manner of 'reading' quite different from that developed for the study of written documents. They should also recognize that the representation of historical events, agents, and processes in visual images presupposes the mastery of a lexicon, grammar, and syntax – in other words, a language and a discursive mode – quite different from that conventionally used for their representation in verbal discourse alone. All too often, historians treat photographic, cinematic, and video data as if they could be read in the same way as a written document. We are inclined to treat the imagistic evidence as if it were at best a complement of verbal evidence, rather than as a supplement, which is to say, a discourse in its own right and one capable of telling us things about its referents that are both different from what can be told in verbal discourse and also of a kind that can only be told by means of visual images.

Some information about the past can be provided only by visual images. Where imagistic evidence is lacking, historical investigation finds a limit to what it can legitimately assert about the way things may have appeared to the agents acting on a given historical scene. Imagistic (and especially photographic and cinematic) evidence provides a basis for a reproduction of the scenes and atmosphere of past events much more accurate than any derived from verbal testimony alone. The historiography of any period of history for which photographs and films exist will be quite different, if not more accurate, than that focused on periods known primarily by verbal documentation.

So, too, in our historiographical practices, we are inclined to use visual images as a complement of our written discourse, rather than as components of a discourse in its own right, by means of which we might be able to say something different from and other than what we can say in verbal form. We are inclined to use pictures primarily as 'illustrations' of the predications made in our verbally written discourse. We have not on the whole exploited the possibilities of using images as a principal medium of *discursive* representation, using verbal commentary only diacritically, that is to say, to direct attention to, specify, and emphasize a meaning conveyable by visual means alone.

Rosenstone properly insists that some things – he cites landscapes, sounds, strong emotions, certain kinds of conflicts between individuals and groups, collective events and the movements of crowds – can be better represented on film (and, we might add, video) than in any merely verbal account. 'Better' here would mean not only with greater verisimilitude or stronger emotive effect but also less ambiguously, more accurately. Rosenstone appears to falter before the charge, made by purists, that the historical film is inevitably both too detailed (in what it shows when it is forced to use actors and sets that may not resemble perfectly the historical individuals and scenes of which it is a representation) and not detailed enough (when it is forced to condense a process that might have taken years to occur, the written account of which might take days to read, into a two or three-hour presentation). But this charge, as he properly remarks, hinges on a failure to distinguish adequately between a mirror image of a phenomenon and other kinds of representations of it, of which the written historical account itself would be only one instance. No history, visual or verbal, 'mirrors' all or even the greater part of the events or scenes of which it purports to be an account, and this is true even of the most narrowly restricted 'micro-history.' Every written history is a product of processes of condensation, displacement, symbolization, and qualification exactly like those used in the production of a filmed representation. It is only the medium that differs, not the way in which messages are produced.

Jarvie apparently laments the poverty of the 'information load' of the historical film, whether 'fictional' (such as *The Return of Martin Guerre*) or 'documentary' (such as Rosenstone's own *The Good Fight*). But this is to confuse the question of scale and level of generalization at which the historical account ought 'properly' to operate with that of the amount of evidence needed to support the generalizations and the level of interpretation on which the account is cast. Are short books about long periods of history in themselves non-historical or anti-historical in nature? Was Edward Gibbon's *Decline and Fall*, or for that matter Fernand Braudel's *The Mediterranean*, of sufficient length to do justice to its subject?[1] What is the proper length of a historical monograph? How much information is needed to support any given historical generalization? Does the amount of information required vary with the scope of the generalization? And, if so, is there a normative scope against which the propriety of any historical generalization can be measured? On what principle, it might be asked, is one to assess the preference for an account that might take an hour to read (or view) as against that which takes many hours, even days, to read, much less assimilate to one's store of knowledge?

According to Rosenstone, Jarvie complemented his critique of the necessarily impoverished 'information load' of the historical film with two other objections: first, the tendency of the historical film to favor 'narration' (Rosenstone himself notes that the two historical films he worked on 'compress[ed] the past to a closed world by telling a single, linear story with, essentially, a single interpretation') over 'analysis'; and, second, the presumed incapacity of film to represent the true essence of historiography, which, according to Jarvie, consists less of 'descriptive narrative' than of 'debates between historians about just what exactly did happen, why it happened, and what would be an adequate account of its significance.'[2]

Rosenstone is surely right to suggest that the historical film need not necessarily feature narrative at the expense of analytical interests. In any event, if a film like *The Return of Martin Guerre* turns out to resemble a 'historical romance,' it is not because it is a narrative film but rather because the romance genre was used to plot the story that the film wished to tell. There are other genres of plots, conventionally considered to be more 'realistic' than the romance, that might have been used to shape the events depicted in this story into a narrative of a different kind. If *Martin Guerre* is a 'historical romance,' it would be more proper to compare it, not with 'historical narrative' but with the 'historical novel,' which has a problematic of its own, the discussion of which has concerned historians since its invention in much the same way that the discussion of film today ought properly to concern them. And it ought to concern them for the reasons outlined in Rosenstone's essay, namely, because it raises the specter of the 'fictionality' of the historian's own discourse, whether cast in the form of a narrative account or in a more 'analytical,' non-narrative mode.

Like the historical novel, the historical film draws attention to the extent to which it is a constructed or, as Rosenstone calls it, a 'shaped' representation of a reality we historians would prefer to consider to be 'found' in the events themselves or, if not there, then at least in the 'facts' that have been established by historians' investigation of the record of the past. But the historical monograph is no less 'shaped' or constructed than the historical film or historical novel. It may be shaped by different principles, but there is no reason why a filmed representation of historical events should not be as analytical and realistic as any written account.

Jarvie's characterization of the essence of historiography ('debates between historians about just what exactly did happen, why it happened, and what would be an adequate account of its significance') alerts us to the problem of how and to what purpose historians transform information about 'events' into the 'facts' that serve as the subject matter of their arguments. Events happen or occur; facts are constituted by the subsumption of events under a description, which is to say, by acts of predication. The 'adequacy' of any given account of the past, then, depends on the question of the choice of the set of concepts actually used by historians in their transformation of information about events into, not 'facts' in general, but 'facts' of a specific kind (political facts, social facts, cultural facts, psychological facts). The instability of the very distinction between 'historical' facts on the one side and non-historical ('natural' facts, for example) on the other, a distinction without which a specifically historical kind of knowledge would be unthinkable, indicates the constructivist nature of the historian's enterprise. When considering the utility or adequacy of filmed accounts of historical events, then, it would be well to reflect upon the ways in which a distinctively imagistic discourse can or cannot transform information about the past into facts of a specific kind.

I do not know enough about film theory to specify more precisely the elements, equivalent to the lexical, grammatical, and syntactical dimensions of spoken or written language, of a distinctly filmic discourse. Roland Barthes insisted that still photographs do not and could not predicate – only their titles or captions could do so. But cinema is quite another matter. Sequences of shots and the use of montage or closeups can be made to predicate quite as effectively as phrases, sentences, or sequences of sentences in spoken or written discourse. And if cinema can predicate, then it can just as surely do all the things that Jarvie considered to constitute the essence of written historical discourse. Moreover, it should not be forgotten that the sound film has the means by which to complement visual imagery with a distinctive verbal content that need not sacrifice analysis to the exigencies of dramatic effects. As for the notion that a filmed portrayal of historical events could not be 'defend[ed]' and 'footnote[d],' respond to objections, and 'criticize the opposition,' there is no reason at all to suppose that this could not in principle be done.[3] There is no law prohibiting the production of a historical film of sufficient length to do all of these things.

Rosenstone's list of the effects of historians' prejudices against 'historiophoty' is sketchy but full enough. He indicates that many of the problems posed by the effort to 'put history onto film' stem from the notion that the principal task is to translate what is already a written discourse into an imagistic one. Resistance to the effort to put history onto film centers for the most part on the question of what gets lost in this process of translation. Among the things supposedly lost are accuracy of detail, complexity of explanation, the auto-critical and inter-critical dimensions of historiological reflection, and the qualifications of generalizations necessitated by, for instance, the absence or unavailability of documentary evidence. Rosenstone seems to grant the force of Jarvie's claim that the 'information load' of the filmed representation of historical events and processes is inevitably impoverished when he considers the question of whether a 'thinning of data' on the screen 'makes for poor history.' While pointing out that film permits us to 'see landscapes, hear sounds, witness strong emotions . . . or view physical conflict between individuals and groups,' he seems unsure whether historiophoty might not 'play down the analytical' aspects of historiography and favor appeals to the emotive side of the spectator's engagement with images. But, at the same time, he insists that there is nothing inherently anti-analytical about filmed representations of history and certainly nothing that is inherently antihistoriological about historiophoty. And, in his brief consideration of the film documentary, Rosenstone turns the force of the anti-historiophoty argument back on those who, in making this argument, appear to ignore the extent to which any kind of historio*graphy* shares these same limitations.

He grants, for example, that, although the film documentary strives for the effect of a straightforwardly direct and objective account of events, it is always a 'shaped' – fashioned or stylized – representation thereof. '[W]e must remember,' he writes, 'that on the screen we see not the events themselves . . . but selected images of those events.' The example he gives is that of a film shot of a cannon being fired followed by another shot of an explosion of the (or a) shell some distance away. Such a sequence, he suggests, is, properly speaking, fictional rather than factual, because, obviously, the camera could not have been simultaneously in the two places where first the firing and then the explosion occurred. What we have, then, is a pseudo-factual representation of a cause–effect relation. But is this representation 'false' thereby, that is to say, is it false because the explosion shown in the second shot is not that of the shell fired in the first shot but rather is a shot of some other shell, fired from who knows where?

In this case, the notion that the sequence of images is false would require a standard of representational literalness that, if applied to historiography itself, would render it impossible to write. In fact, the 'truthfulness' of the sequence is to be found not at the level of concreteness but rather at another level of representation, that of typification. The sequence should be taken to represent a *type* of event. The referent of the sequence is the *type* of event depicted, not the two discrete events imaged, first, the firing of *a* shell and, then, *its* explosion. The spectator is not being 'fooled' by such a representation nor is there anything duplicitous in such a rendering of a cause-and-effect sequence. The veracity of the representation hinges on the question of the likelihood of this *type* of cause-and-effect sequence occurring at specific times and places and under certain conditions, namely, in the kind of war made possible by a certain kind of industrial-military technology and fought in a particular time and place.

Indeed, it is a convention of written history to represent the causes and effects of such events in precisely this way, in a sequence of images that happens to be verbal rather than visual, to be sure, but no less 'fictional' for being so. The concreteness, precision of statement, and accuracy of detail of a sentence such as, 'The sniper's bullet fired from a nearby warehouse struck President Kennedy in the head, wounding him fatally,' are not in principle denied to a filmed depiction either of the event referred to in the sentence or of the cause-and-effect relation that it cites as an explanation. One can imagine a situation in which enough cameras were deployed in such a way as to have captured both the sniper's shot and the resultant effect with greater immediacy than that feigned in the verbal representation and, indeed, with greater factual precision, inasmuch as the verbal utterance depends on an inference from effect to cause for which no specific documentation exists. In the filmed representations of this famous event, the ambiguity that still pervades our knowledge of it has been left intact and not dispelled by the specious concreteness suggested in the provision of the 'details' given in the verbal representation. And if this is true of micro-events, such as the assassination of a head of state, how much more true is it of the representation in written history of macro-events?

For example, when historians list or indicate the 'effects' of a large-scale historical event, such as a war or a revolution, they are doing nothing different from what an editor of a documentary film does in showing shots of an advancing army followed by shots of enemy troops surrendering or fleeing, followed by shots of the triumphant force entering a conquered city. The difference between a written account and a filmed account of such a sequence turns less on the general matter of accuracy of detail than on the different kinds of concreteness with which the images, in the one case verbal, in the other visual, are endowed. Much depends on the nature of the 'captions' accompanying the two kinds of images, the written commentary in the verbal account and the voice-over or subtitles in the visual one, that 'frame' the depicted events individually and the sequence as a whole. It is the nature of the claims made for the images considered as evidence that determines both the discursive function of the events and the criteria to be employed in the assessment of their veracity as predicative utterances.

Thus, for example, the depiction, in Richard Attenborough's film *Gandhi*, of the anonymous South African railway conductor who pushed the young Gandhi from the train, is not a misrepresentation insofar as the actor playing the role may not have possessed the physical features of the actual agent of that act. The veracity of the scene depends on the depiction of *a* person whose historical significance derived from the *kind* of act he performed at a particular time and place, which act was a function of an identifiable type of role-playing under the kinds of social conditions prevailing at a general, but specifically historical, time and place. And the same is true of the depiction of Gandhi himself in the film. Demands for a verisimilitude in film that is impossible in any medium of representation, including that of written history, stem from the confusion of historical individuals with the kinds of 'characterization' of them required for discursive purposes, whether in verbal or in visual media.

Even in written history, we are often forced to represent some agents only as 'character types,' that is, as individuals known only by their general social attributes or by the kinds of actions that their 'roles' in a given historical event permitted them to play, rather than as full-blown 'characters,' individuals with many known attributes, proper names, and a range of known actions that permit us to draw fuller portraits of them than we can draw of their more 'anonymous' counterparts. But the agents who form a 'crowd' (or any other kind of group) are not more misrepresented in a film for being portrayed by actors than they are in a verbal account of their collective action.

Too often, discussions of the irredeemably fictional nature of historical films fail to take account of the work of experimental or avant-garde filmmakers, for whom the analytic function of their discourse tends to predominate over the exigencies of 'storytelling.' Rosenstone cites a number of experimentalist films that not only depart from but actually seek to undermine the conventions of commercial (especially the Hollywood variety of) filmmaking. A film such as *Far from Poland*, he points out, not only does not feature storytelling at the expense of analysis but actually brings under question the conventional (nineteenth-century) notions of 'realistic' representation to which many contemporary historians, analytical as well as narrational, still subscribe. He specifically likens the work of experimental filmmakers to that of Bertolt Brecht in the history of the theater. But he might just as well have likened it to the work of those historians of the modern age who have taken as their problem less the 'realistic representation' of 'the past' than what Jarvie himself calls the question of 'what would be an adequate account' of 'what exactly did happen, why it happened, and . . . its significance.' This is surely the lesson to be derived from the study of recent feminist filmmaking, which has been concerned not only with depicting the lives of women in both the past and present truthfully and accurately but, even more important, with bringing into question conventions of historical representation and analysis that, while pretending to be doing nothing more than 'telling what really happened,' effectively present a patriarchical version of history. The kind of experimentalist films invoked by Rosenstone do indeed 'subvert' the kind of 'realism' we associate with both conventional films and conventional historiography, but it is not because they may sacrifice 'accuracy of detail' in order to direct attention to the problem of choosing a way to represent the past. They show us instead that the criterion for determining what shall count as 'accuracy of detail' depends on the 'way' chosen to represent both 'the past' and our thought about its 'historical significance' alike.

Notes

1 Edward Gibbon, *The History of the Decline and Fall of the Roman Empire*, London, 1776–88; Fernand Braudel, *The Mediterranean and the Mediterranean World*, New York: Simon and Schuster, 1972.

2 Robert A. Rosenstone, 'History in Images/History in Words: Reflections on the Possibility of Really Putting History onto Film,' *American Historical Review*, reproduced above; and I. C. Jarvie, 'Seeing through Movies,' *Philosophy of the Social Sciences*, 1978, vol. 8, p. 378.

3 Jarvie, 'Seeing through Movies,' p. 378.

PART 2

Shaping historical film

MAKING A HISTORY INVOLVES MAKING DECISIONS. This is because the past is not ready packaged for telling and understanding. There is no necessary or absolute start or end point to an event that happened in the past. Nor is there any one necessary or absolute form of telling or ordering it. A fact only becomes a historical fact, Carr once argued, when it is deemed significant by selection, interpretation and ordering:

> The facts speak only when the historian calls on them: it is he who decides to which facts to give the floor, and in what order or context.[1]

For some scholars, the form of a history is secondary to its content; the narrative structure and emphases of their works are suggested by the events themselves. In David Carr's view, for example, those who make history draw out narrative forms that are implicit 'in the events themselves'.[2] Many more scholars, though, argue that histories are more or less authorial constructions. As Phillips and Phillips explain, the activities of filmmakers as shapers of the past are like those of all historians:

> films treat the historical record as mere raw material, to be adapted to the needs of the screenplay. Chronology is expanded, compressed, reversed, or falsified to suit the dramatic trajectory. Historical personages are revised, deified or demonized, conflated or created from whole cloth to serve the director's will.[3]

What is debated is the extent to which a history is an expression of a 'director's will', and whether expressions of will in history correspond to those of fiction makers.

In *Metahistory*, for example, Hayden White advances that histories are characterised by various conventional modes of emplotment (story or plot type), ranging from satire, in which historical agents are ultimately captive to the situations in which they find themselves, to comedy, where events tend to a beneficial resolution, and Roland Barthes has written of the 'reality effects' that historians employ to suggest that their works are transparent descriptions of the past.[4]

The readings in Part 2 are all contributions to the discussion on what I have called the 'shaping' of historical films, or the role of form in histories. The first reading is a journal article by Jean-Louis Comolli, which was translated into English for the journal *Screen* in 1978. In it, Comolli suggests that historical films are part of a 'game' of belief and disbelief, and that viewers are like 'impatient gamblers' who believe that they can win despite the odds. Comolli's argument is that while actors in fiction films portray characters that do not exist, actors in historical films portray figures that they are not. On this count, historical films may be more artificial in asking viewers to believe in what they see than fiction films. Conversely, he suggests that viewers derive pleasure from the performances that they see, even though they recognise them as artificial. Historical film always entails, therefore, a 'trampoline' of belief and disbelief, of pleasure in deceit and discomfort at the truth.

While Comolli's focus rests upon the body of the actor, many more publications on films see the 'director's will' at work in the activity of editing. The extract from the end of Gilles Deleuze's *L'Image-temps: Cinéma 2* (1985), which was translated as *Cinema 2: The Time-Image* in 1989, is a good case In point. Deleuze's work presents a taxonomy of images, the chief of which are the 'movement image' and the 'time image'. Movement images are characterised by 'continuity', camera movements that follow characters, transitions from event to event that are achieved by matches on action (e.g. following an actor through a door in an edited sequence) or continuity checks. Movement images are suggestive of fluid movement rather than a succession of separate and even disparate elements. Movement images dominated filmmaking until the advent of World War II, when images were liberated from prevailing belief systems to deliver 'shocks of force' or 'time images'. Time images remind us through conventions such as abrupt editing jumps or mismatches on action that what we see is interpretative rather than representative of 'reality', and that the relations between phenomena are more or less contingent.

Mary Ann Doane's work, particularly the book *The Emergence of Cinematic Time* (2002), pushes scholarly research on editing back to the beginnings of cinema, and suggests that the emergence of 'cinematic time' was a response to the restructuring of time in modernity. The extracts reproduced in this *Reader* convey her argument that the emergence of a measured and calibrated time to meet the needs of industrialisation and the commodification of labour was potentially threatened by the emergence of a cinematic temporal logic unlike linear industrial time. Doane focuses on three editing techniques that fostered the emergence of ideas of cinematic space and time. The first are jump cuts that replay an event – and thus time – from different positions; the second are chase scenes, which appear to stretch time and connect different spaces together in a fluid movement; and the third are parallel edits that move viewers back and forward between two different events and thus suggest a world outside the currently seen frame. All three devices inject time with 'desire, anticipation, [and] expectation', feelings that might run contrary to rationalised industrial time. What emerged in cinema, though, was a temporal hybrid: editing can help to push a narrative in a linear fashion towards a resolution, but it can also rupture or perforate expected narratives or draw phenomena together in novel or unexpected ways. Just as there is cinematic time, there is also historical time. To date, however, there has been no study of the conventions that suggest historical time in the manner of Doane's study of cinematic time. Nor has there been a detailed study of the intersection of historical time and cinematic time in historical films. Doane's and Deleuze's works therefore offer us intimations of future historiography.

Maureen Turim's *Flashbacks in Film* (1989) – an extract of which is reproduced here – examines the emergence and continuing use of one particular editing convention: the movement from a scene set in one time to one from an earlier time or 'flashback'. Flashbacks were used at the same time that filmmakers experimented with parallel editing, chase scenes and jump cuts and functioned to foster suspense to suggest character motivation. During the silent era, though, flashback became a form of filmic shorthand to indicate the thoughts, psyches and experiences of characters. Moreover, flashback increasingly signalled the start of a character's facing up to or working through a past trauma, and this, Turim claims, might have performed a therapeutic function for film viewers who themselves felt isolated in their traumatic experiences.

Turim's writing draws out a point that might be read as latent in the extracts from Deleuze and Doane: that film forms might be associated with particular social effects. If flashback-laden films like Ingmar Bergman's *Wild Strawberries* (1957) suggest a therapeutic role for memory and history on film, what can be said about historical comedies? Are they, as Northrup Frye suggested, transgressive 'safety valves'?[5] The word 'transgressive' is important here, for it reminds us that some conventions and narrative forms are more customary in historical studies than in others. Looking at the lively and divided response to 'Holocaust comedies' such as *Life is Beautiful* (1997) and *Train of Life* (1998), it seems that the use of comedic forms of narration in historical studies is not habitual or even assured. There has been much discussion on whether the constellation of events that are organised under the concept of the Holocaust can be represented in film or writing at all, let alone through narratives that tend to a beneficial resolution. Are there words or images that can help us to know or to begin to understand the Holocaust, or do these ultimately diminish the horror and provide us with a representation that is ultimately reassuring and superficial? What is interesting about these questions is that they are asked quite often about the Holocaust, but far more rarely about other historical events. Should we wonder about the 'fit' of narrative forms for all events? This is a useful question to have in mind when reading the extracts from Sander Gilman's journal article from 2000, 'Is Life Beautiful?', and Lawrence Baron's book *Projecting the Holocaust into the Present* (2005). I have included both not simply because they provide analyses of *Train of Life* and *Life is Beautiful*, but because their varying understandings of the social and temporal dimensions of the Holocaust lead them to different groups of films. Baron's decision to incorporate films that examine the continuing impact of the Holocaust on the lives of survivors, for instance, allows him to examine the use of comedy to explore the ideas of guilt and social dislocation. His work reminds us that selecting the scope for a history is as important as selecting the events and phenomena that populate it.

Notes

1 E. H. Carr, *What is History?*, ed. R. W. Davies, rev. edn, Harmondsworth: Penguin, 1986, p. 11.

2 D. Carr, 'Narrative and the Real World: An Argument for Continuity', *History and Theory*, 1986, vol. 25(1), pp. 117–31.

3 C. Phillips and W. D. Phillips, Review of *Columbus*, in M. Carnes (ed.), *Past Imperfect: History According to the Movies*, New York: Henry Holt, 1995, p. 63.

4 H. White, *Metahistory: The Historical Imagination in Nineteenth-Century Europe*, Baltimore, MD: Johns Hopkins University Press, 1975; R. Barthes, 'The Reality Effect', in *The Rustle of Language*, trans. R. Howard, Oxford: Basil Blackwell, 1986, pp. 141–8.

5 N. Frye, *Fables of Identity: Studies in Poetic Mythology*, New York: Harcourt, 1963.

Jean-Louis Comolli

HISTORICAL FICTION

A body too much?

'Historical Fiction: A Body Too Much?', *Screen*, 1978, vol. 19(2), pp. 41–53. Discursive notes edited.

WHAT IS TO BE MADE, in films, of fictional effects? How and on what basis do cinematic fictions work? What is in play, what tricks, in the conjunction of the machine of Fiction and the machine of Representation? I should like to approach these questions through a special type of fiction, historical fiction.

Why? There is no 'historical film' that is not fiction first: how indeed could the past be filmed live? Nor any that, however serious its documentation, does not fictionalise the most referenced historical argument. However, even in the case of a work of phantasy this inevitable putting into fiction comes to a stop at one or other of the limits of the historically referential: a minimum of information, a minimum of historical knowledge have to be provided and a minimum of period effects have to be produced too.

It is my hypothesis that the cinematic representation of History defies Fiction although it holds only through it. In such a paradoxical situation, both required, and prevented, irresistible and imprisoned, historical fiction becomes a kind of analyser which pushes to their most revealing limit the conditions of exercise and stakes at play in all cinematic fiction. If one of the great questions of the cinema, founding and launching the fictional mechanism, is *how does one believe in it?*, with historical fictions one has to believe in it with additional difficulties, against more obstacles and above all to believe in it despite what might seem to rationalise that belief, despite even the indices of truth and the referential proofs which are used to replace the game of belief by an order of knowledge.

Filming a fiction, staging it, mounting it in the field of a look begins by assigning to characters, those of the script, physical trajectories through concrete locations (speech too being a trajectory). To this end these imaginary characters have to be endowed with bodies, faces, looks and voices. Bodies which are quite real since they are those of the actors: the ones we see. The body filmed is not an imaginary body, even if the fiction refers it to some purely invented character and whatever the phantasies for which it is the support.

It is not imaginary to the extent that we see its image and know, as soon as we are in the spectator's place, that a real body, the actor's, is required for there to be an image of a body. The body of the imaginary character is the image of the real body of the actor. This body caught in our look appears to us as an attribute of the character? I do not think so. I know this is what the notion and practice of *typage* would like to convince us of. But it seems that things happen otherwise than Eisenstein's lectures tell us (I am not talking about his films, in which, as Barthes has emphasised,[1] the consistency of the denotation and connotation of the bodies is fairly weak) and otherwise than in the *class normativity* one fears they might imply (a worker is like a worker, etc).

I think rather that it is the character who, being filmable only by proxy, via an interposed actor, has for us the value of an attribute of the actor's body. The character reaches us as a bodily effect in the image. He may have been long worked over, defined, constituted in a script, but it is not the order of investigation but the order of exposition that is enounced in a film: first to appear will be the body, the body as an *empty mask*, and the character will only appear later and bit by bit as effects of this mask, effects in the plural, changing, unstable, never quite achieved, thwarted, incomplete.

If the mise-en-scène of a fiction is thus the attribution to real bodies of imaginary characters, things are slightly more complicated with historical fictions: all the characters in them are not phantastic; often they presuppose a referential model; or they have one and must make the best of it; when they do not use this model as surety, only entering the film as representatives of the historical referent, having no other diegetic consistency than to guarantee, by a rapid and not unobtrusive appearance, by a presence often no more than photographic, that this is the serious realm of History, real History. In short, most of these characters have played, or are supposed to have played, their parts, big or small, on the stage of History before they came to rest on that of the film. These characters have a past, they have a history before the film began and without needing it: other scriptwriters, the historians, have dealt with them.

The actor Ardisson, in Renoir's *La Marseillaise*, plays the character Jean-Joseph Bomier, a figure from the lower classes of Marseilles, enthusiastic and scatter-brained, 'spontaneously anarchist', hence the stake and the main target for the propagandist efforts of the organised militant Arnaud (Andrex).[2] Like everything we finally come to know about this character, we learn this only from the development of the fiction. All we can know about him is what the film tells us. Perhaps Bomier existed, perhaps there was a 'real' Bomier, but that does not matter, for us he only exists in the film, there are no other traces of him than those left by Ardisson's body in Renoir's images. For us, Bomier is a fictional character who, despite his role in a 'historical film', has all the properties of an imaginary character.

In the same film, Louis XVI is Pierre Renoir. But there could hardly be a less imaginary character than Louis XVI: historical, the name was borne by a body (even a sacred body), and the image of this body has come down to us, not in one but in many films, and before the films in numerous portraits. Ardisson, for as long as the film lasts, lends his body to a fictional name, a bodiless name. Pierre Renoir can only confront his body with the supposed (and supposedly familiar) body of Louis XVI: interference, even rivalry between the body of the actor and that other body, the 'real' one, whose (historical) disappearance has left traces in images other than cinematic ones which have to be taken into account.

If the imaginary person, even in a historical fiction, has no other body than that of the actor playing him, the historical character filmed has at least two bodies, that of the imagery and that of the actor who represents him for us. There are at least two bodies in competition, one body too much. And if for us Ardisson is unimpeachably the Marseillais Bomier, whom we cannot see in any other way, whose image we can compare with no other, only refer it to itself as the film imposes it, there will on the contrary always be some doubt as to the pertinence of Pierre Renoir to Louis XVI.

Ardisson's task is, so to speak, simple: Bomier can only be him. Of course it is also necessary that Bomier be, for initially he is nothing, he is only Ardisson so long as Ardisson does not produce the effects that constitute Bomier. But these effects will all go to Bomier's credit. Without any reservations, without the slightest doubt, even if they are contradictory and sometimes excessive: Bomier is not a character all of a piece and in particular he is a character who has to change lines under Arnaud's influence. For this change to be manifest and convince the spectator more effectively, Bomier will be led, over his dead body (he too denies), to positions he had earlier condemned: he will come to appreciate the words of the 'Marseillaise' which he had condemned as appallingly bombastic,[3] or claim to be a supporter of the delegation of power he had constantly stormed against. Which, be it said in parenthesis, enables Renoir, by an accumulation of contrasting effects and a whole play of ruptures, to dispense with the fatal moment of 'attaining consciousness' which so encumbered *La Vie est à Nous*.

So Ardisson's facial contortions, his omni-directional impulsiveness, his overacting in mimicry, gesture and voice, all contribute to a split character, full of holes and residues, but the character is there for all that: such can only be Bomier, with self-evident authority. Even inconsistent, the character is consistent with the actor. And nothing can disturb this consistency, either from within the fiction (which adopts the character's inconsistency, plays on to make it acceptable) or from outside the film: in the name of what could we doubt this representation of Bomier?

No doubts? And yet here too we know that Ardisson is not Bomier. But this indisputable certainty which places every spectator in the position of nobody's fool from the moment the film begins is quite unproductive for us: it remains of the order of a frozen, fixed, unadventurous knowledge (we know, but how much rather would we not know . . .). Of itself, it is incapable of gaining us the slightest pleasure, and we accept it as the inevitable precondition for the spectacle to be possible at all (there have to be actors, machines, theatres, etc), the condition that every spectator knows and immediately recognises its nature as simulacrum, is perfectly aware of and necessarily accepts the break and the distance between him or her and the scene. We experience this knowledge and certainty with a certain fatalism (it has to be . . .), I would go so far as to say with boredom: we are in the position of those impatient gamblers who know the rules of the game and who one asks to remember those rules before playing: quick, the game is beginning!

This boring knowledge has to be lost as soon as possible and these rules played. The certainty we always have, bearing it in mind, that the spectacle is not life nor the film reality, that the actor is not the character and that if we are there as spectators it is because we know it is a simulacrum,[4] is a certainty we have to be able to doubt. Its only value is that it is put at risk: it only interests us if it can (temporarily) be abolished. The 'I know very well' irresistibly calls for the 'but all the same', includes it as its value, its intensity. The one is inseparable from the other, is valueless without the other. We know, but we want something else: to believe. We want to be fooled, without ever quite ceasing to know that we are. We want both, both to be fools and nobody's fools, to oscillate, swing from knowledge to belief, from distance to adhesion, from criticism to fascination.

And in fact we never forget that Pierre Renoir is not Louis XVI, that Ardisson is not Bomier. But at the same time we believe that they are. If at least the actor and the film play them sufficiently *with us*. The spectacle is always a *game*. It requires the participation of the spectators not as consumers but as players, accomplices, masters of the game, even, if they are also its stakes. The simulacrum does not fool a 'passive' spectator (there are no 'passive spectators'): the spectator has to participate in his own fooling; the simulacrum is the *means* whereby he is helped to fool himself. The spectator, never 'passive', works: but his work, contrary to current orthodoxy, is not just decoding, reading, elaboration of signs and mobilisation of knowledge. First of all and just as much, if not more, it is to play the game, to fool himself for pleasure and despite this knowledge that strengthens his position as nobody's fool, to maintain, if the spectacle, the game, will allow, the mechanism of denegation at its regime of highest intensity. The more one knows the more difficult it is to believe and the more it is worth managing to do so.

That is why we enjoy the performances of Ardisson and Pierre Renoir in different ways. Ardisson is not Bomier? We agree and at the same time are quite happy for him to be so. Nothing prevents us giving him the benefit of our complicity: now it's his turn to play. He must convince us of what we know to be untrue but ask only to believe so that the game can begin and go on (the game stops, even if the spectacle does not, when we no longer believe). Between him and us the game is simple and, so to speak, without handicaps: at the outset we grant that the actor may be Bomier because for us Bomier can only be this actor. It is up to him to do the rest, to fulfil his part of the bargain and, with the help of fiction and mise-en-scène, progressively (even if jerkily) construct the character, fortifying the initial supposition of identity more and more. What happens then works less unequivocally in the mode of denegation: more in that of confirmation. Or rather, the denegatory formula is reversed and becomes: 'I know very well you are Bomier – but all the same, what an actor Ardisson is!' A new knowledge is constituted against the background of the first, denegated, no doubt too easily denegated, knowledge. And this new knowledge both satisfies us – the bargain is well fulfilled – and disappoints us a little: it does not raise the stakes, it turns on itself in a loop of confirmation, each thing in its place, the body with the character and the actor with the performance.

There is the risk of a loss of tension, a regime of lesser pleasure, if the character is taken as given, regarded as so automatic that all there is left to enjoy is the actor's talent: lack of interest in the character, decathexis from the fiction. This is what would happen in *La Marseillaise*, too, if Bomier was not built precisely out of inconsistencies and infringements of the code, in a *belying* figure. In the first stages of the fiction we learn to divine the character (the mask is only gradually filled in) and as everything is done to make him predictable for us we finally come to know him almost too well: a lapse into the overcoded. But, just as our predictions become so certain that they no longer interest us, belies them. He is no longer where we expected him, and the more marked he has been, the more he unmarks himself: new bet, higher stakes, the fictional energy is set going again, and it is this that enables us to believe (again) in this quite incredible disavowal of Bomier.

Pierre Renoir, it is clear, faces a far more taxing bargain. We really do know that he is not Louis XVI and never quite will be. Something undecidable floats around him, a blur in the image, a duplication: there is a ghost in this body. At any rate there is some historical knowledge, some referent constituting a screen for the image and preventing the actor and the mise-en-scène from playing on self-evidence (it can only be me) or assertion (it is me!).

The mechanism has to be more devious, not so much to struggle against this disturbing effect as rather to use it and play on it: this will proceed from the double affirmation (it's him and it's me) which realises the always improbable conjunction of two identities, two bodies which exclude one another while coinciding. No fit between character and actor,[5] or one that is fleeting, lightning-like, immediately destroyed by a return of the discrepancy between body acting and body acted. Pierre Renoir's Louis XVI never quite comes off, it can only be at the limit, and that is why despite everything we can believe in it because it is worked out *starting from this 'despite'* as well: the difficulty of the playing is represented in the game itself.

As a result we are summoned to the delicate exercise of a double game: it is him and it is not, always and at the same time; we believe in it and we do not, at the same time. Neither of the terms ever really prevails over the other, each keeps the other as a ground against which it stands out, each bounces off the trampoline of the other. They are held together for us by this oscillating movement, by the to-and-fro which makes us pass from one to the other without ever abandoning either. And this game of proximity and distance, of complicity and criticism, to which we are thus introduced, far from leaving us in an unsatisfied reserve or leading us to detachment, fuels and reignites our desire to believe (all the same) better than would any fit between actor and character, any self-evidence, any well-furbished credibility. For now the denegation is working at full throttle, neither of the two contradictory propositions that constitute it making an end of the other and each, even, improving on the other. The moment Pierre Renoir, by acting whose springs I shall analyse later, manages what is not easy, to make us believe he is Louis XVI, while not preventing us from continuing to think that he is not, a dynamic of increasing intensity is set up. The more he is him, the more difficult it is to believe it: the more we believe in it, the more we know all the same that he is not him, and the more we believe in it all the same. The pleasure here is not without its unease, it derives from the unease that reignites it.

All cinematic fictions are stretched more or less tightly by this knot of denegation.[6] But historical fiction (at least its masterpiece, *La Marseillaise*) takes things further, and brings into play a movement of denegation to infinity. The coded is more visible, the supposedly known more awkward, the belief more problematic: there is *more to denegate*, a body and a knowledge too much. The irrational leap that marks the spectator's every entry into fiction, and whose gain of pleasure the latter risks quickly exhausting if it does not organise its repetition and amplification, is more difficult, more dangerous, in the case of historical fiction, since the belief and denial on which it is based are barred at every moment by the discourses of reason and have to prevail despite them, in an outburst of even greater irrationality.

Only one body in our example, can be 'too much': the one whose image we see, the body of Pierre Renoir, which belies as much as it figures that of Louis XVI. How can one play with a body too much? With one's own body too much? Why, by making this surplus visible, by disturbing the spectator's look with a bodily supplement, in other words by playing the most difficult game, by doing the opposite of what happens (today still) in most 'historical films'.

The latter usually try to ensure that the actor's body is forgotten, to cancel it, to keep it hidden, at least, beneath the supposedly known and intendedly pre-eminent body of the historical character to be represented. This is done by banking on the (necessarily blurred) memory the spectator has of that historical body and imagining that therefore all that needs to be done is to cobble together a resemblance (vague and inaccurate like all resemblance), or to force the inadequate physique of the actor with make-up (which will always be denoted as such: it is the nature of make-up to be visible), for the image of the historical body present in the spectator's memory to allow identification between the character and the actor's body (it really is him!) and for that image having thus performed this service to be entirely consumed in the soldering of copy and model.

No question in *La Marseillaise* of attempting to obliterate the memory image. On the contrary, its persistence is allowed to float, it is played on as a kind of embarrassment, a screen, a rival for the current image. As if it were necessary that it could survive throughout the struggle unleashed against it by the image of the actor's body for that struggle really to take place. But for this to be true, the body too much, retained in the act of its repudiation, must not remain in the state of a memory trace: otherwise the image of the film could prevail over the image from memory. It must also be inscribed in the actuality of the vision, it must be manifest and come back from the screen into the spectator's look. In fact this can only be done if it is supported and carried by the only body visible at that moment, the actor's.

Pierre Renoir is not content not to conceal his own body behind the supposed body of Louis XVI, not to apply it to the supposedly known model. He brings this body, his own, to the fore: he emphasises its reality and presence, multiplies its effects. Far from making the spectator forget it, he points it out to him: henceforth this body will not be something automatic. It begins to count, to weigh. The self-evidence of the image of a body as a result of which it is seen without being seen, the apparent naturalness, the familiarity of the body are thwarted here: Pierre Renoir plays his body as a problematic, paradoxical, body, strange to itself. (I note, in parenthesis, that all this is not just a matter of acting and the actor's technique: neither reaches us except doubly inscribed in the dispositions of the fiction and the frames of the mise-en-scène; hence as effects.)

How is this body made too present? How is it made, not just sufficiently visible to escape the normal fate of most filmed bodies, insignificant, accessory, on the edge of non-visibility, but also so unbypassable, unforgettable? By making it the very centre and object of the scene, by displaying it in all its states. In all the sequences in *La Marseillaise* in which Pierre Renoir plays Louis XVI it is the royal body itself that is questioned, in question. Fiction and mise-en-scène, far from seeking to avoid this problematic body, to minimise it by decentring it, by filming it in ceremonies and amidst crowds, appearing along with others, take the opposite course and make this body the major preoccupation both of the character and of those surrounding him. It is dressed, powdered, fed; it is also venerated (or not); it is taken for walks, protected, hidden . . . Valets, aristocrats, soldiers are at its service. Jean Renoir is not trying to trick either history or the spectator: he takes seriously the central place of the Body of the King in the monarchic system, he marks its devalorisation at the moment of the Revolution, he spares no avatar of the royal but devalued body of Louis XVI, in the end he takes the wager of his representation to its ultimate limits.

The first time we see it, in the scene of the *lever du Roi*, the royal body seems to us both caught up in, and prisoner to, the ritual mise-en-scène of the Court, which mediates its approach with a whole series of relays; and somewhat astray, not quite in the right place, already a little too much. Of course, the alienation effect produced by this lies in the contrast between the solemnity of the approach and the prosaic character of this body in night cap and gown. It lies perhaps above all in the discovery that this so carefully guarded body is nothing but the body of the actor, without make-up and as it were naked, deprived of the artifices of resemblance as much as the character it is supposed to embody is of the marks of royalty. Thus from the start we are made to feel quite sharply that on the one hand it is the body of Pierre Renoir that will command the scene, but on the other that the royal body has seen its best days and will have trouble holding its place. This impression is immediately strengthened: this body is dependent on the influence or assistance of other bodies subordinate to it, it is awkward, clumsy, incapable of autonomy; both futile and gross, childlike and graceless; no authority emanates from it, no confidence; in short, it is a body visibly ill at ease wherever it is (except at table), almost always embarrassed and seemingly embarrassing its supposed master first of all. Pierre Renoir brings off the coup of making this work with and in his own body (which certainly does not embarrass him so much), of, as it were, figuring a body in its own despite, discrepant, displaced, always somewhere in between actor and character. The maintenance of such an uncertainty as to the identity of the body of the actor with that of the character raises the stakes in the fictional game, as we have seen; and this embarrassment which threatens to block the fiction can, as is the case here, be fictionalised in its turn: we thus discover, through emotion[7] as much as information, that Louis XVI is at ease neither in his body nor in his role.

The scene which epitomises all these surpluses and deficiencies, the paradoxes of the royal body, is the one in which, before the battle for the Tuileries Palace, Louis XVI unenthusiastically agrees to review the troops defending him. Hardly has his valet finished dressing him for this exhibition, which is by no means to his taste, than we see him caught in a certain embarrassment: his wig has slipped and is on askew. With some irritation he has it adjusted and at last advances into the throng of brilliant nobles of the court, who, not ungrotesquely, go down on one knee and, their swords drawn, sing a fashionable royalist song (‘*Oh Richard, oh mon Roi!*’). Louis XVI stares at them dumfounded; he does not know what expression to put on or what to say; distraction captures this heavy body and it becomes almost obscene juxtaposed to these elegant chevaliers. He goes on. The cries of ‘*Vive le Roi!*’, mechanically repeated by Grenadiers and Swiss Guards only draw a half-smile from him, particularly since his wig is still troubling him. Lower down, in the courtyard, the battalions of the National Guard, royalists and others. First there are acclamations, more spontaneous than those of the mercenaries: he is now almost reassured: the people recognise him and are cheering him. He wants to go on despite attempts to dissuade him: the remaining companies to be reviewed, the ones who have been put in the front line, are the least certain. And their welcome is indeed an attack: they shout to his face ‘*Vive la Nation!*’ Once again the royal body collapses; we see his face disintegrate; he stops, arms dangling, unable either to respond with contemptuous silence or to order a punishment; he guiltily lowers his head, his wig goes awry again and he adjusts it mechanically. He is pulled away and brought to safety. He rapidly disappears from the scene which shifts to a confrontation between two officers, one of whom wants to punish the insult to the King while the other prevents him with the most peremptory firmness. Thus the displacement and repetition of the conflict in a minor scene no more penalises the outrage on the King's person which remains unpunished: not only does the royal body no longer embody power, already there is no power left at all.

‘An admirable touch’, notes André Bazin,[8] in passing, ‘Louis XVI is hindered by the fact that his wig is askew’: admirable indeed, for the sudden effect of condensation it produces. The wig here functions both as metaphor: it is in the place of the crown which is also slipping from the King's head; and as metonymy: it is this part which first detaches itself from the disintegrating royal body. Never has this body stopped falling apart as it was constructed before our eyes. It is no longer in any way sacred for its subjects who dare to hold themselves up in its presence and as if equal to it (*La Marseillaise* could also be summarised as the path taken by the body of the people to reach power and to overthrow it, as the body of the people rising and breaking like a wave, before being taken in hand by new masters and, finally, regimented: the march on Valmy). It is an encumbrance to its last supporters, quite happy to be rid of it through the intercession of the big bourgeoisie (Roederer, all in black and revolutionary titles, spiriting the royal body away and at the same time conducting its retreat like a funeral). It is unbearable even to its closest and most faithful friends, distraught at its constant inadequacy for its role. Finally it embarrasses the King himself. In short, this body is decidedly too much, and eventually it is too much *for us* too.

Hence when the accumulation of embarrassing effects by the fiction and by the actor's playing make this body more and more unbearable for us, too, today's spectators, and we catch ourselves relieved at its setting aside, that is the moment when we have *really* believed in Louis XVI in this film. Yet all we have seen is Pierre Renoir's body and we have never, in all the time it has been present in the image, been able to believe that this body could quite have been that of Louis XVI.

And the moment this body has become, so to speak, so much too much that it has to disappear, we believe in it as we have never believed in it before . . . By inscribing it in the private and public mises-en-scène of the Court, in parades and struggles, the mise-en-scène (of the film) has shown us the royal body only when caught in the looks of its subjects. It has duplicated our look with theirs. As if the actor had acted for our eyes, but also for those of the characters, the unease felt by Louis XVI at being a body exposed to the looks of his subjects, *but also* to our looks. The spectacle of this body gradually becomes as painful for the spectators in the film as for the spectators of the film. The duplication of looks is accompanied by an overlapping of places.[9] The result is a kind of double transfer so that we recognise more and more the embarrassment we, the spectators, feel in the fictional embarrassment of the characters and of the King himself at the untenable place of the royal body; and in return make our own some of their reasons for no longer holding to that body or to that place. We have never seen anything but Pierre Renoir's body, but this body has made us see the body too much of Louis XVI with, dare I say, the eyes of his contemporaries, and made us condemn it as they did: may it disappear!

Notes

1 Cf. Roland Barthes 'The third meaning' in *Image-Music-Text*, trans. S. Heath, London: Fontana, 1977.

2 Remember the date, 1937, and the circumstances of this film: the wave of enthusiasm for the Popular Front and rise of the *national* theme in left-wing discourse. As if in echo to the praise of the 'Marseillaise' pronounced by Maurice Thorez in 1936, the film co-operative and the CGT launched the film project and tried to finance it by a national subscription.

3 His words: 'There is something wild and bombastic in this song which I do not like.'

4 The spectacle, and the cinema itself, despite all the *reality effects* they may produce, always offer themselves to spectators *for what they are*. There are no spectators *unaverted* to the spectacle, even if they allow themselves (temporarily) to be caught by the fictioning machine and fascinated by the simulacrum: that is exactly *why* they went.

5 As André Bazin notes, 'miscasting' is almost a rule in Renoir's films: 'None of the major actors in *The Rules of the Game* is in his element (with the exception of Gaston Modot and Paulette Dubost). And who would claim that the cast of *The Lower Depths* stepped from the Gorkii play? Gabin as a hero in a Russian novel is a long shot at best; and it would be difficult to conceive of a more spectacular bit of miscasting than Valentine Tessier in *Madame Bovary*', *Jean Renoir*, ed. François Truffaut, trans. W. W. Halsey II and William H. Simon, New York: Delta Books, 1973, p. 74. Or again, about *The Human Beast*: 'Renoir founds [his justification of the characters] not on psychology but on a metaphysics of actors. What we see on the screen is not the murderous rage of Lantier, but that of Jean Gabin. Even when the actor does not correspond physically or morally to the character in the book, the "error" of casting offers more advantages than disadvantages, because the presence of the actor, his powers of suggestion, are clearly superior to what is in the book' (ibid. p. 69).

6 Which is active in a film at more levels than that of fiction alone. For example, that of the 'impression of reality' whose artificial character is never quite forgotten.

7 For this impossible body moves us, moves us because of all the difficult and painful things the mise-en-scène makes it suffer. The 'warm sympathy' for his characters

usually attributed to Renoir here shows its true colours: quite the opposite of kindness or any kind of softness or pity.

8 *Jean Renoir*, p. 67.

9 Far and near, here and there, double inscription of the spectator's place in the auditorium and in the scene. Siegfried Kracauer, 'Photography,' in *The Mass Ornament: Weimar Essays,* trans. and ed. Thomas Y. Levin, Cambridge, MA: Harvard University Press, 1995, p. 49.

Mary A. Doane

THE REPRESENTABILITY OF TIME

The Emergence of Cinematic Time, Cambridge, MA: Harvard University Press, 2002, pp. 1–32.

IN DECEMBER 1895, the same month as that of the first public screening of films of the Lumière Cinématographe, a story titled 'The Kinetoscope of Time' appeared in *Scribner's Magazine*.[1] The story conveys something of the uncanniness of the new technology's apparent ability to transcend time as corruption by paradoxically fixing life and movement, providing their immutable record. It condenses many of the fears, desires, anxieties, and pleasure attached to the idea of the mechanical representability of time. At the beginning of 'The Kinetoscope of Time' the unnamed protagonist finds himself in an unrecognizable and seemingly placeless place, barely furnished and surrounded by walls heavily draped in velvet. The only furnishings are four narrow stands with 'eye-pieces' at the top, which, though unnamed, are clearly kinetoscopes, the individual viewing machines invented by Thomas Edison and preceding the cinema. A message projected on the curtains invites the protagonist to look through the eyepieces in order to view 'a succession of strange dances.' He does so and proceeds to describe a series of scenes that unfold (including the story of Salomé, a scene from *The Scarlet Letter*, and a scene from *Uncle Tom's Cabin* in which Topsy dances). When these cease, the captivated spectator is invited to move to another kinetoscope to view scenes of combat as 'memorable' as those of the dances. Here he witnesses scenes from the *Iliad*, *Don Quixote*, *Faust*, and the Custer massacre.[2] When the protagonist raises his eyes after this series he becomes aware that he is no longer alone; a mysterious but distinguished-looking middle-aged man is suddenly present. This man appears to claim great age by suggesting that he himself was present at, among others, the filmed scenes of *Salomé* and the *Iliad*. But when the protagonist asks if he is 'Time himself,' the figure laughs and denies it. The mysterious man proceeds to offer him two more viewings – one of the protagonist's own past, the other of his future, including 'the manner of your end,' but this time at a price: 'The vision of life must be paid for in life itself. For every ten years of the future which I may unroll before you here, you must assign me a year of your life – twelve months – to do with as I will.' The protagonist refuses this Faustian contract and is haughtily dismissed by the kinetoscope's proprietor. After making his way with difficulty through a dark and winding tunnel, the young man finds himself in the 'open air:' 'I was in a broad street, and over my head an electric light suddenly flared out and whitewashed the pavement at my feet. At the corner a train of the elevated railroad rushed by with a clattering roar and a trailing plume of white steam. Then a cable-car clanged past with incessant bangs upon its gong. Thus it was that I came back to the world of actuality.' But within this 'world of actuality,' the protagonist discovers in a shop window an engraving of the man he has just met. His costume clearly indicates to the protagonist that he lived in the last century, and a legend below the engraving identifies him as Monsieur le Comte de Cagliostro.[3]

The protagonist's viewing of these filmed records of other times and other places occurs in a placeless and timeless space that resembles in many ways (its darkness and otherness to the world outside, its nonidentifiability) the cinema theaters of a much later period. And in the world that the young spectator returns to, normalcy is signified by the technologies of modernity – electric lighting, elevated trains, cable cars – and the series of shocks associated with them. The story conjoins many of the motifs associated with the emerging cinema and its technological promise to capture time: immortality, the denial of the radical finitude of the human body, access to other temporalities, and the issue of the archivability of time. The stories, unlike the space of their projection, are all familiar, and they reinscribe the recognizable tropes of orientalism, racism, and imperialism essential to the nineteenth-century colonialist imperative to conquer other times, other spaces. In the story of Salomé, the narrator-protagonist claims that 'the decorations were Eastern in their glowing gorgeousness,' and that 'in the East women ripen young.' In the scene from *Uncle Tom's Cabin*, Topsy was 'one of the blackest of her race,' and 'her black eyes glittered with a kind of wicked drollery.' In Custer's last stand, the 'red Indians were raging, with exultant hate in their eyes,' while the white soldiers were 'valiant and defiant' in meeting their fate. These are the recorded times, the other temporalities, that allow the protagonist to disavow, for a while, his own temporality of clattering trains and clanging cable cars. The 'kinetoscope of time' constitutes, in Michel Foucault's terms, both a heterotopia and a heterochrony, offering its spectator an immersion in *other* spaces and times, with the assurance of a safe return to his or her own. What the new technologies of vision allow one to see is a record of time.

The story suggests that the mysterious proprietor of the kinetoscope is contaminated by the attributes of his own machine – specifically its ability to access other times (the protagonist's past, his future) and the denial of mortality (the proprietor does not know death). Its rhetoric echoes that which accompanied the reception of the early cinema, with its hyperbolic recourse to the figures of life, death, immortality, and infinity. The cinema would be capable of recording permanently a fleeting moment, the duration of an ephemeral smile or glance. It would preserve the lifelike movements of loved ones after their death and constitute itself as a grand archive of time. As André Bazin would later point out, photographic technology 'embalms time, rescuing it simply from its proper corruption.'[4] But because time's corruption is 'proper' to it, its fixed representation also poses a threat, produces aesthetic and epistemological anxiety. 'The Kinetoscope of Time' registers this threat as the complicity of the machine with the demonic; hence the protagonist's refusal to look.

Although popular accounts tended to endow the cinema with determinate agency – that is, cinematic technology made possible a new access to time or its 'perfect' representation – in fact the emerging cinema participated in a more general cultural imperative, the structuring of time and contingency in capitalist modernity. Although the rupture here is not technologically determined, new technologies of representation, such as photography, phonography, and the cinema, are crucial to modernity's reconceptualization of time and its representability. A sea change in thinking about contingency, indexicality, temporality, and chance deeply marked the epistemologies of time at the turn of the last century. The reverberations of this break are still perceptible today in the continual conjunction of electronic technologies and questions of instantaneity and the archivability of time. As Andreas Huyssen points out, 'the issue of media . . . is central to the way we live structures of temporality in our culture.'[5] Film, television, and video are frequently specified by the term *time-based media*.

When Walter Benjamin wrote, with respect to Baudelaire's poetry and its relation to early modernity, 'In the *spleen*, time becomes palpable: the minutes cover a man like snowflakes,' he was not isolating an attitude unique to Baudelaire.[6] One could argue more generally that at the turn of the century time became palpable in a quite different way – one specific to modernity and intimately allied with its new technologies of representation (photography, film, phonography). Time was indeed *felt* – as a weight, as a source of anxiety, and as an acutely pressing problem of representation. Modernity was perceived as a temporal demand. Toward the end of the nineteenth century there was a rapid diffusion of pocket watches in the general population. The German historian Karl Lamprecht noted the importation of 12 million watches for a German population of about 52 million in the 1890s.[7] In 1903 Georg Simmel linked the precision of the money economy to the precision 'effected by the universal diffusion of pocket watches.' Simmel associated this new obsession with temporal exactitude to the heightened tempo and the 'intensification of nervous stimulation' of urban life: 'Thus, the technique of metropolitan life is unimaginable without the most punctual integration of all activities and natural relations into a stable and impersonal time schedule.'[8] Modernity was characterized by the impulse to *wear* time, to append it to the body so that the watch became a kind of prosthetic device extending the capacity of the body to measure time. The acceleration of events specific to city life was inseparable from the effects of new technologies and a machine culture made possible by developments in modern science. In the realm of physics and beyond, the refinement of the Second Law of Thermodynamics (the law of entropy) engendered a conceptualization of time as the tightness of a direction, an inexorable and irreversible linearity. In the late nineteenth and early twentieth centuries, time became increasingly reified, standardized, stabilized, and rationalized.

It is within the context of a modernity defined by rapid industrialization and the diffusion of new technologies as well as the rapid changes of urban life that contingency emerges as a site of awe and fear, constituted as both lure and threat. Its lure is that of the passing moment, the fascination of the ephemeral, but Walter Benjamin delineates the dark underside of such a relation to contingency as shock or trauma. The concept of shock has received a great deal of attention in contemporary theory, which has linked it to the various blows and assaults upon the subject associated with urban life and modern technologies – traffic, railway travel, electric lighting, newspaper advertising. This is substantiated by Benjamin's own explanation of the 'complex kind of training' to which technology has 'subjected the human sensorium.'[9] But in Benjamin's lengthy appeal to Freud to delineate the psychical mechanism of the distinction between the shock experience associated with mechanical reproduction and the auratic experience associated with traditional art forms, it becomes clear that shock is also, and perhaps most importantly, a way of conceptualizing contingency in modernity.

Freud, in *Beyond the Pleasure Principle*, claims that 'consciousness arises instead of a memory-trace' and therefore that the two systems are incompatible. Instead, memory fragments are 'often most powerful and most enduring when the incident which left them behind was one that never entered consciousness.' In Proustian terms, this means that the involuntary memory is composed of contents that were never experienced consciously; they somehow managed to bypass the level of consciousness. Consciousness, for Freud, does not remember. Its most important function is rather to protect the organism against excessive stimuli, to act as a stimulus shield in operation against external energies. According to Benjamin, 'The threat from these energies is one of shocks. The more readily consciousness registers these shocks, the less likely they are to have a traumatic effect.'[10]

This stimulus shield would, of course, be tougher, more impenetrable, in a highly developed technological society. In Benjamin's argument, such a society requires a heightened consciousness to parry the shock effects of urban existence. The human organism increasingly becomes surface. For Benjamin, what are lost in this process are memory traces and the full experience of the event exemplified by storytelling, as opposed to the communication of information or mere sensation. This is why it is no longer possible to write like Proust. Shock is, therefore, as opposed to the auratic, a kind of surface phenomenon; experiences do not 'take,' they simply slip away:

> The greater the share of the shock factor in particular impressions, the more constantly consciousness has to be alert as a screen against stimuli; the more efficiently it does so, the less do these impressions enter experience (*Erfahrung*), tending to remain in the sphere of a certain hour in one's life (*Erlebnis*). Perhaps the special achievement of shock defense may be seen in its function of assigning to an incident a precise point in time in consciousness at the cost of the integrity of its contents.[11]

Three points need to be made about Benjamin's activation of Freud (and Proust) in his conceptualization of shock. First, shock is specified as that which is unassimilable in experience, a residue of unreadability. In being parried by consciousness it never reaches the subjective depths (of the unconscious, of experience) that could confer upon it a stable meaning. This is the sense in which shock is aligned with the contingent. Second, shock is defined in terms that associate it with a pathology. The subject must defend, himself/herself against it at the risk of losing psychical integrity or equilibrium. Consciousness is above all 'protective.' Third, the defense against shock embodies a privileged relation to time. The rationalization of time (its division into discrete entities – seconds, minutes, hours, and its regulation by the clock) is a symptom of the foreclosure of meaning in the defense against shock (an incident is 'assigned a precise point in time in consciousness at the cost of the integrity of its contents'). Rationalization supplants, displaces, or, in a sense, *mimics* meaning.

Nevertheless, shock is not to be avoided or rejected in a historically regressive nostalgia for the auratic. Instead, it must be *worked through*. Benjamin refers to Baudelaire – who in his estimation is the literary figure most sensitive to the phenomenological and epistemological crises of modernity – as a 'traumatophile type,' actively searching out the shocks of an urban milieu. Similarly, photography and film have a special relation to shock and, in the case of film, a potentially redemptive one. The snapping of the camera shares with other modern technologies the drive to condense time, the aspiration for instantaneity. But photography's impact upon the perception of the 'moment' is historically decisive:

> Of the countless movements of switching, inserting, pressing and the like, the 'snapping' of the photographer has had the greatest consequences. A touch of the finger now sufficed to fix an event for an unlimited period of time. The camera gave the moment a posthumous shock, as it were.

Here, shock is aligned with photography's ability to arrest the ephemeral, to represent the contingent. But Benjamin reserves his strongest enthusiasm for film, in which 'perception in the form of shocks was established as a formal principle.'[12] Benjamin tends to align shock in film – and hence its 'formal principle' – with montage. The very rapidity of the changing images in film is potentially traumatic for the spectator and allows the cinema to *embody* something of the restructuration of modern perception. For Benjamin, the shock experience of film makes it adequate to its age, unlike other aesthetic forms, with their adherence to the aura.

Despite Benjamin's explicit equation of filmic shock and montage, it is clear from his theoretical activation of Freud and Proust and his delineation of shock as a surface phenomenon unassimilable to meaning, that the cinema's shock effect is ineluctably associated with its indexicality, its ability to register or represent contingency. Montage functions for Benjamin not so much to confer order or meaning but to rapidly accumulate and juxtapose contingencies. In this, the film form mimics and displays for the spectator the excesses of a technologically saturated modern life. And, comparing this shock-producing montage to work on the assembly line (where gestures are isolated and disconnected) and to the unretentive and mechanical gestures of gambling (the *coup*), Benjamin is necessarily ambivalent about the ideological effects of the cinema (a form that both refuses the depth of experiential meaning – *Erfahrung* – and, at the same time, is a sensitive indicator of and participant in a vast reorganization of subjectivity in modernity). His ambivalence here mirrors that associated with the image of contingency as both lure and threat.

Cinema is a crucial participant in an ongoing rethinking of temporality in modernity. The relations between cinema and the other disciplines – psychoanalysis, physiology, physics, statistics, philosophy – are not simple formal analogies or evidence of some general *Zeitgeist*. The pressure to rethink temporality in the nineteenth century is a function of the development of capitalist modernity and its emphases upon distribution, circulation, energy, displacement, quantification, and rationalization. These developments require new conceptualizations of space and time and the *situatedness* of the subject. How does the subject inhabit this new space and time? What are the pressures of contingency and the pleasures of its representability? The ideologies of instantaneity, of temporal compression, of the lure of the present moment that emerge in this period have not disappeared; they confront us now in the form of digital technologies.

The new standards of accuracy, memory, and recordkeeping in modernity traversed the disciplines and in fact encouraged their interaction. Within the terms of their own internal evolution, and acknowledging their relative autonomy, these disciplines were approaching a version of the same problem – the representability of time. Marey in physiology and Freud in psychoanalysis wrestled with the apparent conflict between the accurate recording of time and its legibility. The ability to represent time as irreversible in physics opened up the possibility of an entirely different way of conceptualizing history, as Michel Serres has compellingly demonstrated; and a new paradigm of historical thought had an effect upon the conceptualization of cinema as historical record. The mutual resonances and transformations between these different epistemological frameworks indicate a powerful – and contagious – response to historical trauma, a trauma that involves a refiguring, indeed rupturing, of what had previously been understood as an indivisible temporal continuum, the support and guarantee of a coherent subjectivity. Change becomes synonymous with 'newness,' which, in its turn, is equated with difference and rupture – a cycle consistent with an intensifying commodification.

The significance of the cinema lies in its apparent capacity to perfectly *represent* the contingent, to provide the pure record of time. And this effort is particularly legible in the most dominant genre of the early cinema – the actuality, which appeared to capture a moment, to register and repeat 'that which happens.' The hundreds of films in the Lumières' catalogues cover a vast array of activities whose only common denominator (despite the attempt to subject them to a taxonomy) is that they are filmable: a baby eating, a train arriving at a station, workers leaving a factory, photographers arriving at a conference, a snowball fight, the demolition of a wall. The actuality dominated the first decade of film production and produced continual evidence of the drive to fix and make repeatable the ephemeral. Much of the rhetoric accompanying the reception of the earliest films is a sheer celebration of the cinema's ability to represent movement. While photography could fix a moment, the cinema made archivable duration itself. In that sense, it was perceived as a prophylactic against death, ensuring the ability to 'see one's loved ones' gesture and smile long after their deaths.[13] What was registered on film was life itself in all its multiplicity, diversity, and contingency.

This archival desire is intimately linked to the technological assurance of indexicality. The fidelity of the image to its referent was no longer dependent upon the skill or honesty of a particular artist. The imprint of the real was automatically guaranteed by the known capability of the machine. For the first time, an aesthetic representation – previously chained to the idea of human control – could be made by accident. This strengthened the medium's alliance with contingency. Film was perceived as the imprint of time itself (as in 'The Kinetoscope of Time'), a time unharnessed from rationalization, a nonteleological time in which each moment can produce the unexpected, the unpredictable, and temporality ratifies indeterminacy. Film, in its mechanical and unrelenting forward movement, appears as the incarnation of the thermodynamic law of irreversibility, and as such gives witness to time as the erosion of organization and the free field of chance. Film seems to respond to the dilemma of the representability of time with an easy affirmation. The indexicality of the cinematic sign appears as the guarantee of its status as a record of a temporality outside itself – a pure time or duration which would not be that of its own functioning. This is what imbues cinematic time with historicity. Because it seems to function first and foremost as a *record* of whatever happens in front of the camera, the cinema emerges from and contributes to the archival impulse of the nineteenth century. In it, images are *stored*, time itself is stored. But what is it that is being archived? Once the present as contingency has been seized and stored, it ineluctably becomes the past. Yet this archival artifact becomes strangely immaterial; existing nowhere but in its screening for a spectator in the present, it becomes the experience of presence (this is the sense in which film is usually associated with the present tense rather than the past). What is archived, then, would be the experience of presence. But it is the disjunctiveness of a presence relived, of a presence haunted by historicity. In his essay on photography, Kracauer claims, 'A shudder runs through the viewer of old photographs. For they make visible not the knowledge of the original but the spatial configuration of a moment.'[14] Similarly, film makes visible not a knowledge of the original but a certain passing temporal configuration. The grandchildren in Kracauer's essay shudder when confronted with the photograph of the grandmother because they see not the grandmother but an image of time, and a time that is not necessary but contingent. This is the pathos of archival desire.

In a sense, the goal of pure inscription or recording was, from the first, self-defeating. The act of filming transforms the contingent into an event characterized by its very filmability, reducing its contingency. The event was there to be filmed. Our current interest in the daily and mundane phenomenon of workers leaving the Lumière factory in 1895 lies in the fact that it constitutes the subject matter of one of the earliest films. Although it proffers to the spectator a wealth of detail and contingency – the different types of clothing of various workers, the use of bicycles, the direction of gazes, etcetera – its significance is ultimately constrained by its association with the 'birth' of the cinema. And even in their own time, these early films functioned as both record and performance. The cinema's decisive difference from photography was its ability to inscribe movement through time, and, as Tom Gunning has pointed out, much of the fascination of the earliest Lumière screenings was generated by beginning with a projected still photograph (a form of representation thoroughly familiar to the spectator) and subsequently propelling it into movement so that the temporal work of the apparatus could be displayed as a spectacle in its own right.[15]

The representation of time in cinema (its 'recording') is also and simultaneously the production of temporalities for the spectator, a structuring of the spectator's time. The cinema is perceived as both record and performance. Recent work on early cinema has tended to focus on its performative dimension. Gunning and André Gaudreault, in their conceptualization of the 'cinema of attractions,' argue that early films were above all a form of direct display to the spectator, of showing or showmanship.[16] Unabashedly exhibitionistic, they differ from the classical cinema in their direct address, their frequent recourse to a gaze aimed at the camera. The 'cinema of attractions' in its emphasis on theatrical display, is opposed to the diegetic absorption of the later classical cinema. It is a confrontational cinema, emphasizing shock and surprise.

Yet it is important to emphasize that notions of film as record and film as performance/display are not necessarily contradictory or incompatible. While the earliest screenings of film clearly functioned as demonstrations of the capabilities of the machine itself (so much so that advertisements frequently mentioned the name of the machine/apparatus – the Biograph or Vitascope – rather than the titles of films), one of the most prominent capabilities exhibited was that of indexicality, the ability to represent motion and temporal duration. Contingency was itself a display. Gunning and Gaudreault buttress their argument about the cinema of attractions by situating the cinema in the context of other popular forms of entertainment, including fairs, vaudeville, and the magic theater. The cinema's central role as entertainment does not preclude its intimate relation with new epistemologies, its inextricability from the reorganization of knowledge taking place in modernity. For photographic media offered new standards of accuracy, memory, knowability. The cinema, unlike fairs, vaudeville, and magic theater, requires a permanent inscription, an archival record. While all of these forms celebrate the ephemeral, it is the cinema which directly confronts the problematic question of the *representability* of the ephemeral, of the archivability of presence.

Ultimately, the focus of archival desire in the cinema is an impossible one – the reproduction of presence, a presence perceived to be the victim of rationalization and estrangement. Yet the archive's historicizing impulse, together with its inextricability from the concept of value, resonates uneasily with the desire to represent presence and instantaneity, with cinema's alliance with contingency and ephemerality, and with its apparent ability to represent anything whatsoever.

The cinema engages multiple temporalities, and it is helpful, at least temporarily, to disentangle them. There is the temporality of the apparatus itself – linear, irreversible, 'mechanical.' And there is the temporality of the diegesis, the way in which time is represented by the image, the varying invocations of present, past, future, historicity. Flashbacks would be the most prominent example of how the temporal content of the narrative can seemingly contest or counter the irreversibility of the apparatus itself. And finally, there is the temporality of reception, theoretically distinct but nevertheless a temporality which the developing classical cinema attempted to fuse as tightly as possible to that of the apparatus, conferring upon it the same linear predictability and irreversibility. Historically, experimentation with this form of temporality has been relegated to an avant-garde at the margins of mainstream cinema. Everything about the theatrical setting – the placement of the screen in relation to the audience, the darkness of the auditorium and its enclosed space – encourages the spectator to honor the relentless temporality of the apparatus.

It is possible to look away or to exit momentarily, but in the process something is lost and is felt as such. Similarly, the historical trajectory of the cinema has seemed to effect a reduction in the function of film as pure record of a time and a movement outside itself. Even in the early days of the cinema, the use of camera stoppage and editing allowed the film to construct its own temporality, independently of the external event or situation. The specific technology of the cinema – its apparent ability to represent the contingent without limit – posed the threat of an overwhelming detail, a denial of representation itself. The frame, of course, constitutes a spatial limit, but it is intriguing to note that histories and theories of early cinema continually pinpoint the temporal limit of the *cut*, the interruption in the linear forward movement of the film strip, as the crucial moment in the elaboration of film language. The cinema moves from the status of a machine that amazes and astonishes through its capacity as a record of time and movement to a machine for the production of temporalities that mimic 'real time.' Nevertheless, the production of temporalities in the classical cinema is ultimately not separable from the idea of the image as a record of time outside itself. At the macroscopic level, in its maintenance of continuity and the illusion of 'real time,' the film mimics and reiterates the microscopic level of the shot itself. In this way, it borrows and activates the fascination of the shot's privileged relation to contingency and a temporality emancipated from rationalization. Contingency becomes a form of graspable effectivity.

The fully developed classical cinema, like statistics, acknowledges contingency and indeterminacy while at the same time offering the law of their regularity. In 1848 Quetelet, in an attempt to banish chance, wrote: 'What we call an anomaly deviates in our eyes from the general law only because we are incapable of embracing enough things in a single glance.'[17] The cinema emerges as the materialization of the drive to 'embrace enough things in a single glance.' An advertisement for the American Biograph Company in 1900 proclaimed: 'Our Films Are Seven Times the Size of Others, We Show Twice as Many Pictures Per Second, and Our Pictures on the Canvas are LARGER, BRIGHTER, STEADIER and More INTERESTING Than Others . . . We have a Stock of Over Three Thousand Subjects and They are Coming all the Time from Europe, Asia, Africa and America.'[18] Indexicality has acted historically not solely as the assurance of realism but as the guarantee that anything and everything – any moment whatever – is representable, cinematographic. Contingency is brought under the rein of semiosis. But the earliest films display more vividly the fact that chance and contingency are the highly cathected sites not only of pleasure but of anxiety. The threat is that of an excess of designation, an excess of sensation that excludes meaning and control. The developing classical conventions structure time and contingency in ways consonant with the broader rationalization and abstraction of time in an industrialized modernity. Efficiency becomes a crucial value, and time is filled with meaning. Nevertheless, contingency is by no means banished. The structuring of time also involves its (structure's) denegation. Cinema comprises simultaneously the rationalization of time and an homage to contingency. Classical cinematic form involves the strict regulation of a mode that never ceases to strike the spectator as open, fluid, malleable – the site of newness and difference itself.

Notes

1 Brander Matthews, 'The Kinetoscope of Time,' *Scribner's Magazine* 1895, vol. 18(6), pp. 733–744, reproduced in George C. Pratt, *Spellbound in Darkness: A History of the Silent Film*, Greenwich, CT: New York Graphic Society, 1973, pp. 8–14.
2 The confusion of fiction and nonfiction here indicates a strong sense of an inherently historiographic tendency in the apparatus itself.
3 Count Alessandro di Cagliostro (1743–1795) was a celebrated Italian charlatan who posed as an alchemist, dispenser of aphrodisiacs and elixirs of youth, medium, and soothsayer. Fashionable society of pre-Revolutionary Paris was enamored with him, and many believed him to be several hundred years old. Cagliostro was eventually denounced by his own wife for heresy and imprisoned in the fortress of San Leo in the Apennines, where he died.
4 André Bazin, *What Is Cinema?* trans. and ed. Hugh Gray, vol. 1, Berkeley, CA: University of California Press, 1967, p. 14.
5 Andreas Huyssen, *Twilight Memories: Marking Time in a Culture of Amnesia*, New York: Routledge, 1995, p. 4.
6 Walter Benjamin, 'On Some Motifs in Baudelaire,' in *Illuminations*, trans. Harry Zohn, ed. Hannah Arendt, New York: Schocken, 1969, p. 184 (hereafter 'Motifs').
7 Stephen Kern, *The Culture of Time and Space, 1880–1918*, Cambridge, MA: Harvard University Press, 1983, p. 110.
8 Georg Simmel, 'The Metropolis and Mental Life,' in *The Sociology of Georg Simmel*, trans. and ed. Kurt H. Wolff, London: Collier-Macmillan, 1950, pp. 412, 410, 413.
9 Benjamin, 'Motifs,' p. 175.
10 Sigmund Freud, *Beyond the Pleasure Principle*, in *The Standard Edition of the Complete Psychological Works of Sigmund Freud*, trans. and ed. James Strachey, vol. 18, London: Hogarth Press, 1955, p. 25; Benjamin, 'Motifs,' p. 161.
11 Benjamin, 'Motifs,' p. 163.
12 Benjamin, 'Motifs,' pp. 174–175.
13 See Noël Burch, *Life to Those Shadows*, Berkeley: University of California Press, 1990, p. 21.
14 Kracauer, 'Photography,' p. 56.
15 Tom Gunning, 'An Aesthetic of Astonishment: Early Film and the (In)Credulous Spectator,' in *Viewing Positions, Ways of Seeing Film*, ed. Linda Williams, New Brunswick, N.J.: Rutgers University Press, 1995, p. 118.
16 See Tom Gunning, 'The Cinema of Attractions: Early Film, Its Spectator and the Avant-Garde,' in *Early Cinema: Space, Frame, Narrative*, ed. Thomas Elsaesser, London: British Film Institute, 1990, pp. 56–62.
17 Quoted in Porter, *The Rise of Statistical Thinking*, p. 105.
18 Pratt, *Spellbound in Darkness*, p. 18.

Maureen Turim

FLASHBACKS IN FILM

Memory and history

Flashbacks in Film: Memory and History, New York: Routledge, 1989, pp. 1–12.

MOST READERS ARE PROBABLY FAMILIAR with what we mean by a flashback in film. For many, Hollywood classics have defined this familiarity with the flashback technique including such famous examples in Orson Welles's *Citizen Kane* (1941), cited in virtually every dictionary of film that attempts a definition of the flashback. A body of literature discussing the flashback exists, ranging from scriptwriting manuals to introductory books on film study. In its classic form, the flashback is introduced when the image in the present dissolves to an image in the past, understood either as a story-being-told or a subjective memory. Dialogue, voice-over, or intertitles that mark anteriority through language often reinforce the visual cues representing a return to the past. Both earlier and later in film history, other forms of flashbacks occur that are less obviously marked. We therefore need a more general definition for the flashback that includes all types of flashbacks. In its most general sense, a flashback is simply an image or a filmic segment that is understood as representing temporal occurrences anterior to those in the images that preceded it. The flashback concerns a representation of the past that intervenes within the present flow of film narrative. As we shall see shortly, there is a great deal more to be said about the definition of the flashback and the implications of this term.

Memory, in its psychoanalytic and philosophical dimensions, is one of the concepts inscribed in flashbacks. Memory surges forth, it strengthens or protects or it repeats and haunts. A plethora of depicted memories are offered across the history of flashback use, each slightly different in form, ideology, tone. Some are subjective, interiorized; others represent a telling-in-language whose degree of subjectivity might be considerably less. To analyze this constant play of difference, the films need to be examined as fragments of a cinematic discourse on the mind's relationship to the past and on the subject's relationship to telling his or her past.

The cinematic presentation of memory in these films can be compared with the knowledge proposed by various disciplines that research and speculate on memory processes. We shall find that this comparison shows some mirroring and some fascinating discrepancies, some anticipations of the future of science by art and some anachronisms used blithely because they correspond to some dramatic imperative of a given mode of fiction.

If flashbacks give us images of memory, the personal archives of the past, they also give us images of history, the shared and recorded past. In fact, flashbacks in film often merge the two levels of remembering the past, giving large-scale social and political history the subjective mode of a single, fictional individual's remembered experience. This process can be called the 'subjective memory,' which here has the double sense of the rendering of history as a subjective experience of a character in the fiction, and the formation of the subject in history as the viewer of the film identifying with fictional characters positioned in a fictive social reality. The play of different voices within film narration, however, implies certain departures or divisions within this formation of subjectivity. Even flashbacks that are themselves marked by subjectivity or the single focalization of a character may engender a representation of history not so subjectively circumscribed, or so unified. The telling or remembering of the past within a film can be self-conscious, contradictory, or ironic. Some flashback narratives actually take as their project the questioning of the reconstruction of the historical. A close study of the variations in flashbacks is actually a means of questioning the conceptual foundations of history in its relationship to narrative and narrative in its relationship to history.

The analysis of flashbacks in film is first of all a history of formal changes in storytelling techniques. As such, this study owes much to Russian formalist methodology in establishing a theory and method for analyzing the permutations of form found in flashback films. The formalists introduced the basic distinction in terminology between story and plot.[1] The term 'story' refers to narrative events as understood in a 'real' temporality, a logic of linearity and causality that refers to the ordering of time in the 'natural' world. Plot is the inscription of events in their actual presentation in the narrative (the book as read or film as viewed). Thus plot order can vary from story order to various effects, and story order is often left for the reader/viewer to conceptualize according to different cues of dating and reference.

Another concept Russian formalism introduced was the notion of a 'device,' a construct within form that complicates the formal patterning of the textual object, providing form with variations. The flashback can be seen as one such device, as it rearranges plot order. In some ways the device is similar to the notion of the figure within earlier rhetorical theory, but it is at once a larger category and one which has a different status. Rhetoric in the earlier tradition saw figures as creating meanings that the reader/analyst's job was to explicate and evaluate. The formalists inverted the device/signification relationship previously assumed in explanations of how texts functioned. Content exists to naturalize or justify the device, except in cases where the device is bared in displays of narrative reflexivity.[2] The great contribution of early formalism was to accentuate *another* history of textual development by inverting the value assigned to content over form.

While acknowledging the debt to formalist theory, let me also suggest that the formalism that informs this study is not a formalism conceived of as separate from or in opposition to a larger sense of historical development; quite the contrary. My premise is rather that the history of the flashback from 1902 through 1985 is also a complex fragment of more general developments within film history and social history. By slicing through film history focusing on a single narrative technique we can examine important changes in cinematic representation and ideology, not always discussed in formalist studies as such.

We can easily suggest that the flashback developed as a means of mimetic representation of memory, dreams, or confession, and in so doing we are not necessarily returning to an outmoded thematic treatment of technique. We can instead see flashbacks simultaneously as both devices to be covered with referential and narrative justification and as a means of portraying thought processes or circuitous investigations of enigmas. We can see that it is this weave of motivation that makes the inscription of flashbacks in fact so fascinating.

We might also extrapolate a complex pattern of evolution and influence among novel, play, and film. Film influences the modern novel to duplicate a cinematic sense of the flashback mimetically, while the traditional novel, especially the 19th-century novel, can be seen as already containing the literary equivalent of a filmic flashback, though 'naturalized' in language.[3]

The history of the flashback device is not linear, however, and formalist method can help overcome a tendency to make history into a linear or developmental progression. The development of the flashback is not a linear progression from an awkward form to an increasingly complex and sophisticated inscription. If we can apply terms to periods of flashback uses like 'primitive,' 'classical,' and 'modernist,' we also find that there are asynchronic developments that place some of the most modernist and innovative uses of the flashbacks in films of the twenties. The modernist innovations of flashbacks during the sixties are a reprise of the flashback concepts developed in the twenties avant-garde. Further, the earliest flashbacks of silent American films are rich and suggestive images. Though they may appear more simple in form (a single shot tableau or a reprise of shots already seen) this inherent simplicity of imagery actually functions to create an expansion of meanings. These tableaux function as context-dependent signifiers and concentrated junctures in narrative coding. The flashbacks of the Hollywood sound period present a different kind of semiotic complexity, for the sound/image relationships weave between different temporalities and focalizations. The most recent Hollywood flashbacks, conversely, are often less sophisticated than those found in films of earlier periods; they are redundant in their internal coding and serve primarily to deliver missing narrative exposition.

The link between the 19th-century novel and early film was astutely made by Sergei Eisenstein in his essay, 'Dickens, Griffith and the Film Today.'[4] Eisenstein cites passages from *A Tale of Two Cities*, *Nicholas Nickleby*, and *Hard Times* to show literary equivalents to cinematic montage. Parallel montage, the cutting from one series of actions in one space to another simultaneous series in another space, is the main object of Eisenstein's attention. He also discusses the use of 'close-up' details in descriptive passages and the montage insert of an element of the action in a kind of 'skipped' order. Eisenstein mentions Stefan Zweig's discussion of the masked autobiographical memory traces that give *David Copperfield* a richness of details as it describes the hero's reminiscences. Flashback narration as such, however, is not one of the elements that Eisenstein discusses as a point of comparison between Dickens and Griffith, though it certainly is among their shared narrative techniques; temporal shifts are less Eisenstein's concern in this essay than are spatial shifts and metaphoric montage.

The literary equivalent to the flashback is often less distinct and abrupt than the cinematic flashback in its temporal shifts. Verbal storytelling can ease temporal shifts through the sustaining power of the narrative voice, whether that of authorial omniscience or of a character in first-person narration. An arsenal of verb tenses and qualifying clauses render these shifts as an invisible act of language. The concept 'flashback' as developed by the cinema makes us more aware of these temporal shifts in literary narration. After cinema makes the flashback a common and distinctive narrative trait, audiences and critics were more likely to recognize flashbacks as crucial elements of narrative structure in other narrative forms. This may be particularly true for the popular conception of narrative temporality among a general audience, but it is perhaps also a factor in scholarly recognition of modes of narrative temporality, first in formalist literary theory and more recently in structuralist theory. Both the formalists of the early years of the 20th century and the post-World War II structuralists developed their narrative theories with film as a common cross-reference to their usually primary focus on literary narration. As Gérard Genette acknowledges in the context of a discussion of the contribution of the Russian formalists, 'Everyone knows that the birth of the cinema altered the status of literature: by depriving it of certain of its functions, but also by giving it some of its own means.'[5] The flashback may well be one of the functions that cinema altered and gave back to literature. It seems likely that the manner in which the cinematic flashback manipulates narrative temporality highlights literature's differential treatment of temporal modalities.

Two major figures in structuralist and semiotic theory, Gérard Genette and Roland Barthes, introduced a series of concepts concerning narrative textuality that provide a background against which a theory of the flashback can be constructed. I will therefore summarize briefly the relevant aspects of their approaches to the text. We should keep in mind, however, that their models are usually literary, especially significant in light of the preceding discussion of the difference, historically and semiotically, between literary and filmic texts.

In his essay 'Discours du récit' in *Figures III*, Genette considers the ordering of narrative events one of the basic aspects of narrative construction.[6] He establishes a series of useful terms to describe variations in order. 'Anachrony' is the general term he proposes for any temporal rearrangement, while 'analepse' indicates a movement from a narrative present to the past (as in a flashback) and 'prolepse' indicates a movement from a narrative present to a disjunct future (as in a flashforward). Both the analepse and prolepse can be distinguished further by the opposition interior/exterior; an interior analepse is one that returns to a past of the fiction that remains within the temporal period of the rest of the narration. All flashbacks which repeat incidents narrated previously or referred to elliptically within the prior linear development of the narration are interior analepses. Exterior analepses jump back to a time period prior to and disjunct from the moment of the narrative's beginning.

The interior/exterior distinction is related to Genette's notion of the 'portée' of the analepse, that is, how long ago the past event occurred. Flashbacks can skip back over years, decades, days, hours, or just a few moments. 'Amplitude' is Genette's term for the duration of the event within the analepse, or to put it more simply, how much of the past is told in the flashback. A flashback can cover a period of time in the past understood as being several years long or, conversely, just a few moments. The term 'duration' then is freed to mean the actual length of the flashback as it is told. In literature this can be measured in lines or pages, while in film we speak of minutes. Each of these concepts, amplitude, portée, and duration, is significant in the analysis of the flashback as a narrative device; each not only contributes to the more precise description of differences between flashbacks, but the nature of the structural view implied in these terms allows us to conceive of the flashback in the context of the narrative structure as a whole.

Genette also develops the notion of ellipses (periods of time that are left out of narration) beyond its definition in standard literary analysis. We can combine these terms to formulate analytical statements about flashbacks; for example, we find that analepses sometimes retrospectively fill in ellipses. This combination of devices is one of the ways narratives build suspense by withholding the revelation of information until an efficacious moment, often the climax of the story. The combination of terms can also provide a description of another kind of flashback; we can say that in these cases analepses themselves contain ellipses. Sometimes flashbacks carry this to an extreme, bracketing several incidents together to relate the past paradigmatically. The incidents narrated within the analepse can themselves be organized achronologically.

Genette often diagrams passages from literature as part of his analysis of their structure, creating a visual description of order, portée, amplitude, and duration.

Genette's purpose in *Figures III* seems divided between the illustration of types of temporal organization and the analysis of the function of specific types in Proust. This division in his theoretical purpose has two consequences, the first of which is that his terminology is cumbersome, especially in transliteration into English. While a passage from Proust can be used to explain the notion of amplitude, the converse is not so evident. In actual textual analysis, one can speak directly and perhaps more convincingly of the actual arrangement of temporality in the passage. It therefore seems unnecessary to use Genette's terms for the dimensions of flashbacks in all the actual analyses in this book – 'amplitude' or 'portée' can be discussed in simple language, by analyzing, for example, how a certain flashback inserts a reference to a day in time several years earlier, for example. This seems more direct than saying the amplitude of the flashback is restricted (one day) while its portée is fairly extensive (several years). The decision on my part to use more direct language may have the unfortunate consequence of making what are elements of the theoretical dimensions of temporal organization seem like mere description; it is therefore in reference to Genette's exposition of what is at stake for narrative in temporal organization that I hope such specific analyses of analepse structure can be read.[7]

The second drawback to Genette's project is its potential for remaining at the level of typology. Genette's major contribution in 'Discours du récit' is not the typology itself, but his sensitive analysis of Proust's language in relationship to temporality, its rich comparison with a wide range of literature, and the theoretical speculations that occur over the course of the essay. Genette demonstrates how much the organization of events in narrative can vary and how significant this process of variation can be. Ultimately, this essay points out much of what is most innovative about Proust's writing. In abstracting the level of temporal organization from its naturalized embedding in the narrator's voice, Genette points to how Proust's work achieves its density in constructing time, language, and subjective experience. Though the distinctions Genette introduces are mostly applied to examples from literature, they allow us to develop a concept of a specifically filmic treatment of narrative time.[8]

This relevance to film analysis is suggested indirectly by Genette in the selection of a quote from Christian Metz at the very opening of 'Discours du récit':

> [Narrative is] a doubly temporal sequence, . . . There is the time of that which is told and the time of the plot (the time of the signified and the time of the signifier). This duality is not only that which makes possible all temporal distortions that are commonly found in narratives (three years in the life of the hero summarized in two lines of a novel, or in a few shots of a montage sequence in cinema, etc.); more fundamentally it invites us to remark that one of the functions of narrative is to create one time in another time.[9]

While Genette goes on from here to discuss that filmic unfolding is perhaps more fixed than reading time, he accepts the basic parallel between the two narrative processes. Is the figure of duality in itself adequate to describe narrative temporality? Has the binary opposition of the formalist story–plot distinction reemerged as the image of a dual narrative temporality? Similarly, Gilles Deleuze introduces the term 'bifurcation' in his *Cinema 1: The Movement Image* to discuss the temporality of the flashback, though he means for the term to indicate a multiple splitting beyond the pair of temporalities bifurcation implies.[10] While this duality may be a basic structuring principle of film that the flashback makes particularly evident, temporality in the filmic narrative may not be so simply double. Analysis of focalization, as proposed by Marc Vernet, is one way of modifying the notion of dual temporality in film: this concept becomes extremely useful in his analysis of the function of voice-off narration in the flashback sequences of film noir.[11] In a more general sense, when we consider narrative as a weave of voices and as a construction of narrative codes as introduced by Roland Barthes, we can see how temporality is multiply inscribed.

Roland Barthes's work on narrative coding, first in a series of articles, then in his book *S/Z*, is another structural view of the ordering of narrative exposition.[12] Less concerned with temporality per se than is Genette, Barthes nonetheless provides important constituents of our theory of the flashback by defining narrative as organized by five different codes, or sets of information. Barthes's analysis in *S/Z* strives in his reading of Balzac's 'Sarrasine,' to counteract the linearity he sees as recapitulated in the traditional 'explication des textes' as well as in prior structural studies that stop at 'the major structures.' This goal becomes all the more difficult since the analysis itself proceeds through the short story from phrase to phrase in order to comment upon the 'lexias' of the text, small units of coded significations. Yet Barthes insists he wants to disperse the text. His phrase is étoilé,' which is rendered in the English translation as 'starred'; this unfortunately suggests 'marking' rather than the French connotation of a systematically spread out universe of stars. His goal is to avoid 'assembling' the text, which leads him to statements like the following when speaking of sequential actions: 'we shall not attempt to put them in any order.' Barthes wishes to highlight 'the plural meaning entangled' in actions. He contributes to a theory of the flashback precisely because in delineating five narrative codes he breaks with a simple story/plot polarity and provides a more multi-faceted view of narrative inscription, reference, and signification. Barthes's analysis highlights other functions that we might consider for the flashback besides that of affecting order, and allows us to consider temporality itself as more multiple.

A linear, causal temporality is implicit in the proairetic code, or the code of actions as it can be called. This linear sequence of cause and effect forms a hypothetical logic, a kind of assumed background against which narrative events unfold. It is based on a sense of the 'way things work in the real world,' from the way a street is crossed to what happens when an engine fails on a plane. It borrows heavily from the physical properties of existence and movement in time and space, what might be called the 'laws of nature.' This logic of time and space is ultimately what helps the viewer to distinguish a flashback from a purely imaginary sequence or an arbitrary narrative disruption. The abstract logic of a hypothetical time-line of events is a necessary prerequisite to understanding a narrative in which any elements are left out or told in an altered chronology. We acquire this abstract logic initially by experiencing chronologies both as observers of the world and as consumers of chronologically narrated tales. This learned expectation which develops as our abstract logic for understanding stories can be referred to indirectly and differentially by the achronological tale, the fantastic or the absurd story. If the logic of narrative is set up against the physical properties of the world as we know it, the play of narrative is as departure and deviation.

Many kinds of flashbacks are, in addition, hermeneutically determined. The hermeneutic code, or code of enigmas, is one way in which narrative organizes the exposition of events so as to keep interest invested in a posed question, the answer to which is delayed. Barthes sees it as the code most intimately entwined with the proairetic code; in his section called, 'The Full Score,' he develops an analogy to musical composition that implies a hierarchy of relations amongst the codes, with the proairetic and the hermeneutic forming a combined flow that sustains the more flashy and disjunct flourishes of the other three codes (pp. 28–30).

Some flashbacks directly involve a quest for the answer to an enigma posed in the beginning of a narrative through a return to the past. The frame-tale which opens with a consequence, such as murder, the erection of a monument, etc., and then flashes back to tell how or why this event came to be, is one example. Another is the narrative which employs a flashback just prior to the climatic revelation of the enigma, to provide a missing aspect of the enigma. Other narratives use a series of flashbacks to develop an enigma and delay its resolution before reaching the final flashback of revelation, or conversely, revealing the solution to the enigma by other means.

Flashbacks can also be important sources of association of a character or place with certain connotations, a process Barthes calls the semic code. By suddenly presenting the past, flashbacks can abruptly offer new meanings connected to any person, place, or object. Flashbacks then gain a particularly rich dimension in the coding of the psychology of character, and because their evidence is the past, they immediately imply a psychoanalytic dimension of personality.

Flashbacks can be devoted to citing historical and scientific knowledge of the culture within fiction, Barthes's referential code. Flashbacks sometimes are the primary sites for fixing referential meaning in texts which otherwise evade direct references to history. They become a means for developing an ideology of history that colors the 'eternal' or 'timeless' connotations evoked by certain types of stories. This is why I have chosen the phrase 'subjectivizing of history' to explore the function of flashbacks in creating specific ideologies of history.

Every flashback draws an antithesis between past and present, but there are various ways this antithesis can be animated within what Barthes calls the symbolic coding of the narrative, the code that constructs the textual play of power and desire. Subjective truths and the emotional charge of memory are often values associated with flashbacks. These charged sequences are inserted into the less individuated, more 'objective' present unfolding of events, often combating and overturning a certain view of the law. Knowledge of the past is often presented as a privilege afforded by the fiction, access to which is transformative, but temporary and didactic. Nostalgia is a figure ambiguously attached to the flashback; the past is an object of desire, due to its personal, intense, and even liberating attributes, but it is also dangerous and frightening. Flashbacks in most cases terminate at precisely the point at which they must be sealed off, in which the imperatives of fixing interpretations and reaching judgments in the present must be imposed. Made aware of the past, the spectator is freed to forget it once again. This symbolic order vacillates between knowing and forgetting, the shifts determined by the positioning of the spectator within the structured operations of narrative temporality.

Another type of textual investigation termed 'deconstruction' by Jacques Derrida (but practiced by others as well who do not necessarily employ this term) goes against the grain of the text's own weave of representation.[13] Rather than just analyzing elements or even the structures of a text, deconstruction allows us to see the structuring of the text as itself a configuration. In a sense, deconstruction follows from the structural perspective, but also follows through, beyond its points of departure and its goals, into the realm of an analysis of philosophical configurations.

For example, consider the way in which Barthes analyzes in *S/Z* the 'truth' of the fiction molded by hermeneutic code, the 'truths' the text cites in its referential code, and the 'natural' logic of the proairetic code. Deconstruction puts a sharper edge on these various ways of slicing through the truth values assigned by a text to itself and its implicit philosophical discourse. Deconstruction's debt in regard to the decentering of truth to the writings of Nietzsche is another reason why it is particularly useful for this study as Nietzsche's writings discuss the figures of repetition and fate that the flashback, particularly during the forties, presents.

The quotes surrounding the 'true' and the 'natural' are one way of granting a questioning force to the inscription of these terms that will not allow their use to conform with an ideal reality. Derrida substitutes another mark, that indicates an erasure that retains the trace, an X crossing out the representation of truth to indicate the double energy of a deconstructive mode that allows one never to fix on what is present nor on what is absent, but inscribes the conflict between the opposition present/absent in the realm of representation. This conflict is deeply embedded in the functioning of language itself. Psychoanalysis was able to indicate certain figures in dream representation and in parapraxis that presented a limited model for a deconstructive reading. Marxist analysis of ideology also contributed to an understanding of significant absences and figural representations within discourse.[14] However, both psychoanalysis and Marxism have their own borders through which they frame truths. Deconstruction attempts, in its shifting energies, to show frames rather than to construct them, and in showing them to permeate these structures of thought.

Deconstruction, for this reason, is complex and threatening. Some dismiss it, some simplify or deform it to their own ends; unfortunately its proposals can easily be downshifted to a return to absolute formalism, a mechanical description of the form of representational tropes. However, in the writings of the most vibrant deconstructive analysts, there is always more at stake. Form is not reinforced, but divided and multiplied in an investigation that allows this division and multiplication to affect the process of textual analysis.

For an investigation of the flashback, this has significant consequences: inherent in the flashback as trope is a certain assumption of temporality and order. The very term 'chronological' implies an implicit clockwork logic to events. Our notion of duration is in this context something measurable and absolute. Yet, we know that it is also possible for events to cease to be discrete and for duration to be differentially measured or entirely called into question. In these instances we begin to see how the notion of chronology is marked as a culturally determined means of representation. The camera and projector, like the printed pages of a book before it, imply a certain temporality, an unfolding that other representational apparati do not. Perhaps the film does so even more than the book, whose pages can more easily be turned in various orders against the flow of the printing; but this is more of a physical difference than a theoretical one, for all it takes is a multiple video display bank to project a film as the disordered sum of its temporal units. The point is that in traditional practice, we have a very fixed frame through which we read and watch films. All inversions of temporality that occur within their representations are framed by this assumed clockwork mechanism and measured against it. If structuralism maps the ordering of texts, deconstruction allows us to see the view of the world implicit in the design of the map itself.

So far in developing a theory of the flashback, I have been reviewing relevant theories of narrative structuring whose reference is literature. Equally relevant is the concept of temporality as expressed in images and the way in which verbal commentary that may accompany them affects this image temporality.

Many theorists of photography have remarked on the evidential quality of photography, the manner in which it appears to bear witness to the scenes it depicts. The viewer often interprets a photo as documenting fragments of the real world.

André Bazin, for one, championed this indexical aspect of the photographic sign, assigning an ontological status to photography's ability to imprint a mimetic image of a perceived reality. Bazin extended this ability to 'mummify' the world, to capture and preserve it as 'it really was' to the cinematic image.[15] Roland Barthes borrows from Bazin's phenomenological approach to the photograph, contending that photos provide evidence that what we see imaged within them once existed. Barthes says the photo implies the 'having been there' of the scene or objects depicted; according to Barthes, its assumed tense is the past.[16]

Cinema's ability to display motion in time is seen by Bazin, as it was by many earlier film theorists, as in addition to the realist vocation of photography. This establishes film as an even more powerful medium of realism than photography. Bazin championed putting this realist capacity to the service of filmic fiction as a means of creating stories that closely described a perceived reality. According to Barthes, however, cinema partakes of a different implied temporality; on one level, the cinema implies the same past tense as the photograph, presenting 'the having been there' of the actors. However, the fictional functioning of film presents what Barthes calls another 'pose,' effacing this indication of the past existence of the referent in favor of a presence of a character within the ongoing present of the story, that is, the impression of an imaginary reality. Of course, the cinema that Barthes is considering is the fiction film rather than other types of film, such as archival documentary footage and home movies.

Some documentary footage is understood by its spectators in much the same way as is archival photography, as a document of a reality that once existed at the moment the images were taken. However, when incorporated into a documentary film such archival footage can be introduced into a narration that incorporates a nearly fictional presentation, as it strives to transport the spectator to another scene, another time. The 'nearly present' is an important mode for documentary films that chronicle current events, with the simultaneous broadcast capacity of television striving to make the image 'live' and therefore a present reality. Home movies have much the same status as family photographs as regards this question of temporal reference; they offer an image of the past of the individuals and places depicted and are understood as records of this past in much the same way as the photo album has become the archive of the family. The response to such images can vary from one which understands their pastness, to one that relives the past as part of an ongoing present, positions marked respectively by such verbal responses as 'there was X when he was a baby,' and 'there is X swimming.'

If documentary modes of filmic representation can indicate a definitive past, even if in some instances they edge towards the present, what of the temporality of the image within the fiction film? Barthes's formulation of the different temporal understanding of photographic and cinematic images coincides with a certain widely held belief that cinema is understood in the present tense. One supporting argument for this belief, in fact, involves flashbacks. The argument claims that within a given flashback segment, the spectator experiences the film in exactly the same way that one experiences any other segment of a fiction film, as an ongoing series of events happening to the characters in their immediate temporal experience, that is their 'present.' As this type of statement is most often made in the context of a comparison of literary and filmic modes of narration, the contrast is drawn between the variety of tenses available to the writer of literature and the singularity of tense available in cinema. Literature can qualify its mode of narration, while cinema simply presents actions. This position holds that beyond the initial entrance into and exit from a flashback, the spectator has no temporal markings of anteriority for the events depicted, and should a spectator begin watching the film in the middle of the flashback, he or she would never know that the flashback segments were actually meant to depict the past.

Such arguments ignore the way a filmic text codes its temporality. First it does so as a product of its diachronic unfolding; segments are defined temporally in relation to what preceded or what will follow them. Secondly, the temporal reference of a filmic segment is defined by a complex combination of visual and auditory indications, which can include: voice-over narration, filmic punctuations such as dissolves, changes in image qualities such as color to black and white, changes in elements of mise-en-scène such as costumes indicating an earlier time period or make-up differences that indicate younger periods in a character's life, and changes in non-diegetic music. This does not mean that the filmic image has the semantic fluidity and precision of verbal expression when it comes to articulating temporal references; language provides a subtle delineation of different modalities of temporal reference that are only available to film through the use of language either in the form of voice-over or written intertitles or subtitles. The history of the flashback in film, however, constitutes just this struggle to code a cinematic past.

Finally, a remark on the assumption that it is the equivalent of a present-tense narration that is created by filmic fictions as part of the impression of an imaginary reality; even films whose fiction creates an ongoing present for its characters are not necessarily received by its viewers entirely within this imaginary frame. Sometimes spectators maintain their distance and experience the narrative as a story that is being narrated, as a story from a past or from another scene to which they do not have an unmediated access. This distance may be encouraged by the film by internal distancing devices of several kinds, such as voice-over narration, stylized mise-en-scène, or the foregrounding of historical references. Some film narratives acquire through these means a sense of a past-tense narration which is somewhat analogous to the distancing modalities of the past-tense in literary discourse. Similarly, a 'painterly' or 'theatrical' mise-en-scène operates differently from images whose mise-en-scène is in a realistic mode. Bazin and Barthes tend to assume a style of photographic image that utilizes codes of analogy that have come to be phenomenologically invisible. It is for this reason that Barthes makes such a strong distinction between looking at a photograph and looking at a drawing, a distinction that is no longer appropriate for pictorial photography, for example, any more than it is appropriate for German expressionist film.

Fiction film, then, has many ways to develop temporalities through which the cinematic image can be understood. More complicated flashback structures tend to emphasize the means by which film presents its fiction. The imaginary entrance into a present reality is provided, but the spectator is made aware of the threshold and the process of transversing it. The spectator in this case is acutely aware of the filmic fiction as a story-being-told. Multiple flashbacks, embedded flashbacks, abrupt modernist flashbacks can make spectators more aware of the modalities of filmic fiction, of the processes of narrative itself. These manipulations of narrative temporality can serve to self-consciously expose the mechanisms of filmic narration, the artifice through which time becomes an expressive element of narrative form. However, various techniques simultaneously can be used to naturalize these temporal manipulations, such as locating them in the psyche or the storytelling capacity of a character within the fiction. A spectator then is suspended between two different ways of looking at temporal manipulations within filmic imagery, one that is aware of the formal operations of narrative and one that forgets these elements due to naturalizing processes within the fiction.

This split between knowledge and forgetfulness through which the flashback operates within filmic fiction is similar to the more general split belief system that operates in fiction's formulation of the 'impression of reality' as it has been described by Christian Metz.[17] One knows that one is watching a film, but one believes, even so, that it is an imaginary reality. The difference I am pointing out here is that the flashback structure tends to override this split constituting the impression of reality with a second level rearticulating a similar conflict of beliefs. On this level, the spectator is again presented with a duality, and this time the balance often tilts towards a knowledge of structure, an awareness of the process of telling stories about the past. This may be a reason flashback structures are negatively received as too artificial and as slowing the action by many critics, some filmmakers, and undoubtedly other people as well. They have a potential for disturbing a participatory viewing of a film and encouraging a greater intellectual distance, although, again, the countervailing forces that naturalize the flashbacks as personal memories can produce just the opposite effect – no emotional distance, extreme identification.

It is in this context that we can explore the ideological implications of the flashback as a framing device for stories and for representation of history within these stories. For if the flashback presents a narrative past, this past often refers to an historical past. The rendering of this historical past is colored by both the general processes of fictional transformation, and by the specific framing and focalization of this fictional version of the historical past as a flashback.

One of the ideological implications of this narration of history through a subjective focalization is to create history as an essentially individual and emotional experience. Another is to establish a certain view of historical causality and linkage. By presenting the result before the cause, a logic of inevitability is implied; certain types of events are shown to have certain types of results without ever allowing for other outcomes than the one given in advance. Many flashback narrations contain an element of philosophical fatalism, coupled with a psychoanalytic fatalism. This fatalism presents a cynical view of history cyclical, guaranteed to repeat that which we have already seen; the release from the repetitions inherent in history is then forged in a singular solution that serves a prevailing ideology, such as patriotic identification or a retreat into the 'personal' as a microcosmic, idealized world. Further, the history narrated in flashback is often a didactic history, containing moral lessons. The lessons vary from one historical period or location to another, which is one of the reasons it is useful to organize this study in historical periods. Considering the nationality of production is another means of analyzing differences in the lessons about history that flashbacks try to teach.

However, it is possible in a more modernist and experimental reinscription of history in the flashback to call all these ideological implications into question. In these cases, changes in the form of the flashback and the voice-over narration can not only reorient the stated ideology but question the ideological processes of making and telling histories.

In psychoanalysis, the case history and the 'cure' is a process through which the patient retells the past and deciphers dreams that are in many ways reworkings of this personal past history. The analyst hears the many versions and symbolic representations of this story and in a sense becomes an accomplice in determining the form of its unfolding.

Flashbacks in film often parallel this operation as they present a past, like a dream, waiting to be interpreted. Sometimes the psychoanalytic analogy is directly taken up by the fiction with the flashback narrative becoming the story of the patient in analysis, as is the case in the twenties with G.W. Pabst's *Secrets of a Soul* (1926) and in the forties with Curtis Bernhardt's *Possessed* (1947). More often, the psychoanalytic analogy is indirect; there is no analyst within fiction listening to the flashback narration. Even so the spectator can 'hear' the flashback from the position of the analyst, which includes the possibility of identification with the narrator of the flashback. The flashback invites this analytic reception, as it is offered as an explanation from the past for the situation in the present. However, when the texts themselves indicate a Freudian reading of the flashback material, they often utilize a simplified and determinist version of psychoanalysis, for example, the 'popularized Freud' that combines interpretations by both American psychoanalysts and the mass media. This version of Freud often manifests a dark, fatalistic view of the human psyche when given expression in fiction.

We need to consider the psychoanalytic theory on another level as well in building a theory of the functioning of flashbacks. Flashbacks often present images which are to be understood as memories. These films portray their own versions of how memories are stored, how they are repressed, how they return from the repressed. These representations can be compared to Freud's representations of the memory system, the unconsciousness, and his theory of the return of the repressed.[18] Then we can also look at how psychoanalytic theory and psycho-perceptual theory after Freud produced modifications and changes in his model. The comparison between representations of memory within the fiction of the films and representations of memory in scientific theory has as its goal not just the critique of the fictional representation by an application of the scientific, but also a critique of applied psychoanalysis as a tool for reading texts. If the films deviate from scientific knowledge, they do so for their own purpose and create their own effects. The kind of psychoanalytic methodology one needs to confront such textual strategies is of another order. For example, flashback films make specific use of the theory of associative memory, the way an event or sensation in the present brings forth a memory trace that was since forgotten. The elements placed into association in this way become linked in the text's symbolic code. The analyst, in playing with the association of these elements, can work against the grain of a habitual reading of what the film is supposed to mean, and find that the film is saying other things quite 'unconsciously.' Thus the way psychoanalysis figures into our analysis of the functioning of flashback is as both a reference and a tool in understanding the manifest representation of memory in the film and as a part of a deconstructive reading of the structure of the symbolic order of the film, in which the flashbacks play a key function.

Notes

1 Yuri Tynianov, 'Plot and Story-line in the Cinema,' *Russian Poetics in Translation*, 1978, vol. 5, p. 20.
2 Boris Tomashevsky, 'Thematics,' *Russian Formalist Criticism: Four Essays*, ed. Lee Lemon and Marion Reis, Lincoln, NE: University of Nebraska Press, 1965, pp. 78–85, and Victor Shklovsky, 'On the Connection Between Devices of Sloshes Construction to General Stylistic Devices,' trans. Jane Knox, *20th Century Studies*, 1972, no. 7/8, p. 54.
3 Keith Cohen, *Film and Fiction: Dynamics of an Exchange*, New Haven: Yale University Press, 1979.
4 Sergei Eisenstein, 'Dickens, Griffith and the Film Today,' *Film Form*, trans. Jay Leyda, New York: Harcourt and Bruce, 1969.
5 Gérard Genette. 'Poétique et l'histoire,' *Figures III*, Paris: Editions du Seuil, 1972, pp. 13–20.
6 Genette, 'Discours du récit;' *Figures III*, pp. 71–121, trans. as *Narrative Discourse: An Essay in Method*, tr. Jane E. Lewin, Ithaca, NY: Cornell University Press, 1980, pp. 33–85.
7 In his 'Aprés-propos' that closes *Figures III*, Genette recognizes this problem and suggests that he expects that posterity will not hold on to a large number of his terminological inventions and distinctions (p. 269).
8 Critiques of the application of Genette's work to film narratives include Michèle Lagny, Marie-Claire Ropars and Pierre Sorlin, 'Le Recit saisi par le film,' *Hors Cadre*, 1984, no. 2, pp. 99–124; and Francis Jost, 'Discours cinématographique, narration: deux façons d'envisager le problème de l'énonciation,' *Théorie du film*, ed. Jean-Louis Leutreat and Jacques Aumont, Paris: Editions Albatros, 1980, pp. 121–31.
9 Christian Metz, *Essais sur la signification au cinéma*, vol. 1, Paris, Klincksieck, 1968, p. 27, as quoted in 'Discours du récit,' p. 77 (my translation – note that Metz's original passage is slightly different from the way he is quoted by Genette and I have added the brackets at the beginning to indicate that Metz's 'le récit est' is taken from the previous sentence of the original. I have translated this use of *récit* in its more general sense as equivalent to the American 'narrative,' while using 'plot' to translate the more restricted meaning of *récit* in the next sentence).
10 Gilles Deleuze, *Cinéma II: L'Image-Temps*, Paris: Editions de Minuit, 1985, pp. 66–75. Deleuze is interested in what he calls the 'nappes de temps,' the sheets or layers of time and looks to the films of Welles and Resnais for examples of this layering. Yet he wants to separate Resnais's success from his play with flashback structures, seeing it rather in his work on all forms of the imaginary (p. 160).
11 Marc Vernet, 'Narrateur, personnage et spectateur dans le film de fiction à travers le film noir,' unpublished Ph.D. dissertation, L'Ecole des Hautes Etudes, 1985. Vernet argues that differences in enunciation between film and literature circumscribe the applicability of a theory built on verbal textuality to the visual constructs of film.
12 Roland Barthes, *S/Z*, trans. Richard Miller, New York: Hill and Wang, 1974.
13 Among the writings of Jacques Derrida most relevant here are: *De la Grammatologie*, Paris: Editions de Minuit, 1967, *Ecriture et la différance*, Paris: Seuil, 1967, and *Glas*, Paris: Editions Denoël/ Gonthier, 1981. See also Marie-Claire Ropars, *Le Texte divisé*, Paris: Presses Universitaires de France, 1981 for an excellent discussion and practice of a Derridean analysis of films. I also mean to include the writing of Jean-François Lyotard and much of the writing of Julia Kristeva, among others, within a more general sense of what we might mean by deconstruction.
14 Pierre Macherey, *Pour une théorie de la production littéraire*, Paris: Maspero, 1970. See also the Marxist criticism of Fredric Jameson, Terry Eagleton, Raymond Williams, among others and the influence of Macherey on *Cahiers du cinéma* in the early seventies.

15 André Bazin, 'Ontology of the Photographic Image,' *What is Cinema?*, vol. 1, trans. Hugh Grey, Berkeley, CA: University of California Press, 1967, pp. 9–16.

16 Roland Barthes, *La Chambre Claire: Note sur la photographie*, Paris: Editions de 1'étoile, Gallimard, Seuil, 1980.

17 Christian Metz, *Essais sur la signification au cinéma*, vol. 2, Paris: Klinksieck, 1973 and *The Imaginary Signifier: Psychoanalysis and the Cinema*, trans. Celia Britton, Annwyl Williams, Ben Brewster, and Alfred Guzetti, Bloomington, IN: Indiana University Press, 1977, pp. 42–57.

18 The writings of Sigmund Freud on these issues include *Interpretation of Dreams*, *Beyond the Pleasure Principle*, 'Notes on the Mystic Writing Pad,' 'The Uncanny,' and 'Jensen's *Gradiva*'.

Gilles Deleuze

CINEMA 2

The time-image

Cinema 2: The Time-Image, trans. H. Tomlinson and R. Galeta, London: Athlone, 1989, pp. 270–9.

WE CAN NOW SUMMARIZE the constitution of this time-image in modern cinema, and the new signs that it implies or initiates. There are many possible transformations, almost imperceptible passages, and also combinations between the movement-image and the time-image. It cannot be said that one is more important than the other, whether more beautiful or more profound. All that can be said is that the movement-image does not give us a time-image. Nevertheless, it does give us many things in connection with it. On one hand, the movement-image constitutes time in its empirical form, the course of time: a successive present in an extrinsic relation of before and after, so that the past is a former present, and the future a present to come. Inadequate reflection would lead us to conclude from this that the cinematographic image is necessarily in the present. But this ready-made idea, disastrous for any understanding of cinema, is less the fault of the movement-image than of an over-hasty reflection. For, on the other hand, the movement-image gives rise to an image *of* time which is distinguished from it by excess or default, over or under the present as empirical progression: in this case, time is no longer measured by movement, but is itself the number or measure of movement (metaphysical representation). This number in turn has two aspects: it is the minimum unity of time as interval of movement or the totality of time as maximum of movement in the universe. The subtle and the sublime. But, from either aspect, time is distinguished in this way from movement only as indirect representation. Time as progression derives from the movement-image or from successive shots. But time as unity or as totality depends on montage which still relates it back to movement or to the succession of shots. This is why the movement-image is fundamentally linked to an indirect representation of time, and does not give us a direct presentation of it, that is, does not give us a time-image. The only direct presentation, then, appears in music. But in modern cinema, by contrast, the time-image is no longer empirical, nor metaphysical; it is 'transcendental' in the sense that Kant gives this word: time is out of joint and presents itself in the pure state.[1] The time-image does not imply the absence of movement (even though it often includes its increased scarcity) but it implies the reversal of the subordination; it is no longer time which is subordinate to movement; it is movement which subordinates itself to time. It is no longer time which derives from movement, from its norm and its corrected aberrations; it is movement as *false movement*, as aberrant movement which now depends on time. The time-image has become direct, just as time has discovered new aspects, as movement has become aberrant in essence and not by accident, as montage has taken on a new sense, and as a so-called modern cinema has been constituted post-war. However close its relations with classical cinema, modern cinema asks the question: what are the new forces at work in the image, and the new signs invading the screen?

The first factor is the break of the sensory-motor link. For the movement-image, as soon as it referred itself back to its interval, constituted the action-image: the latter, in its widest sense, comprised received movement (perception, situation), imprint (affection, the interval itself), and executed movement (action properly speaking and reaction). The sensory-motor link was thus the unity of movement and its interval, the specification of the movement-image or the action-image *par excellence*. There is no reason to talk of a narrative cinema which would correspond to this first-movement, for narration results from the sensory-motor schema, and not the other way round. But precisely what brings this cinema of action into question after the war is the very break-up of the sensory-motor schema: the rise of situations to which one can no longer react, of environments with which there are now only chance relations, of empty or disconnected any-space-whatevers replacing qualified extended space. It is here that situations no longer extend into action or reaction in accordance with the requirements of the movement-image. These are pure optical and sound situations, in which the character does not know how to respond, abandoned spaces in which he ceases to experience and to act so that he enters into flight, goes on a trip, comes and goes, vaguely indifferent to what happens to him, undecided as to what must be done. But he has gained in an ability to see what he has lost in action or reaction: he SEES so that the viewer's problem becomes 'What is there to see in the image?' (and not now 'What are we going to see in the next image?'). The situation no longer extends into action through the intermediary of affections. It is cut off from all its extensions, it is now important only for itself, having absorbed all its affective intensities, all its active extensions. This is no longer a sensory-motor situation, but a purely optical and sound situation, where the seer [*voyant*] has replaced the agent [*actant*]: a 'description'. We call this type of image opsigns and sonsigns, they appear after the war, through all the external reasons we can point to (the calling into question of action, the necessity of seeing and hearing, the proliferation of empty, disconnected, abandoned spaces) but also through the internal push of cinema being reborn, re-creating its conditions, neo-realism, new wave, new American cinema. Now, if it is true that the sensory-motor situation governed the indirect representation of time as consequence of the movement-image, the purely optical and sound situation opens onto a direct time-image. The time-image is the correlate of the opsign and the sonsign. It never appeared more clearly than in the author who anticipated modern cinema, from before the war and in the conditions of the silent film, Ozu: opsigns, empty or disconnected spaces, open on to still lifes as the pure form of time. Instead of 'motor situation – indirect representation of time', we have 'opsign or sonsign – direct presentation of time'.

But what can purely optical and sound images link up with, since they no longer extend into action? We would like to reply: with recollection-images or dream-images. Yet, the former still come within the framework of the sensory-motor situation, whose interval they are content to fill, even though lengthening and distending it; they seize a former present in the past and thus respect the empirical progression of time, even though they introduce local regressions into it (the flash-back as psychological memory). The latter, dream-images, rather affect the whole: they project the sensory-motor situation to infinity, sometimes by ensuring the constant metamorphosis of the situation, sometimes by replacing the action of characters with a movement of world. But we do not, in this way, leave behind an indirect representation, even though we come close, in certain exceptional cases, to doors of time that already belong to modern cinema (for instance, the flashback as revelation of a time which forks and frees itself in Mankiewicz, or the movement of world as the coupling of a pure description and dance in the American musical comedy). However, in these very cases, the recollection-image or the dream-image, the mnemosign or the onirosign, are gone beyond: for these images in themselves are virtual images, which are linked with the actual optical or sound image (description) but which are constantly being actualized on their own account, or the former in the latter to infinity. For the time-image to be born, on the contrary, the actual image must enter into relation with its *own* virtual image as such; from the outset pure description must divide in two, 'repeat itself, take itself up again, fork, contradict itself'. An image which is double-sided, mutual, both actual and virtual must be constituted. We are no longer in the situation of a relationship between the actual image and other virtual images, recollections, or dreams, which thus become actual in turn: this is still a mode of linkage. We are in the situation of an actual image *and* its own virtual image, to the extent that there is no longer any linkage of the real with the imaginary, but *indiscernibility of the two*, a perpetual exchange. This is a progress in relation to the opsign: we saw how the crystal (the hyalosign) ensures the dividing in two of description, and brings about the exchange in the image which has become mutual, the exchange of the actual and the virtual of the limpid and the opaque, of the seed and the surrounding.[2] By raising themselves to the indiscernibility of the real and the imaginary, the signs of the crystal go beyond all psychology of the recollection or dream, and all physics of action. What we see in the crystal is no longer the empirical progression of time as succession of presents, nor its indirect representation as interval or as whole; it is its direct presentation, its constitutive dividing in two into a present which is passing and a past which is preserved, the strict contemporaneity of the present with the past that it will be, of the past with the present that it has been. It is time itself which arises in the crystal, and which is constantly recommending its dividing in two without completing it, since the indiscernible exchange is always renewed and reproduced. The direct time-image or the transcendental form of time is what we see in the crystal; and hyalosigns, and crystalline signs, should therefore be called mirrors or seeds of time.

Thus we have the chronosigns which mark the various presentations of the direct time-image. The first concerns the *order of time*: this order is not made up of succession, nor is it the same thing as the interval or the whole of indirect representation. It is a matter of the internal relations of time, in a topological or quantic form. Thus the first chronosign has two figures: sometimes it is the coexistence of all the sheets of past, with the topological transformation of these sheets, and the overtaking of psychological memory towards a world-memory (this sign can be called sheet, aspect, or *facies*). Sometimes it is the simultaneity of points of present, these points breaking with all external succession, and carrying out quantic jumps between the presents which are doubled by the past, the future and the present itself (this sign can be called point or accent). We are no longer in an indiscernible distinction between the real and the imaginary, which would characterize the crystal image, but in undecidable alternatives between sheets of past, or 'inexplicable' differences between points of present, which now concern the direct time-image. What is in play is no longer the real and the imaginary, but the true and the false. And just as the real and the imaginary become indiscernible in certain or very specific conditions of the image, the true and the false now become undecidable or inextricable: the impossible proceeds from the possible, and the past is not necessarily true. A new logic has to be invented, just as earlier a new psychology had to be. It seemed to us that Resnais went furthest in the direction of coexisting sheets of past, and Robbe-Grillet in that of simultaneous peaks of present: hence the paradox of *Last Year in Marienbad*, which participates in the double system. But, in any event, the time-image has arisen through direct or transcendental presentation, as a new element in post-war cinema and Welles was master of the time-image . . .

There is still another type of chronosign which on this occasion constitutes *time as series*: the before and after are no longer themselves a matter of external empirical succession, but of the intrinsic quality of that which becomes in time. Becoming can in fact be defined as that which transforms an empirical sequence into a series: a burst of series. A series is a sequence of images, which tend themselves in the direction of a limit, which orients and inspires the first sequence (the before), and gives way to another sequence organized as series which tends in turn towards another limit (the after). The before and the after are then no longer successive determinations of the course of time, but the two sides of the power, or the passage of the power to a higher power. The direct time-image here does not appear in an order of coexistences or simultaneities, but in a becoming as potentialization, as series of powers. This second type of chronosign, the genesign, has therefore also the property of bringing into question the notion of truth; for the false ceases to be a simple appearance or even a lie, in order to achieve that power of becoming which constitutes series or degrees, which crosses limits, carries out metamorphoses, and develops along its whole path an act of legend, of story-telling. Beyond the true or the false, becoming as power of the false. Genesigns present several figures in this sense. Sometimes, as in Welles, they are characters forming series as so many degrees of a 'will to power' through which the world becomes a fable. Sometimes it is a character himself crossing a limit, and becoming another, in an act of story-telling which connects him to a people past or to come: we have seen the paradox by which this cinema was called '*cinéma vérité*' at the moment that it brought every model of the true into question; and there is a double becoming superimposed for the author becomes another as much as his character does (as with Perrault who takes the character as 'intercessor' or with Rouch who tends to become a black, in a quite different non-symmetrical way). It is perhaps here that the question of the author and the author's becoming, of his becoming-other, is already posed in its most acute form in Welles. Sometimes again, in the third place, characters dissolve of their own accord, and the author is effaced: there are now only attitudes of bodies, corporeal postures forming series, and a gest which connects them together as limit. It is a cinema of bodies which has broken all the more with the sensory-motor schema through action being replaced by attitude, and supposedly true linkage by the gest which produces legend or story-telling. Sometimes, finally, the series, their limits and transformations, the degrees of power, may be a matter of any kind of relation of the image: characters, states of one character, positions of the author, attitudes of bodies, as well as colours, aesthetic genres, psychological faculties, political powers, logical or metaphysical categories. Every sequence of images forms a series in that it moves in the direction of a category in which it is reflected, the passage of one category to another determining a change of power. What is said in the most simple terms about Boulez' music will also be said about Godard's cinema: having put everything in series, having brought about a generalized serialism. Everything which functions as limit between two series divided into two parts, the before and the after constituting the two sides of the limit, will also be called a category (a character, a gest, a word, a colour may be a category as easily as a genre, from the moment that they fulfill the conditions of reflection). If the organization of series generally takes place horizontally, as in *Slow Motion* with the imaginary, fear, business, music, it is possible that the limit or category in which a series is reflected itself forms another series of a higher power, henceforth superimposed on the first: as in the pictorial category in *Passion* or the musical one in *First Name Carmen*. There is in this case a vertical construction of series, which tends to return to coexistence or simultaneity, and to combine the two types of chronosigns.

The so-called classical image had to be considered on two axes. These two axes were the co-ordinates of the brain: on the one hand, the images were linked or extended according to laws of association, of continuity, resemblance, contrast, or opposition; on the other hand, associated images were internalized in a whole as concept (integration), which was in turn continually externalized in associable or extendable images (differentiation). This is why the whole remained open and changing, at the same time as a set of images was always taken from a larger set. This was the double aspect of the movement-image, defining the out-of-field: in the first place it was in touch with an exterior, in the second place it expressed a whole which changes. Movement in its extension was the immediate given, and the whole which changes, that is, time, was indirect or mediate representation. But there was a continual circulation of the two here, internalization in the whole, externalization in the image, circle or spiral which constituted for cinema, no less than for philosophy, the model of the True as totalization. This model inspired the noosigns of the classical image, and there were necessarily two kinds of noosign. In the first kind, the images were linked by rational cuts, and formed under this condition an extendable world: between two images or two sequences of images, the limit as interval is included as the end of the one *or* as the beginning of the other, as the last image of the first sequence or the first of the second. The other kind of noosign marked the integration of the sequences into a whole (self-awareness as internal representation), but also the differentiation of the whole into extended sequences (belief in the external world). And, from one to the other, the whole was constantly changing at the same time as the images were moving. Time as measure of movement thus ensured a general system of commensurability, in this double form of the interval and the whole. This was the splendour of the classical image.

The modern image initiates the reign of 'incommensurables' or irrational cuts: this is to say that the cut no longer forms part of one or the other image, of one or the other sequence that it separates and divides. It is on this condition that the succession or sequence becomes a series, in the sense that we have just analysed. The interval is set free, the interstice becomes irreducible and stands on its own. The first consequence is that the images are no longer linked by rational cuts, but are relinked on to irrational cuts. Godard's series is an example, but they can be found everywhere, notably in Resnais (the moment around which everything turns and repasses in *Je t'aime je t'aime*, is a typical irrational cut). By relinkage must be understood, not a second linkage which would come and add itself on, but a mode of original and specific linkage, or rather a specific connection between de-linked images. There are no longer grounds for talking about a real or possible extension capable of constituting an external world: we have ceased to believe in it, and the image is cut off from the external world. But the internalization or integration of self-awareness in a whole has no less disappeared: the relinkage takes place through parcelling, whether it is a matter of the construction of series in Godard, or of the transformations of sheets in Resnais (relinked parcellings). This is why thought, as power which has not always existed, is born from an outside more distant than any external world, and, as power which does not yet exist, confronts an inside, an unthinkable or unthought, deeper than any internal world. In the second place, there is no longer any movement of internalization or externalization, integration or differentiation, but a confrontation of an outside and an inside independent of distance, this thought outside itself and this un-thought within thought. This is the unsummonable in Welles, the undecidable in Resnais, the inexplicable in the Straubs, the impossible in Marguerite Duras, the irrational in Syberberg. The brain has lost its Euclidean co-ordinates, and now emits other signs. The direct time-image effectively has as noosigns the irrational cut between non-linked (but always relinked) images, and the absolute contact between non-totalizable, asymmetrical outside and inside. We move with ease from one to the other, because the outside and the inside are the two sides of the limit as irrational cut, and because the latter, no longer forming part of any sequence, itself appears as an autonomous outside which necessarily provides itself with an inside.

The limit or interstice, the irrational cut, pass especially between the visual image and the sound image. This implies several novelties or changes. The sound itself must become image instead of being a component of the visual image; the creation of a sound framing is thus necessary, so that the cut passes between the two framings, sound and visual; hence even if the out-of-field survives in fact [*en fait*], it must lose all power by right [*de droit*] because the visual image ceases to extend beyond its own frame, in order to enter into a specific relation with the sound image which is itself framed (the interstice between the two framings replaces the out-of-field); the voice-off must also disappear, because there is no more out-of-field to inhabit, but two heautonomous images to be confronted, that of voices and that of views, each in itself, each for itself and in its frame. It is possible for the two kinds of images to touch and join up, but this is clearly not through flashback, as if one voice, more or less off, was evoking what the visual image was going to give back to us: modern cinema has killed flashback, like the voice-off and the out-of-field. It has been able to conquer the sound image only by imposing a dissociation between it and the visual image, a disjunction which must not be surmounted: irrational cut between the two. And yet there is a relation between them, a free indirect or incommensurable relation, for incommensurability denotes a new relation and not an absence. Hence the sound image frames a mass or a continuity from which the pure speech act is to be extracted, that is, an act of myth or story-telling which creates the event, which makes the event rise up into the air, and which raises itself in a spiritual ascension. And the visual image for its part frames an any-space-whatever, an empty or disconnected space which takes on a new value, because it will bury the event under stratigraphic layers, and make it go down like an underground fire which is always covered over. The visual image will thus never show what the sound image utters. For example, in Marguerite Duras, the originary dance will never rise up again through flashback to totalize the two kinds of images. There will be none the less a relation between the two, a junction or a contact. This will be the contact independent of distance, between an outside where the speech-act rises, and an inside where the event is buried in the ground: a complementarity of the sound image, the speech-act as creative story-telling, and the visual image, stratigraphic or archaeological burying. And the irrational cut between the two, which forms the non-totalizable relation, the broken ring of their junction, the asymmetrical faces of their contact. This is a perpetual relinkage. Speech reaches its own limit which separates it from the visual; but the visual reaches its own limit which separates it from sound. So each one reaching its own limit which separates it from the other thus discovers the common limit which connects them to each other in the incommensurable relation of an irrational cut, the right side and its obverse, the outside and the inside. These new signs are lectosigns, which show the final aspect of the direct time-image, the common limit: the visual image become stratigraphic is for its part all the more readable in that the speech-act becomes an autonomous creator. Classical cinema was not short of lectosigns, but only to the extent that the speech-act was itself read in the silent film, or in the first stage of the talkie, making it possible to read the visual image, of which it was only one component. From classical to modern cinema, from the movement-image to the time-image, what changes are not only the chronosigns, but the noosigns and lectosigns, having said that it is always possible to multiply the passages from one regime to the other, just as to accentuate their irreducible differences.

Notes

1 Paul Schrader has spoken of a 'transcendental style' in certain cinema-authors. But he uses this word to indicate the sudden arrival of the transcendent, as he thinks he sees it in Ozu, Dreyer, or Bresson (*Transcendental Style in Film: Ozu, Dreyer, Bresson*, extracts in *Cahiers du cinéma*, 1978, no. 286). It is thus not the Kantian sense, which in contrast opposes the transcendental and the metaphysical or transcendent.

2 More precisely, crystal-images are connected to the states of the crystal (the four states that we have distinguished), while crystalline signs or hyalosigns are connected to its properties (the three aspects of the exchange).

Sander L. Gilman

IS LIFE BEAUTIFUL? CAN THE SHOAH BE FUNNY?

Some thoughts on recent and older films

'Is Life Beautiful? Can the Shoah Be Funny? Some Thoughts on Recent and Older Films', *Critical Inquiry*, 2000, vol. 26(2), pp. 279–308.

DURING THE PAST FEW DECADES there has been much speculation about the impossibility or the appropriate way of imagining or representing the Shoah. Humor has rarely figured in this discussion. Even the appropriation of forms such as the commix (the illustrated novel) by artist/authors such as Art Spiegelman has self-consciously stripped these forms of any comic, humorous, or witty content or intent.[1] Indeed, Spiegelman's text works against the popular American assumption that 'serious' themes cannot be dealt with in the form of the illustrated text. In Israel such appropriations even in the form of the commix seem not to have been imaginable.[2] In Japan, on the other hand, one of the most powerful series of Osamu Tezuka's *manga* (commix) *Also Tell Adolph* (*Adolph ni Tsugu*) (1983), which received the Kodansha Manga Award in 1986, chronicles the Shoah as seen from the point of view of the Japanese.[3] Neither Spiegelman's nor Tezuka's commix is comic.[4]

If even the commix has avoided the comic in representing the Shoah, let us pause for a moment and ask one of our title questions again: Can the Shoah be funny? Can horror be understood through laughter? Who laughs? (*quid rides?*) was the ancients' question. The audience, the victim, the perpetrators? Is laughter the intention of the creator of a work of art or the response of an audience? Is laughter intentional or – as in the 1994 case of the Oakland high school students who laughed at a screening of *Schindler's List* at a school assembly – situational?[5] (Anything and everything at a school assembly is understood by high school students as potentially the butt of laughter.) But then even more basic to our question: What is the Shoah? Is the Shoah a specific moment in time, a specific set of horrors, or is it a metaphor for all genocides, past, present, and future? Is it European history or is it an American 'problem'? as Peter Novick asks.[6] Clearly it is the attempt to murder all of Europe's Jews, an attempt that succeeded in murdering millions of Jews along with millions of others. But any understanding of the Shoah must acknowledge that its meaning and function have changed over the fifty years since it occurred. The murder of the Jews moved from being one aspect of the crimes of the Nazis to being their central, defining aspect over half a century. Over the past decade or so, it has evolved from a specific, historical moment to the metaphor for horror itself. Can the Shoah be funny? This question must be framed in both its historical and its ethical dimension.

Central to any discussion of humor in the Shoah seems to be an understanding of what concept of humor is evoked. Virtually all of the theoretical views of the comic in the West are ways of speaking about narratives – the stories that are told which encapsulate humor. If you take as a starting point Thomas Hobbes's notion that humor is in complex ways wedded to notions of power or the illusion of power, then humor is a weapon aimed at those perceived as weaker or stronger than oneself. Yet if Sigmund Freud's image of humor (*Witz*) is employed, then the tendentious laughter that results is a sign of an attack on the object of the joke, an attack shared with the listener, reader, or viewer. Is humor a gratification of the forbidden or unspeakable desires that Hobbes's notion of humor places in the public sphere? Henri Bergson saw in humor the desire to humiliate and to 'correct' those who are perceived as different in a public manner. These are quite contradictory models of humor, and yet they all rely on one marker – the physiological production of laughter – for the clear distinction of what is humorous.[7] Laughter is, of course, the prime marker of the comic whatever the theoretical explanation of why we laugh.[8] Can we imagine laughing at representations of the Shoah? Is there an earned laughter that teaches and a false laughter that obfuscates?

The late Terrence Des Pres, writing shortly after Spiegelman's *Maus* was first collected in book form, wrote of the clear proscription against laughter in representations of the Holocaust. He saw a form of 'Holocaust etiquette,' which 'dictates that anything pertaining to the Holocaust must be serious, must be reverential in a manner that acknowledges (and supports) the sacredness of its occasion.' He argued that laughter, humor, and the comic mode are helpful as coping mechanisms. Tragedy is rooted, according to Des Pres, in an unmediated claim of realism; the comic makes no claim on realistic representation.[9] The comic, to counter A. C. Bradley, the great Shakespearean scholar of the turn of the century, is more than a world of drama that falls between the tragedies, which dealt with the permanents of life, and the comedies, with the accidents.[10] In refusing to accept mimesis as possible, the comic rejects the idea that the Shoah is historically bounded. The comic allows for distance, self-possession, evaluation, and protest in regard to the finality of the 'final solution to the Jewish Question.' Des Pres wrote: 'In the realm of art, a comic response is more resilient, more effectively in revolt against terror and the sources of terror than a response that is solemn or tragic . . . Comic art resists that which has come to pass.' Holocaust laughter, he says, is 'life-reclaiming.'[11]

It is clear, in spite of Des Pres's title, that no one ever actually *laughed* while reading *Maus.* It was never received as the equivalent to Roadrunner cartoons or to the 'Itchy and Scratchy Show.' And that is certainly even more the case with Tezuka's work, which does not replace human figures with animal analogies. What is striking is that even when 'humorous' modes of expression are used in representing the Shoah, laughter is rarely the desired reaction. Certainly there are some contexts in which laughter is desired, but these have been clearly circumscribed. That there are tasteless jokes about the Shoah there is no doubt. And people are supposed to laugh at them (or perhaps at their tastelessness)! Allen Dundes and his colleagues in the United States and in (then) West Germany collected sets of Auschwitz jokes, which, by their very nature, are understood as the perpetrators 'laughing' at the victims.[12] Their tone is similar to the 'little moron' jokes of the 1950s while their content often verges on the obscene or the anti-Semitic. They are read as comic because their narrative voice seems to be neutral. That is, they are understood as being told about 'Jews' rather than by 'Jews.' The 'Jew' in these jokes is the object, and there is no sense of identification with the Jew. Thus laughter can occur in a joke about the Shoah only when the Jew is literally moved to the margins of the joke. They become, at least in Dundes's reading, a means of distancing the teller and the listener from the horrors of the Shoah.

But with the exception of such 'jokes,' none of the comic representations of the Shoah are intended to evoke laughter. All assume that the author and the reader (the teller and the listener now as disembodied entities) will not laugh, even at the comic turns of the fiction. Serious fiction dealing with the Shoah, with a few exceptions such as Edgar Hilsenrath's *The Nazi and the Barber* (1973) and Leslie Epstein's *King of the Jews* (1979), has avoided the very use of the comic for narrative devices.[13] And the exceptional cases use black comedy – heavy in a satirical voice or with irony layered upon a bleak vision of the Shoah. Much like the work of Spiegelman, himself the child of a survivor, there is a need to bend the form to the topic, rather than the other way around. Such works can generate no laughter.

But more than this seems to be necessary for such works to be accepted. To have been accepted into high culture as an adequate representation of the Shoah, such texts have to be seen as stemming from the pen of 'Jews.' And one should note at this point that the authors of such texts are more often than not clearly self-identified as Jews. Spiegelman and Epstein have this declared on the jackets of their books. Hilsenrath has been paraded by his publishers as a survivor of the Nazi ghettos in Transnistria. His persona was key to the reception of *The Nazi and the Barber* in both the United States and Germany. One can note that Hilsenrath's novel was first published in the United States in an English translation in 1973; it had to wait for four years before it found a German publisher. And when it was finally published in German its author left out its critical, satirical conclusion. When asked, he noted that such a text could be read by Americans but would be misunderstood by Germans. Being heard as a comic 'Jewish' voice in Germany in the 1970s was something quite different, at least in regard to the meaning of the Shoah, than being heard as a comic 'Jewish' voice in America. Such a comic voice is of course not the voice of the comic. There is no intention for the reader of either version of the novel to laugh.

The evocation of identity and life experience as a means of permitting the use of the comic in a limited sense to represent the Shoah seems vital. Certainly, even in the historical and autobiographical accounts of life in the Third Reich and among Jews during the Shoah, there are glimmers of discussions of humor.[14] Recently a few of the videotaped memoirs of survivors of the Nazi camps and ghettos stressed the pragmatic function of humor as a means of coping or even of survival.[15] Such laughter is a response to the reality of the Shoah as individual experience. It seems to be, at least in the survivors' accounts, a rather surprising means of keeping one's sense of control in a situation where no control was possible. Yet laughter on the part of the interviewer or on the part of the viewer is missing.

Laughter, however, does not moderate the representation of the Shoah. Spiegelman can never truly understand his father's life; jokes and humor in the camps seem virtually foolish in their inadequacy. No one can laugh at or even with his figures. Their laughter (if it occurs) seems inexplicable, while the laughter in the accounts of the actual survivors seems comprehensible. And for those who have had no exposure to the events, except through the cultural representations of the Shoah, comedy seems to have been simply more problematic than the tragic. Laughter cannot ever be evoked. Why is it that, if humor does have a function in ameliorating the effects of the Shoah, we are so very uncomfortable imagining laughter in the context of the Shoah? Indeed, can there be anything funny about representing the Holocaust?

One might say that laughter in regard to the notion of a *Jewish* Shoah is especially marginalized since there remains in today's world the strong image of a Jewish comic voice evoking laughter.[16] The great comic tradition of modern Jewish letters runs from Shalom Alechim to Josef Roth to Philip Roth to Woody Allen to Simon Louvish. (Never mind from Eddie Cantor to Lennie Bruce to Jerry Seinfeld.) The Jewish voice seems to be one in which the comic and humor dominate. (Of course, there is another voice, that of deep pessimism, which runs from Shalom Asch to I. J. Singer to Aaron Appelfeld, but let us bracket that for the moment.) Jewish voices can be – indeed are often – understood today as comic voices *evoking laughter*. And yet in regard to the Shoah this comic voice is marginalized if not suppressed.

Thus the question of whether the Shoah can be marginalized does revolve around a series of interlocking questions. First, is it appropriate to use the comic (and its physiological response, laughter) in representing events of transcendental horror? How much does the redefinition of the horrors of World War II (after 1945) into the central position of the Jewish Shoah (by the 1970s) preclude or enable laughter to be imagined as a possible effect of representation? And how much does the presupposition of the image of the Jew as the comic and as the victim enable or preclude Jewish or non-Jewish uses of laughter in making representations of the Shoah publicly acceptable?

Recently the discussion of the comic as a means of representing the Shoah has arisen in relation to the cinema, seemingly an adequate vehicle for the translation of the past into the present. That is, only in the cinema the comic, and its corollary, laughter, seem to have a role in an adequate representation of the Shoah. (One might note that the comic in the cinema from its very origin is coupled with laughter; film comedies from the silent screen on intend for their audiences to laugh in the anonymity of the darkened theater. Our sense of distance is much greater than when we, face to face with another, are told a joke or read a novel. We are isolated in the cinema while still a part of a collective.) Certainly in most films on the Shoah, from Alain Resnais's *Night and Fog* (1956) to Claude Lanzmann's *Shoah* (1985) to Steven Spielberg's *Schindler's List* (1993), laughter is not only missing but also inconceivable.[17] These films also provide a trajectory. They move from the image of the Shoah in which the victims are literally missing or present as photographs from the liberation of the camps to accounts in which living survivors provide narratives of the past (and in the case of Spielberg's film accounts of their meaningful survival). And yet there is a series of films in which the comic seems to be appropriate – at least to some viewers and critics.[18]

The comic is possible when imagining the Third Reich and the Nazis as the enemy. It is a means of assuring the viewer that the 'victim' is smarter and more resilient than the aggressor. The victim must be in a position to win or to at least survive the world of the Nazis. Not all film evocations of the Third Reich seem to need to (or want to) evoke the Shoah. Partially this has to do with when the work was made and the meanings attached to the Shoah at the time. But it was possible to write a comedy long after the 1940s about the Third Reich, such as the long-running TV series *Hogan's Heroes* (1965–1971), without evoking the Shoah. Indeed, such representations are possible only if the survival of the 'victims,' here the Allied prisoners of war, is never drawn into question. Like its model, the German-Jewish director Billy Wilder's *Stalag 17* (1951), a murder mystery set in a prisoner-of-war camp, the central problem of the show is the necessary preservation of the prisoners' lives. The laugh track on this series was possible only if the idea of the Shoah and its horrors were eliminated from the audience's consideration and Hogan and his men will survive all that is done to them. No randomness is permitted and thus the inherent randomness of the Shoah must be eliminated in such representations.

The earliest comic films dealing with the Third Reich and its treatment of the Jews were made before or at the very beginning of the murder of Europe's Jews.[19] No reference to the Shoah is possible in such films, a fact not lost on their makers. The Anglo-Jewish actor Charlie Chaplin's Jewish barber in his *The Great Dictator* (1940) (with Paulette Goddard as his Jewish wife) presents a critique of Fascist racism that historically prefigures the Shoah. (Here one can also mention the Three Stooges short *You Natzy Spy!* of 1940 as a further example of such pre-Shoah parodies of the Nazis.) Chaplin himself commented well after the war that 'had I known of the actual horrors of the German concentration camps, I could not have made *The Great Dictator*; I could not have made fun of the homicidal insanity of the Nazis.'[20] Nor could his audience have laughed.

Yet the evocation of laughter by this film *today* is possible because the film's treatment of anti-Semitism makes it seem relatively harmless in retrospect. Indeed, in the German-Jewish director Ernst Lubitsch's *To Be or Not to Be* (1942), Jack Benny stars as the actor Joseph Tura, about whom it is said by a Nazi officer: 'What he did to Shakespeare we are doing to Poland.'[21] In the film there is no intimation of the persecution of the Jews. The response of at least one critic was to wonder why audiences should 'laugh at some broad anti-Nazi satire while we are weeping over the sad fate of Poland.'[22] For Lubitsch the answer was clear: 'American audiences don't laugh at these Nazis because they underestimate their menace, but because they are happy to see this new order and its ideology ridiculed.'[23] Even though Chaplin and Benny were Jewish (as were Jerome Lester Horwitz, a.k.a. Curly Howard, Louis Fienberg, a.k.a. Larry Fine, and Moses Horwitz, a.k.a. Moe Howard), the reference for the film in the 1940s was anti-Semitism, not the potential or actual destruction of European Jewry. Such films seem today to be relatively harmless period pieces in their evocation of laughter. And we do laugh at them now as they were laughed at in the 1940s.

In Mel Brooks's remake of *To Be or Not to Be* (1983), the omnipresence of the Shoah in the American audience's mind could not be avoided.[24] Indeed, Brooks played a triple role: the actor-protagonist, Hamlet, and Hitler. The strained nature of the remake was to no little degree the result of that oppressive if unspoken presence of the Shoah in the audience's awareness. That Brooks too is Jewish did not ameliorate this sense of unease, but it did give the film a level of public acceptability. Comedy in this context was only possible with the bracketing of the Final Solution. And such a bracketing was impossible, at least in America when the Shoah became the stuff of mass culture following the showing of the NBC-TV series *Holocaust: A Story of Two Families* on 16 April 1978. This series was even more widely viewed than the 1977 TV miniseries on the African American experience, *Roots.* Brooks's most successful use of an anti-Nazi satire, the musical-within-the-film *Springtime for Hitler* in his first film *The Producers* (1968), worked only because it was *not* supposed to work. It was to be the ultimate bad-taste flop for the producer Max Bialystok (Zero Mostel) but almost destroys him because it becomes a popular success. After the 1970s such images of the Nazis could be made only with the implicit evocation of the Shoah. After the 1970s in American (and American-Jewish) public sensibility, the horrors of World War II had become defined by the Shoah.

S. N. Behrman, the American playwright, like Brooks reworked an earlier, pre-Shoah text, Franz Werfel's 'comedy after a tragedy' *Jakobowsky and the Colonel*, after 1945. Originally written in 1941–42 and published at the end of the war, Werfel's sad comedy is turned into a preachy and rather heavy-handed Broadway comedy of manners with some reflection on the global nature of prejudice. (It became a sort of comedic *South Pacific.*) When the Jewish comic Danny Kaye redid Behrman's text as a film in *Me and the Colonel* (1957), there seems to be no trace of the ultimate future of such Polish Jews as the title character. All is reduced to a cat-and-mouse game eventually to be won by the pursued, not the pursuers. The comic here, as in *To Be or Not to Be*, is invoked as a means of avoiding any representation of the Shoah. Laughter can exist because the Shoah is unmentioned (and unmentionable).

More recently there have been a number of films by self-identified Jewish authors and directors that used the comic as a means of representing the Shoah. The Australian-Jewish director of operas Elijah Moshinsky created his black comedy *Genghis Cohn* (1993) for BBC-TV. It starred Robert Lindsay, Diana Rigg, and the South African-Jewish actor Anthony Sher as the title character. It was adapted by Stanley Price from the Franco-Jewish author Romain Gary's novel *The Dance of Genghis Cohn* (*La Danse de Genghis Cohn*) (1967). Moshinsky's film is an account of a former Nazi camp commander at Dachau, living incognito in a quiet village after the war, who finds his sins coming back to haunt him as the ghost of a Jewish comedian he put to death lures him into becoming a Jew. Laughter results in this film from the audience's identification with the ghost, who, as a convention in the film, marks not the dead of the Shoah, but their continued existence (as memory) in the present. Since the murder of Cohn did not result in his obliteration but in his continued existence, laughter can result.

Moshinsky's film uses the conventional ghost-as-living-being (as in *The Ghost and Mrs. Muir* [1947]). The Canadian film *Punch Me in the Stomach* (1994), from a screenplay by the performance artist Deb Filler and Francine Zuckerman, and starring Filler, uses the convention of the monologue film (such as Jonathan Demme's film of Spalding Grey's *Swimming to Cambodia* [1986]) to evoke laughter. The monologue is the autobiographical adaptation of comedienne Filler's one-woman stage show in which she plays the role of thirty-six different characters from her extended family. She is self-identified in the film as the daughter of a concentration camp survivor. She presents an account of how her father requested her to accompany him on a tour of the concentration and death camps he had been in during the Shoah. She narrates this experience, but only after framing this with other stories about her own family and upbringing.

Many of her stories are invented, as she tells her audience toward the end of the show, such as the one about her father as a survivor-as-television-star. Her father did indeed become famous in Australia because he was a survivor and because of his daughter's stage work, but that was life imitating art, not vice versa. During the television scene, the schematic course of her father's testimony suddenly gets interrupted when he says, 'and also, sounds funny I know, but you had to keep your sense of humor.' Then he tells the story about his first night in the barracks. There was not enough space. He and his fellow inmates were crammed so tightly into a bed that they could turn over only together and on command. 'We laughed, we had to,' he says. 'What else could you do? We laughed the whole first night in Auschwitz.' Laughter is, in the memory of the survivor, a coping mechanism. When he travels to Theresienstadt decades later with his daughter the visit ends, too, in Filler's enactment of it, with a powerful comic twist. Returning from the rundown toilets of the museum, and holding in her hand a broken toilet chain, she and her father burst into laughter. 'We were laughing so hard we couldn't stop.' The laughter, however, is the laughter of the participants, not of the viewers of the film. Indeed, the viewers' reaction is dumbfoundedness as the daughter narrates her father's laughter.

One can mention the extraordinary, supposedly autobiographical German-language film by the Hungarian-Jewish playwright and theater director George Tabori, *Mother's Courage* (1995), directed by the Dutch filmmaker Michael Verhoeven, the director of one of the best films of the German response to the Shoah, *The Nasty Girl* (1990).[25] Using the putative account of his mother's one-day trip to and back from Auschwitz to Budapest, Tabori notes the often-arbitrary nature of personal survival and destiny. 'Where were you? Why were you out so long without letting us know?' they demand in the film when she returns after her day at Auschwitz. The cultured and soft-spoken Mrs. Tabori, played by British actress Pauline Collins, is an unlikely match for her captors. Yet, she quietly sizes up her ill-bred Fascist jailers and determines a courageous way out. As she manages her escape, we are well aware that she is the only passenger on that crowded transport who does. The comedy in Tabori's account lies in the contrast between the audacious nature of his mother's actions and the accident of her survival. Laughter from the audience results because of the seeming implausibility of both the actions and the attitudes. The comic is the result of different readings of Jewish 'chutzpah' and German 'obduracy.'

The comic in all of the films results from a double presence: the speaking daughter of the survivor on stage; the eighty-year-old Tabori in Verhoeven's film framing his mother's life; and the dead comic, as a ghostly presence in the present, manipulating the world of the Nazi by forcing him to convert to Judaism. Laughter haunts these films because of the ghostly presence of past throughout, but a past that exists in living form in the present. As with the dramatization of the diary of Anne Frank, the dead are brought back to life, if but for the moment.[26] This coupled with the claim of the authenticity of a living Jewish voice provides the potential for the audience's laughter.

Filler, Verhoeven, and Moshinsky use the comic and its power to evoke laughter in very different ways to translate the Shoah for the viewer of the 1990s. All three films, however, had very limited release and very limited critical responses. (Here one can mention the unreleased 1972 Jerry Lewis concentration camp film *The Day the Clown Cried*, about Helmut Drook, a clown who is forced to entertain children on their way to the gas chambers to keep them quiet.) They were unsuccessful as generally accepted representations of the Shoah because they used (or evoked) humor as their central narrative strategy. And as self-conscious products of Jewish directors, they made a claim on the comic voice of the Jew. However, in the context of the world of *Schindler's List*, the general public did not accept any such comic voice.

On the contrary, most recently the use of cinematic humor has been seen as a strongly positive factor in the success of Roberto Benigni's tragicomedy *Life Is Beautiful* (*La vita è bella*) (1998) released by Miramax Films. The Italian film opened its American run on 22 October 1998 in New York and Los Angeles, having won the Cannes Grand Jury Prize as well as the Jerusalem Film Festival Award. In March 1999 the film won an Oscar for best foreign film and Benigni as well an Oscar for best male actor. This double win indicates some level of commercial and critical acceptance in the United States. Verhoeven's and Moshinsky's films have had neither an American commercial release nor a critical rationale. Benigni, however, has an international reputation as a latter-day Jerry Lewis or Jacques Tati or Cantiflas, an international comic actor whose presence evokes specific comic turns well beyond the national culture in which he was initially best known. In Jim Jarmusch's *Down by Law* (1986) and *Night on Earth* (1991), he presented his physical comedy (similar to that of Robin Williams or Jim Carrey) to a 'high art' audience – which loved it. Of course, Benigni also replaced the late Peter Sellers in Blake Edwards' sequel *Son of the Pink Panther* (1993), which was a critical as well as a commercial disaster. In all of these humorous films laughter was the intended (if sometimes missed) goal.

Throughout the film, indeed up to the very end, Benigni's physical comedy underlines the childlike nature of the actor and the necessity of representing the image of innocence. This is his image in the international cinema. It is not a 'Jewish' image, as Benigni is neither Jewish himself nor has he self-consciously played Jewish characters in the past. Indeed, his selection of the theme and setting seems to have more to do (at least according to his own account) with his desire to play a figure *in extremis* rather than a figure in a movie about the Shoah. He noted that the germ of the film took shape in a conversation with his coauthor Vincenzo Cerami in 1995 with the 'idea of a man in the most extreme circumstances who tries to convince himself he's not there.'[27] But what better setting than the Shoah for such testing of character and actor alike?[28] The idea of doing a comic film about the Holocaust was first dismissed by Benigni, who imagined it as 'Donald Duck in an extermination camp.'[29] And yet when working on the film with Cerami he began to refigure his own identity as the child of a survivor. His father had fought as a member of the Italian army until Italy was forced to switch sides in 1943. He was then rounded up and sent to work as a laborer in Germany. Benigni reads his father's account as follows: 'He was an antifascist, but he was not political . . . So he suddenly was captured by the Nazis and put in a work camp in Germany for two years. He came back like a skeleton, covered with insects . . . And when he came back he told stories about what a nightmare it was, like Primo Levi did in his book.'[30] The work camps, no matter what their horrors, were, of course, not Auschwitz. In order retrospectively to give him the moral authority to make this film, Benigni reshapes his history so as not to appear merely like 'Donald Duck in an extermination camp.' He needs to claim to be making a quasi-autobiographical film about the Shoah.

Needless to say *Life Is Beautiful* did not have a uniformly positive reception. Many critics actively loathed it. In its reception and its structure Benigni's film in a strange way picks up the theme and the tone of the concentration camp as a site for the grotesque and the unreal begun in Italian film with the work of Lina Wertmuller, especially her film *Seven Beauties* (1976).[31] There slapstick humor was used to frame the concentration camp experience of a small-time Casanova, a non-Jew, Pasqualino Frafuso (played by Giancarlo Giannini). (Wertmuller was the first woman director to receive an Oscar nomination.) And like that film Benigni's has been the subject of both praise and of attack. During a press conference at the Cannes festival, one French journalist stood up to accuse Benigni of mocking the victims of the Holocaust, declaring that he was 'scandalized' by the picture. A reporter from the *International Herald Tribune* stated that she 'loathed this film,' and *The Guardian* (London) wrote that it is 'a hopelessly inadequate memorial to the vile events of the Holocaust.'[32] In a recent symposium of the U.S. Comedy Arts Festival in Aspen, the film director James L. Brooks called '*Life Is Beautiful* a movie about the comic spirit.' He noted that 'he was dumbfounded by criticism from people offended by what they have perceived to be its lighthearted treatment of the Holocaust.'[33] While the Italian press was generally ecstatic by Benigni's winning the Oscar, the *Corriere della sera* asked on its front page whether the comic was the best possible way for Italian culture to be judged abroad. It answered the question by having Dario Fo note in an op-ed piece that 1999 was the year that he, a comic writer, won the Nobel Prize for Literature.[34] For Italian commentators, there is no question of the substance of the film, only its Italian provenance. We must ask along with the doubters, What would be an adequate cinematic representation if Benigni's comic spin were not?

Let us turn to the first attempt to use the comic in representing the Shoah cinematically. There has been some discussion recently as to whether Benigni 'appropriated' bits of the French-Romanian director Radu Mihaileanu's comic fable of the Shoah entitled *Train of Life* (*Train de vie*) (1998).[35] Lionel Abelanski stars as Shlomo, the town idiot, who masquerades as a German officer to commandeer a train and rescue the inhabitants of a *shtetl.* More important for our purposes than this shadow source is the first film to use humor and laughter in representing the *Jewish* Shoah. There is no question as to its identity: the 1974 film *Jacob the Liar*, directed by Frank Beyer from a film script by the child-survivor author, Jurek

Becker. It was produced by DEFA (Deutsche Film-Aktiengesellschaft), the state-owned studio of the German Democratic Republic (GDR), which produced over 750 feature films and countless documentaries and shorts between 1946 and 1992. Major directors such as Slatan Dudow, Wolfgang Staudte, Kurt Maetzig, and Konrad Wolf, as well as Beyer, worked for DEFA.

The resonance of Becker's image of the Jew in *Jacob the Liar* is both that Jakob is every man but that he is a particularly Jewish everyman. What is clearly the case is that Roberto Benigni's figure is Jewish only within the Italian model of the 'hidden Jew.' Certainly the notion in the film is that the viewer 'sees' Guido as a Jew only when his uncle complains that he has been made the brunt of anti-Semitic attacks. Only then does the marginal figure that we see on the road become a version of the wandering Jew. The Italian model was that Jews were literally invisible within Italian culture and that only the bestiality of the Germans differentiated them from their non-Jewish Italian neighbors. While Italian Fascist anti-Semitism is evoked, it is of a rather comic type, such as the painting of anti-Semitic slogans on the side of a horse. This myth is perpetuated in the film, even though there are clearly socially isolating moments stressed, such as the response of Dora's mother who is alienated from her daughter. This juxtaposition again emphasizes the 'good' Italians and their relationship to 'their' Jews as opposed to the bad, murderous Germans of the camps.

Benigni's character is not seen at the beginning of the film as a Jew. His character from the standpoint of the non-Italian viewer is not 'Jewish' in terms of the cultural semiotics of this category. Or, rather, he fulfills the stereotypes and self-image of the Italian Jew as held by Jewish survivors such as Primo Levi, that they were well integrated into Italian prewar society and no different from other Italians. Becker's world is the world, not of such cultural invisibility, but of the inherent visibility of the antihero, who is labeled as Jewish from the opening moment of the film. The flashbacks to the prewar world of Jakob Heym as the owner of a small restaurant, with a love life and a place in the world, provides a continuity to the Jakob of the camps. His viewers and readers understand Jurek Becker's world as authentic because of his biography. It is the world of the Jew in the Shoah. This world is defined as a discontinuous world, a world that had been ruptured by the Shoah. There is no real possibility of any sort of continuity that extends past the death camps. Benigni's non-Jewish world is a world that promises these continuities between the past, the Shoah, and the future.

Becker works self-consciously against type in this film. He avoids the pious cliches of the socialist realistic representation of victim or hero, of anti-Fascism as an ideology. What he does use are the assumptions about Jewish difference, which dominate German (and Western) culture, and he turns them on their head. These turn out to be qualities ascribed to the 'stage' Jew, the schlemiel, which run counter to the heroic. The character of Jakob Heym becomes a positive figure in his status as a 'little man.' He is the schlemiel who cannot avoid the randomness of the world in which he exists but can through simple actions attempt to ameliorate its suffering.

Benigni too attempts to use these images. But, unlike Becker, who is self-consciously using this vocabulary as an antidote to the heroic, Benigni simply uses them for their own worth, for their own value. The fairy-tale sequence in *Jacob the Liar* is different in kind than the game plot in *Life Is Beautiful.* While both center on acknowledging the fantasy world of the child, in preserving it, in focussing on the difference between the expectations of adults and that of children, Becker's goal is the momentary suspension of anxiety, which seems to be the purpose of his film. Benigni's goal within the plot is the physical rescuing of the child. In this way, Benigni makes a claim for the true heroism of the father, who puts his life ahead of the life of his son and *succeeds* in rescuing him. This is the promise of laughter in comic representations of the Third Reich from *The Great Dictator* to *Hogan's Heroes*. When we laugh at the protagonist in his attempts to ameliorate the life of his son both under Fascism and finally to save his life in the death camp, we acknowledge the fact that these attempts must be successful. Laughter as evoked by the comic turns in this film is our guarantee of the happy ending, the rescue of the child.

However, it is a rather complicated happy ending. Not only have all of the actions of Guido resulted in his son being rescued, but the reunion of mother and son provide the perfect resolution to Guido's disruption of Dora's Catholic world. The son, who by Nazi law was Jewish but by Jewish law is not Jewish, and the non-Jewish mother are seen in the final shot as a Madonna and son, a reconstituted 'Italian' family, with its divisive 'Jewish' aspect missing. This seems to be a perfect happy ending for a film about the ability for any individual to shape history. Here the rescue of mother and child reconstitutes the Italian utopia, which existed before Guido interrupted it by his conquest of Dora. The promised future, an impossibility in Becker's world, is guaranteed by the selfless act of sacrifice by the father. Laughter is the key in our understanding of both of these films. Becker's laughter is undermined. We laugh because we are confronted with our own assumptions about the rules by which the world of the camps functions. Benigni's laughter is proof that whatever else will happen the promise of the film, the rescue of the child, must take place. Our expectations are fulfilled, and we feel good about our laughter.

Such a promise is impossible in the world of Becker's understanding of the Shoah; not purposeful action by adults but the accident of chance allows children to survive, and this underpins the falsity of Roberto Benigni's claim. In the Shoah, individual action could not guarantee the salvation of any individual. Theodor Adorno tells of overhearing two women leaving a production of *The Diary of Anne Frank* in Frankfurt in the 1960s. One turns to the other and says: 'Yes, but that girl at least should have been allowed to live.'[36] This is the motto of Benigni's film. Becker's deep pessimism knows that at the end those who are spared, like the narrator of *Jacob the Liar*, are spared accidentally, and have the obligation to tell their stories. That these stories are comic is the result of the pattern of accident. Here A. C. Bradley is right, but for the wrong reason. Accident is the wellspring of comedy and laughter, not because it is the opposite of tragedy but because it is the instantiation of the random in life, over which one can only laugh or weep. Becker provides the ability to do both in *Jacob the Liar* and makes it possible to use the elicitation of laughter as a means of representing the unrepresentable, not only the Shoah, but the randomness of life. Benigni's promise is that there are no accidents, that at the end of the comedy the gods in the machine will arrive to resolve the action and rescue those in danger.

The central difference between Becker and Benigni, however, lies in the movement of time and the permanence of the cultural record. Becker's film script (and his novel) entered into the world in which the struggle against Fascism, the Shoah, and the survivor were all constituent parts of both the experience and the ideology of his experience. Whether acknowledged or repressed the murder of the Jews was a fact in the lives of the survivors (like Max Becker and his son) as well as in the Germany in which they chose to live. This would have been true in different ways in West Germany or Poland in the 1950s and 1960s. By the 1990s the Shoah has begun to become history rather than memory (even, as in the case of Becker, constructed memory). The cultural model of Chaplin's and Lubitsch's image of Fascism is just as much a part of the visual history of our time as are Resnais and Spielberg. The heroic, as in Spielberg's complex and contradictory image of Oskar Schindler, can now be an acceptable part of the telling of the Shoah's *history*. Benigni can select a mode of evoking laughter as long as he ties it to the heroic. And the heroic, in this case, must be a success. No laughter could result if, by the conclusion of the film, not only the father, but also the child (and his mother) were dead. Oskar Schindler's tale makes sense as a narrative of the Shoah in the 1990s because it recounts his success in rescuing 'his' Jews. His is a world of the survivor, not the world of the victim. Purposeful action can change the world. It can avert the accidents of history. The world historical personality can change the shape of history.

Laughter is again possible in the 1990s as it was in the early 1940s. But it is also made possible by a filmmaker who is self-consciously understood as not being Jewish, as not needing the authenticity that a Jewish public identity would bring to the telling of the tale. This is, of course, also analogous to the cases of Chaplin and Lubitsch. While the Nazis labeled both as Jewish, in neither case was this an aspect of their public persona in the early 1940s. The movement to history means that the claims for authenticity that made a film such as *Jacob the Liar* even conceivable for the general audience (if not for the survivor such as Max Becker) are no longer needed. The Shoah is becoming (has become?) a factor of general historical experience of the West rather than of the experience only of those who were or were imagined to be the primary victims. In this case it is also analogous to the earliest comic films as anti-Semitism was seen as a sign of the general inhumanity of Fascism rather than as its most evil and salient feature.

Notes

1 Unless otherwise noted, all translations are my own. See Art Spiegelman, *Maus: A Survivor's Tale*, 2 vols, New York, 1986, 1991. See also the following: Spiegelman, 'Art Spiegelman: Un Subtil Sens de l'équilibre (An Exquisite Sense of Balance),' interview by Barry Schwabsky, *Art Press* 1994, no. 194, pp. 27–32; 'A Conversation with Art Spiegelman,' interview with Susan Jacobowitz, *Artweek*, 16 December 1993, pp. 15–16; and 'The Cultural Relief of Art Spiegelman: A Conversation with Michael Silverblatt,' *Tampa Review* 1992, vol. 5, pp. 31–36.

2 See Sheva Fogel, 'Drawing on Politics and Chutzpah: A Look at Israel's Comics and Cartoons,' *The Comics Journal*, 1991, no. 141, pp. 31–34.

3 See Frederik L. Schodt, *Manga! Manga! The World of Japanese Comics*, Tokyo: Kodansha International, 1983.

4 See Joseph Patrick Witek, '"Stranger and More Thrilling Than Fiction": Comic Books as History' unpublished Ph.D thesis, Vanderbilt University, 1988 and Bernd Dolle-Weinkauff, 'Das "Dritte Reich" im Comic: Geschichtsbilder und darstellungsaesthetische Strategien einer rekonstruierten Gattung,' *Jahrbüch fur Antisemitismusforschung* 1993, vol. 2, pp. 298–332.

5 See 'Laughter at Film Brings Spielberg Visit,' *New York Times*, 13 April 1994, p. B11.

6 See Peter Novick, *The Holocaust in American Life*, New York: Houghton Mifflin, 1999.

7 Aristotle's, too, if the book on *Comedy* had not been lost. Aristotle notes in the *Poetics*, 5.1449a2–3, that comic laughter is critical of the ridiculous, but that it is a ridiculous which 'is not painful or destructive'; this passage is discussed in detail in Gerald F. Else, *Aristotle's 'Poetics': The Argument*, Cambridge, MA: University of Michigan Press, 1963, pp. 184–89.

8 We can mention one exception – the German idea of a comedy without laughter, which builds upon Denis Diderot's idea of the comédie sérieuse. Diderot's view dominates the history of 'high' German comedy (but not the popular comedy) through the twentieth century. It is actually bad form to laugh during a performance of Lessing's *Nathan the Wise.* See Helmut Arntzen, *Die ernste Komödie: Das deutsche Lustspiel von Lessing bis Kleist*, Munich: Nymphenburger, 1968.

9 See Terrence Des Pres, 'Holocaust Laughter,' *Writing into the World: Essays, 1973–1987*, New York: Penguin, 1991, p. 278.

10 See A. C. Bradley, *Shakespearean Tragedy: Lectures on 'Hamlet,' 'Othello,' 'King Lear and 'Macbeth'*, London: Macmillan, 1905.

11 Des Pres, *Writing into the World*, pp. 280–81, 286.

12 See Alan Dundes and Thomas Hauschild, 'Auschwitz Jokes,' *Western Folklore* 1983, vol. 42, pp. 249–60; Uli Linke and Dundes, 'More on Auschwitz Jokes,' *Folklore*, 1988, vol. 99(1), pp. 3–10; and Dundes and Hauschild, 'Kennt der Witz kein Tabu? Zynische Erzählformen als Versuch der Bewältigung nationalsozialistischer Verbrechen,' *Zeitschrift für Volkskunde* 1987, vol. 83(1), pp. 21–31. See also Paul Lewis, 'Joke and Anti-Joke: Three Jews and a Blindfold,' *Journal of Popular Culture*, 1987, vol. 21, pp. 63–73.

13 See Sander Gilman, *Jews in Today's German Culture*, Bloomington, IN: University of Indiana Press, 1995, as well as Miriam Maltz, 'Depicting the Holocaust: Literary Techniques in Leslie Epstein's *King of the Jews*,' *Jewish Affairs*, 1992, vol. 47, pp. 79–85.

14 See Hans-Jochen Gamm, *Der Flüsterwitz im Dritten Reich*, Munich: List, 1963, and Steve Lipman, *Laughter in Hell: The Use of Humor during the Holocaust*, Northvale, NJ: Jason Aronson, 1991.

15 See the taped video records of David W., 1921–, Holocaust testimony (HVT-1687) [videorecording], interviewed by Helen Cohn and Lidya Osadchey, 31 Jan. 1991, Fortunoff Video Archive for Holocaust Testimonies, Yale University Library Box 208240, call number MS1322. He states that he was born in Chzarnów, Poland, in 1921. He notes the 'importance of being with his brother, humor, and his barber skills to his survival.' See also the interview with Agatha R., who was born in Mukachevo, Czechoslovakia (interviewed by Sidney M. Bolkosky, Fortunoff Video Archive for Holocaust Testimonies, Yale University Library Box HV1–739, call number MS1322), in which she states the role of 'inmate humor' in survival.

16 The most succinct summary of this view (on which many books have been written) is Irving Saposnik, 'The Yiddish Are Coming! The Yiddish Are Coming! Some Thoughts on Yiddish Comedy,' in *Laughter Unlimited: Essays on Humor, Satire, and the Comic*, ed. Reinhold Grimm and Jost Hermand, Madison, WI, 1991, pp. 99–105.

17 See especially Tony Barta, 'Film Nazis: The Great Escape,' in *Screening the Past: Film and the Representation of History*, ed. T. Barta, Westport, CT: Praeger, 1998, pp. 127–48, and *Spielberg's Holocaust: Critical Perspectives on Schindler's List*, ed. Yosefa Loshitzky, Bloomington, IN: University of Indiana Press, 1997. See also Dominick LaCapra, *History and Memory after Auschwitz*, Ithaca, NY: Cornell University Press, 1998); Ilan Avisar, 'Holocaust Movies and the Politics of Collective Memory,' in *Thinking about the Holocaust: After Half a Century*, ed. Alvin H. Rosenfeld, Bloomington, IN: University of Indiana Press, 1997, pp. 38–58; Janet Lungstrum, 'Foreskin Fetishism: Jewish Male Difference in *Europa, Europa*,' *Screen*, 1998, vol. 39, pp. 53–66; Morris Zyrl

and Saul S. Friedman, 'The Holocaust as Seen in the Movies,' in *Holocaust Literature: A Handbook of Critical, Historical, and Literary Writings*, ed. Saul S. Friedman, Westport, CT: John Trotter, 1993, pp. 604–22.

18 See A. Roy Eckardt, 'Comedy Versus Tragedy: Post-*Shoah* Reflections,' Oxford: Oxford Centre for Hebrew and Jewish Studies Lecture Series, 1990; and Carol Faye Stern Edelman, '(1) Attitudes Toward Violence the Subculture of Violence Revisited; (2) Conflict and Control Functions of Sexual Humor; (3) Resistance to Genocide: Victim Response During the Holocaust' unpublished Ph.D thesis, University of Arizona, 1987.

19 For the general context, see Lester D. Friedman, *Hollywood's Image of the Jew*, New York: Ungar, 1982; Neal Gabler, *An Empire of Their Own: How the Jews Invented Hollywood*, New York: Anchor, 1988; and Mark Winokur, *American Laughter: Immigrants, Ethnicity, and 1930s Hollywood Film Comedy*, New York: St Martins, 1993.

20 Quoted in David Robinson, *Chaplin: His Life and Art*, New York: HarperCollins, 1985, p. 485.

21 Quoted in Leland A. Poague, *The Cinema of Ernst Lubitsch: The Hollywood Films*, Cranbury, NJ: AS Barnes, 1978, p. 90.

22 Uwe Naumann, *Zwischen Tränen und Gelächter*, Koln: Pahl-Rugenstein Verlag, 1983, p. 292.

23 William Paul, *Ernst Lubitsch's American Comedy*, New York: Columbia University Press, 1983, p. 243.

24 See Mordecai Newman, 'Naughty Nazis: A Review of "To Be or Not to Be,"' *Jewish Frontier*, 1984, no. 51, pp. 24–26.

25 See Caroline Alice Wiedmer, 'Reconstructing Sites: Representations of the Holocaust in Postwar Literary, Cinematic, and Memorial Texts,' unpublished Ph.D thesis, Princeton University, 1994.

26 See Lawrence Graver, *An Obsession with Anne Frank: Meyer Levin and the Diary*, Berkeley, CA: University of California Press, 1995.

27 Beth Pinsker, 'Did Another Shoah Comedy Inspire Benigni?' *Forward*, 5 February 1999, p. 1.

28 Roberto Benigni's model was echoed by Fernando Trueba's *Girl of My Dreams* (*La Niña des tus ojos*) (1998), starring Penélope Cruz playing Macarena Granada, a Spanish actress making a film about German–Spanish friendship for the UFA in 1938.

29 Roberto Benigni, 'Life Is Beautiful: An Interview with Roberto Benigni,' interview by Prairie Miller, www.allmovie.com/cg/x.dll?UID=8:20:45|AM&Pp=avg&sql=MIP|81377

30 Roberto Benigni, 'Life Is Beautiful: An Interview with Roberto Benigni.'

31 See for example the discussion in Ralph Tutt, 'Seven Beauties and the Beast: Bettelheim, Wertmuller, and the Uses of Enchantment,' *Literature/Film Quarterly*, 1989, vol. 17, pp. 193–201.

32 Quoted in Erika Milvy, '"*I Just Wanted to Make a Beautiful Movie*,"' *Salon*, 30 Oct. 1998, www.salonmag.com/ent/movies/int/1998/10/30int.html

33 Bruce Weber, 'What's So Funny?: Decoding That Enigma Called Humor and Failing Gleefully,' *New York Times*, 9 March 1999, p. B9.

34 See *Corriere della sera*, 23 March 1999.

35 See Pinsker, 'Did Another Shoah Comedy Inspire Benigni?' *Forward*, p. 14.

36 Theodor W. Adorno, 'Was bedeutet: Aufarbeitung der Vergangenheit,' *Eingriffe*, Frankfurt am Main: Suhrkamp, 1968, pp. 143–44.

Reading 11

Lawrence Baron

SERIOUS HUMOR

Laughter as lamentation

Projecting the Holocaust into the Present, New York: Rowman and Littlefield, 2005, pp. 130–50. Text and discursive notes edited.

THE PHRASE 'HOLOCAUST HUMOR' seems like an oxymoron. It violates three cardinal rules that Terrence Des Pres felt unofficially governed Holocaust discourse: (1) that the Holocaust be portrayed as a unique event, (2) that representations of the Holocaust be accurate, and (3) that the Holocaust be approached solemnly.[1] Yet, even the Jews languishing in the ghettoes or anticipating their deaths in the camps exchanged jokes to ridicule their executioners, extract hope out of despair, or cope with the absurdity of their dilemma. Their resort to humor provided a defense mechanism to sublimate their rage against their oppressors and transform their misery into something bearable.[2]

Before the Holocaust had reached its awful apex, filmmakers armed with their cameras took humorous potshots at Hitler and his henchmen. Charlie Chaplin's *The Great Dictator* (1940) satirized Hitler as an egotistical demagogue whose guttural anti-Semitic tirades wilted microphones and who juggled the globe like a child playing with a ball. Chaplin demolished the myth of Aryan purity by playing both the Jewish barber and the Phooey (Chaplin's epithet for the führer). He concluded the movie by having the barber drop his charade as Hynkel and deliver a serious speech condemning fascism and racism. In retrospect Chaplin regretted his comic treatment of Nazi oppression: 'Had I known of the actual horrors of the German concentration camps, I could not have made fun of the homicidal insanity of the Nazis.'[3]

Ernst Lubitsch's *To Be or Not to Be* (1942) elicits laughter by having a troupe of actors outwit their oppressors. The movie opens with footage of battle-ravaged Warsaw and features an excerpt from one of Hitler's radio addresses. These actualities serve as a framework for Lubitsch to satirize 'the Nazis and their ridiculous ideology.' Lubitsch draws attention to the plight of the Jews by putting Shylock's famous speech from *The Merchant of Venice* (i.e. 'Hath not a Jew eyes?') into the mouth of a Jewish extra, who rehearses these lines backstage, on a debris covered street, and in front of an audience of German soldiers and an actor masquerading as Hitler. Lubitsch does not trivialize the severity of the German occupation, but rather, as Annette Insdorf maintains, fights 'horror with the ammunition of sharp humor.' Mel Brooks's remake of *To Be or Not to Be* (1983) lacks the political pungency of the original.

By the late 1950s, a few new films were produced that employed humor to mock Nazi racism and sympathize with its victims, as table 1 indicates. The first postwar comedy about the German persecution of Jews did not appear until 1958. Adapted from Franz Werfel's play *Jacobowsky and the Colonel*, *Me and the Colonel* replicates *To Be or Not to Be*'s formula of fugitives evading the Germans through a series of clever deceptions. It features humorous banter between a Polish Jew and an anti-Semitic Polish aristocrat, who grow to respect each other as they stay one step ahead of their common enemy. Sander Gilman's criticism of the film's omission of direct references to the Shoah exhibits an extremely narrow concept of what constitutes a Holocaust movie and ignores how Jewish refugees like Werfel derived vicarious revenge from out-smarting the Nazis on screen.

Made in the same year, Kurt Hoffmann's *Aren't We Wonderful* satirizes the historical amnesia of many West Germans who conveniently forgot the Third Reich as they switched allegiances to the democracy that replaced it. Staged as a series of cabaret skits linked by the experiences of recurring characters from the 1930s until the 1950s, the movie depicts Nazism as a lower-class phenomenon that middle-class Germans tolerated more out of conformity than conviction. Its hero, Hans Böckel, never loses his liberal moorings and does the right things, like saving a Jewish friend, refusing to support Hitler to advance his career, and fighting neo-Nazism in the postwar period. Although Hoffmann assumes that the audience would identify with Böckel's disdain for Hitler, he insinuates that many decent Germans had retreated inward and relinquished control of their country to fanatics. To awaken them from their complacent slumber, Hoffmann tickled their funny bones rather than rattling the skeletons in their closets.

Comedies remained rare, even as the output of Holocaust feature films doubled in the 1960s and 1970s. The odd-couple scenario provided the most common vehicle for pairing victims with those who might betray or befriend them: *The Shop on Main Street* mines the incongruous relationship between Tono and Rosalie to keep the

Table 1 Holocaust comedies as percentage of Holocaust films

	1945–1959	*1960–1969*	*1970–1979*	*1980–1989*	*1990–1999*
Comedies	4	6	8	10	26
Percentage of films	3.6	4.4	6.4	4.4	11.7

film's tone light until its tragic ending. Claude Berri's *The Two of Us* (1966) and *Harold and Maude* (1971) elicit laughs by mismatching the lead characters. In the former, an anti-Semitic French peasant unwittingly shelters a Jewish boy who has been taken to the countryside to escape the Germans. Every canard the old man utters about Jews is discredited by his affection for the child. *Harold and Maude* pairs a morbid teenage boy with a free-spirited eighty-year-old woman. Maude's unbridled libertinism reflects her aversion to any authority as a Holocaust survivor. Her past is discreetly hinted at through a glimpse of the numbers tattooed on her arm and her fond memories of prewar Vienna. Appreciative of the second chance afforded by her survival, she teaches Harold, who regularly stages phony suicide attempts to attract his mother's attention, to relish life.[4]

Mel Brooks premised *The Producers* (1968) on the assumption that any comic portrayal of Hitler would offend Americans. Upon the advice of his new accountant, impresario Max Bialystock scours scripts for a play so terrible that it will fold the first night, entitling him to keep the money raised to produce it. The musical *Springtime for Hitler* seems destined to flop, but audiences find its tastelessness campy. Brooks does not simply let kitsch prevail. He lampoons the composer of the romp, Franz Liebkind, who alternates between being an American patriot and regressing into a loyal Nazi. Liebkind hopes to prove that Hitler was a better dancer than Winston Churchill.[5]

Making comedies about concentration camps remained taboo until the 1970s. The checkered fate of Jerry Lewis's *The Day the Clown Cried* (1972) is a case in point. Lewis plays a clown imprisoned in a transit camp for cracking derogatory jokes about Hitler. There he regains his passion for performing by entertaining Jewish children before they are deported. The movie was never released, but a dramatic version of a similar story provided the plotline for *The Last Butterfly* (1990).[6]

Lina Wertmueller's *Seven Beauties* (1975) became the first film to extract laughter from the plight of an inmate at Auschwitz. Wertmueller sandwiches the pathetic attempts of her sleazy protagonist to survive between footage of the devastation caused by World War II and the imminence of death in the camp where he is interned. The antihero, Pasqualino, murders a pimp who had 'corrupted' his sister. Sentenced to serve as an orderly in a hospital, he rapes a comatose patient. At Auschwitz, he is ordered to select seven men for execution and kill his best friend. To get an extra ration of food, he seduces the repulsively obese female commandant who has made his existence miserable. In the process, the victimizer becomes the victim.[7] The film sparked a controversy between Terrence Des Pres and Bruno Bettelheim over whether it glorified survival at any cost. In retrospect, its portrayal of Pasqualino's dilemma accords closely with Lawrence Langer's theory that camp inmates were forced to make 'choiceless choices' designed to demoralize them either way.[8]

Jewish desperation provided the sardonic theme of the other notable Holocaust comedy produced in the 1970s. Frank Beyer adapted *Jacob the Liar* (1974) from Jurek Becker's novel of the same name. Becker and his family had been confined in the Lodz ghetto before they were deported to various concentration camps.[9] Jacob hears a radio broadcast about the Soviets' advancing on the eastern front. The Jews of the ghetto cling to this bit of hopeful news. Jacob sustains their optimism by monitoring the progress of the war as broadcast on a radio he purportedly owns. The expectation of liberation soon deters Jews from committing suicide or organizing resistance. When Jacob confides to a friend that he has no radio, his friend hangs himself. The closing scene shows Jacob trying to buoy the spirits of a girl by vouching for the truth of a fairy tale he once had told her about clouds consisting of cotton balls. The film ends as Jacob, the girl, and other deported Jews gaze at clouds through a slit in the side of a railroad car.[10] This strategy of concocting a lie to conceal the dispiriting truth serves as the premise of subsequent comedies, like *Life Is Beautiful* (1997) and *Train of Life* (1998).

Although the number of Holocaust feature films released in the 1980s increased over the prior decade, the percentage constituted by comedies decreased. In the wake of the success of the television miniseries *Holocaust*, the decision to build an American Holocaust museum, and the increased prominence of the Holocaust in public education and the mass media, the unwritten rules mandating tragic depictions of the Holocaust were rigorously adhered to by the movie industry. The rise in the proportion of Holocaust films adapted from memoirs and nonfiction sources militated against the production of comedies with Holocaust themes. Gilman has observed that the irreverent satire of *The Producers* worked with audiences in the 1960s because the movie appeared 'at a moment in time when the name Hitler was not solely identified with the *Shoah*.'[11] By the 1980s, the use of comedy to depict the worst genocide of the twentieth century seemed too offensive.

Woody Allen's *Crimes and Misdemeanors* (1989) was one of the few movies from the 1980s to mix comedy into a film with a subplot about a Holocaust survivor and Jewish faith after Auschwitz. Unlike *Deconstructing Harry* (1997), in which Harry tastelessly quips that six million Jewish dead is 'a record made to be broken,' Allen reserved his one-liners in the former film for his failed love life and career as a filmmaker and dealt with the crimes of murder and the Holocaust in a more serious vein. His nemesis, Lester, a successful television director, pontificates that 'comedy is tragedy plus time' and cites jokes about Lincoln's assassination as proof of this axiom. In the documentary Allen's character makes about Lester, he likens Lester, in his arrogance, to Mussolini not Hitler. Within the core stories in which two antagonists prevail, Allen cites the Holocaust as a metaphor for a world in which God and moral justice do not exist.[12]

Time may not have healed the wounds of the Shoah, but it has altered the modes of representing the event in feature films. Almost 12 percent of the Holocaust films made in the 1990s were comedies. Three factors fostered this sharp increase: the search for original approaches to subject matter, the presumed familiarity of the public with the basic facts of the Holocaust, and the passing of a generation of filmmakers who experienced World War II as adults and rise of those who were

Table 2 Backgrounds of filmmakers of Holocaust comedies made in the 1990s

Jewish child survivors	2
Gentile minors in Europe during the war	6
Children of survivors	7
Born 1945–1960 in war-zone states	5
Born after 1960 or in neutral states	3
Insufficient background information	3

minors during the war or who were born after it.[13] Alan Berger surmises that children of Holocaust survivors (and, I would argue, of children raised in nations in the 1940s and 1950s where the memory of the war remained vivid) have found that humor 'permits them both to accept their helplessness to undo the past and also to explore their relationship to their parents' past.'[14] Table 2 reveals the high proportion of directors and writers of Holocaust comedies who share this background.

Detractors and fans of Roberto Benigni associate his comedic style with bawdiness, pratfalls, sight gags, and a rapid-fire stream of jokes.[15] His film persona has made it difficult for critics to accept his films as highbrow entertainment. Benigni sought to prove that his brand of humor could accommodate serious subjects. He chose to place his buffoonish character in an extermination camp, which he regarded as 'the symbol of our century, the negative one, the worst thing imaginable.' The theme was personal to him as well because his father had been confined in a German labor camp for siding with the Italian monarchy's shift of allegiance to the Allies in the autumn of 1943. Benigni recalled how his father spoke about this ordeal: 'Night and day fellow prisoners were dying all around him. He told us about it, as if to protect me and my sisters, he told it in an almost funny way – saying tragic, painful things, but finally his way of telling them was really very particular. Sometimes we laughed at the stories he told.'[16]

Benigni cast himself as a lovable jokester who protects his young son from the horrors of a death camp by pretending it is part of a game to win a tank. This narrative device struck many critics as an exploitative gimmick to elicit laughs by desecrating the memory of those who died in the extermination centers. Charles Taylor's scathing review of *Life Is Beautiful* typifies the resistance the film encountered: 'The point, I think, is the sheer callous inappropriateness of comedy existing within the physical reality of the camps – even the imagined reality of a movie.'[17]

Anticipating such criticism, Benigni took a number of precautions to insure that his 'fable' of a child surviving in a concentration camp did not deviate too far from the truth. He recruited Marcello Pezzetti of the Contemporary Jewish Documentation Center of Milan to serve as the historical consultant for *Life Is Beautiful.* Pezzetti had extensive experience in interviewing Italian survivors of Auschwitz and put Benigni in contact with some of them, particularly those who had been adolescents when they were inmates. A survivor designed the uniforms worn by the prisoners in the film. Schlomo Venezia, the sole surviving Italian member of the *Sonderkommando*, which collected the clothes of those about to die and disposed of their corpses afterward, advised Benigni on staging the scene where Guido's uncle and other Jews undress before being gassed.[18] Most of the children who survived Auschwitz were the twins whom Dr. Mengele kept alive as guinea pigs for medical experiments.[19] Some however, survived in concentration and labor camps because adult prisoners hid and nurtured them. Benigni knew the story of a four-year-old child who was smuggled into Buchenwald in a suitcase and protected by the camp's underground.[20] This incident became the basis for a novel by Bruno Apitz and Frank Beyer's adaptation of it into the East German film *Naked among Wolves* (1962).[21]

One of the most common charges leveled at *Life Is Beautiful* is that it consists of two discordant halves. The first part is a light comedy about coincidences that lead to the marriage of Guido the waiter and his beautiful wife Dora. The second is a tragedy about the family's deportation and internment. To shield his son from the reality of camp life, Guido fabricates far-fetched rationales to convince his son, Giosué, that the cruelties he witnesses and hears about in the death camp have been fabricated by the other prisoners to scare him into quitting the game and losing the tank.[22] Maurizio Viano's insightful analysis of *Life Is Beautiful*, to which I am indebted, sees this dualism as an artistic device: 'Spatially, the two opposites are kept separate and yet over-determine one another, a bit like the Yin-Yang symbol, where the black and the white are well defined and symmetrically juxtaposed but each contains a speck of the other as a memento of their interdependence.'[23]

The title of the movie seemingly implies an unqualified optimism contradicted by the fact that Guido is executed the night before the camp is liberated. The film's original working title was *Buongiorno Principessa* (Good Morning, Princess) since this was how Guido first greeted Dora when she fell out of a barn loft into his arms. After the film was completed, Benigni read a letter written by Leon Trotsky shortly before his assassination. Therein, the exiled revolutionary expressed his gratitude toward his wife and for his Mexican asylum: 'Life is beautiful. Let the future generations cleanse it of all evil, oppression, and violence, and enjoy it to the full.' By referring to this passage, Benigni celebrates life and acknowledges how ephemeral it is.[24]

Many critics faulted Benigni for minimizing Guido's Jewish identity. It is not until his uncle's painted horse gallops onto the screen that Guido's religious background is disclosed. As one reviewer put it, '[Guido's] innocent in a generic way.'[25] Benigni left clues for more knowledgeable viewers. Guido's last name is Orefice, which is a common Italian Jewish name literally meaning 'goldsmith.' His son's name is the Italian equivalent of Joshua.[26] If one looks for biblical analogies, Joshua leads the Israelites into the Promised Land because Moses died before he could reach it. There are two other reasons, however, for concealing Guido's origins until the middle of the picture. The first is historical. Many Italian Jews were highly acculturated and supportive of Mussolini's regime until 1938.[27] The second stems from Benigni's intent to have Italians empathize with his clownish persona and then ask themselves, Why did they go after Benigni? The next logical question is why persecute the Jews at all.[28]

In what strikes me as an egregious case of intellectual casuistry, Kobi Niv argues that the name Giosué is actually 'synonymous with Jesus.' Accordingly Guido's name sounds like the Italian for Judas. Thus, Niv maintains that Guido deceived Giosué like Judas deceived Jesus by concealing the truth from him, but eventually redeemed himself by dying so that Giosué could be reborn when the camp was liberated by the Allies. As if this reasoning were not sufficiently convoluted, Niv cites an insignificant piece of dialog spoken by Guido at the beginning of the movie. Upon repairing his car, Guido casually says, 'I'm going to wash my hands.' Niv claims this line replicates how Pontius Pilate washed his hands of the responsibility for ordering the crucifixion of Jesus. Since Niv accuses Benigni of minimizing the Jewish genocide to highlight the redemptive power of marital and parental love, he postulates that Guido's words announce 'the purpose of the film we are about to see: it seeks to wash Europe's hands, the hands of Christian civilization, clean of the Jewish blood it spilled during World War II.'[29]

Life Is Beautiful has a cinematic lineage in the *Comedia del' italiano*, which parodies serious themes of national identity and the collective memory of fascism. Films like

Luigi Comencini's *Everybody Go Home* (1960), Federico Fellini's *Amarcord* (1974), Giuseppe Tornatore's *Cinema Paradiso* (1988), and Gabriele Salvatores's *Mediterraneo* (1991) have spun humorous tales from the combustible mixture of Italian customs, everyday concerns, government repression, and war.[30] Marcus observes that Benigni was also influenced by the Italian dramatist Luigi Pirandello, who distinguished between the comic, which arises from an awareness of disparate perspectives, and humor, which results from philosophical reflection on the meaning of this disparity. Benigni accomplishes this by doubling the perspective of the audience. It experiences the story from the viewpoint of Giosué recounting his father's game; unlike the boy, it also recognizes from its prior awareness of the Holocaust how implausible Guido's explanations of the daily routines in the death camp really are.[31]

Although the Italian movie market is saturated with Hollywood and multinational productions, *Life Is Beautiful* outsold the imports at the box office at home and became both the most financially successful film in Italian cinematic history and the most successful foreign film in American cinematic history. It not only won the Grand Jury Prize at Cannes and the Oscar for Best Foreign Language Film but also captured the Jerusalem Film Festival Award for the Best Jewish Experience.[32] One hears the echo of Bettelheim's cynical critique of the popularity of *The Diary of Anne Frank* in Niv's attribution of *Life Is Beautiful*'s international acclaim to a 'profound, and still growing, need to blot this horrific event out of history, to erase it from the collective memory of Western, Judeo-Christian, European–American civilization, thus enabling this civilization to free itself of the guilt of having committed the Holocaust.'[33]

While Bettelheim's analysis possessed some validity in the 1950s, when public awareness of the Holocaust was still limited, Niv's lacks credibility because it fails to take into account the popularization of the Holocaust that has occurred in the interim. The surfeit rather than paucity of images about the Holocaust by the 1990s motivated some directors to experiment with genres like comedy to represent the event. I find Hilene Flanzbaum's explanation for the positive reception of *Life Is Beautiful* more convincing because she acknowledges the innovative impulse among filmmakers:

> Benigni plays to a sophisticated audience – one that has seen plenty of graphic and horrific cinematic scenes – some about the Holocaust and some not. His job then is to defamiliarize this violence: he does this by focusing on only one aspect of psychological suffering experienced in the Holocaust. For the parents in the audience who have lost sleep over what they might do to protect their own child, the film proved overwhelming. Benigni accomplishes a great deal when he defamiliarizes the Holocaust enough to make viewers feel it all over again.[34]

In his autobiographical novel *Night*, Elie Wiesel recalls that Moché, the beadle of his synagogue, returned after being deported and frantically reported to the remaining Jewish residents of Sighet that the Germans had killed everyone else on his transport. He implored his neighbors to heed his warning. They dismissed him as a madman. Two years later, the Germans deported the Jews of Sighet to Auschwitz.[35] What if the Jews of Sighet had believed the beadle and taken his advice? What if the beadle had devised a daring escape plan so implausible that it was bound to confound the Nazis? Rumanian director Radu Milhaileanu explores this premise in *Train of Life*. In an opening headshot, the village fool, Shlomo, recalls what happened to his shtetl during World War II. Next, he rushes through the forest to the front of his synagogue. Frenzied music, rhythmic screams, and the sound of breaking glass reflect his panic. As he approaches the little synagogue, he falls on the ground, rolls onto his back, and beats his chest and forehead with his fists. The rabbi summons the town's sages to listen to Shlomo's eyewitness report about the Germans slaughtering the Jews in a nearby town. Like many of Wiesel's characters, Shlomo blames God for allowing the Germans to do this and questions whether heaven can ever reside in Jewish hearts again. While many of the village elders doubt the incredible tale told by Shlomo, the rabbi believes him and wonders how they can save the Jews in the shtetl. Shlomo proposes that they buy an old train, refurbish it to look like a German transport, and deport themselves to Palestine. To complete the deception, some of the Jews will learn German, wear Nazi uniforms, and pretend to be guards. Like the inane inhabitants of Chelm, the wise men of the town approve of Shlomo's scheme. After all, is Shlomo's plan anymore preposterous than the notion that a civilized country like Germany would liquidate European Jewry?[36]

The facial close-up of Shlomo that opened the movie ends it as well, but in the end Shlomo's narration starts sounding improbable. He reports that most of the Jews [escaped and] settled in India, and most of the gypsies [who later joined them] went to Palestine. The camera then reveals that Shlomo is wearing a concentration camp uniform and is standing behind a barbed wire fence. Grinning sheepishly, he confesses, 'Well that's the true story of my shtetl . . . well almost true.' He softly sings about his shtetl. His is a tale told by a fool, full of fanciful thinking, eulogizing a community and culture that no longer exists. The credits roll over a black background with a violin sustaining mournful chords.

Train of Life went into production before *Life Is Beautiful* was released. Mihaileanu had mailed the script to Benigni and offered him the part of Shlomo, but Benigni declined since he was busy making his own comedy about the Holocaust. Mihaileanu submitted his movie to the Cannes Film Festival, where it was rejected because of its irreverent mix of humor and the Holocaust. Yet, the more renowned Benigni got his picture screened at Cannes after adopting a recommendation made by the festival's director to pitch his story as a fable rather than as reality. Mihaileanu subsequently accused Benigni of plagiarizing the bracketing structure of Shlomo's recollections in *Train of Life* by sandwiching his story between voice-overs of Giosué recounting how his father had sacrificed himself.[37]

Actually, the two movies represent different perspectives on the Holocaust. *Life Is Beautiful* reflects the comedic persona of Benigni in particular and Italian comedies about everyday life under fascism in general. Although the audience eventually learns that Guido is Jewish, his slapstick antics and satirical jibes possess little that is distinctively Jewish. Mihaileanu, on the other hand, once belonged to Bucharest's Yiddish theater ensemble. His movie is steeped in Eastern European Jewish folklore, literature, politics, and religiosity. His parents survived the camps while other members of his family perished. Whereas the survival of Giosué and Dora leaves the audience with hope, Shlomo's final soliloquy and internment shatter the alternate reality he has imagined and conjure up the obliteration of the community he fondly recalls. To Mihaileanu, 'Jewish humor has always been a shield against madness. Comedy is tragedy's balm. We don't laugh at a tragic event. But we continue to laugh in order to persevere.'[38]

Like many Eastern European directors after the collapse of the Soviet Union, Mihaileanu required financing from Western European studios to produce his picture.[39] Although the use of French as the film's language initially interferes with the credibility of its characters as Jews from the shtetl, they break into Yiddish expressions and Hebrew prayers frequently enough to imbue the movie with a Jewish sensibility.[40] On this point, Mihaileanu might have emulated Yolande Zauberman's decision in *Ivan and Abraham* (1993) to retain the dialects spoken by ethnic groups who comprised the populations in Eastern Europe since this reflects the cultural and linguistic barriers that divided them.

Mihaileanu fled Romania in 1980 when it was under communist rule. His caricature of the doctrinaire Yossi mirrors his own disillusionment with Marxism. This had been the theme of his first feature film, *Betrayal* (1993). The scene of the train being bombarded draws freely from Emir Kusterica's *Underground* (1995), a zany satire about the Yugoslavian communist partisans, Titoism, and the recent ethnic wars in Bosnia and Serbia. Mihaileanu depicts the incoming shells in cartoon style. They whiz randomly, exploding on impact, except for a dud that skids along the ground upon landing. The frenetic musical score sounds like a Spike Jones composition.[41]

Although *Train of Life* stood in the box-office shadows of *Life Is Beautiful*, it received many prestigious prizes, including the Audience Award from the Sundance Film Festival and the Italian Academy Award for Best Foreign Language in a year when its main competitor was *Shakespeare in Love*. Mihaileanu clearly felt an obligation as a child of survivors to preserve the memory of the murdered European Jews. Interviewed by his father, he described his film as 'an allegory nourished by our blood, our culture, and our memory, a deep desire to re-create the world of the shtetl I never knew, but which our family experienced in the flesh.'[42] He also hoped that his film would serve as a warning to halt the rise of neo-Nazism in Germany and Austria and 'ethnic cleansing' in the former Yugoslavia.[43] Although driven from their homes, the Jews in *Fiddler on the Roof* eventually find refuge in Palestine, Poland, or the United States. Mihaileanu's colorful characters board a train bound for a death camp.

Notes

1 Terrence Des Pres, 'Holocaust Laughter,' in *Writing into the World: Essays, 1973–1987*, New York: Penguin, 1991, 277–78.

2 Steve Lipman, *Laughter in Hell: The Use of Humor during the Holocaust*, Northvale, NJ: Jason Aronson, 1991; Chaya Ostrower, *Humor as a Defense Mechanism in the Holocaust*, unpublished PhD thesis, Tel Aviv University, 2000; Lynn Rapaport, 'Laughter and Heartache: The Functions of Humor in Holocaust Tragedy,' in *Gray Zones: Ambiguity and Compromise in the Holocaust and Its Aftermath*, ed. John Roth and Jonathan Petropolus, New York: Berghahn, 2005.

3 *The Great Dictator*, directed by Charles Chaplin; Jodi Sherman, 'Humor, Resistance, and the Abject: Roberto Benigni's *Life Is Beautiful* and Charlie Chaplin's *The Great Dictator*,' *Film and History* 2002, vol. 32(2), 74–76.

4 Aneta Champman, 'Let Life Begin – *Harold and Maude*,' in *The Film Comedy Reader*, ed. Gregg Rickman, New York: Limelight Editions, 2001, 303–8.
5 Gregg Rickman, '*The Producers*,' in *The Film Comedy Reader*, 298–302.
6 Omer Bartov, *The 'Jew' in Cinema: From the Golem to Don't Touch My Holocaust*, Bloomington, IN: Indiana University Press, 2005, 162–65; David Gussak, 'Survival as a Work of Art: Representing Theresienstadt,' in Caroline Joan Picart, *The Holocaust Film Sourcebook*, Westport, CT: Praeger, 2004, 2, 180–82.
7 Ernest Ferlita and John R. May, *The Parables of Line Wertmueller*, New York: Paulist Press, 1977; Kriss Ravetto, *The Unmaking of Fascist Aesthetics*, Minneapolis, MN: University of Minnesota Press, 2001, 187–225.
8 Bruno Bettelheim, *Surviving and Other Essays*, New York: Alfred A. Knopf, 1979; Terrence Des Pres, 'The Bettelheim Problem,' in *Writing into the World*, 63–87; John Michalczyk, 'In the Eye of the Storm: Controversies Surrounding Holocaust Films,' paper presented at the Popular Culture Association Conference, San Diego, California, March 24, 2005.
9 Sander L. Gilman, *Jurek Becker: How I Became a German: Jurek Becker's Life in Five Worlds*, Washington, DC: German Historical Institute, 1999; David Rock, *Jurek Becker: A Jew Who Became a German?*, New York: Berghahn, 2000.
10 Annette Insdorf, *Indelible Shadows: Film and the Holocaust*, 3/e, New York: Cambridge University Press, 2003, 142–44.
11 Sander L. Gilman, 'Is Life Beautiful?' 74 [reading 10].
12 Woody Allen, *Woody Allen on Woody Allen: In Conversation with Stig Bjorkman*, New York: Grove, 1994, 209–26; Peter J. Bailey, *The Reluctant Film Art of Woody Allen*, Lexington, KY: University of Kentucky Press, 2003, 131–44; David Desser and Lester D. Friedman, *American-Jewish Filmmakers*, Urbana, IL: University of Illinois Press, 1993, 92–101; Sander Lee, *Eighteen Woody Allen Films Analyzed: Anguish, God, and Existentialism*, Jefferson, NC: McFarland and Co., 2002, 139–63.
13 Rick Altman, *Film/Genre*, London: British Film Institute, 1999, 179–94; Sabine Hake, *German National Cinema*, New York: Routledge, 2002, 186–92.
14 Alan Berger, *Children of Job: American Second-Generation Witnesses to the Holocaust*, Albany, NY: State University of Press of New York, 1997, 150–52.
15 Carlo Celli, *The Divine Comic: The Cinema of Roberto Benigni*, Lanham, MD: Scarecrow Press, 2001, 1–41.
16 Benigni quoted in Alexandra Stanley, 'The Funniest Italian You've Probably Never Heard Of,' *New York Times Magazine*, October 11, 1988, 44.
17 Charles Taylor, 'The Unbearable Lightness of Benigni,' *Salon*, October 30, 1998, 4.
18 Celli, *Divine Comic*, 111–16, 153–54.
19 Lucette Matalon Lagnado, *Children of the Flames: Dr. Josef Mengele and the Untold Story of the Twins of Auschwitz*, New York: Morrow, 1991; Deborah Dwork, *Children with a Star: Jewish Youth in Nazi Europe*, New Haven, CT: Yale University Press, 1991, 209–49, 309 n.99.
20 Celli, *The Divine Comic*, 152; Insdorf, *Indelible Shadows*, 289–90.
21 Bruno Apitz, *Nackt unter Wöelfen: Roma* (Halle: Mitteldeutscher Verlag, 1958; Bill Niven, 'Der Not gehorchend, nicht dem eigenen Triebe, ich tüs der Werbung nur zuliebe! The Genesis of Bruno Apitz's Nackt unfer Wölfen,' *German Studies Review* 2005, vol. 28(2), 265–83.
22 Peter Bondanella, *Italian Cinema from Neorealism to the Present*, 3/e, New York: Continuum, 2001, 449–50.
23 Maurizio Viano, '*Life Is Beautiful:* Reception, Allegory, and Holocaust Laughter,' *Jewish Social Studies: The New Series* 1999, vol. 5(3), 53–56.
24 Viano, '*Life Is Beautiful*,' 52.
25 Michael Fox, 'Beautiful Italian Fable Dumbs Down Holocaust Horrors,' *Jewish Bulletin of Northern California*, October 30, 1998, 2.

26 Viano, *Life Is Beautiful*, 61–62.
27 Susan Zuccotti, *The Italians and the Holocaust: Persecution, Rescue, and Survival*, New York: Basic Books, 1987; Alexander Stille, 'Jews in Fascist Italy,' *Life Is Beautiful* Tribute Page, at www.geocities.com/Broadway/Wing/6027.index.html (accessed July 25, 2002).
28 Celli, *The Divine Comic*, 51.
29 Kobi Niv, *Life is Beautiful, But Not for Jews: Another View of the Film*, Tel Aviv: NB Books, 2000, 85–101.
30 Marcia Landy, *Italian Film*, New York: Cambridge University Press, 2000, 98–120, 253–57, 363–65; Bondanella, *Italian Cinema*, 142–95, 347–83, 435–61.
31 M. J. Marcus, 'The Seriousness of Humor in Roberto Benigni's *Life is Beautiful*', in id. *After Fellini: National Cinema in the Postmodern Age*, Baltimore, MD: Johns Hopkins University Press, 2002, 277–81; Caroline Joan Picart and Jennifer Perrine, 'Laughter, Terror, and Revolt in Three Recent Holocaust Films,' in Picart, *Holocaust Film Sourcebook*, vol. 1, 402–7.
32 'Awards,' and 'Business Data,' *La vita e bella*, at www.imdb.com; Carlo Testo, *Italian Cinema and Modern European Literatures: 1945–2000*, Westport, CT: Praeger, 2002, 139–48.
33 Niv, *Life Is Beautiful*, 103.
34 Hilene Flanzbaum, 'But Wasn't It Terrific? A Defense of Liking *Life Is Beautiful*,' *Yale Journal of Criticism*, 2001, vol. 14(1), 273–86.
35 Elie Wiesel, *Night*, trans. Stella Rodway, New York: Avon, 1969, 12–32.
36 See Solomon Simon, *The Wise Men of Helm and Their Merry Tales*, New York: Behrman House, 1945; Isaac Bashevis Singer, *The Fools of Chelm and Their History*, trans. Elizabeth Shub, New York: Farrar, Straus, and Giroux, 1973.
37 Anne Thompson, 'The Evolution of "Life,"' *Premiere Magazine*, April 1999, 1–2.
38 'Production Notes,' and 'An Interview between Father and Son,' *The Shtetl Times*, *Train of Life* Press Kit. Stefan Steinberg, 'An Interview with Radu Mihaileaunu: The Director of *Train of Life:* "We have to learn to articulate these deep emotions"'; March 31, 2000, at www.wsws.org/articles/2000/mar2000/radu-m31.shtml (accessed July 12, 2002).
39 Anne Jackel, 'Too Late? Recent Developments in Romanian Cinema,' in *The Seeing Century: Film, Vision, and Identity*, ed. Wendy Everett, Amsterdam: Rodopi, 2000, 106–7.
40 *The BFI Companion to Eastern European and Russian Cinema*, ed. Richard Taylor, Nancy Wood, Julian Graffy, and Dina Iordanova, London: British Film Institute, 2000, 701.
41 Wade Major, '*Train of Life*,' at www.boxoffice.com/scrpts/fiw.dll?getreview&whare=names&terms=train-of-lif (accessed July 31, 2002); Stefan Steinberg, '"Not to Banalize, not to Rewrite, but to Keep the Discussion Going": Radu Mihaileanu's *Train of Life*,' November 26, 1998, at www.wsws.org/arts/1998/nov1998/tra-n26.shtml (accessed July 31, 2002); *Underground*, directed by Emir Kusterica (France, Germany, Hungary, 1995). See Goran Goric, *Notes from the Underground: The Cinema of Emir Kusterica* (London: Wallflower Press, 2001).
42 'An Interview between Father and Son,' *The Shtetl Times*, *Train of Life* Press Kit, 3.
43 Steinberg, 'Not to Banalize,' 2.

PART 3

Historical films and identity

HISTORY IS OFTEN ASSUMED TO PLAY A ROLE in the shaping of individual, group and national identity. That is, histories are seen as encouraging us to think of ourselves as selves that persist over time and to connect or disconnect ourselves from others in imagined groups. Those imagined groups might be local, short-lived and transient, or may persist over many generations and cover populations across the globe. Identity is thus not a property of persons, but more properly refers to the processes by which we imagine ourselves as individuals or as a part of various groups. Historians have written a great deal on the ways in which individuals have in different times and places thought of themselves and placed themselves and others in groups. Imperial, postcolonial and women's historians, for instance, have been interested in the ways in which forms of representation and language foster economic, political and social inequalities. As a form of representation, film is thought to play a key role in fostering identity formation. This is thought to be due not only to its global reach, but also to its purported influence on viewer beliefs, aspirations and behaviours.

The readings in Part 3 offer an introduction to the ways in which scholars connect historical films with current-day problems and notions of identity. In that sense, they all affirm Pierre Sorlin's observation (see reading 1) that historical films tell us more about their presents than the past. Moreover, they show us the remarkable variety of pasts that are assumed to point to the present. Assembling a representative body of readings on identity and historical film is impossible because of the sheer number and global scope of publications on the topic. I have therefore selected a range of publications on historical films and US identity as a case study of the ways in which films are read as being about the present. This case study, I believe, is not only useful because of the global position of the US as a film exporter and as a political and economic power, but also because it highlights the sheer range of histories that are assumed to play a role in identity formation. If the authors of all of the extracts reproduced in this section are to be believed, then ancient Rome and Britain in the dark ages, as well as World War II, the Vietnam War and the United Nation's Operation in Somalia in 1992–3, are thought to offer diagnoses of recent social, economic and political problems in the US.

Part 3 opens with Robert Burgoyne's application of Alison Landsberg's concept of 'prosthetic memory' to the film *Forrest Gump* (1994). Prosthetic memory, we recall from the Introduction, refers to the ways in which film viewers take on experiences represented in films. Burgoyne's reading of *Forrest Gump* forms part of his argument in the book *Film Nation* (1997) that 'the link between national identity and narrative is especially apparent in the American cinema'. In distinction from his readings of *Glory* (1989), *Thunderheart* (1992), *Born on the Fourth of July* (1989) and *JFK* (1991), however, he sees *Forrest Gump* as encouraging the construction of single, unproblematic, conservative narrative of nation. Through its use of an 'everyman' lead character and visual effects to place that man – and thus for Burgoyne, viewers – in the past, Burgoyne sees *Forrest Gump* as presenting a more palatable account of events in order to construct a 'virtual nation' whose historical debts have all been forgiven and whose disabilities have been corrected. In so doing, the 'traumas' of the 1960s and 1970s – notably racial antagonism and the fight for women's rights – are repressed.

Repression is also a key theme in Gaylyn Studlar and David Desser's analysis of *Rambo: First Blood Part II* (1985), which was first published as a review in *Film Quarterly* in 1988. Desser and Studlar see in *Rambo* the rehabilitation of the US's history in Vietnam through a double act of displacement. First, *Rambo*, like other combat films made in the US in the 1980s and early 1990s, replaces the question 'Were we right to fight in Vietnam?' with another, 'What is our obligation to the veterans of the war?' In this act of substitution, the victims of the war become the draftees or enlisted men who live with a war that is never over. Second, when John Rambo is offered the chance to rescue MIAs, his asking 'Are they going to let us win this time?' indicates a chance for redress. That redress takes place not through government action, however, but through the violent acts of a hypermasculine, half-breed – half German, half American Indian – body. The US's confidence in its past – undermined so painfully by the Vietnam War, and also by the feminist movement – is thus restored not through collective political acknowledgement of 'trauma', but through a lone fetishised male body. As with repressions by the 'young and childish', Desser and Studlar conclude that in US Vietnam War films we encounter a 'luxuriating in the symptoms of a desperate ideological repression manifested in the inability to speak of or remember the painful past, a cultural hysteria in which violence must substitute for understanding, victimization for responsibility, the personal for the political'.

Marilyn B. Young sees repression and displacement in the service of 'kicking the Vietnam syndrome' at work in a wider range of films than that examined by Burgoyne, Desser and Studlar. For her, a key feature of combat films ranging from

Saving Private Ryan (1998) to *Black Hawk Down* (2001) is the marginalisation of political questions – many of which do not elicit clear or comforting answers – by what she calls a 'band of brothers' motif. In *Saving Private Ryan*, the Second World War is reduced to the rescue of one man, and in *Black Hawk Down*, the US's disastrous experiences in Somalia as part of a UN Operation in 1992–3 are localised in the relationship between soldiers. As the character Hoot (Eric Bana) explains: 'When I get home and people ask me, "Hey, Hoot, why do you do it, man? What are you? Some kind of war junkie?" I won't say a goddamn word. Why? They won't understand. They won't understand why we do it. They won't understand that it's about the men next to you. And that's it. That's all it is.' US soldiers sacrifice their lives only for one another, and their demonstrations of courage and suffering allow all conflicts – including the Vietnam War represented in *We Were Soldiers* (2002) – to become ones that can be memorialised proudly.

The idea of historical film as a mechanism that allows viewers to repress or rewrite 'history that hurts' – as Desser and Studlar call it – takes in ancient as well as modern settings. In Susan Aronstein's view, for instance, the filmic adaptation of Arthurian legend in *First Knight* (1995) aims to reassure viewers that Bill Clinton's intervention in Bosnia would allow the US to fulfil its 'humanitarian responsibilities to a global village' without being bogged down in a 'deadly quagmire'. The connection between Arthur and the fight for freedom and democracy through 'necessary violence' is also present in the post-September 11 adaptation of the legend, *King Arthur* (2004), which while it offers a 'direct condemnation of the cold war rhetoric and attitudes that led to the war in Iraq', and questions the distinction between 'patriot' and 'terrorists', nonetheless sees Arthur become 'the ultimate patriot, the man defending his country against the invading forces of chaos'.

Finally, in Monica Silveira Cyrino's estimation, *Gladiator* (2000) is as much about the US's need to think about itself as a secure social, economic and political superpower – as demonstrated through its liking of large televised sporting events and quest for conservative home, family and spiritual values – as it is about ancient Rome. Indeed Cyrino sees the revival of the 'swords and sandals' genre of films set in the ancient world as answering the US's need for social and international security, even before the events of September 11.

In combination, these appraisals of a varied range of historical films reveal the extent to which scholars see film as fostering identity formation. Moreover, it is clear that they see film as fostering the repression of any 'history that hurts'. Whether all historical films foster the repression or rewriting of history in the service of social integration and even depoliticisation is the focus of Part 4.

Robert Burgoyne

PROSTHETIC MEMORY/ TRAUMATIC MEMORY

Forrest Gump (1994)

'Prosthetic Memory/Traumatic Memory: *Forrest Gump* (1994)', *Screening the Past,* no. 6, 1999, at www.latrobe.edu.au/screeningthepast/.

IN THIS ESSAY I would like to consider some of the ramifications of a widely accepted yet undertheorized idea: that the preeminence of the moving image in contemporary culture has reshaped our collective imaginary relation to history. This widely circulated observation has been the subject of much anguished commentary from the widest possible range of critics. Concern about the cinema's ostensible distortion of historical reality or of the culture's willingness to substitute glossy images for historical understanding and insight emanate from left, right, and center. Although I disagree with many of these arguments, which tend to ignore the complex and sophisticated theories of history underpinning many historical films, the real issue driving these critiques is a fundamental one: films that take history as their subject are so controversial, I believe, mainly because of the extraordinary social power and influence that seem to have accrued to what has been called the cinematic rewriting of history. Although academic and even mainstream critics tend to focus on questions concerning the limits of fact and fiction and the erosion of the presumed boundary between realist and imaginative discourse that these films bring into relief, these questions are, I think, secondary to this more central concern with the seemingly unbounded social power wielded by the cinema in its representation of the past.

Now to some extent, the impression of overwhelming cinematic influence over the historical imagination is exaggerated. Films that take history as their subject are bounded by the public sphere in which they participate. Usually, a cascade of reviews, editorial commentary, academic criticism, rejoinders, defenses, conference presentations, web sites, and even, in the case of Oliver Stone's *JFK* (1991), town meetings, serve to keep these films 'in check'.[1] Nevertheless, the ferocity of the controversies over films such as *JFK*, *Schindler's List* (1993), *Malcolm X* (1992), *Nixon* (1995), *Jefferson in Paris* (1995), and *Forrest Gump*, to name a few, point to the idea that film has somehow claimed the mantle of authenticity and meaningfulness with relation to the past – not necessarily of accuracy or fidelity to the record, but of meaningfulness, understood in terms of emotional and affective truth. Film, in effect, appears to invoke the emotional certitude we associate with memory. Like memory, film is associated with the body; it engages the viewer at the somatic level, immersing the spectator in experiences and impressions that, like memories, seem to be 'burned in'.[2]

In this essay, I would like to develop the notion of film as an apparatus of cultural memory, and to compare it with the recent fascination with other popular forms of engagement with the past, such as experiential museums, historical reenactments and historical theme parks, and the burgeoning popularity of historical pageants, such as the Dream Cruise in Detroit, in which tens of thousands of classic car collectors parade down Woodward Avenue over the course of a summer weekend.

I will begin by summarizing an important argument that has been made by Alison Landsberg, who has coined the striking term 'prosthetic memory' to describe the way mass cultural technologies of memory enable individuals to experience, as if they were memories, events through which they themselves did not live.[3] She cites the growing popularity of experiential museums, such as the Holocaust Museum, historical reenactments, including the recent D-Day celebrations, and historical films such as *Schindler's List* as evidence of a widespread cultural desire to reexperience the past in a sensuous form, and stresses the power of what she calls experiential mass cultural forms to make historical or political events meaningful in a personal, local way. The new modes of experience, sensation, and history that are made available in American mass culture, she writes, 'have profoundly altered the individual's relationship to both their own memories and to the archive of collective cultural memories'. Defining the concept of prosthetic memory as 'memories that circulate publicly, that are not organically based, but that are nonetheless experienced with one's own body – by means of a wide range of cultural technologies,' Landsberg argues that prosthetic memories, especially those afforded by the cinema, 'become part of one's personal archive of experience'. Citing psychological investigations from the 1930s on 'emotional possession' as well as works by Siegfried Kracauer and Steven Shaviro on the relation between film and somatic response, Landsberg maintains that 'the experience within the movie theater and the memories that the cinema affords – despite the fact that the spectator did not live through them – might be as significant in constructing, or deconstructing, the spectator's identity as any experience that s/he actually lived through'. The artificial but real experiences afforded by the cinema 'might actually install in individuals "symptoms" through which they didn't actually live, but to which they subsequently have a kind of experiential relationship'. Although the production and dissemination of memories that are defined not by organic, individual experience but by simulation and reenactment are potentially dangerous, posing the threat of alienation and revisionism, prosthetic memories also enable a sensuous engagement with past lives and past experiences that, Landsberg argues, can serve as 'the basis for mediated collective identification'.[4]

These arguments appear to have a particular salience for understanding the popularity and the larger cultural significance of a film such as *Forrest Gump*. In many ways, the film appears to literalize the concept of prosthetic memory. It explicitly takes on the role of offering an experiential relationship to history, inserting the main character, and by extension, the viewer, into what appears to be a physical, literal relationship to actual historical figures, splicing the character Gump into fictionalized interactions with archival film images of JFK, LBJ, George Wallace, Nixon, and John Lennon. What Landsberg calls the 'widespread desire on the part of Americans to experience and to live history,' the desire to experience history in a 'personal, bodily way,' is exemplified in *Forrest Gump*. The most spectacular and provocative aspect of the film's seizure of memory – its use of digital technology to 'master' the past by 'remastering' archival material in order to graft the figure of the main character into historical film and television footage – clearly is meant to solicit a mnemonic and mimetic response on the part of the viewer, suturing the viewer into a past they had not led, enabling the viewer to inhabit, through identification with the main character, an actual historical scene; the cinema in *Forrest Gump* is thus revealed, in the most emphatic way, to be an instrument that allows individuals to 'experience a bodily, mimetic encounter with a collective past they never actually led'.[5] This suturing of the spectator, through identification with the character Forrest Gump, into an actual historical scene collapses the distinction between the personal and the historical and foregrounds the multiple and complicated relations between individual and collective memory and history in the age of cinema and media culture.

Memory, in the traditional sense, describes an individual relation to the past, a bodily, physical relation to an actual experience that is significant enough to inform and colour the subjectivity of the rememberer. History, on the other hand, is traditionally conceived as impersonal, the realm of public events that have occurred outside the archive of personal experience. But in contemporary media culture, the most significant 'historical' events are often transformed into 'experiences' that shape and inform the subjectivity of the individual viewer: with the media continually and effortlessly re-presenting the past, history, once thought of as an impersonal phenomenon, has been replaced by 'experiential' collective memory. Landsberg sees this as a positive development, arguing that the mimetic, bodily experience of the historical past afforded by the mass media can make particular histories or pasts available to people across existing stratifications of race, class, gender, and generation. History, she argues in effect, must become like memory in order to inform subjectivity, in order to change and alter consciousness, which is the basis for any kind of political alliance or action. The mass media can give people an experience of history that is felt at the deepest emotional and somatic level, felt as memory is felt, giving rise to identification and empathy across existing social divisions.

I find these ideas compelling, and I feel they go a long way toward explaining the desire, the cultural appetite for experiences that go beyond our own temporal framework, a desire realized and reinforced in the burgeoning popularity of official and vernacular forms of public rememoration. The fascination with memory and history in contemporary society can be seen, from the perspective opened up by the concept of prosthetic memory, as a salutary development: prosthetic memories can become the grounds for political alliances and for new collective frameworks that cut across existing social divisions. Insofar as prosthetic memories are not intrinsic to any individual, not limited to the organic experience of any one person or group, they are equally available to everyone, and thus have democratizing potential. As Landsberg concludes, 'prosthetic memories have the potential to generate something like public spheres of memory'.[6]

However, there is another, less optimistic way of viewing the rising importance and influence of social memory and its interconnection with the mass media. The physical, experiential relation to the historical event and the historical past that mass technology affords may inhibit the narrative closure that storytelling, and narrative history, allow. Rather than generating historical amnesia, as is so often claimed, film and media may generate its opposite, an inability to stop obsessing about an event. As Thomas Elsaesser has written:

> [W]hat of the memory of events which live in the culture because of the images they have left, etched on our retinas, too painful to recall, too disturbing not to remember? 'Do you remember the day Kennedy was shot?' really means 'Do you remember the day you watched Kennedy being shot all day on television?' No longer is storytelling the culture's meaning-making response; an activity closer to therapeutic practice has taken over, with acts of re-telling, remembering, and repeating all pointing in the direction of obsession, fantasy, trauma.[7]

In Elsaesser's formulation, the mass media create cultural memories that resist the kind of narrative closure associated with story-telling, with narrative history. He asks what obscure urge is satisfied by the compulsion to repeat that seems to drive the mass media in its continuous presenting and re-presenting of historical trauma. Hayden White has described twentieth century historical events as 'modernist;' the lack of closure, the fragmentation and dissociation of one event from another, the inability of historians and the public at large to 'master' and contain events in narrative form, may be a consequence, he writes, of the unprecedented scale and compound contexts of 'modernist' historical events, such as the Holocaust, the Vietnam War, or the assassination of JFK.[8] Taking White's hypothesis one step further, Elsaesser suggests that the lack of closure in modernist historical events may be a property of the mass media itself and its take on history, which tends to create in the spectator symptoms of obsession and trauma. In the optimistic account of prosthetic memory provided by Landsberg, the somatic powers of mass technology to produce something like symptoms in the spectator create the potential for empathic identification, for new collective frameworks, for public spheres based on memory. In Elsaesser's less sanguine perspective, the burning in of memories via the media – burned in to the point that they create symptoms in the spectator – speak not to empathy and new social alliances but rather to cultural obsession, fantasy, and trauma.

In the film *Forrest Gump*, we can find both aspects of the contemporary historical imagination at work. The public reception the film received gives credence to the notion of a public sphere based on memory – a sphere of social discourse and contestation around history. But from another perspective, the response to the film betrays a good deal of cultural obsession, fantasy, and trauma. The film itself dwells on the subject of memory and its relation to history; it illustrates at the formal, narrative, and thematic levels the current preeminence of memory in the construction of concepts of the historical past and particularly, in the construction of concepts of nation and national belonging. Memory is thematized here as the connective tissue that binds the characters to the narrative of nation, as the webwork that supplies the forms and sites of identification that are essential to the emotions of national belonging. The film places in relief the power of memory and narratives of memory to create subjective connections to the national past, to call forth the sense of 'I' and 'We' that makes the national narrative compelling and meaningful: in this respect, it appears to illustrate the positive potential of mediated memory to create an interface with 'past lives, past experiences, past bodies,' so as to ground individual subjectivities 'in a world of experience larger than one's own modal subjectivity'.[9]

In foregrounding memory as the connective tissue of nation, however, *Forrest Gump* reveals itself to be a film that functions, more deliberately than most, as an ideological force seeking to redefine national identity. In evoking memory as the register of national belonging, the film can effectively construct an image of nation that can exist apart from, or float free of, the historical traumas of the sixties and seventies. The guileless hero Gump, who comes across as a kind of national saint, narrates his own story in a way that emphasizes certain zones of social and cultural coherence within the deeply fractious social reality of the period, reordering the past in such a way that the political and social ruptures of the sixties can be reclaimed as sites of national identification. The film can thus be seen, from this angle, as an apparatus that functions precisely like a prosthesis, supplementing or even replacing organic memory, which in the context of the sixties might be defined as dysfunctional, cultural memories that in their organic form cannot be integrated into the larger projects of nation, that have been exceptionally difficult to assimilate, such as the Vietnam War. Social memory in *Forrest Gump* is in effect refunctioned in a way that allows it to be integrated into the traditional narrative of nation, producing an image of social consensus built around memory.

In using the concept of prosthetic memory in this fashion, I depart from Landsberg's approach by emphasizing its relation to another apparatus of memory, that of the national narrative. *Forrest Gump*, I feel, revises the contested and multiple memories of the sixties in such a way that they become prosthetically enhanced – functional for the purposes of a traditional, ultra-conservative narrative of nation. The film sets forth a narrative of memory whose transparent purpose seems to be that of 'managing' the national traumas, the crises in national identity, that defined the sixties and seventies and that continue to trouble the nation's self-image. The diverse and contested cultural memories of the sixties are refunctioned and redefined in Forrest Gump so as to produce an improved image of nation, at once potent, coherent, and 'of the people' – a virtual nation in which the positive elements of national identification are segregated from the historical actions undertaken in its name. As Tom Conley aptly puts it, the project of national reclamation undertaken by Forrest Gump depends on the film's 'wiping the slate clean of female presence,' and on erasing the national canvas of social, and particularly, racial antagonism.[10]

The role of film and video as an apparatus of memory, a technology that burns in memories so as to create a form of bodily relation to events that one has not organically experienced, is emphatically on display in *Forrest Gump*. Its powerful appeal to a form of ethnic nostalgia, or to what Michael Kammen more positively calls the 'emotional discovery of America,' is an exemplary instance of the widespread cultural desire to connect to the past and to embrace experiential forms of knowledge.[11] But the film also displays a particular kind of postmodern hubris, the faith that the cinema can 'redeem the past, rescue the real, and even rescue that which was never real'.[12] In trying to rescue that which was never real, the film discloses the profoundly unstable ground that memory, unaccompanied by history, unannotated by fact, provides as a source of experiential knowledge and collective identification.

Notes

1 See Thomas Elsaesser, 'Subject positions, speaking positions: from *Holocaust*, *Our Hitler*, and *Heimat* to *Shoah* and *Schindler's List*,' in *The Persistence of History: Cinema, Television, and the Modern Event*, ed. Vivian Sobchack, New York: Routledge, 1995, p. 167.

2 Friedrich Nietzsche, *On the Genealogy of Morals*, trans. W. Kaufmann, New York: Vintage, 1969, p. 61: '[i]f something is to stay in memory, it must be burned in.'

3 See Alison Landsberg, 'Prosthetic memory: the logics and politics of memory in modern American culture,' Ph.D. dissertation, University of Chicago, 1996. See also Landsberg's 'Prosthetic memory: *Total Recall* and *Blade Runner*,' in *Cyberspace/Cyberbodies/Cyberpunk: Cultures of Technological Embodiment*, eds. Mike Featherstone and Roger Burrows, London: Sage, 1995, pp. 175–89; and 'America, the Holocaust, and the mass culture of memory: toward a radical politics of empathy,' *New German Critique*, 1997, vol. 71, pp. 63–86.

4 A. Landsberg, 'Prosthetic memory,' p. 4.

5 Ibid., p. 21.

6 Ibid., p. 25.

7 T. Elsaesser, 'Subject positions,' p. 146.

8 Hayden White, 'The fact of modernism: the fading of the historical event,' in V. Sobchack, *The Persistence of History*, pp. 17–38.

9 A. Landsberg, 'Prosthetic memory,' p. 30.

10 Tom Conley, letter to author, 15 October 1995.

11 Michael Kammen, *The Mystic Chords of Memory: The Transformation of Tradition in American Culture*, New York: Knopf, 1991, p. 299.

12 T. Elsaesser, 'Subject positions,' p. 166.

Reading 13

D. Desser and G. Studlar

NEVER HAVING TO SAY YOU'RE SORRY

Rambo's rewriting of the Vietnam War

'Never Having to Say You're Sorry: Rambo's Rewriting of the Vietnam War', *Film Quarterly*, 1988, vol. 42(1), pp. 9–16.

'HISTORY IS WHAT HURTS,' writes Fredric Jameson in *The Political Unconscious*. 'It is what refuses desire and sets inexorable limits to individual as well as collective praxis.'[1] The pain of history, its delimiting effect on action, is often seen as a political, a cultural, a national liability. Therefore, contemporary history has been the subject of an ideological battle which seeks to rewrite, to rehabilitate, controversial and ambiguous events through the use of symbols. One arena of on-going cultural concern in the United States is our involvement in Vietnam. It seems clear that reconstituting an image – a 'memory' – of Vietnam under the impetus of Reaganism appears to fulfill a specific ideological mission. Yet the complexity of this reconstitution or rewriting has not been fully realized, either in film studies or in political discourse. Neither has the manner in which the Reaganite right coopted often contradictory and competing discourses surrounding the rehabilitation of Vietnam been adequately addressed. A string of 'rightwing' Vietnam films has been much discussed, but their reliance on the specific mechanism of *displacement* to achieve a symbolic or mythic reworking of the war has not been recognized. Also insufficiently acknowledged is the fact that, far from being a unique occurrence, the current attempt to rewrite Vietnam, and the era of the 1960s more broadly, follows a well-established pattern of reworking the past in postwar Japan and Germany. Although it would be naive to advance a simple parallelist conception of history that foregrounds obvious analogies at the expense of important historical differences, the rewriting of the Vietnam War evidences a real, if complicated, link to previous situations where nations have moved beyond revising history to rewriting it through specific cultural processes.

That America's 'rewriting' of the Vietnam War is ideological in nature, of a particular political postwar moment, is clear *a priori*. But the site at which it is occurring is perhaps less clear and therefore more significant. For what is being rewritten might justifiably be called a 'trauma,' a shock to the cultural system. Commonly used phrases such as 'healing the wounds of Vietnam' are quite revelatory of this idea, but do not grasp the difficulty of any cultural recuperation from shock. In reality, the attempt to cope with the national trauma of Vietnam confronts less a physical than a psychic trauma. The mechanisms through which healing can occur, therefore, are more devious, more in need, if you will, of 'analysis.'

The central question in the problem of the Vietnam War in history is: How can the US deal with not only its defeat in Vietnam, but with the fact that it never should have been there in the first place? By answering this question, the United States would confront the potentially painful revelations of its involvement in Vietnam, which is reminiscent of those questions faced by other nations: How can Japan cope with its role in the Pacific aggression of WWII? How can the West Germans resolve the Nazi era? These questions are virtually unanswerable without admission of guilt. But if, as Freud maintained, individuals find guilt intolerable and attempt to repress it, why should cultures be any different?[2] And if guilt, in spite of repression, always finds an unconscious avenue of expression in the individual's life, we must similarly mark a return of the repressed in cultural discourse as well.

In one respect, the return of the repressed explains the number of Vietnam films appearing simultaneously, or at least in waves of films during the 1980s. Given the nature of film production, the box-office success of any individual film cannot account for so many Vietnam films appearing within a short period of time. Nor can the popularity of such films, left and right, automatically be taken as an indicator of psychic healing. On the contrary, their coexistence might be read as a register of the nation's ambivalent feelings over the war, and ambivalence, Freud tells us, is one of the necessary ingredients in the creation of guilt feelings.[3]

Psychoanalytic therapy maintains that to be healed, one must recall the memory of the trauma which has been repressed by a sense of guilt. Otherwise, a 'faulty' memory or outright amnesia covers the truth, which lies somewhere deep in the unconscious. The more recent the trauma, the more quickly the memory can be recalled; the more severe the original trauma, the more deeply the memory is buried, the more completely it is repressed. In this respect, cultures can be said to act like individuals – they simply cannot live with overwhelming guilt. Like individual trauma, cultural trauma must be 'forgotten,' but the guilt of such traumas continues to grow. However, as Freud notes, the mechanism of repression is inevitably flawed: the obstinately repressed material ultimately breaks through and manifests itself in unwelcome symptoms.[4] In 1959 Theodor Adorno, calling upon the psychoanalytic explanation of psychic trauma in his discussion of postwar Germany, observed that the psychological damage of a repressed collective past often emerges through dangerous political gestures: defensive overreaction to situations that do not really constitute attacks, 'lack of affect' in response to serious issues, and repression of 'what was known or half-known.'[5] Popular discourse often equates forgetting the past with mastering it, says Adorno, but an unmastered past cannot remain safely buried: the mechanisms of repression will bring it into the present in a form which may very well lead to 'the politics of catastrophe.'[6]

One example of the politics of catastrophe was Germany's own unmastered response to World War I. Although Hitler's rise to power was complex (as is America's rewriting of the Vietnam War), there was a crucial element of psychic trauma that enabled Hitler to step in and 'heal' the nation. In *The Weimar Chronicle*, Alex de Jonge offers a telling account of an element of this trauma. At the end of the war, the Germans were unable to comprehend that their army, which proudly marched through the Brandenburg gate, had been defeated. Instead of blaming the enemy, or the imperial regime's failed policy of militarism, the Germans embraced the myth of the 'stab in the back.' Defeat was explained as a conspiracy concocted by those Germans who signed the surrender.[7] William Shirer has noted that the widespread 'fanatical' belief in this postwar myth was maintained even though 'the facts which exposed its deceit lay all around.'[8] This act of 'scapegoating' evidences both the desire to rewrite history and to repress collective cultural guilt and responsibility. Resistance to the truth meant that, for Nazi Germany, ideology functioned as 'memory,' fantasy substituted for historical discourse, and the welcome simplicity of myth replaced the ambiguity of past experience. While WWI should have logically signalled an end to German militarist impulses, it served as merely a prelude to a 'founding myth' for its most virulent expression.[9]

This example, replayed in many more contemporary realms, including the current discourse surrounding Vietnam, allows us to posit a 'will to myth' – a communal need, a cultural drive – for a reconstruction of the national past in light of the present, a present which is, by definition of necessity, better. Claude Lévi-Strauss has suggested that primitive cultures which have no past (i.e., do not conceive of or distinguish between a past and present) use myth as the primary means of dealing with cultural contradictions. Modern societies, of course, are cognizant of a past, but frequently find it filled with unpleasant truths and half-known facts, so they set about rewriting it. The mass media, including cinema and television, have proven to be important mechanisms whereby this rewriting – this re-imaging – of the past can occur. Indeed, it was Hitler's far-reaching use of the media that allowed him to solidify the National Socialist state and set his nation on its monstrous course in a carefully orchestrated exploitation of the will to myth.[10]

A common strategy by which 'the will to myth' asserts itself is through the substitution of one question for another. This mechanism is invoked by Lévi-Strauss as he notes how frequently one question, or problem, mythically substitutes for another concept by the narrative patterns of the myths. In dream interpretation, psychoanalysis calls this strategy 'displacement.' If we allow the notion that cultures are like individuals (and recall the commonplace analogy that films are 'like' dreams), we should not be surprised to find displacement occurring in popular discourse. Displacement accounts for the phenomenon of 'scapegoating,' for instance, on both individual and cultural levels. But there are more devious examples, more complex situations in which the displacement goes almost unrecognized, as has been the case thus far with the current wave of Vietnam films and the project of rewriting the image of the war.

In the case of the recent rightwing Vietnam War films, the fundamental textual mechanism of displacement that has not been recognized is that the question 'Were we right to fight in Vietnam?' has been replaced (displaced) by the question 'What is our obligation to the veterans of the war?' Responsibility to and validation of the veterans is not the same as validating our participation in the conflict in the first place. Yet answering the second question 'mythically' rewrites the answer to the first.

One of the key strategies in this displacement of the crucial question of America's Vietnam involvement is that of 'victimization.' The Japanese have used this method of coping with their role as aggressor in World War II, just as the Nazis used it to rewrite WWI. The Japanese soldiers who fought in the war now are regarded as victims of a military government that betrayed the soldiers and the populace. The Japanese do not try to justify their actions in the war nor even deal with the fact that their policies started the war in the first place. Rather, they try to shift (displace) blame for the war onto wartime leaders who are no longer alive. Contemporary Germany, too, relies on this strategy in an attempt now to rehabilitate West Germany's Nazi past. Strangely enough, its appropriation was given public sanction by President Reagan in his visit to Bitburg cemetery.

That America's problem of/with the Vietnam War might be related to Germany's Nazi past and the controversy over Reagan's visit to Bitburg is addressed in an interesting, if disturbing way, in a letter quoted by Alvin Rosenfeld. The letter writer claimed that Reagan's trip to Bitburg signified 'that we are beginning to forgive the German people for their past sins, in much the same way that America has begun to seek forgiveness for Vietnam.'[11] But is America (or, for that matter, West Germany) actually seeking 'forgiveness' for the past? Reagan told the Germans at Bitburg what they wanted to hear, that the German soldiers buried in the military cemetery were themselves victims of the Nazis 'just as surely as the victims of the concentration camps.'[12] The American resistance to admitting culpability for Vietnam, like the Bitburg affair, revolves around a collective cultural drama of memory and forgetting. In essence, what we find in Japan's revision of its wartime history, Reagan's Bitburg speech, and many of the Vietnam films of the 1980s, is that the appeal to victimization via 'the will to myth' is a powerful rhetorical tool to apply to the problem of guilt. To be a victim means never having to say you're sorry.

Two waves of Vietnam War films in the 1980s have been claimed: the rightwing revisionism of *Uncommon Valor* (1983), *Missing in Action* (1984), and *Rambo: First Blood II* (1985); and the ostensibly more realistic strain of Vietnam films emerging with *Platoon* (1986), *Hamburger Hill* (1987), and *Full Metal Jacket* (1987). At first glance, the comic book heroics of the earlier films seem antithetical to the 'realism' of the later ones, but in spite of such differences the films are actually very much alike in their dependence on the strategy of victimization. The films all work to evoke sympathy for the American GI (today's veteran) and pay tribute to the act of remembering the war as private hell. While the rightwing films, especially *Rambo*, justify a private war of national retribution for the personal sacrifice of vets, the realist films demonstrate the process of victimization of the draftee or enlisted man. *Platoon* even goes so far as to transpose its conflict from the specificity of Vietnam into the realm of the transcendental: the two sergeants, Barnes and Elias, become mythic figures, warrior archetypes, battling for the soul of Chris (Christ?). The crucifixion image as Barnes kills Elias is too clear to miss, while Chris becomes the sacrificial victim who survives.

The rightwing films, especially *Rambo*, most clearly demonstrate the strategy of mythic substitution or displacement in the use of an oft-repeated rumor: that American MIAs are still being held captive in southeast Asia. That *Rambo* was not only the most commercially successful of all the Vietnam films thus far, but also became culturally ubiquitous (a television cartoon series, formidable tie-in merchandise sales, and, like *Star Wars*, becoming part of political discourse) speaks to the power of the will to myth. The need to believe in the MIAs gives credence to the view that the Vietnamese are now and *therefore have always been* an inhuman and cruel enemy. Vietnam's alleged actions in *presently* holding American prisoners serves as an index of our essential rightness in fighting such an enemy *in the past*. Moreover, our alleged unwillingness to confront Vietnam on the MIAs issue is taken to be an index of the government's cowardice in its Vietnam policy: Confrontation would mean confirmation. The American bureaucracy remains spineless: They didn't let us win then, and they won't let us win again.

Consequently, while it appears to embrace the militaristic ideology of the radical right, *Rambo* simultaneously delegitimizes governmental authority and questions the ideological norms of many other Vietnam films. Within its formula of militaristic zeal, *Rambo* sustains an atmosphere of post-Watergate distrust of government. The MIAs, John Rambo's captive comrades, are regarded only as 'a couple of ghosts' by the cynical official representative of the government, Murdock, who lies about his service in Vietnam. He is willing to sacrifice the MIAs to maintain the status quo of international relations. President Reagan's portrait graces the wall behind Murdock's desk, but Murdock is a 'committee' member, aligned, it seems, with Congress, not with the avowed conservatism of the executive branch. Colonel Trauptman, Rambo's Special Forces commander and surrogate father-figure, reminds Murdock that the United States reneged on reparations to the Vietnamese, who retaliated by keeping the unransomed captive Americans. Failure to rescue the MIAs is the direct result of their economic expendability. Murdock says the situation has not changed; Congress will not appropriate billions to rescue these 'ghosts.'

Abandoned once by their country (or rather, 'government'), the POWs/MIAs are abandoned yet again in a highly symbolic scene: airdropped into Vietnam to find and photograph any living MIAs/POWs, Rambo locates an American; the rescue helicopter hovers above them as Vietnamese soldiers close in. Murdock abruptly aborts the mission. Rambo is captured and submitted to shocking (literally) tortures. His Russian interrogators taunt him with the intercepted radio message in which he was ordered abandoned. Rambo escapes, but not before he swears revenge against Murdock.

The mythical MIA prisoners may represent the ultimate *American* victims of the war, but *Rambo: First Blood II* also draws on the victimization strategy on yet another level, through the continued exploitation of its vet hero, John Rambo. The film opens with an explosion of rock at a quarry. A tilt down reveals inmates at forced labor. Colonel Trauptman arrives to recruit Rambo for a special mission. Separated by an imposing prison yard fence, Rambo tells Trauptman that he would rather stay in prison than be released because 'at least in here I know where I stand.' The Vietnam vet is the eighties version of the World War I vet, the 'forgotten man' of the Depression era. Like James Allen in Warner Brothers most famous social consciousness film, *I am a Fugitive from a Chain Gang* (1932), Rambo is a Congressional Medal of Honor winner who feels 'out of step' with a society that has used and discarded him. Condemned as a common criminal, Rambo is released from military prison and promised a pardon because his unique combat skills are again required by the government. He does not realize that he is also needed for political purposes. He will provide the gloss of a veteran's testimonial to the mission's findings, which have been predetermined: no Americans will be found.

As far removed from an appeal to victimization as Rambo's aggressive received myth-image might appear to be, his personal mission of victory and vengeance crucially hinges on his status as present and past victim, as neglected, misunderstood, and exploited veteran. Ironically, in a film that has no memory of the historical complexities of the Vietnam War, Rambo's personal obsession with the traumatic past of Vietnam is cited as the truest measure of his unswerving patriotism. Even Colonel Trauptman feels compelled to tell him to forget the war. Rambo replies: '. . . as long as I'm alive – it's still alive.'

Stallone explained the film in an interview: 'I stand for ordinary Americans, losers a lot of them. They don't understand big, international politics. Their country tells them to fight in Vietnam? They fight.'[13] Rambo and the captive MIAs are the innocent victims of wartime and postwar government machinations that preclude victories. By implicating American policy and government bureaucracy in past defeat and current inaction, the film exonerates the regular soldier from culpability in American defeat as it pointedly criticizes a technologically obsessed, mercenary American military establishment. This echoes both the Japanese strategy of blaming dead leaders for WWII and Reagan's declaration at Bitburg that the Holocaust was not the responsibility of a nation or an electorate, but an 'awful evil started by one man.'[14] Similarly, in his statements on Vietnam, Reagan has employed a strategy of blaming Vietnam defeat on those who cannot be named: 'We are just beginning to realize how we were led astray when it came to Vietnam.'[15]

'Are they going to let us win this time?' Rambo first asks Trauptman when the colonel comes to pull Rambo out of the stockade rock pile for sins committed in the presequel. Trauptman says that it is up to Rambo, but the colonel is unaware that Murdock is merely using Rambo to prove to the American public that there are no POWs. As the film's ad proclaims: 'They sent him on a mission and set him up to fail.' Rambo is the fall guy forced into extraordinary 'moral' action by the ordinary immoral inaction of bureaucrats. According to official standards, Rambo is an aberration, the loose cannon on the deck who subverts the official system, but in doing so he affirms the long-cherished American cult of the individual who goes outside the law to get the job done. He ignores the 'artificial' restraints of the law to uphold a higher moral law, but (unlike Ollie) Rambo manages to avoid the final irony of conspiracy-making.

In rewriting the Vietnam defeat, *Rambo* attempts to solve the contradiction posed by its portrayal of the Vietnam vet as powerless victim *and* suprematist warrior by reviving the powerful American mythos of a 'regeneration through violence.' Identified by Richard Slotkin as the basis of many frontier tales, this inter-text illuminates the way in which *Rambo*'s narrative structure resembles that of the archetypal captivity narrative described by Timothy Flint, whose *Indian Wars of the*

West, Biographical Memoir of Daniel Boone (1828–33) typified this form of early frontier story. In this formula, a lone frontier adventurer is ambushed and held captive by Indians. They recognize his superior abilities and wish to adopt him, but he escapes, reaches an outpost, and with the help of a handful of other settlers wins a gruesome siege against hundreds of his former captors.[16] Sanctified by the trial of captivity, the hunter confronts an Otherness, represented by the wilderness and the Indians, that threatens to assimilate him into barbarism. Through vengeance, he finds his identity – as white, civilized, Christian male.

Rambo's war of selective extermination inverts the wartime situation of Vietnam into a hallucinated frontier revenge fantasy that literalizes Marx's description of ideology: 'circumstances appear upside down . . .'[17] Rambo is an imperialist guerrilla, an agent of technocrats, who rejects computer-age technology to obliterate truckloads of the enemy with bow and arrow. Emerging from the mud of the jungle, from the trees, rivers, and waterfalls, Rambo displays a privileged, magical relationship to the Third World wilderness not evidenced even by the Vietnamese. As Trauptman remarks: 'What others call hell, he calls home.'

Charmed against nature and enemy weapons, Rambo retaliates in Indian-style warfare for the captivity of the POWs, the death of his Vietnamese love interest, and his own wartime trauma. He stands against a waterfall, magically immune to a barrage of gunfire. His detonator tipped arrows literally blow apart the enemy who is subhuman, the propagandist's variation on the Hun, the Nip, the Nazi. Held in contempt even by their Russian advisors, the Vietnamese are weak, sweating, repulsive in their gratuitous cruelty and sexual lasciviousness. Rambo annihilates an enemy whose evil makes American culpability in any wartime atrocities a moot point. In *The Searchers*, Ethan Edwards says: 'There are humans and then there are comanch.' In *Rambo*, there are humans and then there are gooks who populate a jungle which is not a wilderness to be transformed into a garden, but an unredeemable hell which automatically refutes any accusation of America's imperialist designs.

With regard to the captivity narrative, it is also significant that Rambo is described as a half-breed, half German and half American Indian, a 'hell of a combination,' says Murdock. The Vietnam vet's otherness of class and race is displaced solely onto race. The Indianness of costume signifiers: long hair, bare chest, headband, and necklace/pendant ironically reverse the appropriation of the iconography of Native Americans by the sixties counterculture as symbolic of a radical alternative to oppressive cultural norms.[18] Ironically, the film's appropriation of the iconography of the noble savage also permits Rambo to symbolically evoke the Indian as the romanticized victim of past government deceitfulness disguised as progress (i.e., genocide). These invocations of Indianness should not overshadow the fact that Rambo is a white male, as are most of the men he rescues. Thus the film elides the other question of color – the fact that 'half the average combat rifle company . . . consisted of blacks and Hispanics.'[19] American racism, and the class bias of the culture found the US armed services in Vietnam consisting of a majority of poor whites and blacks, especially among the combat soldiers, the 'grunts.' The captivity narrative overshadows the historical narrative of rebellion in the ranks of the grunts (fragging – the killing of officers) and the feeling of solidarity that soldiers of color felt for their Vietnamese opponents.

The reliance on the captivity narrative and Indian iconography evidences a desperate impulse to disarticulate a sign – the Vietnam veteran – from one meaning (psychopathic misfit, murderer of women and children) to another, the noble savage. Stallone admitted in an interview that the rushes of the film made Rambo look 'nihilistic almost psychopathic.'[20] The film cannot repress an ambivalence toward the Vietnam veteran, in spite of the noble-savage iconography. By emphasizing the efficiency of Rambo as a 'killing machine' created by Trauptman, Stallone's protagonist becomes an American version of Frankenstein's monster. He begins to evoke figures from genre films such as the Terminator, or Jason in *Friday the 13th*, in his sheer implacability and indestructibility. One critic has written that Michael, the hero of *The Deer Hunter*, confronts the perversity of Vietnam's violence 'with grace.'[21] Rambo, as the embodiment of the return of the repressed, can only confront perversity with perversity.

Through the castrated/castrating dialectic of sacrifice and sadistic violence, Rambo redeems the MIAs and American manhood, but in spite of his triumph of revenge, he has not been freed of his victim status at the end of the film. Trauptman tells him: 'Don't hate your country . . .' Rambo's impassioned final plea states that all he wants is for his country to love the vets as much as they have loved their country. Trauptman asks, 'How will you live, John?' Rambo replies, 'Day by day.' The ending suggests that the screenwriters absorbed much from Warner Brothers' *I am a Fugitive from a Chain Gang* in which veteran Allen, duped by bureaucrats, is returned to prison and denied his promised pardon. He escapes a second time to tell his fiancée, 'I hate everything but you . . .' She asks, 'How do you live?' Allen: 'I steal.' While Allen disappears into darkness, Rambo's walk into the Thai sunset also serves to recall the ending of numerous Westerns in which the hero's ambivalence toward civilization and the community's ambivalence toward the hero's violence precludes their reconciliation. Like Ethan Edwards, Rambo is doomed to wander between the two winds, but to a 1980s audience, no doubt, the ending does not signal the awareness of the tragic consequences of unreasoning violence and racial hatred as in Ford's film, but the exhilarating possibility of yet another Stallone sequel.

Like populist discourses such as Bruce Springsteen's 'Born in the USA,' *Rambo* plays upon a profound ambivalence toward the Vietnam vet, the war, and the US government but, like Springsteen's song, *Rambo* has been incorporated into the popular discourse as a celebration of Americanism. In its obvious preferred reading, the film is decoded by its predominantly post-Vietnam, male audience as a unified, noncontradictory system.[22] This kind of integration into the cultural discourse is possible because the will to myth overrides the ideological tensions that threaten the coherence of the film's textual system. The film does not require a belief in history, only a belief in the history, conventions, and mythmaking capacity of the movies.

In a challenging essay in *Postmodernism and Politics*, Dana Polan speaks of cinema's 'will-to-spectacle,' the banishment of background, the assertion that 'a world of foreground is the only world that matters or is the only world that is.'[23] If one eliminates the past as background, events can be transformed into satisfying spectacle, hurtful history into pleasurable myth. Drawing on this will-to-spectacle, the mythogenesis of *Rambo* lies, not in history, but in the *ur*-texts of fiction that provide its mythic resonance as a genre film and its vocabulary for exercising the will to myth.

In fact, virtually all background is eliminated in *Rambo*, and the spectacle becomes the half-clad, muscle-bound body of Sylvester Stallone: the inflated body of the male as the castrated and castrating monster. John Rambo is the body politic offered up as the anatomically incorrect action doll – John Ellis describes an ad for the film showing Rambo holding 'his machine gun where his penis ought to be.'[24] Rambo declares that 'the mind is the best weapon,' but Stallone's glistening hypermasculinity, emphasized in the kind of languid camera movements and fetishizing close-up usually reserved for female 'flashdancers,' visually insists otherwise.

Rambo's narcissistic cult of the fetishized male body redresses a perceived loss of personal and political power at a most primitive level, at the site of the body, which often defined the division of labor between male and female in pretechnological, patriarchal societies. The male body as weapon functions as a bulwark against feelings of powerlessness engendered by technology, minority rights, feminism – this helps explain the film's popularity not only in the US but overseas as well, where it similarly appealed to working-class, male audiences.[25] Most of all, however, the film speaks to post-Vietnam/post-Watergate America's devastating loss of confidence in its status as the world's most powerful, most respected, most moral nation. Our judgment and ability to fight the 'good' war as a total war of commitment without guilt has been eroded by our involvement in Vietnam, as surely as a sense of personal power has been eroded by a society increasingly bewildering in its technological complexity.

Attempting to deliver its audience from the anxiety of the present, Rambo would seek to restore an unreflective lost Eden of primitive masculine power. Yet Rambo must supplement his physical prowess with high-tech weapons adapted to the use of the lone warrior-hero. A contradictory distinction is maintained between his more 'primitive' use of technology and that of the bureaucracy. Rambo's most hysterical, uncontrollable act of revenge is against Murdock and Murdock's technology. He machine-guns the computers and sophisticated equipment in operations headquarters. Uttering a primal scream, he then turns his weapon to the ceiling in a last outburst of uncontrollable rage. Such an outburst is the predictable result of the dynamics of repression, for the film cannot reconstitute institutional norms except through the mythological presence of the super-fetishized superman, who functions as the mediator between the threatened patriarchal ideology and the viewer/subject desperately seeking to identity with a powerful figure. As a reaction formation against feelings of powerlessness too painful to be admitted or articulated, Rambo's violent reprisals, dependent on the power of the over-fetishized male body, may be read as a symptomatic expression, a psychosomatic signifier of the return of the repressed, suggesting profound ideological crisis in the patriarchy.

Freud warned that within the context of repression and unconscious acting out, the young and childish tend to 'luxuriate in their symptoms.'[26] *Rambo* demonstrates a cultural parallel, a luxuriating in the symptoms of a desperate ideological repression manifested in the inability to speak of or remember the painful past, a cultural hysteria in which violence must substitute for understanding, victimization for responsibility, the personal for the political. While *Rambo* reflects ambiguous and often inchoate drives to rewrite the Vietnam War, it also shows how in the will to myth the original traumatic experience is compulsively acted out in a contradictory form that leaves the origins of ideological anxiety untouched: the need to reconcile repressed material remains.

Notes

1 Fredric Jameson, *The Political Unconscious: Narrative as a Socially Symbolic Act*, Ithaca, NY: Cornell University Press, 1981, p. 104.
2 Sigmund Freud, 'Repression,' *General Psychological Theory*, ed. Philip Rieff, New York: Macmillan-Collier, 1963, p. 112.
3 Sigmund Freud, 'Repression,' pp. 114–15.
4 Sigmund Freud, 'Repression,' pp. 112–13.
5 Theodor Adorno, 'What Does Coming to Terms with the Past Mean?' *Bitburg in Moral and Political Perspective*, ed. Geoffrey H. Hartman, Bloomington, IN: Indiana UP, 1986, p. 116.
6 Theodor Adorno, 'What Does Coming to Terms with the Past Mean?,' p. 128.
7 Alex de Jonge, *The Weimar Chronicle*, London: Paddington P, 1978, p. 32.
8 William Shirer, *The Rise and Fall of the Third Reich*, Greenwich, CT: Fawcett, 1960, pp. 55–6.
9 Alex de Jonge, *The Weimar Chronicle*, p. 32.
10 Robert Herzstein, *The War that Hitler Won: The Most Infamous Propaganda Campaign in History*, New York: Putnam's, 1978.
11 Alvin Rosenfeld, 'Another Revisionism: Popular Culture and the Changing Image of the Holocaust,' in G. Hartman, *Holocaust Remembrance: The Shapes of Memory*, Oxford: Blackwell, 1993, p. 96.
12 Alvin Rosenfeld, 'Another Revisionism,' p. 94.
13 Richard Grenier, 'Stallone on Patriotism and "Rambo,"' *New York Times* 6 June, 1985, p. C21.
14 Ronald Reagan, 'Never Again . . .' in *Bitburg and Beyond*, ed. Ilya Levkov, New York: Shapolsky, 1987, p. 131.
15 Francis Clines, 'Tribute to Vietnam Dead: Words, A Wall,' *New York Times* 11 Nov., 1982, p. B15.
16 Richard Slotkin, *Regeneration Through Violence: The Mythology of the American Frontier, 1600–1860*, Middletown, CT: Wesleyan UP, 1973, p. 421.
17 Karl Marx and Frederick Engels, *The German Ideology*, London: Lawrence & Wishart, 1965, pp. 37–8.
18 Richard Slotkin, *Regeneration Through Violence*, p. 558.
19 Gabriel Kolko, *Anatomy of a War: Vietnam, the United States, and the Modern Historical Experience*, New York: Pantheon, 1985, p. 360.
20 Richard Grenier, 'Stallone on Patriotism and "Rambo,"' p. C21.
21 Judy Kinney, 'The Mythical Method: Fictionalizing the Vietnam War,' *Wide Angle* 7(4) (1985), p. 40.
22 John Ellis, '"Rambollocks" is the Order of the Day,' *New Statesman* 8, Nov. 1985, p. 15.
23 Dana Polan, '"Above All Else to Make You See": Cinema and the Ideology of Spectacle.' *Postmodernism and Politics*, ed. Jonathan Arac, Minneapolis, MN: U of Minnesota P, 1986, p. 60.
24 John Ellis, '"Rambollocks" is the Order of the Day,' p. 15.
25 John Ellis, '"Rambollocks" is the Order of the Day,' p. 15.
26 Sigmund Freud, 'Remembering, Repeating, and Working-Through,' *The Standard Edition of the Complete Psychological Works*, ed. and trans. J. Strachey, London: Hogarth, 1953–66, vol. 12, pp. 147–56.

Reading 14

Marilyn B. Young

IN THE COMBAT ZONE

'In the Combat Zone', *Radical History Review*, 2003, no. 85, pp. 253–64.

IN THE AFTERMATH OF THE U.S. VICTORY in the Gulf War, the first president George Bush was optimistic that the country had 'kicked the Vietnam syndrome'. But the syndrome continued to manifest itself in the popular imagination of war. The *Rambo* series had tried to reverse the verdict of defeat, but it left standing the public conviction that Vietnam was not a good war. Despite a victory intended to vanquish the memory of Vietnam, the only notable movies made about Desert Storm – *Courage Under Fire* (dir. Edward Zwick, 1996) and *Three Kings* (dir. David O. Russell, 1999) – were haunted by it. *Courage Under Fire*, in its insistence that post-Vietnam America must have heroes, underlined their absence. *Three Kings* explains why, opening with black-and-white text informing us that the war is over, even as a soldier shouts the question: 'Hey! Are we still killing people?' No one seems to know the answer. The soldier peers through the scope on his gun and sees an Iraqi on a distant hilltop, white flag in one hand, weapon in the other. Before either the audience, or the soldier, can tell whether the man intends to shoot or surrender, the American fires and the man falls dead. 'Congratulations,' his buddy says. 'You got yourself a raghead. I didn't think I'd get to see anyone shot in this war'.

We next observe one of those interviews with the troops that, like ads for the military, punctuated television coverage of the war. Both the press and the troops who so enthusiastically performed for them are mocked: 'They say you exorcised the ghost of Vietnam in [this war with its] clear moral imperative,' the reporter informs the soldiers, who readily agree: 'We liberated Kuwait'. The rest of the movie makes deadly fun of this answer. 'I don't know what we did here,' George Clooney's Special Forces officer bitterly complains to a friend, 'just tell me what we did here'. 'Do you want to occupy Iraq,' the friend answers, 'and do Vietnam all over again?' But in effect, the Gulf War, as *Three Kings* presents it, *is* Vietnam all over again. No clear moral imperative exists; on the contrary, Shiites and Kurds are cynically encouraged to rebel against Saddam Hussein and then abandoned to their fate. Even the bad guys drive the point home: 'Do [*sic*] your army care about the children in Iraq?' one of Saddam's Republic Guard soldiers, pausing in the act of torturing an American captive, asks. 'Do your army come back to help the people? . . . My son was killed in his bed. He is one year old. He is sleeping when the bomb come . . . Can you think how it feels inside your heart if I bomb your daughter?' Individual Americans, like Clooney, through their honesty, virility, and disregard for authority, redeem the country's honor, but only in opposition to, or apart from, the government, never in support of its stated aims. In this, *Three Kings* is a sardonic retelling of what Pat Aufderheide has described as the 'noble-grunt' Vietnam War movie. The enemies are not Vietnamese or Iraqi, but rather 'the cold abstract forces of bureaucracy and the incompetence of superiors'.[1]

For the past few years, the only refuge for the righteous fighting man has been World War II.[2] Unsurprisingly, George W. Bush used it as his first point of reference in the immediate aftermath of September 11 (as had his father, on the eve of Desert Storm): the attack was another Pearl Harbor; the enemy was fascist, totalitarian, a spoke in an axis of evil. Only in World War II, the film historian Thomas Doherty pointed out, can Americans find 'the consolation of closure and the serenity of moral certainty. For Hollywood and American culture the Second World War would always be a safe berth'.[3] Fought for an unquestionably just cause, ending in total victory, World War II could be reliably invoked to remind Americans of their own best selves. Vincent Canby observed that movies about Vietnam had made war itself seem bestial; *Saving Private Ryan* made war 'good again'.[4] This was war as men of Steven Spielberg's generation played it on the street when they were boys: storming beaches, house-to-house fighting, sharpshooters in doorways, vulnerable human beings against tanks, always outnumbered.[5]

No one can identify with a B-52 and, as Michael Sherry pointed out long ago, we rarely witness bombing raids from below.[6] Ground combat proves much more satisfying. The camera always faces out against the enemy, or inward at the grievous wounds enemy fire causes. The individual soldier fighting for his life becomes the victim of war; those he kills, since they are so evidently bent on his destruction, the perpetrators of violence. His innocence is ours. Spielberg's achievement went beyond nostalgia. By enabling identification with the individual combat soldier, his World War II epic extended a pardon to soldiers everywhere. On the large and small screens of the country, a handful of heroes fight off the enemy horde (variously composed of Germans, Japanese, Iraqis, Somalis, or Vietnamese), World War II tropes mixing freely with those of old-fashioned Westerns. While Ryan's war has nothing to do with contemporary American high-tech military tactics, *Saving Private Ryan* established a useful paradigm. The tight focus on the situation of the combat solider is inherently dramatic and, by screening out everything save the immediate context in which he fights, recent war movies, wherever they are set, serve as all-purpose propaganda instruments. The Vietnam War movies of the late 1980s similarly kept the focus on the individual fighting man, erasing history and politics in favor of 'an emotional drama of embattled individual survival'.[7] But the differences prove crucial: in *Platoon* (dir. Oliver Stone, 1986), *84 Charlie Mopic* (dir. Patrick Sheane Duncan, 1989), *Full Metal Jacket* (dir. Stanley Kubrick, 1987), and *Casualties of War* (dir. Brian de Palma, 1989), the mission is explicitly meaningless, the officers useless or worse, the men abandoned by authority, the struggle a civil war. 'We didn't fight the enemy,' the hero of *Platoon* concludes, 'we fought ourselves and the enemy was us'. The mission in *Saving Private Ryan* is assumed to be good, the Germans are the enemies, and who wouldn't want to fight under Tom Hanks?

So attractive, in retrospect, is this old-style ground war that HBO made it into a ten-hour series based on the book credited to Stephen Ambrose, *Band of Brothers*. I watched only one-third of the episodes; after that the rituals of male bonding become wearying. It is not that one missed the presence of women, since, except for sex, men, who cared for each other as tenderly as any woman could, competently handled the things women usually do. The often gentle universe of *Band of Brothers* reinforces the manifest content of the series: once upon a time, America was very, very good. Magically, its old goodness constitutes an ongoing one as well, if only Americans can be brought to remember and cherish the good past. Like the cold war movies of the 1950s – and in direct contrast to the late Vietnam War movies – *Band of Brothers* and *Saving Private Ryan* revel in a 'sentimental militarism' that relies not on ideology, but faith in benevolent male authority.[8]

And something more interesting goes on in *Band of Brothers* than this filiopious history. At the very end, a defeated German general is allowed to address his massed troops, now, like himself, prisoners of war. He tells them how proud he is of them and how well they have fought, with what courage and bravery. The listening Americans are moved: he has described their war as well as his own. War stories written from inside out vary by geography, but they always tell the same story: death, fear, brotherhood. Bravery, courage, and the capacity to commit atrocities are not determined by the cause in which they are displayed. 'It's about the man next to you,' one of the characters in *Black Hawk Down* says, 'that's all it is'. The flat statement, that one kills and dies for the man next to you, never leads to the obvious question: what are both of you doing there? Some historians, like Gerald Linderman, have written the inside story of war with attention to its contradictions, as tragedy rather than heroic epic.[9] Contemporary war movies, from *Saving Private Ryan* to *We Were Soldiers*, follow Ambrose's lead. They abstract war from its context, leaving it standing on its own, self-justifying, impervious to doubt, a fact of nature.

The Pacific theater has been a less popular location in which to revisit World War II; perhaps jungle warfare recalls Vietnam too directly. Terrence Malick's *The Thin Red Line* (1998) was a resounding box office failure, in part because, as Neil Gabler pointed out, in its sharp caricature of the indifference of military authority to the lives of the troops, it was the 'last of the Vietnam-era movies'.[10] Jerry Bruckheimer chose a safer subject, the attack on Pearl Harbor. The only way to watch *Pearl Harbor* is on video, with your finger poised over fast-forward. The product of $127 million worth of special effects, *Pearl Harbor* seems oddly dated. The computer graphics look as unreal, in their high realism, as the tiny galleons that fought on the Spanish Main in Hollywood's days of yore. The love story is faithful to the genre as it was practiced in the 1940s magazine *True Romance*. The acting is silent-movie grandiose; the sentiments neo-Hallmark. The only surprise is that the filmmakers, intent on a happy ending to the carnage of Japanese-wrought destruction, offer us only Doolittle's raid on Tokyo rather than Hiroshima.

Hollywood nostalgia for World War II is not only about doing an end run around Vietnam or salvaging war as a fruitful human activity. It is also intended to hold a mirror to our own corrupt times. In the fat, soft days before the recession and September 11, the generation that fought World War II was praised, in antique slang, as 'the greatest'. Succeeding generations could aspire to being good, maybe great, but by definition they could not be the greatest. 'It is as though,' Ian Buruma wrote after seeing *Pearl Harbor*, 'we should feel nostalgic for times when dying for the nation was called for. We are supposed to believe that people at war were better human beings, and we should be more like them'. The filmmakers, Buruma concluded, were not cynical, but something worse: 'I have a feeling [they] are deeply sincere. They believe in their own spectacle . . . So who needs reality? Just sit back and enjoy the show. Until the next war. And then we die, ingloriously'.[11] Though not, Buruma should have added, in the movies.

Meanwhile, films whose themes proved too close for comfort, like *Collateral Damage* (dir. Andrew Davis, 2002), about a terrorist attack, were delayed, while movies about old wars were advanced. The chair of Paramount explained why *Black Hawk Down*, about the intervention in Somalia, would appear on local screens sooner than expected: 'It's about the sacrifices that soldiers make so the rest of us can be safe'. Mark Bowden, who wrote the book on which the movie is based, pronounced himself well satisfied with the treatment. 'Many people read *Black Hawk Down* as an argument not to use military force,' Bowden told the *Times* reporter, 'which I never intended . . . This movie says that we have the capability of doing this kind of thing. It's ugly and it's terrible, but we have these very brave young men who do this, and we need to use them now and then'.[12]

Black Hawk Down begins with a scrolling text informing the audience of the humanitarian purpose of the U.S. intervention – famine relief – a purpose that could not be fulfilled so long as the evil warlord Aidid controlled the capital Mogadishu.[13] The film wisely skips the unopposed made-for-TV amphibious landing on the beach at Mogadishu.[14] Instead, it focuses entirely on the effort to rescue the crew of a helicopter shot down in the course of a mission to snatch several of Aidid's key lieutenants from their meeting place in the crowded city. Thousands and thousands of armed and apparently crazed Somalis (called, throughout the movie, 'skinnies,' a reference to the famine, though in fact, most of the Somalis look more like stereotypical muscled boys in the hood) besiege the small band of American troops. The film makes no reference to the constant and indifferent use of excessive force by the United States that led Alex de Waal to conclude that 'literally every inhabitant of large areas of Mogadishu considered the UN and U.S. as enemies, and were ready to take up arms against them' by the time of the rescue mission.[15] But then, as Jerry Bruckheimer explained, 'We never set out to tell that story. We wanted to make a film about what these young guys were sent out to do and what they did to survive'.[16]

Initially, the makers of *Black Hawk Down* considered drawing an explicit connection between U.S. withdrawal from Somalia and the growth of al-Qaeda, but they dropped the idea because they thought 'the connections were apparent'.[17] Vice president Cheney, secretary of defense Rumsfeld, deputy secretary of defense Paul Wolfowitz, secretary of the army Thomas E. White, assorted generals, and Oliver North, identified in the ArmyLINK News as a 'political analyst,' attended a special screening of the movie. Ridley Scott told the audience he had made the movie to 'set the record straight'. He wanted to disabuse the public of the notion that the military had 'messed up on Somalia,' when in fact 'it was heroic in a very unstable part of the world'. White agreed: the movie reflected the 'values of valor and self-sacrifice' of the military in its current war against terrorism and indeed throughout its history.[18] Yet with all its patriotic trappings, the implications of *Black Hawk Down* are potentially dangerous to war makers: what is it about America's good intentions that they go so quickly awry? What, after all, did the deaths of a thousand Somalis and eighteen Americans accomplish? The implication of the film's ending, that the United States should not have withdrawn its troops so precipitously, does not resolve but compounds the confusion. What, other than more dead Somalis and Americans, would continued military action have achieved? Could something have been wrong with American intentions?[19]

For all its heroics, *Black Hawk Down* could not erase Vietnam, another war said to have begun with good intentions that went unaccountably wrong. Nor did *Saving Private Ryan* do the job. Giorgio Mariani may be correct when he writes: 'the "monument" that Spielberg erects to his father's generation ties past and present together in a seamless web, thereby absolving the nation not only from the sin of Vietnam, but also from all the other "mistakes" of the half century separating us from the end of World War II'.[20] But this is only generally true. Absolution, to be effective, must be specific. To erase Vietnam, Hollywood would have to go back to Vietnam, where the unraveling of the war story began. In 1941, in an effort to take the bad taste out of World War I and the powerful antiwar movies that dominated the interwar years, Hollywood released *Sergeant York* (dir. Howard Hawks, 1941), a moving tale of a pacifist turned war hero. 'We can sit in the theater and see [York] go fight a better World War I for us,' Jeanine Basinger has written. Films like *Sergeant York*, she explained, 'wipe out earlier images and replace them with new ones, appropriate for the times'.[21] To create a 'new mythos' for World War II, Thomas Doherty wrote, 'Hollywood had to recast the Great War as a reasonable national enterprise, not as the crazy slaughterhouse depicted in literature and film for the previous twenty years . . . Outright obliteration was a prerequisite'.[22]

To fight this new war, the films, literature, and histories of Vietnam must be obliterated. *We Were Soldiers*, in what may be the first of many returns to Vietnam, is the twenty-first century's *Sergeant York*.[23] Like *Black Hawk Down*, *We Were Soldiers* was released ahead of schedule and the test screening pleased Paramount: 'The movie has very, very patriotic American values. The audience embraced those values'. Joseph Galloway, who, with Lieutenant Colonel Harold Moore, wrote the book on which the movie is based, expressed delight with the film. As he explained to a reporter, 'audiences would be drawn to the story because it is not defeatist about what eventually became the misadventure of Vietnam'. The book, like the movie, is relentlessly patriotic. 'This,' the prologue reads, 'is about what we did, what we saw, what we suffered in a thirty-four-day campaign in the Ia Drang Valley of the Central Highlands of South Vietnam in November 1965, when we were young and confident and patriotic'. It was a 'love story,' about men 'proud of the opportunity to serve [the] country'. It was also a story about the 'far more transcendent love' that comes to men 'unbidden on the battlefields . . . We killed for each other, we died for each other, and we wept for each other. And in time, we came to love each other as brothers. In battle our world shrank to the man on our left and the man on our right and the enemy all around'.[24] The film version makes it also a story about family values, a manly reporter ready to pick up a gun, and worthy enemies.

As it happens, Moore's unit, the First Battalion, Seventh Cavalry Regiment, First Division, was also Custer's, and in the movie, before leaving for Vietnam, Moore is shown thoughtfully leafing through an illustrated account of the battle of Little Big Horn, along with a French book describing what is called the 'massacre' of French troops in a battle along Route 19, near where he will soon find himself fighting for his life. Mel Gibson's brow furrows as he contemplates the fate of the French (a brief scene shows Vietnamese soldiers slaughtering French prisoners) and of Custer's men.[25] The domestication of the Vietnamese enemy, common during the war itself, strikes an odd, discordant note. After all, the Indians, in the last couple of decades of films and novels, have been victims, which would make Moore and his men the executioners, and that can't be right. Still, the scene is crucial, the first of many reversals of the images of the Vietnam War. The victims of massacres in Vietnam, it turns out, were white men. My Lai disappears; instead of burning villages, the film shows well-armed, uniformed Vietnamese regulars; napalm strikes burn Americans and Vietnamese alike (the B-52 sorties crucial to the battle are never shown); the American commander is everywhere in the midst of the battle, barely protected and always in danger; the Vietnamese commander gives his orders from the safety of a clean, well-kept, underground tunnel complex (in fact, the Vietnamese command post was not sheltered).[26] Americans die in great numbers, but they are anyhow victorious over the far more numerous Vietnamese, and a soldier's last words express gratitude that he has sacrificed his life for his country. Gone is the resentment of authority the Vietnam movies of the late 1980s expressed; in this Vietnam, as in *Black Hawk Down*, no one gets left behind.[27]

Vietnam has become a war of which Americans can feel proud. The pride derives from the demonstration of courage and the memory of suffering, irrespective of the cause in which the one is displayed and the other endured. Both are proof that the nation, if it would only embrace its heritage, now explicitly including Vietnam, has not gone soft. Ridley Scott, the director of *Black Hawk Down*, decided not to depict the dragging of a dead American through the streets of Mogadishu. Instead, he showed a helicopter pilot, naked from the waist up, his arms out flung, being lifted out of his craft by the mob, a contemporary deposition scene. After watching the film, George Monbiot wrote that the United States had cast itself 'simultaneously as the world's savior and the world's victim, a sacrificial messiah on a mission to deliver the world from evil'.[28] Monbiot called it a 'new myth of nationhood'. I am not sure how new it is, but I agree that it 'contains incalculable dangers' and that it will be playing on movie screens everywhere in the months and years to come and, more disastrously, in the 'real' world as well.

There is something odd about these recent representations of America's messianic mission. From Private Ryan to the Delta Force officers in Somalia and Hal Moore in Vietnam, these Americans sacrifice their lives only for one another. Private Ryan's war, for example, proves the obverse of movies made during World War II, when the individual had sometimes to be sacrificed for the sake of the mission. Ryan reverses the moral of the story; the lives of a group of men are risked for the sake of a single individual. 'In the new metaphor war movies seem to be presenting,' Neil Gabler wrote, 'Americans are no longer distrustful of authority and no longer doubt the cause. Rather, we trust each other and see the cause as us'.[29] And who can doubt that 'we' are a worthy cause? The legitimacy of the state, incarnate in the nation-at-war, is vested in the wars the United States has waged and the new ones the Bush administration plans to wage, all of them justified by the way they are fought for the 'man on our left and the man on our right and the enemy all around'. Hollywood, and the government, would seem to have 'kicked the Vietnam syndrome'.

Notes

1 Pat Aufderheide, 'Good Soldiers,' in *Seeing through Movies*, ed. Mark Crispin Miller (New York: Pantheon, 1990), 84.

2 One could argue that this has been the case, with interesting variations, since 1945. See Christian Appy, '"We'll Follow the Old Man": The Strains of Sentimental Militarism in Popular Films of the Fifties,' in *Rethinking Cold War Culture*, ed. Peter J. Kuznick and James Gilbert (Washington, DC: Smithsonian Institute, 2001), for a particularly interesting analysis of the way Hollywood translated the 'sentimental militarism' of World War II films for cold war use, a translation marked by ambivalence and ambiguity.

3 Thomas Doherty, *Projections of War: Hollywood, American Culture, and World War II* (New York: Columbia University Press, 1993), 271.

4 Vincent Canby, 'The Horror and Honor of a Good War,' *New York Times*, August 10, 1998.

5 For an especially eloquent evocation of this culture, see Tom Engelhardt, *The End of Victory Culture: Cold War America and the Disillusioning of a Generation* (Amherst: University of Massachusetts Press, 1998).

6 See Michael S. Sherry, *The Rise of American Air Power: The Creation of Armageddon* (New Haven, CT: Yale University Press, 1987).

7 Aufderheide, 'Good Soldiers,' 86.

8 Appy, 'We'll Follow the Old Man,' 94.

9 Gerald F. Linderman, *The War Within: America's Combat Experience in World War II* (New York: Free Press, 1997).

10 Neil Gabler, 'Seeking Perspective on the Movie Front Lines,' *New York Times*, January 27, 2002.

11 Ian Buruma, 'Oh! What A Lovely War,' *Guardian*, May 28, 2001. Buruma compared *Pearl Harbor* to patriotic Japanese war movies, which, unlike their American counterparts, stressed duty, courage, sacrifice, and purity of will rather than the evil of the enemy.

12 Kim Masters, 'Against the Tide, Two Movies Go to War,' *New York Times*, November 4, 2001.

13 In fact, the famine had largely abated before U.S. intervention, and the targeting of Aidid restored his waning power, transforming him into 'the aggrieved party in a war with UN colonialists.' See Stephen R. Shalom, 'Gravy Train: Feeding the Pentagon by Feeding Somalia,' *Z Magazine*, November 1993, available at www.zmag.org/ZNET.htm.

14 See Shalom, 'Gravy Train.' The landing was pure public relations for the Marines. Indeed, the entire operation can be seen as an effort by the Pentagon to demonstrate the need for high defense budgets despite the end of the cold war – use it or lose it. See also Scott Peterson, *Me Against My Brother: At War in Somalia, Sudan, and Rwanda*, New York: Routledge, 2001, 54.

15 Alex de Waal, 'U.S. War Crimes in Somalia,' *New Left Review* 230 (1998): 131–44.

16 Chelsea J. Carter, '"Black Hawk Down" Movie Turns Grim Somalia Fight into a Dramatic Tale of Heroism,' *Valley News* (White River Junction, VT), February 2, 2002.

17 Robert K. Elder, 'The War Stories of *Black Hawk Down*,' January 21, 2002, available at www.metromix.com/movies.

18 Joe Burlas, '"Black Hawk Down" Reflects Army Values,' *Army LINK News*, January 16, 2002, available at www.dtic.mil/armylink/news /Jan2002/a20020116bhdown. html.

19 In one of the endless migration tales of the American empire, Sinp Sithavaday, an eighteen-year-old whose family had fled Laos in 1979, found himself in Somalia, a member of the Tenth Mountain Division's second battalion, Eighty-Seventh Infantry. Interviewed by his local newspaper, Sithavaday, without directly criticizing the movie, talked about the 'growing hubris' of U.S. troops: 'We thought, we have rocket launchers, night goggles, infrared designators, all kinds of technical stuff. We are the meanest.' After a few months, he had become dubious about his mission: 'There was a lot of anger at the U.S. They saw us flexing our muscles and killing them.' Like the soldiers sent to Indochina a decade before his birth, Sithavaday complained: 'How can you tell a farmer from a militia member?' Melanie Leslie-Finn, 'Lyme Man Looks Back on His Tour of Duty in Somalia,' *Valley News*, February 2, 2002.

20 Giorgio Mariani, '"Mission of Mercy/Mission of Murder": Spielberg's *Saving Private Ryan* and the Culture of Baby Boomers,' *Acoma* 18 (2000): 4, English version available atwww.acoma.it/n18/inglese /mission2a.htm.

21 Jeanine Basinger, *The World War II Combat Film: Anatomy of a Genre*, New York: Columbia University Press, 1986, 100.

22 Doherty, *Projections*, 100.

23 The passage of time has made the displacement easier. For example, *Coming Home*, a 1978 antiwar movie, was summarized in the February 25, 2002 *New York Times* TV late movie listings this way: 'Jane Fonda, Jon Voight, Bruce Dern. Strong, stinging triangle of wife and Vietnam vets.'

24 Kim Masters, 'Against the Tide, Two Movies Go to War,' *New York Times*, November 4, 2002; Harold G. Moore and Joseph Galloway, *We Were Soldiers Once . . . and Young: Ia Drang – the Battle that Changed the War in Vietnam*, New York: HarperPerennial, 1993, 3–4.

25 See Charles J. Hanley et al., *The Bridge at No Gun Ri*, New York: Holt, 2001. The history of the Seventh Cavalry includes several massacres going the other way: the Battle of the Washita, in 1868, when the cavalry ordered a large group of Amerindians into a constricted area and then slaughtered them; Wounded Knee, in 1890, when it massacred 370 Sioux, many of them women and children; the massacre of Korean villagers in July 1950.

26 The ABC documentary, *We Were Young and Brave*, produced in 1994, is very clear on this point: air power was the deciding factor in the battle. A Vietnamese colonel describes watching, unprotected, as a 'sea of fire' engulfed his troops: 'If you saw it you would think we all died.'

27 See Aufderheide, 'Good Soldiers,' especially 94.

28 George Monbiot, 'Both Saviour and Victim,' *Guardian Weekly*, February 7–13, 2002, 13.

29 Neil Gabler, 'Seeking Perspective.'

Susan Aronstein

REVISITING THE ROUND TABLE
Arthur's American dream

'Revisiting the Round Table: Arthur's American Dream', in *Arthurian Knights: Cinema and the Politics of Nostalgia,* Basingstoke: Palgrave Macmillan, 2005, pp. 191–213, 245–6.

IN JULY 1995, as America debated foreign policy and its role in a post-cold war world, Jerry Zucker offered American audiences a new big-screen version of the legend of King Arthur – the first since *Excalibur*. Released the same summer as *Braveheart*, *Apollo 13*, and *Ace Ventura*, *First Knight* performed indifferently at the box office; although the film is visually stunning, it is hampered by a confused script – promoted to showcase the love-triangle ('their greatest battle would be for her love') but functioning more as a political allegory than a love story. The film's blatant topicality, combined with its unfortunate casting of Richard Gere as Lancelot – who, Anthony Lane complained, presented 'a new take on [the character], Arthurian Gigolo' – played anachronistically, even for a Hollywood production. Richard Schickel, reviewing it for *Time*, headlined the film, '*First Knight* Reinvents Camelot for the Clinton Era,' and concluded, with some resignation that 'every era has the right – maybe even the duty – to reinvent the Arthurian legend according to its own lights'. Those 'lights,' as Andy Pawelczak argued in *Films in Review*, produced 'a tendentiously, liberal movie . . . for Camelot, read America in the Kennedy era of muscular Cold War liberalism when the country still believed its mission was to defend weaker states'.[1]

Pawelczak's identification of *First Knight* with cold war liberalism stems, in part, from the film's cinematic origins in 1950s' Hollywood Arthuriana. In its equation of Camelot and America, its focus on the Arthur/Lancelot/Guinevere love-triangle, its chronicle of the hailing and interpellation of a knight, its exploration of threatened borders, and its visual and editorial style, *First Knight* is a direct descendent of *The Knights of the Round Table* that conservatively rewrites *The Sword of Lancelot*'s 1960s' take on the legend. However, thematically, this film is not a cold war film; it refracts its central themes through a Clinton-era lens, substituting brotherhood for patriarchy, service for leadership, responsibility for manifest destiny, and a global village for American expansionism. Furthermore, in its radical rewriting of the love-triangle, the film bypasses Arthurian tragedy; Camelot is preserved to be led by another 'first among equals,' to continue to assure that 'all mankind under god' live by 'laws that make men free'.[2]

As *First Knight* rewrites Arthurian legend to produce a late-twentieth-century Arthur, it focuses both on the construction of the 'next' leader – a deeply Americanized Lancelot – and on larger questions of foreign policy, explicitly addressing the role 'Camelot' must play in the world. As such, the film's love story is politicized; Lancelot's conversion from mercenary entertainer to Arthur's 'first knight,' the marriage of Arthur and Guinevere, and the resulting love-triangle all carry with them questions of the individual versus the community, of isolationism versus responsibility, themes that are established in the film's opening narrative crawl:

> At long last, the wars were over. Arthur the great king of Camelot had devoted his life to building a land of peace and justice and now he wished to marry.
>
> But the peace was not to last. The most powerful of Arthur's knights had long been jealous of the King's glory. Now he found cause to quarrel with Arthur and left Camelot with hatred in his heart.
>
> And so the land was divided again between those who rallied to Prince Malagant, seeking the spoils of war and those who stayed loyal to the king.

By opening later than cold war Arthuriana (after Arthur's consolidation of the kingdom) and identifying Malagant in the opening crawl, *First Knight* eliminates both the post-World War II references to America's role in defeating Hitler and cold war obsessions with the disguised enemy within to focus on the question of how to maintain peace once the major (cold) war has been won – how to assure the continuation of order in the face of petty rebellions and dictatorial tyrants. Malagant and his army are introduced into a scene of pastoral production – a prosperous village in which people are shown happily working at their daily tasks; the upbeat music switches to ominous tones and the black army rides over the green hills, showing that the borders of this village are unprotected and its denizens are at the mercy of greedy men looking for an excuse for war. The attack that follows emphasizes Malagant's brutality – his human rights' violations – as he cuts down unarmed farmers and traps the villagers in a locked and flaming barn. Claiming that the 'borderlands have been lawless long enough,' Malagant, with his random cruelty and over-sized ego, admonishes, 'know now that I am the law'.

As the scene switches to a nicely democratic Guinevere playing soccer with her subjects, the audience learns that this village lay in Guinevere's care – and that it is her border and her people that are threatened by Malagant's ruthless tyranny; Guinevere, recognizing Malagant for what he is, asks bitterly, 'What does he want? To destroy the whole world and be king of a graveyard?' However, in spite of her assertion 'I'm not the yielding kind,' Guinevere has to admit that 'if Prince Malagant doesn't get what he wants, he has the power to take it'.

Lyonesse is a country threatened by a power-mad dictator with no regard for human rights; Guinevere knows that in order to protect her land she must turn to a power beyond her borders and make an alliance with Camelot – in spite of the fact that what she wants is 'to marry and live and die at Lyonesse'. Although *First Knight* desperately tries to mitigate the fact that the marriage between Arthur and Guinevere is a political alliance, in this film it functions symbolically as just that – the marriage between a lesser country and Camelot, a political treaty with a superpower that 'wears (that) power so lightly' and with 'such gentleness in (its) eyes'.[3] Arthur may promise that 'Camelot will protect Lyonesse whether you marry me or not' and Guinevere may insist that she wants to marry the man 'not your crown, nor your army, not your golden city,' but her initial decision to go to Camelot belies all these later protests of disinterested union. Arthur and Camelot signify protection, as is emphasized when Guinevere walks toward her future husband, flanked by vast lines of military men.

First Knight makes it clear, however, that an alliance with Arthur and Camelot is not only prudent, it is also right. Camelot is the golden city – the City on the Hill – sanctioned by divine election, as a mise-en-scène full of crosses – Celtic stone crosses, stained glass crosses, even cross-shaped Windows in the city's outer defenses – declares. Camelot is God's city and its citizens look to God to guide them; the Round Table begins all of its councils with prayer: 'God give us the wisdom to discover what is right, the will to do it, and the strength to make it endure'. Arthur articulates 'what is right' for a Christian superpower in the film's central foreign policy debate; Malagant proposes a 'treaty,' in which he and Arthur divide Camelot, and the king angrily responds, 'Where is it written "beyond Camelot live lesser people, people too weak to protect themselves, let them die?"' Malagant retorts, 'Other people live by other laws . . . or is the law of Camelot to rule the entire world?' Arthur dismisses this foreign policy relativism – the argument that other countries are none of Camelot's business: 'There are laws that enslave men and laws that make them free. Either what we hold to be right and good and true is right and good and true for all mankind under God or we're just another robber tribe'. Arthur's heated declaration of universal good – and Camelot's moral duty to enforce it – plays right into the neo-Wilsonian idealism of Clinton's foreign policy team; it also serves as a call to action: 'there's a peace that is only to be found on the other side of war and if that war comes, I will fight it'; to which all of the knights of the Round Table – having discovered 'what is right,' have the 'will to choose it,' affirming 'and I'.

War over Lyonesse, however, as Clinton's call to arms in Bosnia, is not entirely disinterested. It is also a war of containment. One of Arthur's knights asserts that Malagant 'wants Lyonesse as a buffer'; Arthur counters, 'He wants Camelot and he thinks he can win'. Lyonesse is not a buffer, but a border and, as a border, it must be held. In the war that follows – announced as the knights swear fealty to the newly married Lady of Lyonesse – the film obscures the costs of such wars, glossing over American fears of becoming involved in another deadly quagmire and depicting the war as another Gulf War, won quickly and painlessly in one well-planned battle, over soon and with small harm done to Camelot's hosts.

Yet, Camelot is not yet safe; Arthur's dream is still threatened – as it is in all Arthurian tales – by the bad 'son,' in this case (removing all responsibility from Arthur's shoulders) not his own biological son, but a renegade knight, a subject who has rejected the Arthurian ideology. Malagant, once the first of Arthur's knights, has embraced an alternative worldview – one based on power and lordship and operating under two assumptions about men and the world: 'Men don't want brotherhood; they want leadership' and 'the strong rule the weak. That's how God made the world'. With this creed of self-interest and self-advancement, of – to use the proper Arthurian terms – 'might makes right,' Malagant offers Camelot's citizens freedom from Arthur's morality, 'from Arthur's tyrannical dream, Arthur's tyrannical law, Arthur's tyrannical God,' the freedom to be individuals, not members of a community of service.

In order for Camelot to endure, its people must reject this vision of rampant individualism and accept Arthur's assertion that God has made them strong 'so that we can help each other'. *First Knight*'s second narrative chronicles the path by which Lancelot internalizes Arthurian ideology and becomes the son capable of perpetuating Arthur's dream. This second narrative is introduced at the end of the film's opening crawl: 'And then there was Lancelot, a wanderer who had never dreamed of peace or justice or knighthood. Times were hard and a man made his living any way he could. And Lancelot had always been good with a sword'. This description, as Jacqueline Jenkins points out, identifies Lancelot as proto-American, an individual who will rise not by lineage but by skill and merit. Jenkins extends this observation to argue that the film chronicles the Arthurian/European old order's acceptance and adoption of Lancelot's new American ways. However, I would argue that it is Lancelot who must change, who must learn to adopt the ideals of what Malagant scornfully dismisses as 'Arthur's dream'. Once he has done so, he becomes Arthur's first knight, replacing Malagant and ensuring the continuity of Camelot.

As the film opens, Lancelot is very much an Indiana Jones character – cynical and unconstructed, a potential knight without a court. He is indeed 'good with a sword' but instead of employing his sword in the service of others, he does so for himself; he is an entertainer and a huckster, not a knight. As this initial scene makes clear, Lancelot has no one and cares for nothing, not even his own life. He instructs his defeated opponent in how to win in sword play, concluding his foolproof technique with 'and you have to not care if you live or die'. Before he can become Arthur's 'first knight,' Lancelot must convert from this initial indifference to his final position; he must acquire a home, find something worth fighting for, and learn to care – very much – about life and death, not his own, but Camelot's.

As Lancelot moves from huckster to knight, Guinevere functions as both an object of desire and a test; as in *The Knights of the Round Table*, she represents the conflict between personal desire and public duty. However, in *First Knight*, this conflict centers not around a competition between homosocial and sexual bonds but one between two ways of defining the world and one's place in it: as a collection of unconnected individuals, each, 1980s style, in pursuit of personal pleasure and gain or as a community of interconnected citizens, whose destiny, in Clinton's words is 'bound up with the destiny of every other (citizen)'. Lancelot, when he rescues Guinevere from Malagant's forest ambush, makes it quite clear that he subscribes to the former view, both in his distinctly American view of class – 'I'd be just as pleased if you were a dairy maid' – and in his insistence that Guinevere is 'not married yet' and 'free to do as (she) pleases'.[4] Since Lancelot wants her, and he 'can see . . . in (her) eyes' that she wants him, what should happen next, engagement or no, is simple to him. Guinevere, however, much better tutored in the proper hierarchy of duty and desire (a switch in gender roles from a similar scene in *The Sword of Lancelot*), replies, 'I'm not to be had for the wanting'.

This scene sets up Lancelot's motive. From his initial introduction to Camelot, through his becoming a knight, and even into the battle for Lyonesse, he desires not knighthood or community, but Guinevere – in spite of Arthur's many attempts to call him to the ideology of the Round Table. The future first knight comes to the king's attention as he successfully runs the gauntlet as a means of access to, and perhaps a kiss from, the lady. He explains to the impressed king how he succeeded where so many had failed: 'Perhaps fear made them turn back when they should have gone forward,' echoing his sword-fighting tutorial as he asserts that he fears nothing because he 'has nothing to lose'. Arthur admires Lancelot's 'cunning display of style, grace, nerve, and stupidity,' but is taken aback by his philosophy. In his first attempt to convert Lancelot from individual to subject, Arthur offers a new way of looking at the world: 'Here we believe that every life is precious, even the life of strangers. If you must die, die serving something greater that yourself'. Arthur then leads Lancelot further into the castle and shows him the center of Camelot, symbolized by the Round Table, 'no head, no foot, everyone equal, even the King'. On the Table, Lancelot reads Camelot's founding philosophy, 'In serving each other we become free'. Arthur explains, 'That is the heart of Camelot. Stones, timbers, towers, palaces, burn them all. Camelot still lives on. Because it lives in us. It's a belief we have in our hearts'. In this exchange between king and potential subject, *First Knight* glosses the standard American appropriation of Camelot as a proto-democratic institution with a Clintonesque vision of a 'community of hope,' residing in individual hearts and built on mutual service and responsibility, a community in which brotherhood displaces equality as the Table's primary value and service becomes the essential component of freedom.

In spite of Arthur's impassioned presentation, Lancelot rejects his invitation to join Camelot's community of brothers, asserting that he'll be 'on the road again'. His plans are disrupted when Malagant, in a narrative sequence loosely borrowed from Chrétien's *Lancelot*, kidnaps Guinevere, banking on the idea that 'although self-sacrifice is very easy,' Arthur's convictions will crumble if he is asked to sacrifice 'someone (he) loves'. Lancelot, bound by no code, saves Arthur from this agonizing decision. He storms Malagant's underground fortress and, in a swashbuckling display of wits and derring-do, rescues Guinevere. In the scene that follows, he again confronts her with his desire, calling her to his definition of individual subjectivity. Guinevere counters with her own definition and this exchange encapsulates the conflicting calls of desire and duty, individual and community. 'What,' Lancelot asks Guinevere, 'if you were free (and) the world (would) go away and all the people in it but you and me. Do as you want to do. Here. Now'. Guinevere, however, refuses to define the world as a place in which individuals have no purpose beyond the fulfillment of personal desire. She challenges Lancelot's view, which this scene explains – in good bodice-ripper fashion – as the result of childhood trauma. Lancelot again rejects the idea of 'home': 'I am my own master. I go where I please. Nothing to lose'. As he speaks, the film flashes back to a young Lancelot, watching helplessly as his parents are incinerated inside a church. Guinevere responds, 'God save us all from such a day' and, in reply to Lancelot's bitter protest, 'he didn't save me'; 'But he did . . . Use it for some good purpose, otherwise you might as well have died with the others'.

For Lancelot, however, that good purpose remains the fulfillment of personal desire, even as he chooses to abandon his life as a wanderer and become a knight of the Round Table. As in all scenes that chronicle the hailing and interpellation of the chivalric subject, this sequence highlights Lancelot's choice between two competing discourses. In *First Knight*, this choice resonates with Clinton-era overtones. Arthur identifies Lancelot as an individual without a court, but noting that he has 'risked his life for another,' argues that Lancelot 'has come to Camelot for a purpose, even though he doesn't know it himself'. Arthur sees this purpose as the transformation that will allow Lancelot 'to be born again into a new life'. Recognizing that the man before him 'cares nothing for (him)self,' has 'no wealth, no home, no goal, just the passionate spirit that drives (him) on,' Arthur offers Lancelot a proper object for this passionate spirit. This offer, however, is a very non-cold war vision of an Americanized Round Table: 'no life of privilege but a life of service'. Guinevere, torn herself between competing desires, urges Lancelot to remain a knight without a court, arguing to Arthur that Lancelot 'goes his own way alone. In that freedom and solitude is his strength'. Guinevere's plea, however, is self-serving, as she well knows. In the Clinton-era Arthuriana of this film there is no strength in solitude and no freedom without community. Lancelot seems to recognize these truths as he replies, 'Here among you I have found something I value more than freedom'.

Of course, since that 'something' is, at this point, Guinevere; Lancelot has not embraced Arthur's dream of brotherhood, community, and service. Although he takes a very Clintonesque version of the Round Table oath, which replaces Malory's admonitions against murder and outrage and the imperative to give succor to ladies and gentlewomen and Tennyson's moral etiquette manual with a simple vow that equally binds king and knights: 'brother to brother, yours in life and death,' his motive for staying, as becomes clear as he tells Guinevere that he will go if she goes with him, is personal desire.

After Lancelot takes his chivalric vow, the action of *First Knight* progresses from the royal wedding in which Guinevere and her lands – as symbolized in a frame of the bride in a half-circle of knights rather then the customary bridesmaids – achieve the protection she initially sought, to the disruption of the fealty ceremony with the news that Malagant has indeed violated Lyonesse's borders, to the hasty preparations for war. In the subsequent battle for Lyonesse, Lancelot finally accepts the community of the Round Table and binds himself to it, finding both an ideological home and a goal. His military prowess earns him the respect of Arthur's initially skeptical knights, who hand him back his sword, hailing him as 'Sir Lancelot'. This sense of community and its joys is reinforced as he watches Guinevere reunited with her people; in true 1990s fashion, the hard-bodied male hero breaks into a flood of tears, and in it, finds both healing and renewed strength.[5] He tells Guinevere, 'I know what I must do now. I never believed in anything before. I do believe in Camelot and I will serve it best by leaving it'. In this moment, Lancelot, like Jack Lucas, is converted from cynicism to belief, from individualism to service and, like Indiana Jones, from mercenary to citizen. He also recognizes that true love sees and nurtures, as Arthur has done for him 'the best in people' and sacrifices itself for the good of the beloved. He offers Guinevere and Camelot the gift of his absence, declaring that he is 'a man who loved you too much to change you'.

It is at this point, when Lancelot and Guinevere have both accepted their place in the Arthurian order, that they slip into the one fatal kiss that usually sets Arthurian tragedy inexorably in play. This scene quotes both *The Knights of the Round Table*, in that it entraps the otherwise chaste lovers, and *Camelot*, in that it seals the lovers' decision to put duty above desire. By combining these two moments, *First Knight* redeems Camelot, removing the internal conflict and presenting the threat as entirely from the outside. In Camelot there is no adultery (and no incest); will wins over heart.[6] When Arthur accuses Guinevere, it is not of infidelity, but of a betrayal of emotion, 'Your will chose me; your heart chooses him,' Guinevere, in harmony with the film's ideology of community, replies, 'Than you have the best of it. My will is stronger than my heart'.

As Arthur insists that Guinevere and Lancelot stand trial in the public square, it seems that he is making the same mistake as *Excalibur*'s Arthur, abandoning the kingdom in the wake of his personal anguish. However, *First Knight* argues that, in the end, Arthur serves the kingdom by insisting on a law that applies equally to all – thus avoiding the poison of *Camelot*. When he is advised that it would be 'better to settle the matter in private,' he retorts, 'Do you think the honor of Camelot is a private matter? Let everyone see that the law rules in Camelot,' a policy of 'full disclosure' that must have resonated with an American public under an administration plagued by scandals and special prosecutors. In this spirit of honor and disclosure, neither the queen nor Lancelot flee from justice; they stand their trial in the public square; during it, Lancelot demonstrates that he has indeed been 'born again' from the 'wanderer who had never dreamed of justice or knighthood' into an Arthurian knight who embraces a life of service. No longer a man who doesn't care 'if (he) live(s) or die(s),' Lancelot now dedicates his life to the ideal of Camelot. He tells Arthur, 'the Queen is innocent, but if my life or death serves Camelot, take it; do as you will with me. Brother to brother, yours in life and death'. As Lancelot accepts the full meaning of his chivalric vow, Malagant storms the city and Arthur reaffirms his definition of the world and a man's purpose in it: 'to help each other'. He sacrifices his own life to this ideal, commanding his people to fight for his dream, even as Malagant's archers pierce him with arrows; as Arthur dies, Lancelot comes into his full power, leading the citizens of Camelot as they turn back the tyrant and killing the 'bad son' with his own hand.

The battle is won, Camelot is saved, and Arthur passes not to Avalon but into the flames of a Viking funeral.[7] In these final sequences, *First Knight* presents the most radical of its many rewritings of Arthurian cinematic and literary traditions. In spite of Arthur's death and incineration, *First Knight* presents an Arthurian comedy – in the sense that order is restored and the torch is passed on to the next generation. Excalibur, and the political and ideological power it represents, does not return to the Lady of the Lake, but is passed to the good son; Lancelot becomes a king instead of a penitent hermit, and Guinevere does not end her days in a convent but as a queen at Lancelot's side. Because the usually hapless lovers believed in the 'good, the true and the right' and chose to live their lives accordingly, they and the kingdom are spared Arthurian tragedy.

First Knight, like Bill Clinton, offered Americans a community of hope in which citizens served each other and America fulfilled its humanitarian responsibilities to a global village; however, in its debt to the cold war Arthuriana of the 1950s, its insistence on one good and true and right, one set of laws – located in American ideology – that make men free, and its pro-military stance, it also set the stage for a doctrine of democratic conquest. In a post-9/11 world, this doctrine was combined with a revision of the cold war meta-narrative – in which the axis of evil stood in for the forces of communism and the enemy within morphed from the leftist intellectual plotting invasion to the hidden terrorist plotting destruction – and grafted onto Clinton's vision of America's global humanitarian position to call the nation to a war that would bring democracy to the Middle East, secure American borders, and liberate an oppressed people. Given the long history of the connection between these themes and Hollywood Arthuriana, it was not unreasonable to expect that, when Hollywood returned to Camelot in the midst of this war, it would produce a film in the mold of *First Knight* and *The Knights of the Round Table.* And such a film is clearly what audiences and critics expected – in spite of the fact that they had been warned for months that Bruckheimer's film was not your father's King Arthur (no castles, no knights, as Franzoni described it, 'in shiny tin cans, cranking about the countryside carrying on quests').[8] Writing for *The New York Times* two months before the release of Bruckheimer's would-be blockbuster, Sharon Waxman predicted that *King Arthur* would be one of the many unambiguous summer releases about 'vanquishing evil, battling for freedom and dying for honor' that Hollywood was banking on as real life became murkier and the outcome in Iraq less certain.[9]

However, *King Arthur* – in spite of its manifest flaws in pacing, dialogue, and characterization – is much more interesting than that. In fact, the film can be read as a direct condemnation of the cold war rhetoric and attitudes that led to the war in Iraq.[10] By figuring Rome, the supposed ambassador of the *Pax Romana*, as a corrupt imperialist force that – in the name of Christianity and under the cover of God's will – offers its conquered subjects not freedom but exploitation, and portraying Arthur as a well-meaning general who has been duped by empty rhetoric into serving and promoting Rome's ethnocentric ends, *King Arthur* questions America's foreign and martial agenda. It also complicates the central binary of cold war/antiterrorism rhetoric – the clear distinction between self and other, patriot and terrorist – in its characterization of the Woads, whom Rome defines as terrorists and rebels but Merlin, Guinevere, and, finally, Arthur, identify as patriots and freedom fighters. Furthermore, the film, with its over-the-top violence and its dark and moody tone, fractures visions of martial glory and casts serious doubts upon the myth that there is peace on the other side of war.

Indeed, *King Arthur* is about the dismantling of myth; from its very beginning frames – and indeed from its first press releases – the film establishes itself as 'the truth behind the myth,' promising to strip away the layers of fantasy and fable to reveal Arthur's 'true identity'. By taking an obscure hypothesis that identifies the original Arthurian knights as a group of Sarmatian conscripts who served in Britain under a Roman general named Lucius Artorius Castus as his starting point, screenwriter David Franzoni, as Mark Rasmussen observes, provides himself with an empty space, free from other Arthurs and other Camelots, upon which to write his 'true' history.[11] On the other hand, in the very act of setting this version against Arthurian tradition, Franzoni invokes it and his revelation of the 'real story' serves to undermine the myths of national authority and manifest destiny usually associated with the mythic Arthur. This process of separating the man from the myth begins with the film's portrayal of Rome, usually figured in Arthurian narrative as the origin of Arthur's political philosophy and – in American versions – as the birthplace of Western democracy. In *King Arthur*, Rome is nothing more than an aggressive conqueror motivated by a desire for 'more land, more wealth, more people loyal to Rome'. The film opens as the Romans invade Sarmatia and wipe out the resistance, leaving alive only a handful of brave fighters who 'were incorporated into the Roman military,' and striking a bargain that indebted 'their sons and their sons to serve the empire'. 'Better,' the narration concludes, 'that they had died that day'. To the Sarmatians, Rome offered not freedom, but enslavement and exploitation, building and maintaining its empire with the blood of Sarmatian sons.

While Rome has succeeded in wiping out the Sarmatian resistance and in incorporating the country into its economic and military base, it has not, as the main narrative begins, completely subdued the Britons, whom the film introduces when a mob of blue-painted warriors emerge from the mists to ambush the Bishop's carriage; the Woads (an unlikely and ahistoric merging of the Picts and the Celts, amusing in a film that trumpets its historical accuracy) are figured here as 'blue demons who eat Christians alive, British rebels who hate Rome' – security threats too stubborn to see what Rome, with its laws, has to offer their barbaric land. If *King Arthur* maintained this definition and told the tale of the securing of the British lands for the forces of democracy, it would have been exactly the kind of film that Waxman had predicted it would be; however, the Sarmatian sequence has already cast doubt upon Rome's motives and good intentions, and even this scene offers an alternative reading of the Woads: 'men who want their country back' and who are convinced that the shedding of their blood in battle against the Romans will produce 'sacred ground'. These doubts intensify as the film continues and it becomes clear that Arthur's Rome, 'ordered, civilized, (where) the greatest minds from all over the world have come together in one place in order to make men free,' 'does not exist,' except in imperialist rhetoric and a few men's mistaken dreams. Instead, Rome is a corrupt institution, run by an elite intent on exploiting its subjects and not above abandoning them when their purpose has been served or Rome's armies are needed elsewhere.

These attitudes are encapsulated in the Bishop, a man intent on his position, as exemplified by his aide's instructions to Arthur's man – 'My master must be seated at the head (of the table)' – and subsequent horrified reaction to Arthur's council room, 'A round table? What sort of evil is this?' Furthermore, the Bishop is a man utterly without scruples, willing to sacrifice others' lives – his decoy's, Arthur's, and his men's – in order to maintain ethnic and class privileges, and not above using the rhetoric of duty and, when that fails, thinly veiled threats, to accomplish his goals. Piously reminding Arthur and his knights that 'we are all but bit players in an ever-changing world,' the Bishop announces Rome's intent to 'remove itself from the indefensible outpost' of Britain, leaving it to the Saxons, who, Arthur protests, 'only claim what they kill'. He then issues one last set of orders: before Arthur's men can be freed to return home, they must journey north to collect a Roman citizen and his family and escort them south. When Arthur refuses to accept the Bishop's designation of this mission as a duty, the Roman official resorts to threats, pointing out that the men may be free but, without the papers he holds, they will certainly be captured and enslaved: no journey, no paper.

While, as many reviewers noticed, this 'one final mission' motif is not without its cinematic precedents, it must have also had a contemporary resonance with both the writers and actors, who filmed *King Arthur* as the first reports of extended tours in Iraq hit the news, and the film's eventual audiences, who viewed it as those extended tours became a hot topic and questions about the war in Iraq and the administration's motives multiplied. The Bishop's callous dismissal of Arthur's protest – he offers the men, 'who have fought for fifteen years for a cause not their own' 'not freedom but death': 'If your knights are truly the knights of legend perhaps some will survive,' must have struck at least some viewers – the same ones that were helping Michael Moore's *Fahrenheit 9/11* make box-office history – as depressingly similar to their own administration's approach to those who did not belong to its base of 'the haves and the have mores'.

And indeed, Arthur's men are asked to face almost certain death in order to save a handful of the 'have mores': a Roman aristocrat, granted a chunk of Britain by the Pope, and his family, which includes the Pope's favorite godson, destined himself to inherit power and privilege. When Arthur arrives at the estate of Marius, he finds a disturbing abuse of power and privilege. Instead of using his Roman superiority to bring civilization and Christian values to the benighted natives, Marius has used his power as a self-proclaimed 'spokesman from God' to exploit, enslave, and, ultimately, torture the people he is, in the official rhetoric about Rome, supposed to free and enlighten. The village's leader languishes in chains, strung up as a warning against insubordination because he requested that the starving villagers be able to keep a little more of the food they grew for themselves; more horrifying still, Arthur discovers a cache of natives being walled into a dungeon to die, including Guinevere, who, as one of the leaders of the Woad's resistance, is in Rome's eyes a terrorist, fair-game for ruthless torture, the use of 'machines to make me tell them things I didn't know to begin with'. When Arthur attempts to rescue these prisoners, he is hindered by a group of fanatic monks, who accuse them of being 'defilers of the Lord's temple'. These monks – aided by Marius, who identifies the prisoners as pagans who 'refused to do the tasks (i.e. slaving for Marius) that God has set for them' and thus 'must die as an example' – see themselves as the messengers of Christianity in a pagan land; they also see Arthur as a natural ally, 'You are a Roman and a Christian,' they argue, 'you understand. It is God's will that these sinners be sacrificed. Only then will they be saved'.

Between Marius and the monk's definition of Roman-Christian privilege and Arthur's ideal of Rome as the beginning of all man's freedom and Christianity as a religion in which an individual can 'kneel before the God he trusts,' lies an unbridgeable gulf. Instead of reinforcing Marius's claim to be from God, Arthur vehemently denies it: 'Marius is not from God and you, all of you were free from your first breath'. In these scenes, however, Arthur still reads men such as Marius and the Bishop as aberrations, clinging to his ideal of Rome as a city on the hill, a beacon of freedom and equality in a dark land, It takes Marius's troubled son to disillusion him. 'What my father believes,' Alectus insists, 'Rome believes, that some men are born to be slaves'. Arthur demurs, arguing that his hero Pelagius, who teaches that 'all men are free to choose their own destiny,' is the true representative of Rome. Pelagius, Alectus informs Arthur, has been executed, concluding, 'the Rome you talk of doesn't exist, except in your dreams'.

Arthur may see himself as a Roman of the Romans, but he is, as he must learn, the antithesis of all Rome really is and, ultimately, convert from Roman general to British patriot. This conversion however, unlike the hailing and interpellation of earlier Hollywood knights and kings, does not overthrow Arthur's initial values – equality, free will, necessary war – it affirms them. When Arthur argues that the fact that he fought for 'a Rome that did not exist' renders his deeds 'meaningless,' since they were executed for economic gain rather than a higher purpose, Guinevere insists that he has 'bloodied evil men' – that he has executed justice in spite of the motives of his leaders. She also argues, however, that Arthur has been living in an unnatural state as 'the famous Briton who kills his own people,' and offers Arthur a new identity, a Briton, and a new way of seeing the world: the Woads as those who 'belong to the land' and the Romans as the invader 'who takes what doesn't belong to him'. It, she concludes, is 'the natural state of any man to want to live free in their own country'.

Merlin also offers Arthur his true identity, reminding him that his mother was 'of our blood' and his sword, Excalibur, is 'made of iron from this earth, forged in the fires of Britain'. Furthermore, this leader of the Woad's rebellion calls for an end to the violence and enmity between the knights and the resistance, recognizing that on both sides many have lost brothers, but arguing that enmity must be put aside: 'the world we have known and fought for is gone,' he insists, 'We (will) make a new one'. Merlin's call for an emotional truce allows past enemies to unite in a common cause and Arthur's conversion from Roman to Briton offers him a new fight – one that, in his eyes, constitutes a just war: the defense of national borders and the institution of a 'new world' of free will and equality, where men, being equal are 'free to be men'.

The film escapes the hard questions that might be raised if Arthur, in order to usher in this new world, would have had to turn his back on Rome and become a terrorist/freedom fighter himself, battling against the very order he once served. However, because it bases its narrative on common theories that identify the historical Arthur as a Roman-British leader who led the abandoned Celts in their defense against the invading Saxons, *King Arthur* can have its cake and eat it too; Rome is discredited but Arthur is saved from the problematic position of taking arms against an established order. Instead, he is able to become the ultimate patriot, the man defending his country against the invading forces of chaos, which the film goes out of its way to portray as unreconstructed barbarians – who save a woman from rape, only to kill her, ruthlessly sacrifice their own people, and generally burn and pillage everything in sight, ensuring that 'not a man, woman, or child who can ever carry a sword' will survive.

It is in this final, unambiguous fight, that Arthur finds the proper outlet and true purpose for the martial violence that has made up the tale of his life; at this moment, the film seemingly switches from a narrative that questions warrior values and actions as the tool of corrupt and greedy governments to one that glorifies those very values as the necessary means to human freedom. As before, Arthur (and eventually his knights) rides to a battle in which, as Lancelot argues, 'certain death awaits'. Yet, this battle is the right one. Arthur explains, 'All the blood I have shed, all the lives I have taken, have led me to this moment,' a moment that begins with Arthur – in a cinematic frame that, like many others in this film, owes much to Jackson's *Lord of the Rings* trilogy – as a lone knight, back-lit on a misty hill, surveying the massive army below him, ready, as he tells the Saxon leader, to 'fight for a cause beyond Rome's or your understanding'.

Arthur, however, is not doomed to fight alone; motivated more by the male ties that bind than by any recognition of a higher cause, the remaining Sarmatian knights abandon their dreams of home and return to stand by their leader. As the battle looms, Arthur delivers a 'St. Crispin's Day' speech to the troops: 'The gift of freedom is yours by right. But the home we seek lies not in some distant land. It's in us and our actions on this day. If this be our destiny, then so be it. But let history record that as free men we chose to make it so'. This rather uninspiring speech may well be the result of poor or hurried writing, but *Gladiator* makes it clear that Franzoni is more than capable of constructing a rousing rhetorical moment. Furthermore, what makes this speech particularly flat is its lack of any real content. Compare it, for instance to Aragorn's speech before the gates of Mordor in *The Return of the King:* 'A day may come when the courage of men fails and we forsake our friends and break all bonds of fellowship, but it is not this day; an hour will fall when the shattered shields from the age of men come crashing down, but it is not this day. This day we fight, by all that we hold dear on this good earth. I bid you stand, men of the West!' While Aragorn's speech appeals to shared values – to that clear-cut good and evil that Waxman argued Hollywood studios were banking on – and tropes the Battle for Middle Earth as the battle for 'all we hold dear,' Arthur's oration makes a rather vague and lukewarm appeal to the freedom and home that lies within each man and a resigned nod to destiny; rather than 'not this day,' perhaps this day.

The battle that follows reinforces the differences between the epic battle for Middle Earth and Arthur's last stand. Even without the decapitations and Guinevere's killing spree, and with sepia-toned blood spatters and a toned-down version of Arthur's execution of the Saxon chief (all changes that Antoine Fuqua made in search of a PG-13 rating), it is deeply violent. Furthermore, unlike Jackson's *Lord of the Rings* battles, it is shot almost entirely in close and medium shots, cutting rapidly from one bloody scene to another, giving the whole a feel of chaos and uncertainty, slowing down only to linger on Lancelot's death. It is not until the battle is over, and presumably won, that the camera pans back to reveal the whole picture, an endless field of death and carnage. The narrative then cross-cuts to first despairing Arthur – 'My brave knights,' he mourns, 'I have failed you. I neither took you off of this island nor shared, your fate' – and, then, to a multiple funeral. As Arthur sets fire to Lancelot's corpse, the film switches to a shot of running horses, echoing the narrator's opening assertion that 'fallen knights return as great horses,' and providing a reading of the tale, 'For two hundred years knights had fought and died for a land not their own but on that day on Badon Hill, all who fought put their lives in service of a greater cause, freedom. As for the knights who gave their lives that day, their deaths were cause for neither mourning nor sadness . . . Their names would live on in tales passed from father to son, mother to daughter: the legends of King Arthur and his noble knights'.

On the one hand, this voice-over expresses standard American Arthurian themes, identifying Arthur's battles as battles for freedom and democracy, necessary violence in the 'service of a greater cause'. On the other, the audience has been left not with visions of freedom and a new start but with images of mutilated and dead bodies and of Arthur's loss and despair. Furthermore, as the film's opening crawl makes clear, the legends of King Arthur have little to do with what this version argues were the actual events; in fact, in them, these Sarmatian knights are barely recognizable, they have been stripped of their national identity and pressed into the service of various ideological and political agendas. Fuqua and Franzoni meant the film to end here, on a somber note that casts questions on the motives and profits of war and points to the rhetoric with which we frame, justify, and even glorify, the death and loss that war brings. If they had been allowed to do so, *King Arthur* would have been a very different and, I believe, more effective film.[12]

However, in search of a PG-13 rating and a summer box-office hit, the director – 16 days before the film's release – added a happy ending, one that places his film in the tradition of Hollywood Arthuriana and muffles the dissenting voice of the narrative that precedes it. Gathered among the standing stones of a Stonehenge substitute, overlooking the ocean on the first sunny day in the entire movie, Arthur marries Guinevere in a wedding that symbolizes, as Merlin announces, 'Our people are one as you are one . . . Let every man, woman, and child bear witness that from this day, all Britons will be united in a common cause'. Arthur is proclaimed king; the sun glints from Excalibur, and an exuberant salute of fire arrows marks the beginning of a new, proto-American order, in which all men will be equal and all free, as the film's second round of promotional posters promised, to 'choose (their) own destiny'.

King Arthur's fate reminds us that the Arthurian space is always-already occupied: by the hierarchical political and social structures of medieval Europe, by a masculine identity constructed and maintained by violence, by visions of a simpler time, by the longing for a king. These conflicting dreams and desires haunt American Arthurian legend from the very moment of its inception in the nineteenth century, when Progressive reformers appropriated chivalric narratives of democratic possibility to construct proper American workers, the new business elite adopted the symbols and doctrines of neo-feudalism to maintain and justify the status quo, corporate magnates depicted their factories as medieval guilds, the rhetoric of manifest destiny and cultural and commercial imperialism valorized the medieval martial ethos, and Wilsonian reform cast Americans as the new Normans, bringing civilization to a chaotic and barbaric world. In Hollywood, these multiple appropriations of the medieval past inflected Hollywood Arthuriana with conservative values, as the legend was used to shore up the status quo, construct proper American subjects, and affirm America's divinely sanctioned position as global leader in films that range from 1917's *The Knights of the Square Table*, through cold war Arthuriana, and into the Reagan–Bush era.

Even versions of the legend that appropriate Camelot for more radical ends find themselves affected by its persistent pull toward conservatism; for some – the political platform of Young England, the mythopoet's and John Boorman's dream of a true King, and Billy's vision of a utopian medieval past – their own longing for hierarchy and positive masculinity carries with it the seeds of the legend's ultimate turn to conservatism. For others – *The Sword of Lancelot* and *King Arthur* – the narrative itself, so often presented to shore up the establishment and its values, resists all attempts to wrest it away from its traditional form. Only two of the films discussed in this book escape the Arthurian turn to conservatism: *Monty Python and the Holy Grail* and *The Fisher King*; these films, one co-directed and one directed by Terry Gilliam, do so because they recognize that their founding narrative contains within it the very values they are trying to escape and they go out of their way to banish those values from the Arthurian space. *The Holy Grail* completely demolishes Arthurian glamor and *The Fisher King* explicitly rewrites the Grail tale, stripping it of its hierarchical and martial trappings.

The history of Hollywood Arthuriana – *The Knights of the Square Table*'s construction of proper citizens, the HUAC era's hunt for the enemy within, the hijacking of Boorman's *Excalibur*, *First Knight*'s vision of a new manifest destiny, Disney/Touchstone's domestication of *King Arthur* – calls us to heed Eco's warning about the dangers of Western Culture's persistent dream of the medieval past: 'Since the Middle Ages have always been messed up in order to meet the vital requirements of different periods,' it is critical that we ask 'which Middle Ages one is dreaming of'.[13] Hollywood's dream of the Arthurian Middle Ages is a seductive one, one that promises individual and national prosperity, that affirms America as a land of democratic possibility and celebrates its divine destiny; however, instead of being uncritically seduced by this nostalgic vision of an Americanized Camelot's golden days and Arthur's lost chivalric past, we need to ask ourselves what other, less desirable, values these Hollywood knights bring forward into the present.

Notes

1 Anthony Lane, *New Yorker* 71 (July 1995): 84 [84–85]; Richard Schickel, *Time* 146 (July 17, 1995): 58; Andy Pawelczak, *Films in Review* 46 (September–October 1995): 57 [56–57]. For a complete list of reviews see Kevin J. Harty, *Cinema Arthuriana: Twenty Essays*, rev. ed., New York: McFarland, 2002, p. 266.

2 Jacqueline Jenkins, 'First Knights and Common Men: Masculinity in American Arthurian Film,' in *King Arthur on Film: New Essays on Arthurian Cinema*, ed. K. J. Harty, New York: McFarland Publishers, 1999, pp. 81–95; and Robert J. Blanch and Julian N. Wasserman, 'Fear of Flying: The Absence of Internal Tension in *Sword of the Valiant* and *First Knight*,' *Arthuriana* 10 (Summer 2000): 15–32, have discussed this film as an Americanization of the legend; however both articles see Lancelot's individualism as valorized, whereas I argue that it must be left behind and Lancelot integrated into the court. Other critical discussions of the film include R. A. Umland and S. J. Umland, *The Use of Arthurian Legend in Hollywood Film: From Conneticut Yankees to Fisher Kings*, Portsmouth, NH: Greenwood, 1996, pp. 94–100, who also note that Lancelot must transform, but focus their analysis on the film and its love-triangle as melodrama; J. Aberth, *A Knight at the Movies*, London: Routledge, 2003, pp. 16–17, who notes Jenkins's assertion that the film shows a democratized Middle Ages, Shira Schwam-Baird, 'King Arthur in Hollywood: The Subversion of Tragedy in *First Knight*,' *Medieval Perspectives* 14 (1999): 202–213, who discusses the film's happy ending as in keeping

with earlier Arthurian traditions that separate the love-triangle from the fall of the Round Table, and Donald Hoffman's '*First Knight* (1995): An American Gigolo in King Arthur's Court; or 0071/2 ,' 39th International Medieval Congress, Kalamazoo MI, May 2004. Hoffman's paper, delivered as I was finishing this book, and Caroline Jewers's article 'Hard Day's-Knights: *First Knight, A Knight's Tale,* and *Black Knight*,' in *The Medieval Hero and Screen: Representations from Beowulf to Buffy*, ed. Martha W. Driver and Sid Ray (North Carolina: McFarland and Company, 2004), pp. 193–207, published after I had initially sent the manuscript to press, are the only other studies to place the film in a political context.

3 Hoffman, 'American Gigolo,' also notes the connection between Guinevere and the land.

4 Jenkins, 'Common Men,' p. 84, also discusses this scene as an example of Lancelot's democratic view of the world.

5 Jenkins examines this battle as a valorization of Lancelot's fighting techniques and the court's acceptance of them (pp. 84–85); she sees his conversion in the scene that follows as in keeping with the men's movement and the new masculinity of the 1990s (pp. 88–89).

6 Hoffman, 'American Gigolo,' also notes that in this film the threat is from the outside, which, as he observes, only increases the film's ethnocentrism.

7 Hoffman notes that this scene in which 'the expendable old man goes spectacularly to Valhalla' enables the film's happy ending (p. 12).

8 Qtd. in Jeff Jensen, 'Return of the King,' *Entertainment Weekly* (July 16, 2004): 40.

9 Jensen, 'Return of the King,' 39–44, 40; Sharon Waxman, 'At the Movies, at Least, Good Vanquishes Evil,' *The New York Times* (July 14, 2004): web edition.

10 The film was widely reviewed and widely dismissed. For intelligent reviews that place the film in the context of *Cinema Arthuriana*, see Kevin J. Harty's and Alan Lupack's reviews in *Arthuriana* 14.3 (2004): 121–125.

11 The film's use of the Sarmatian hypothesis, which Franzoni latched upon after reading C. Scott Littleton and Linda A. Malcor's *From Scythia to Camelot* (New York: Garland, 1994, 2000), has been the subject of considerable discussion – by Franzoni himself, on Arthurnet, in film-advisor John Matthews's 'A Knightly Endeavor: The Making of Jerry Bruckheimer's *King Arthur*,' *Arthuriana* 14.3 (2004): 112–119. Mark Rasmussen presented his analysis of the film's rhetorical use of this hypothesis in 'Touchstone Pictures and the Historical Arthur,' presented at the (Re) Creating Arthur Conference, Winchester, England, August 6, 2004.

12 For a detailed discussion of the changes Fuqua was forced to make when Disney moved the film from a December to a summer release and requested (read insisted) that it be cut with an eye on a PG-13 rating, see Jensen, 'Return of the King.'

13 U. Eco, 'Dreaming the Middle Ages,' *Travels in Hyperreality*, trans. W. Weaver, New York: Harcourt Brace, 1986, p. 68.

Reading 16

Monica Silveira Cyrino

GLADIATOR (2000)

'Gladiator (2000)', in *Big Screen Rome,* Oxford: Blackwell, 2005, pp. 238–56.

JUST AS EARLIER EPIC FILMS used the framework of ancient Rome to address issues relevant to mid-century America, *Gladiator* functions as an allegory of its time, evoking certain essential themes and concerns unique to contemporary American society in the year 2000.[1] Thus, *Gladiator* provides a new critical tool for the exploration of more recent debates in American politics and culture. Scholars of classics and cinema have elucidated how the earlier toga films ambiguously invited American audiences both to distance themselves from and to identify with the spectacle of Roman power, luxury, and superiority. The process of projection in those mid-century films was a complex one, in that the figure of Rome as a corrupt oppressor troubled and repelled the post-war American viewer, while the self-confident and materially comfortable image of Rome inevitably attracted audience favour in the consumer-oriented American economy of the time.[2] But as the first Roman epic made after the end of the Cold War, *Gladiator* arrived in an altogether different sociopolitical world and thereby introduced a new and extraordinary problem of interpretation. The film's prologue script, scrolled against an austere background, with Lisa Gerrard's haunting female vocals as its only accompaniment, informs the audience rather ominously that Rome is 'at the height of its power'. American movie-goers in the year 2000, confident in their country's unilateral geopolitical dominance, experience a shock of recognition followed by a rush of familiarity when they view the spectacular recreation of ancient Rome onscreen. The Romans depicted in *Gladiator* undeniably stand in for contemporary

Americans, and the film is 'a meditation on the perplexity of the world's sole surviving superpower' (Muschamp, *The New York Times*, April 30, 2000). This bewilderment is represented by two very distinct depictions of Rome in this film, as *Gladiator* poses the question of the very direction and purpose of American cultural and political hegemony.

The main theme of the film is the crucial conflict between two competing visions of what kind of superpower Rome, or by analogy America, should be. *Gladiator* opens in a world completely conquered by Roman military might. As General Maximus tells the emperor Marcus Aurelius in the first act of the film: 'There is no one left to fight, sire'. But the worldwide spread of the *pax Romana*, the Roman peace, does not extend to Rome itself. Instead, the film portrays Rome on the verge of breakdown under increasing pressure from within, where two opposing sides clash in an ideological war between the totalitarian oppression epitomized by the wicked young emperor Commodus, and the just and noble Republicanism embodied by the hero Maximus.[3] In an ingenious plot innovation, *Gladiator* introduces the improbable objective of restoring the Republic in the late empire period of AD 180, and allows this fantasy to represent Good in its everlasting conflict against Evil.[4] Earlier epic films traditionally situated Rome in the role of imperialistic oppressor of implausibly virtuous and racially harmonious groups, the most common narrative formula being the subjugation of Christians, Hebrews, or slaves, while films like *Spartacus* and *The Fall of the Roman Empire* focused on rival Roman factions in their examinations of the corrupting influence of power. *Gladiator* presents an imaginative new development by casting the Roman Empire as the oppressor of its true Republican self. So the cinematic showdown between Maximus and Commodus is a battle for Rome's very soul, as each man tries to define his idea of Rome on his own terms. Maximus' dream of a Republican Rome where family farmers become soldiers only when necessary to fight genuine external enemies is set against Commodus' spectacle of Rome where staged battles mask the internal erosion of an empire.

Gladiator is primarily a story of the hero's alienation.[5] The film offers a compelling analogy between the cinematic theme of Maximus' disaffection from the idea of Rome and the modern individual's current sense of estrangement from the American political apparatus in all its corrupt irrelevance. The story of Maximus' journey of transition from general to slave to gladiator exemplifies such isolation from national or group identity, followed by a decisive turn towards pure self-interested individuation. At the beginning, Maximus the general fights for an idea of Rome, but he's never actually been to the city, suggesting he remains undefiled by the reality of Rome's distorted existence. Maximus demonstrates his patriotism and personal valour on the battlefield, and when he utters the Roman army motto, 'Strength and Honour,' it is clear these are virtues he embodies.

The story of Maximus' alienation from the idea of a degenerate Rome and his deep-seated reluctance about his role in restoring Roman government to the people offers a parallel to post-Cold War America. When Maximus first lays eyes on Rome as a slave, he feels nothing but revulsion for and disconnection from the corrupt image he sees. He tells Proximo before the games: 'I am required to kill, so I kill. That is enough'. But Proximo corrects him: 'That is enough for the provinces, but not enough for Rome'. As Maximus demonstrates his killing proficiency and leadership in the Roman Colosseum, he discovers there is power to be won in the pretend wars staged by Commodus. 'Today I saw a slave become more powerful than the emperor of Rome,' Lucilla tells him, as he realizes the truth of her words: 'The mob *is* Rome'. So the disillusioned general turned free-agent hero is driven by his anger and isolation to reenvision his own ideal of Rome from within the arena.

The arena in *Gladiator* offers another provocative interpretation of the relationship between the people and their rulers. In an interval of real or imagined threats to individual and national security, tensions often arise between the exercise of authoritarian rule to preserve liberty under attack, and the ability to express personal freedoms in an atmosphere of alarm. 'Fear and wonder,' Senator Gracchus describes the condition of the Roman people transfixed by the young emperor's games, 'a powerful combination'. Such a time of anxiety creates an opportunity for leaders to take advantage of the people's lack of understanding and participation in the political process. In *Gladiator*, the stress and uncertainty of Roman life under the despotic rule of Commodus is relieved by the production of a numbing series of gladiatorial games, with posters announcing 150 days of *violentia*, 'violence,' in the arena. The senators articulate the gradual loss of the Romans' ability to contribute to their government, as constraints continue to be imposed on them in their mindless preoccupation with the spectacles offered by the tyrant. 'Take away their freedom,' warns Gracchus, 'and still they roar'.

Gladiatorial violence in the Roman arena rehearsed the dangers of warfare and celebrated the prowess of the Roman military in a vicarious thrill for the spectators . . . Similarly, the modern American sports arena has always been a privileged location for the display of patriotism through the performance of the national anthem and the exhibition of healthy American youth and economic affluence in the colourful pageantry of athletes and cheerleaders. But there has been a notable increase in the martial tenor of these presentations in the pre-game and half-time showcases of professional and collegiate sporting events, with more military marching bands and deafening F-16 jet flyovers, as if to exorcise fears of unseen enemies while flexing American military muscle. Such displays demonstrate how contemporary warfare is waged and won by highly trained military forces whose specialized expertise makes them equivalent to modern-day gladiators. In the Colosseum, the mob of Rome is regaled with gripping and convincingly bloody recreations of great Roman battles, where history can be manipulated or even misrepresented to celebrate the current ruler and his personal ambitions. Similarly, in today's media-saturated environment, the American people are exposed to contemporary politicians and pundits who 'spin' or distort facts for partisan convenience, and news outlets control the flow of information to maximize their commercial advantage. 'The people always love victories,' as Lucilla reminds Commodus.

Another link between *Gladiator* and contemporary society is the movement towards 'simplicity' and the longing to return to the homespun, down-to-earth values of the mid-twentieth-century hearth and family.[6] Americans today are wistful about an earlier period of national history because of the currently widespread perception, clearly idealized, that back then America was more certain of its identity and purpose as the leader of the world. It was a simpler time when an individual could easily achieve the 'American Dream' through the virtues of hard work and commitment to God, family, and country. Maximus, too, looks back to a time when the idea of Rome meant something decent, true, and comprehensible about the validity of empire, a time when his loyalty and service to Rome raised him up from the fields of his farm to become General of the Legions, winning victories for Rome on the field of honor. *Gladiator* as a historical movie hearkens back to an earlier cinematic genre, so it responds to the current 'retro' trend in popular entertainment, the desire to recreate a version of the simple cultural spirit of America in the 1950s and 1960s when epic films were in their heyday. '*Gladiator* reveals another twenty-first-century bias. Contemporary Hollywood family values interject themselves into the ancient Roman zeitgeist'.[7]

The film primarily explores the theme of a return to traditional ideals of home and family using the character of Maximus, a farmer who longs for the countryside. His wish to return home when the soldier's job is done is depicted as the single greatest thing a man can strive to achieve. 'Dirt cleans off a lot easier than blood,' he tells the senators. The ideal has special relevance for American viewers familiar with Founding Father Thomas Jefferson's veneration of his farm at Monticello in Virginia, and his concept of the gentleman farmer as the archetype of American nobility and virtuous citizenship. When Marcus Aurelius asks him after the battle in Germania, 'Tell me about your home,' Maximus delivers a sentimental speech about the simple beauty and jasmine-scented tranquility of his farm in Hispania, with its fecund soil 'black like my wife's hair'. His wistful reverie is given particular meaning and evokes the modern individual's yearning for the simplicity of the land, because actor Crowe said he wrote the speech drawing on his own feelings of homesickness for his Australian ranch. During this scene, Marcus Aurelius tells Maximus his home is 'worth fighting for,' and thereby suggests that the protection of the small family farm is one of the chief purposes of Roman military conquest. The old emperor, beset by doubts about the legacy of his rule, realizes the countryside, and not the city, is the true Rome. The 'homesick' speech anticipates and fortifies the depiction of Maximus as an old-fashioned man of the soil who has been cruelly displaced. Maximus picks up a handful of dirt and smells it before each fight, drawing strength from his sensory connection to the soil. This gesture creates for the film audience a consistently 'grounded' character throughout a series of important onscreen trials: before the battle in Germania, before his first contest in the provincial arena in Zucchabar, before the pivotal battle of Carthage, and before his final, fatal confrontation with Commodus. Writer Franzoni noted: 'Some thought he did it when his life was in danger. But really, the impulse was, he does it when he's about to kick ass'.[8] Maximus cannot lose as long as he keeps in contact with the ground.

This portrayal of Maximus as a simple man of the land responds to modern society's idealization of the countryside and its supposed virtue and purity, just as many American families continue to abandon crime-ridden metropolitan centers in favor of simpler, safer suburban communities. In the cinematic imagination, no city in history is depicted as more treacherous and perverse than ancient Rome, where the inhabitants 'are occupied by an overriding lust for power, lust for wealth, or lust pure and simple'.[9] *Gladiator* revives the spectacle of Roman corruption and debauchery so lavishly portrayed in earlier toga films that equated oppressive political power with social and sexual deviance. As in earlier epics, *Gladiator* employs images of transgressive sexuality to suggest the moral depravity of Roman tyranny. Commodus expresses his incestuous yearnings for his elder sister, Lucilla, in several scenes that connect his aberrant erotic desires with his despotic plans for Rome.

In the same breath that he announces his wish to dissolve the Senate, Commodus invites Lucilla to stay the night with him. After the conspiracy is discovered, he spares Lucilla but demands she provide him with an heir to cement his dynasty, bellowing at her: 'Am I not merciful?' Commodus' perverse sexuality parallels the depiction of the bisexuality of wealthy Crassus hinted at in *Spartacus*, where the inversion of conventional sexual relations also revealed the dysfunction of the Roman value system, and maintained an equation 'between aristocratic promiscuity and political rapacity'.[10]

In profound contrast to these images of Roman sexuality gone awry, Maximus honors his wife and remains celibate through a series of tension-filled encounters with his ex-lover, Lucilla. Their first meeting after years of separation takes place in Germania, where they grieve together over the suspicious death of Marcus Aurelius. This tenuous bond is quickly erased after Maximus has been betrayed, enslaved, and his family murdered by Commodus. Chained to the wall of the gladiators' quarters, Maximus is met by a veiled Lucilla who emerges from the shadows: 'Rich matrons pay well to be pleasured by the greatest champions'. In an angry and sexually charged exchange, Maximus accuses Lucilla of complicity in his family's deaths. Their next encounter occurs at the gladiatorial compound as the coup attempt is set in motion. 'You risk too much,' Maximus tells her, and when she answers brokenly, 'I have much to pay for,' he corrects her, 'You have nothing to pay for'. This single, oblique reference to their previous affair seems to assign the blame for past hurt to Lucilla and accords well with the depiction of Maximus as a gentleman of old-fashioned decency. As she whispers to him, 'I have felt alone all my life, except with you,' all she gets for her declaration is a modest kiss.

In these brief meetings, Maximus and Lucilla negotiate the tricky boundaries of their past relationship and reconstruct it tentatively within the emotional gap created by their other broken bonds. Unlike in earlier epics where the male hero engages in a heterosexual romance that eventually domesticates his coarse masculinity, Maximus and Lucilla circle each other, but never actually come back together. Only when Maximus lies dying in her arms in the final scene are they very nearly restored once again as a couple, since like a good husband, he has provided her with security for herself and her son by his heroism, assuring her with his final breath: 'Lucius is safe'. While Maximus ensures the safe bond between imperial mother and son, throughout the course of the film he longs for and remains devoted to the memory of his own wife and child, even when they are dead. Through the figure of Maximus as an old-fashioned 'soldier of Rome,' a gentleman cultivator of the land, and a faithful Roman husband and father, *Gladiator* suggests a popular reaffirmation of the ideals of family and the values of simplicity.

Another intriguing theme in *Gladiator* that reverberates with contemporary American audiences is the portrayal of Maximus as a man of deep personal spirituality.[11] The scenes where he is praying to his family and caressing tiny images of his wife and son by candlelight are some of the most moving in the film. Individual Roman families engaged in domestic worship of the family *genius*, 'spirit,' and their own ancestors, known as the *penates* or 'household gods,' in personal rites coexisting with the official state religion of the Olympian gods. Maximus is shown at prayer in several key moments, the first occurring in Germania after he has just been asked by Marcus Aurelius to become the Protector of Rome. 'Ancestors, I ask you for your guidance,' he prays. 'Blessed mother, come to me with the gods' desire for my future. Blessed father, watch over my wife and son with a ready sword. Whisper to them that I live only to hold them again, for all else is dust and air. Ancestors, I honor you and will try to live with the dignity that you have taught me'. When Maximus informs his loyal servant, Cicero, they may not be able to return home, it suggests his prayer has inspired him to consider the old emperor's request as an extension of his loyal military service to Rome. The audience again hears the words of Maximus' prayer in a murmured voice-over as he rides home to Hispania, wounded and depleted, in a desperate attempt to save his family: 'All else is dust and air'. Later after a fight in the Colosseum, Cicero returns the cherished miniature figures to Maximus. In a private moment in the gladiator barracks, Maximus prays and speaks to the figures as Juba asks him: 'Can they hear you? Your family, in the afterlife?' In the film's final scene, Juba buries the little images in the sand of the arena, and utters the last words of the film with the privileged voice of hope. 'Now we are free,' Juba tells his dead friend, 'I will see you again. But not yet, not yet'.

By representing Maximus as someone who honors his household gods in the manner of a traditional Roman *paterfamilias*, the 'head of the family,' *Gladiator* combines 'both modern familial sensitivity and ancient Roman Republican virtues'.[12] Maximus expresses his personal spirituality in his tender observance of the family religion. While the private solemnity and quiet spontaneity of this Roman religious practice appeal to the modern viewer, the film's spiritual theme also acknowledges the movement towards alternative and individualized religious expression, and a concurrent disaffection with the inflexible institutions of organized group religions. While spiritual interest is growing strong in most sectors of modern American society, many of the mainstream religions are experiencing a steep decline in active participation and regular attendance at services. Writer Franzoni wanted a hero who 'transcends traditional religious morality,' explaining: 'I believe there is room in our mythology for a character who is deeply moral, but who's not traditionally religious'.[13] *Gladiator* contrasts the arrogance and control of Roman imperial rule with the heartfelt and genuine religiosity of the individual. Just as Maximus removes the 'sign of his gods,' the SPQR emblem of Roman rule, from the flesh of his shoulder, some believers are separating themselves from the hierarchical, strictly structured, and often dysfunctional religions they were born into in favor of a spirituality developed on their own terms.

Popular interest in the afterlife, in particular the possibility of contact with the spirits of family and friends in the next world, is infusing American culture at the turn of the millennium. Maximus encourages his troops to fight bravely until the final moment, with the promise of a peaceful and painless transition to the world beyond: 'And if you find yourself alone, riding through green fields with the sun on your face, do not be troubled, for you are in Elysium, and you are already dead!' In the contemporary American imagination, the line between this world and the next is becoming blurred, and the passage after death is made easier by the comforting presence of our immediate family members and closest friends. The phenomenon of communicating with the dead is readily apparent in the American popular media, in films like M. Night Shyamalan's *The Sixth Sense* (1999) and Steven Soderbergh's *Solaris* (2002), and in television shows like HBO's *Six Feet Under* (2001–5) and NBC's *Medium* (2005–current). These all highlight the theme of reunion, the compelling belief that loved ones are still accessible after death, and it is never too late to reconnect with family members and close friends who have 'crossed over'.

Implicit in these popular constructions of the afterlife is the concept that the boundary between life and death is permeable and will disintegrate under the forces of human love. When Juba asks Maximus if his family can hear his voice in the afterlife, Maximus answers without hesitation: 'Oh, yes'. When Juba presses, 'What do you say to them?' Maximus says: 'To my boy, I tell him I will see him again soon, to keep his heels down while riding his horse. To my wife . . . that is not your business'. His wistful answer evokes the idea of the afterlife current in Roman antiquity that the spirits of the honorable dead could engage in the same activities they enjoyed during their lifetimes. Yet it also resonates with the growing popular notion that the souls of one's deceased loved ones do not reside in a traditionally construed Judaeo-Christian heaven or hell; rather, they exist in some neutral place where they can still communicate with the living. In *Gladiator*, the loss of his family is the single most powerful force motivating Maximus, and the viewers' feelings of assurance that he will be reunited with them after his death imbues the harsh ending of the film with a sense of gratification and positive resolution.

Maximus' yearning for his family in the afterlife is represented in a series of mesmerizing moments, the spiritual meaning of which becomes apparent only in the last scene. At the opening, and punctuating important transitional moments throughout the movie, dream-like images appear that are initially difficult to understand. A man's brawny hand ruffles through a wheat field in the first shot, as children's laughter is heard. A long row of mournful cypress trees stands still against a gray, rocky landscape. There is a desolate stretch of pale stone wall, overgrown with weeds, and above it a dramatic sky streaked with color promises a storm. The vision of wheat fields suggests an association with the story of the Roman goddess of the underworld, Proserpina, who is restored to her mother, Ceres, the goddess of the grain, in the summertime as the crops bear fruit. The field of wheat is thus a symbol of resurrection, the promise of rebirth in a peaceful afterlife, and the happy reunion with loved ones. 'What we do in life, echoes in eternity,' Maximus assures his men.

In *Gladiator*, these images evoke an impression of the advent of death, and mark crucial scenes in Maximus' journey towards his destiny. The film audience glimpses the hand in the wheat field against a flash of gray when Maximus is about to be executed in the first act of the film, and as he begs Quintus to protect his family, his former comrade-at-arms roughly replies: 'You will meet your family in the afterlife'. The dream imagery occurs again at the beginning of the second act, with an image of a bleak, rock-strewn path and the voices of laughing children, as the broken, lifeless Maximus is found upon his family's newly dug graves and taken away by the slave traders to Zucchabar. As Juba tends Maximus' near-fatal wound, he instructs him: 'Don't die'. Again at the transition to the third act, Maximus tells Juba his family is waiting for him in the afterlife, and they share a pledge to meet their families after death. Then, as the provincial gladiatorial troupe approaches the outskirts of Rome, accompanied by children running through fields alongside their caravan, flashes of the stony landscape under a vivid sky again appear onscreen. In the final scene as Maximus dies in the arena, we see a man's bloodied hand pushing through a door in the pale wall, and beyond that, a dream-image of the tree-lined path leading up to Maximus' house in Hispania. Only at this moment do the viewers realize it is Maximus' strong hand ruffling through the wind-blown wheat fields around his own farm, and the sound of the laughing child is that of his own son, who now runs towards his father on the pathway as his beautiful wife waits on the porch, shielding her eyes from the burst of warm sunshine. In the Colosseum, Lucilla closes Maximus' eyes, and as he floats over the sand covered with rose petals, she weeps and tells him: 'Go to them . . . you're home'. Only at the end of the last reel is it evident that this circular film has been one long, mystical flashback at the moment of the hero's death, anticipating his reunion with his beloved family in the afterlife.

As Marcus Aurelius looks wearily around the frozen German battlefield, he sighs: 'So much for the glory of Rome'. The lines etched on the emperor's face describe the trajectory of an absolute empire, from the opportunity to affect positive change in the world, to the responsibility for that involvement to be moral and meaningful, followed by the jaded recognition of the burdens imposed by such imperial obligation, and finally, inescapably, complete exhaustion.[14] America, like Rome, persists. Empire goes forward on its own institutional momentum, even as its internal structure shows signs of fraying. 'My father's war against the barbarians,' Commodus wonders. 'He said it himself, it achieved nothing. But the people loved him'. Just as the ancient Romans watched their empire waver on the edge of internal collapse, *Gladiator* asks Americans to contemplate whether insular considerations and attention to purely national interests will be enough to sustain them in the pursuit of more global ambitions. Unless the obligations that accompany the opportunities of empire are acknowledged, in particular the need to maintain the great esteem once earned from people and nations all over the world, America may be compelled to admit, as Marcus Aurelius does: 'I brought the sword, nothing more'.

Gladiator also persuades its audience to ponder the brittleness of the idea that an empire has the right to export its definition of justice and freedom, and how vulnerable that idea can be both to popular misunderstanding and disregard and the indifference or manipulation of their leaders. 'There was a dream that was Rome,' says the old emperor. 'You could only whisper it. Anything more than a whisper and it would vanish, it was so fragile'. Like the image of ancient Rome envisioned by Maximus, the American Dream occupies a similarly precarious place: 'American power and influence are actually very fragile, because they rest upon an idea, a unique and irreplaceable myth: that the United States really does stand for a better world and is still the best hope of all who seek it' (Tony Judt, *The New York Review of Books*, August 15, 2002). The death of Maximus at the film's conclusion is thus not an unequivocally triumphant moment, since the gladiator does not turn out to be the promised catalyst for sweeping political change. Contemporary viewers are well aware the Republic is not reinstated and the Roman Empire does not come to an end after the removal of Commodus. Rather, the ending suggests the dangers and risks associated with the noble pursuit of an honorable idea of empire that Maximus exemplifies.

Ultimately, viewers must decide if *Gladiator* sends a positive message about heroes and the nature of empire. Like the best epic movies, *Gladiator* raises more questions than it answers. Does it matter that Maximus does not go home again until he is dead? Is fighting the good fight enough? Will his dream of a strong, worthy Rome ever be realized? When Lucilla asks with patrician authority at the end of the film, 'Is Rome worth one good man's life?' a hopeful response follows: 'We believed it once . . . make us believe it again'. The hero himself becomes a dream-image of the idealized Rome he loves so much. As his spirit floats over the petal-strewn sand of the arena and out over the columns and walls of the sunset-streaked city, Maximus becomes a symbol both of the strength and the fragility of Rome.

Notes

1 Monica Cyrino, '*Gladiator* and Contemporary American Society.' In Martin M. Winkler (ed.), *Gladiator: Film and History*. Oxford: Blackwell, 2004, pp. 127–9.

2 Maria Wyke, *Projecting the Past: Ancient Rome, Cinema, and History*. New York and London: Routledge, 1997, pp. 23–32; Sandra Joshel, Margaret Malamud and Maria Wyke, 'Introduction.' In S. R. Joshel, M. Malamud, and D. T. McGuire (eds.), *Imperial Projections: Ancient Rome in Modern Popular Culture*. Baltimore and London: Johns Hopkins University Press, 2001, pp. 6–13; and William Fitzgerald, 'Oppositions, Anxieties, and Ambiguities in the Toga Movie.' In S. R. Joshel, M. Malamud, and D. T. McGuire (eds.), *Imperial Projections: Ancient Rome in Modern Popular Culture*. Baltimore and London: Johns Hopkins University Press, 2001, pp. 24–8.

3 Jon Solomon, *The Ancient World and the Cinema*. Revised and expanded edn. New Haven and London: Yale University Press, 2001, pp. 94–5.

4 Peter Bondanella, *The Eternal City: Roman Images in the Modern World*. Chapel Hill and London: University of North Carolina Press, 1987, pp. 4–5; Martin Winkler, '*Star Wars* and the Roman Empire.' In Martin M. Winkler (ed.), *Classical Myth and Culture in the Cinema*. Oxford and New York: Oxford University Press, 2001, pp. 273–80.

5 Monica Cyrino, '*Gladiator* and Contemporary American Society', pp. 136–7.

6 Monica Cyrino, '*Gladiator* and Contemporary American Society', pp. 140–2.

7 Jon Solomon, *The Ancient World and the Cinema*, p. 93.

8 John Soriano, 'WGA.ORG's Exclusive Interview with David Franzoni.' *The Writers Guild of America, Web Site* 2001, online; www.wga.org/craft/interviews/franzoni 2001.html.

9 Peter Bondanella, *The Eternal City: Roman Images in the Modern World*. Chapel Hill and London: University of North Carolina Press, 1987, p. 4.

10 Alison Futrell, 'Seeing Red: Spartacus as Domestic Economist.' In S. R. Joshel, M. Malamud, and D. T. McGuire (eds.), *Imperial Projections: Ancient Rome in Modern Popular Culture*. Baltimore and London: Johns Hopkins University Press, 2001, p. 105.

11 Monica Cyrino, '*Gladiator* and Contemporary American Society', pp. 140–2.

12 Jon Solomon, *The Ancient World and the Cinema*, p. 95.

13 John Soriano, 'WGA.ORG's Exclusive Interview with David Franzoni'.

14 Monica Cyrino, '*Gladiator* and Contemporary American Society', pp. 148–9.

PART 4

Historical film as reality, documentary and propaganda

HISTORIANS BELIEVE THAT HISTORIES are connected to or reflect lived experiences. In the latter half of the twentieth century, however, an increasing number of scholars asserted that those lived experiences were from the historian's present, and not from the past. As Roland Barthes saw it, for instance, histories form part of a 'discourse of sobriety' riddled with 'reality effects' or conventions such as footnotes, quotations or a seemingly omniscient narrator. Such 'readerly' texts – framed as transparent windows onto a past reality – serve to mask the interests of the white bourgeois Europeans whose interests they apparently serve. 'Writerly' texts, by contrast, highlight the rhetorical techniques they employ and encourage readers or viewers to engage them in multiple ways. Their chief goal, Barthes explains, is 'to make the reader no longer a consumer, but a producer of the text'.[1] Similarly, Jacques Derrida argued that historians have only been able to claim a privileged status for their writings by denying the unstable qualities of language. At best, histories bear the traces of and constantly refer to other texts in an endless chain of signification that he calls *différance*. Without beginnings and ends, historical texts are without pasts, without authors, without even readers.

Following on from Barthes's and Derrida's questions about the relationship between the past, the present and history, a number of historiographers have sought to chart the contemporary cultural and ideological dimensions of histories. Some have also maintained – as with Pierre Sorlin, whose views we met in Part 1 – that historical films point more firmly to their makers' social and political views than written histories. Indeed, as we discovered in Part 3, filmic representations of both the ancient and the modern world have been connected to the promotion of a conservative social and political agenda in the US in the past forty years. It is worth wondering along with Marcia Landy, Keith Jenkins and Martin Davies, however, whether all histories are primarily ideological expressions and thus whether histories are a pervasive form of propaganda.[2] The readings in Part 4 extend the discussion of our understanding of historical films along these lines, asking us to think about the social and political function of historical films in more general terms. Further, they ask us to consider whether there are 'writerly' historical films that encourage their viewers to be producers rather than consumers of texts.

Our exploration begins with Jean Baudrillard's argument that like the characters in the Wachowski brothers' *The Matrix*, we have lost contact with the 'real' in various ways, and have become no more than consumers in a society where the 'hyperreality' of simulations – evidenced in spectacles and the proliferation of images – turns us from class conflict. This is signalled, he argues in an essay from *Simulacra and Simulations*, in part by the loss of history, despite the proliferation of films and television programmes that appear to turn to history and 'fetishize' the 'retro'. This is because these recreations offer us a vision of the past that is more alluring than our present – the hyperreal – and thus allow us to escape from the 'desert of the real' and the burden of social and political agency. Further, these films do not reflect the past, only visions of the past in other films. Historical films are thus for him part of a wider proliferation of simulations that reflect only other simulations and that turn audiences into a 'silent majority'.

Baudrillard's observations on society were influenced in part by those of Roland Barthes, whose short essay from 1964, 'The Romans in Films' is also reproduced in this part of the *Reader*. In this essay, Barthes reads the 'insistent fringes' in Joseph Mankiewicz's *Julius Caesar* (1953) as an explicit sign of 'Roman-ness'. The actors may be known to us from other films, and may act in ways more familiar to us than to Romans, but their hairstyles – like other icons or conventions in historical films such as the yellow star in Holocaust films – signal that what we see is history. The Roman fringe, like footnotes, is a 'reality effect', one that might be utilised so pervasively in 'writerly' texts that its connection with the past 'goes without saying'. Objects in films, like the scholarly devices of historians, therefore, may mask their ideological functions and convince us that what we see or read are unmediated accounts of the past.

In his more extended study of another form of images – photography – Barthes concluded that filmic images are too fleeting to provide space for what he called the 'punctum', painful stimuli that can remind us of our mortality. He writes:

> in front of the screen, I am not free to shut my eyes; otherwise, opening them again, I would not discover the same image; I am constrained to a continuous voracity, a host of other qualities, but not *pensiveness*; whence the interest, for me, of the photogram.[3]

One might be tempted to conclude therefore that all films cannot be other than 'writerly'. This is a claim that Philip Rosen subjects to scrutiny in his book *Change*

Mummified (2001). Just as photographic conventions might serve to reign in what Rosen calls 'socially dispersive subjectivity', so cinema might problematise conventions that foster social integration. And while both referential and fictional elements in historical films might be shaped by an imperative for things to 'make sense', the icons provided in some films so far exceeds that needed to suggest a 'reality effect' that the result is a spectacle that might be celebrated by filmmakers and viewers alike. For Rosen, as for André Bazin, spectators know that what they see is a film and actively construct the illusion of filmic reality, whether that reality suggests a past or a present. Further, for both, film offers better access to history than any other art form because it 'mummifies' and transforms reality, yet it is never apart from subjects who seek meaning in it.[4]

Audiences also play a key role in Michelle Pierson's writings on special effects and authenticity in film. Pierson has written extensively on science fiction films, which she notes in the reading reproduced in this Part, are not dissimilar from historical films in their 'look of having been designed'. Historical films, she stresses, generally do not present viewers with likenesses to 'historical actuality'; rather, they appeal to audiences through conventional, familiar and accessible historical references. They also seek to persuade audiences of their quality through devices such as 'sincere' star performances – as with Ridley Scott's decision to allow Russell Crowe to retain his Australasian accent in *Gladiator* – sepia colour, and production publicity that emphasises the crew's awareness of 'getting things right'.

Pierson's interest in special effects means that her work is largely focused on large-budget feature films. Linda Williams's reading shifts our focus to what are perhaps the most 'reality effect'-laden films: documentaries. As Bill Nichols and Carl Plantinga have shown, documentaries do not all share the same qualities, but are rather related to one another through a 'braid of family resemblances'.[5] Nichols and Plantinga, like Williams, are particularly interested in what Williams calls 'new' documentaries, works which like Errol Morris's *The Thin Blue Line* (1987) foster filmmaker and viewer reflexivity by throwing into relief unquestioned assumptions, offering choices and giving voice to the views of marginalised and silenced people. Finally, we consider a group that has not traditionally been associated with the reflexive appreciation of historical films: children. Henry Giroux's provocative argument is that '[t]he strategies of entertaining escapism, historical forgetting, and repressive pedagogy in Disney's books, records, theme parks, movies, and TV programs produce a series of identifications that relentlessly define America as white and middle class'. It does so, Giroux claims, through a 'pedagogy of innocence' both in animated films aimed at children and in live action films designed for adults, such as *Good Morning, Vietnam* (1989).

Giroux's reading, like all of those reproduced in this Part, remind us that historical films are not realistic in themselves, but realistic because viewers recognise them as such. That is, 'realism' in film is a matter of convention, and different conventions may be used in different times and cultures and for different age groups. Charting those conventions is a historical task, as is ascertaining whether, as a consequence of their 'reality effects', films propagate particular ideological views or render viewers politically inactive. These are tasks that are increasingly occupying the attention of film historians and historical film scholars, and some of the fruits of their labours are reproduced in Part 5.

Notes

1 R. Barthes, *Image-Music-Text*, trans. S. Heath, New York: Hill and Wang, 1977, pp. 52–68.

2 Keith Jenkins, *Re-thinking History*, London: Routledge, 1992; id. *Refiguring History*, London: Routledge, 2003; and Martin Davies, *Historics*, London: Routledge, 2006.

3 R. Barthes, *Camera Lucida: Reflections on Photography*, New York: Hill and Wang, 1972, p. 55.

4 A. Bazin, *What is Cinema?*, trans. H. Gray, vol. 2, Berkeley, CA: University of California Press, 1967, pp. 9–16, 97.

5 C. Plantinga, *Rhetoric and Representation in Nonfiction Film*, Cambridge: Cambridge University Press, 1997, p. 15; and B. Nichols, *Introduction to Documentary*, Bloomington, IN: University of Indiana Press, 2001, p. 21.

Jean Baudrillard

HISTORY

A retro scenario

'History: A Retro Scenario', in *Simulacra and Simulations,* ed. M. Poster, Stanford: Stanford University Press, 1998, pp. 43–8.

IN A VIOLENT AND CONTEMPORARY PERIOD of history (let's say between the two world wars and the cold war), it is myth that invades cinema as imaginary content. It is the golden age of despotic and legendary resurrections. Myth, chased from the real by the violence of history, finds refuge in cinema.

Today, it is history itself that invades the cinema according to the same scenario – the historical stake chased from our lives by this sort of immense neutralization, which is dubbed peaceful coexistence on a global level, and pacified monotony on the quotidian level – this history exorcised by a slowly or brutally congealing society celebrates its resurrection in force on the screen, according to the same process that used to make lost myths live again.

History is our lost referential, that is to say our myth. It is by virtue of this fact that it takes the place of myths on the screen. The illusion would be to congratulate oneself on this 'awareness of history on the part of cinema,' as one congratulated oneself on the 'entrance of politics into the university.' Same misunderstanding, same mystification. The politics that enter the university are those that come from history, a retro politics, emptied of substance and legalized in their superficial exercise, with the air of a game and a field of adventure, this kind of politics is like sexuality or permanent education (or like social security in its time), that is, posthumous liberalization.

The great event of this period, the great trauma, is this decline of strong referentials, these death pangs of the real and of the rational that open onto an age of simulation. Whereas so many generations, and particularly the last, lived in the march of history, in the euphoric or catastrophic expectation of a revolution – today one has the impression that history has retreated, leaving behind it an indifferent nebula, traversed by currents, but emptied of references. It is into this void that the phantasms of a past history recede, the panoply of events, ideologies, retro fashions – no longer so much because people believe in them or still place some hope in them, but simply to resurrect the period when *at least* there was history, at least there was violence (albeit fascist), when at least life and death were at stake. Anything serves to escape this void, this leukemia of history and of politics, this hemorrhage of values – it is in proportion to this distress that all content can be evoked pell-mell, that all previous history is resurrected in bulk – a controlling idea no longer selects, only nostalgia endlessly accumulates: war, fascism, the pageantry of the belle epoque, or the revolutionary struggles, everything is equivalent and is mixed indiscriminately in the same morose and funereal exaltation, in the same retro fascination. There is however a privileging of the immediately preceding era (fascism, war, the period immediately following the war – the innumerable films that play on these themes for us have a closer, more perverse, denser, more confused essence). One can explain it by evoking the Freudian theory of fetishism (perhaps also a retro hypothesis). This trauma (loss of referentials) is similar to the discovery of the difference between the sexes in children, as serious, as profound, as irreversible: the fetishization of an object intervenes to obscure this unbearable discovery, but precisely, says Freud, this object is not just any object, it is often the last object perceived before the traumatic discovery. Thus the fetishized history will preferably be the one immediately preceding our 'irreferential' era. Whence the omnipresence of fascism and of war in retro – a coincidence, an affinity that is not at all political; it is naive to conclude that the evocation of fascism signals a current renewal of fascism (it is precisely because one is no longer there, because one is in something else, which is still less amusing, it is for this reason that fascism can again become fascinating in its filtered cruelty, aestheticized by retro).

History thus made its triumphal entry into cinema, post-humously (the term *historical* has undergone the same fate: a 'historical' moment, monument, congress, figure are in this way designated as fossils). Its reinjection has no value as conscious awareness but only as nostalgia for a lost referential.

This does not signify that history has never appeared in cinema as a powerful moment, as a contemporary process, as insurrection and not as resurrection. In the 'real' as in cinema, there was history but there isn't any anymore. Today, the history that is 'given back' to us (precisely because it was taken from us) has no more of a relation to a 'historical real' than neofiguration in painting does to the classical figuration of the real. Neofiguration is an *invocation* of resemblance, but at the same time the flagrant proof of the disappearance of objects in their very representation: *hyperreal*. Therein objects shine in a sort of hyperresemblance (like history in contemporary cinema) that makes it so that fundamentally they no longer resemble anything, except the empty figure of resemblance, the empty form of representation. It is a question of life or death: these objects are no longer either living or deadly. That is why they are so exact, so minute, frozen in the state in which a brutal loss of the real would have seized them. All, but not only, those historical films whose very perfection is disquieting: *Chinatown*, *Three Days of the Condor*, *Barry Lyndon*, *1900*, *All the President's Men*, etc. One has the impression of it being a question of perfect remakes, of extraordinary montages that emerge more from a combinatory culture (or McLuhanesque mosaic), of large photo-, kino-, historicosynthesis machines, etc., rather than one of veritable films. Let's understand each other: their quality is not in question. The problem is rather that in some sense we are left completely indifferent. Take *The Last Picture Show*: like me, you would have had to be sufficiently distracted to have thought it to be an original production from the 1950s: a very good film about the customs in and the atmosphere of the American small town. Just a slight suspicion: it was a little too good, more in tune, better than the others, without the psychological, moral, and sentimental blotches of the films of that era. Stupefaction when one discovers that it is a 1970s film, perfect retro, purged, pure, the hyperrealist restitution of 1950s cinema. One talks of remaking silent films, those will also doubtlessly be better than those of the period. A whole generation of films is emerging that will be to those one knew what the android is to man: marvellous artefacts, without weakness, pleasing simulacra that lack only the imaginary, and the hallucination inherent to cinema. Most of what we see today (the best) is already of this order. *Barry Lyndon* is the best example: one never did better, one will never do better in . . . in what? Not in evoking, not even in evoking, in *simulating*. All the toxic radiation has been filtered, all the ingredients are there, in precise doses, not a single error.

Cool, cold pleasure, not even aesthetic in the strict sense: functional pleasure, equational pleasure, pleasure of machination. One only has to dream of Visconti (*Guépard*, *Senso*, etc., which in certain respects make one think of *Barry Lyndon*) to grasp the difference, not only in style, but in the cinematographic act. In Visconti, there is meaning, history, a sensual rhetoric, dead time, a passionate game, not only in the historical content, but in the mise-en-scène. None of that in Kubrick, who manipulates his film like a chess player, who makes an operational scenario of history. And this does not return to the old opposition between the spirit of finesse and the spirit of geometry: that opposition still comes from the game and the stakes of meaning, whereas we are entering an era of films that in themselves no longer have meaning strictly speaking, an era of great synthesizing machines of varying geometry.

Is there something of this already in Leone's Westerns? Maybe. All the registers slide in that direction. *Chinatown*: it is the detective movie renamed by laser. It is not really a question of perfection: technical perfection can *be part of* meaning, and in that case it is neither retro nor hyperrealist, it is an effect of art. Here, technical perfection is an effect of the model: it is one of the referential tactical values. In the absence of real *syntax* of meaning, one has nothing but the *tactical* values of a group in which are admirably combined, for example, the CIA as a mythological machine that does everything, Robert Redford as polyvalent star, social relations as a necessary reference to history, technical virtuosity as a necessary reference to cinema.

The cinema and its trajectory: from the most fantastic or mythical to the realistic and the hyperrealistic.

The cinema in its current efforts is getting closer and closer, and with greater and greater perfection, to the absolute real, in its banality, its veracity, in its naked obviousness, in its boredom, and at the same time in its presumption, in its pretension to being the real, the immediate, the unsignified, which is the craziest of undertakings (similarly, functionalism's pretension to designating – design – the greatest degree of correspondence between the object and its function, and its use value, is a truly absurd enterprise); no culture has ever had toward its signs this naive and paranoid, puritan and terrorist vision.

Terrorism is always that of the real.

Concurrently with this effort toward an absolute correspondence with the real, cinema also approaches an absolute correspondence with itself – and this is not contradictory: it is the very definition of the hyperreal. Hypotyposis and specularity. Cinema plagiarizes itself, recopies itself, remakes its classics, retroactivates its original myths, remakes the silent film more perfectly than the original, etc.: all of this is logical, *the cinema is fascinated by itself as a lost object as much as it (and we) are fascinated by the real as a lost referent.* The cinema and the imaginary (the novelistic, the mythical, unreality, including the delirious use of its own technique) used to have a lively, dialectical, full, dramatic relation. The relation that is being formed today between the cinema and the real is an inverse, negative relation: it results from the loss of specificity of one and of the other. The cold collage, the cool promiscuity, the asexual nuptials of two cold media that evolve in an asymptotic line toward each other: the cinema attempting to abolish itself in the cinematographic (or televised) hyperreal.

History is a strong myth, perhaps, along with the unconscious, the last great myth. It is a myth that at once subtended the possibility of an 'objective' enchainment of events and causes and the possibility of a narrative enchainment of discourse. The age of history, if one can call it that, is also the age of the novel. It is this *fabulous* character, the mythical energy of an event or of a narrative, that today seems to be increasingly lost. Behind a performative and demonstrative logic: the obsession with historical *fidelity*, with a perfect rendering (as elsewhere the obsession with real time or with the minute quotidianeity of Jeanne Hilmann doing the dishes), this negative and implacable fidelity to the materiality of the past, to a particular scene of the past or of the present, to the restitution of an absolute simulacrum of the past or the present, which was substituted for all other value – we are all complicitous in this, and this is irreversible. Because cinema itself contributed to the disappearance of history, and to the advent of the archive. Photography and cinema contributed in large part to the secularization of history, to fixing it in its visible, 'objective' form at the expense of the myths that once traversed it.

Today cinema can place all its talent, all its technology in the service of reanimating what it itself contributed to liquidating. It only resurrects ghosts, and it itself is lost therein.

Reading 18

Philip Rosen

DETAIL AND HISTORICITY IN MAINSTREAM CINEMA

Reality and indexicality from Bazin to Barthes

'Detail and Historicity in Mainstream Cinema: Reality and Indexicality from Bazin to Barthes', in *Change Mummified: Cinema, Historicity, Theory*, Minneapolis: University of Minnesota Press, 2001, pp. 166–99.

IN THE 1970S, major tendencies in film theory veered strongly toward treating any cinematic aspiration for the real as an ideological category. This was based in part on a problematic of film spectatorship that generated a series of subsequent discussions and debates. Antirealist assumptions have since persisted in other kinds of accounts of film and types of film theory, and have perhaps too often become unspoken and unexamined. But indexicality and temporality were always the blind spots of 1970s film theory, whatever its strengths (and in my view they were many). In *Camera Lucida*, Barthes – whose earlier work was one of the key reference points for 1970s film theory – initiated a reconsideration of indexicality and pastness, beginning from the relation of subjective desire to the configurations of representational technologies.

So it may be worth finding ways to make *Camera Lucida* a bit less constricting for the consideration of cinema. First, consider some of the grounds for the distinctions made in *Camera Lucida*: the notion of a direct encounter with the real outside signification; an absolute distinction between the private and the public; the book's privileged photograph evincing nostalgia for direct, unmediated access to his mother as the exemplary privatized and particularized experience. Whatever these are in the immediate experience of Barthes's subject, they are themselves all socially mediated, ideologically produced configurations, as Barthes is also aware. Against the experience of the ideal subject that it designates, then, his phenomenology of disruptive particularity still defines that subject within socially given terms.

In that case, Barthes's stance is, precisely, utopian; it can exist in no place except the fantasies of a hypothetical subject. On the one hand, such fantasies paradoxically call into question the very nonideological outside they are supposed to manifest, just because, in the end, a nonideological outside can only be constructed as subjective fantasy. On the other hand, these same fantasies do provide ideals, standards for significant social critique and grounds for resistance; they become a junction of desire and politics. For present purposes, we can go further and treat this utopia as providing a critical standpoint on the history of filmic textuality. But any such critique and any such history would therefore be one routed through the status of the normalized processes of indexical imaging configurations and alternatives to them – both of which engage with fantasy life.[1]

Second, despite its ego-centered phenomenological mode of expression, *Camera Lucida* locates 'realism' as a contested mode of sociality. This means that it is not an automatic effect of a specific medium or technology. According to Barthes, the history of photography is replete with compositional and artistic devices that work to reign in socially dispersive subjectivity. He complains that the mass of photographs are commonly aestheticized, conventionalized, 'informationalized' and/or disseminated so as to sublimate the fantasmatically absolute particularity that photography may engender. Presumably, any social formation requires such operations, which bring to bear on image-production a set of economic, institutional, educational, class, cultural, and/or even legal constraints, regulating the network of available contacts with any postulated real.[2]

But this means that the opposition between heavily socialized and radically dispersive significations of the real exists even *within* the medium that exemplifies Barthes's ideal. It would follow that the converse is possible in his contrary indexical medium, cinema. It becomes thinkable that cinema may retain elements of the threat and problematicity offered by indexicality to the socialized norms for subjectivity. And *Camera Lucida* is driven by its logic to some piecemeal indications that the neutralizing aspects it attributes to cinema are not necessarily universal to the medium, even including occasional claims for disruptive moments in individual films. For present purposes, the most suggestive of such indications is Barthes's remark that when he treats cinema as other to the radically privatized potential of photography, he is referring to narrative cinema: 'The cinema participates in this domestication of Photography – *at least the fictional cinema*, precisely the one said to be the seventh art' [my emphasis].[3]

Suppose we speculate on how this might serve as a heuristics or an optic – a standpoint – for conceiving of the history of film. To begin with, cinema would be treated within a history of indexical representation, as a complex regime circulating around the social management of subjective constructions of the real and accesses to it. This does imply a more flexible attitude toward cinema than one might expect from some of the ontologizing language Barthes uses in characterizing indexical media, for management is not mere suppression. It assumes that there is at least a potential for conflict, for departure from socializing norms. Even mainstream film would also appeal to and moreover provoke such aspirations, if only (in the most restrictive conception) to channel them. Incidentally, there is plenty of historical evidence in institutional and public discourses for the idea that indexical media in general and filmic textuality in particular present potential or actualized sociocultural danger. Direct examples are provided by the often class-bound censorship debates during the first decades of its existence as a mass medium, and film history has remained dotted with such instances right up to more recent and incessant debates over violence in film, children's television, pornography, and so forth.

Of course, this focus on indexicality also leads back to the idea that film draws on and participates in the kinds of aspirations for the real through indexicality that are rooted in the nineteenth century. And with specific reference to cinema, this approach makes the transition from preclassical to classical cinema, which suppressed actuality filmmaking in favor of explicit narrative, a crucial conjuncture in the social history of representation. Fundamental textual practices standardized in the development of classical cinema, tied to the impulse to rationalize production, can be treated as participating in processes of managing and regulating indexicality and the desires associated with it.

Connected to this is a theoretical point having to do with distinctions between media and bearing on textual procedures. Within the Barthesian problematic, mainstream cinema would meet subjective desire for the real and truth more like literature and less like the photograph than one might expect. The submission of foreground-background relations to a narrational rhetoric including the deployment of the reality-effect; the use of preexisting models of visual composition to present a well-organized, harmonious collection of details; the regularization of off screen space; the very imposition of the parameters of a certain range of familiar types of narrative form on cinematic space (which is qualitatively different from the individualized narration of photographic space by subjective fantasy) – all these and other givens of most mainstream film narratives are, among other things, social processes seeking to exploit the opportunities offered by the cinematic medium to tame the indexical image as document. In rationalizing the detail, they align it with certain regimes of social rationality.

History in film

Let us return to the broad textual and spectatorial relations between document and diegesis postulated by the normalized fiction film, with attention to the vicissitudes of indexicality. A profilmic field – from the standpoint of the spectator, a visual field of objects that was indexically imprinted as they existed at some point in the past – is staged or performed as another (fictional) time. The spectator processes this staging in his or her present time. This is already historiographic in a sense, for it locates the film-spectator relation as a point where pastnesses and presentness confront one another. To this extent, then, the chief or dominant lines in the development of mainstream cinema necessarily and already participate in a cultural terrain of historicity. (This is not to say it is the only kind of fabrication of the image ever at work, even in mainstream films.)

But what of explicitly historical representation in film? The 'historical film' can be defined here as a certain conjunction of regimes of narrative and profilmic: in its purest form, it consists of a 'true story' (or elements of a 'true story') plus enough profilmic detail to designate a period recognizable as significantly 'historical,' that is, as signifying a generally accepted minimum of referential pastness.[4] As a definition this may seem slippery, but only because so many of its terms themselves designate discursive and ideological arenas subject to historical change ('regimes,' 'enough,' 'recognizable,' 'generally accepted').

The historical film throws the passages between document and diegesis in the mainstream narrative film into a special kind of relief. In any conventional fiction film, insofar as we apprehend depicted objects as having actually existed in front of the camera, to that extent there is a documentary (or actuality) component to our apprehension. But since a conventional fiction film is not supposed to be understood as a documentary, such details are to be apprehended as in some sense constructed, diegetic. In that case, this indexically imprinted profilmic is organized according to the narrative hierarchies of a 'virtual' time, that of the fictional world. The extra twist of the historical film is that this 'virtual' time also claims to have its own previously documentable 'reality,' that of a researchable historiography. There is a second referential preexistent.

Nevertheless, the sense of explicit historiography is conveyed not as a genuine document, but as diegesis, as in *The Return of Martin Guerre* (taken as a historical film in its 'pure form'). As a narrative film, *The Return of Martin Guerre* must employ textual mechanisms associated with fiction, something unavoidable in any historical reenactment (for example, there must be actors). Yet, precisely as a 'historical film,' it must simultaneously propose some extra supplement of referential truth, but one that can only be signified as diegesis. Consequently, this supplement comes through as a reconstruction, as a restoration rather than a preservation. If I can employ architectural terminology, it is because (as always with the restorationism-preservationism spectrum), the quest for referentiality is an underlying premise for both ends; this means it is generally realized as a simultaneity or oscillation of differing registers of referentiality. What 1970s film theory hypostasized as the cinematic impression of reality is a processing or play of shifting or simultaneous degrees and levels of differentiated spectatorial investment.

But it is worth noting that at least one concept invoked in 1970s film theory can be used to address this play in the historical film, namely the psychoanalytic concept of fetishism. I mention it because it recalls the defensive, disavowing aspects of modern historicity discussed in earlier chapters. In a remarkable 1977 article, Jean-Louis Comolli attempts a description of the representational structure of the narrative historical film. It is on the more or less implicit model of the fetishistic splitting of knowledge and belief (the fetishistic subject unconsciously believes the woman had a penis, but knows she does not – is castrated – and in order to achieve sexual pleasure reinstates that belief in the present via the fetish object). But while Comolli's key example is the body of an actor (Pierre Renoir playing Louis XVI in *La Marseillaise*), his tacit invocation of fetishistic positioning has less to do with corporeal fragmentation than with assumptions about spectatorial investment. Comolli emphasizes that the film image as such documents that Pierre Renoir was actually present during the filming, but this means that the historical personage he plays cannot have been present. In an ordinary fiction film the actor portrays a character who he or she is not, but that character never existed; in a historical film, the actor portrays a *referential* figure who he or she is not. Therefore, although the historical film may claim to deal with real events, it is actually more artificial with respect to a spectator's desire to believe in the reality of the image. According to Comolli, Pierre Renoir highlights this gap through an eccentric performance rather than attempting to suppress it by a naturalistic performance.

On the one hand, then, Comolli infers that a historical film must draw a greater quotient of irrational investment from a spectator to sustain his or her investment in its reality. This is comparable to the belief pole in a fetishistic position, and it resonates with the emphasis on subjective investment in both Bazinian and Barthesian realisms. On the other hand, pleasure is also available from a certain range of artifice and stylization manifesting distance from authenticity. The latter, in effect, acknowledges and addresses the spectator's awareness that the historical film is not 'really' history but a performance. This awareness corresponds to the knowledge pole in a fetishistic position. Any film or part of a film is a play on differing combinations of knowledge and belief, neither of which can be completely eliminated. Textually and institutionally, then, to downplay the knowledge pole in favor of the belief pole is a 'realist' tendency. (Perhaps paradoxically, this means that the belief pole may be aligned with – or propped onto – a rhetoric of disciplined accuracy, research department publicity, and so forth.) At the other end, an option for text and spectator involves highlighting the knowledge pole to include some degree of acknowledgment of the inevitable artificiality of the historical reconstruction. Comolli goes on to argue that pleasure and position may be abetted by setting up a game with the spectator and taking the risk of stretching out the gap between knowledge and belief, something exemplified for him in Pierre Renoir's enactment of Louis.

As a moment in 1970s film theory, Comolli's account of the historical film illustrates something about the range of possibilities in psychoanalytic film theory, which is wider than is sometimes recognized. He postulates spectatorship as a kind of dialectic between a 'realist' quest for the referential, and a certain simultaneous spectatorial awareness of and pleasure in the artifice of the film. One might even say that the latter leaves openings for a degree of critical activity on the part of the spectator. So it should be added that while Comolli emphasizes the actor, this approach is in principle applicable to all profilmic objects in a historical film. But like most 1970s film theory, Comolli does not theorize indexicality, and as a consequence is vague on the roots of the documentary force of the image (the basis for the presumption of the reality of Pierre Renoir's body), and therefore does not fully develop what I call the distinction between documentary and diegetic levels of spectatorial engagement.[5]

For now, I would put it most simply as follows. There is a complex play in the spectatorial apprehension of every image of a historical film like *The Return of Martin Guerre*, among a documentary 'substructure'; the conversion of document into narrationally positioned diegetic detail (details such as the smoke must be situated as narratively significant and/or insignificant as in any fiction film); and then – if we understand the pictured objects as appropriately or reasonably 'authentic' reconstructions of sixteenth-century French life – a conversion back from the diegetic to a quasidocument, which results in a spectatorial comprehension that might be summed up as follows: 'Oh, that's what it looked like, I see how people kept themselves warm in 1560.' What we see, then, is not what actually *was*, but what it would have looked *like* in 1560.

This means that the diegeticized profilmic, as historical representation, inevitably falls short of the kind of documentary authority claimed by the image as an indexical trace of the profilmic. As with Ranke's '*wie es eigentlich gewesen*,' the apprehension of history confronts the gap between likeness and being. The Rankean historians understand this as the break between the discourse produced by the historian and the dream of a hypothetically complete, rigorous documentation that would completely secure the truth of that historiography. In the historical film, it is the disjunction between the image as authenticating document, beginning from the camera's relation to the profilmic during the making of the film, and the imaged as diegesis. All of these divisions are ultimately between a past and a present, which for modern Western historicity is the site of the very necessity for historical representation in the first place.

However, it is also true that my definition of the historical film as the conjunction of a certain regime of story and of mise-en-scène makes it difficult to absolutize a distinction between the historical film and other kinds of mainstream films. On this point, the problematic character of the notion of a 'true story' has been discussed often enough with respect to historiography, but here I would highlight the level of the detail per se. Even though the historical film gives relations between document and diegesis an extra referential twist, there are important similarities and parallels to the organization of document-diegesis relationships throughout classical and mainstream cinema, including films that do not claim to convey a 'true story.' There are even degrees of the historical film; for example, a 'period' romance, adventure film, or literary adaptation usually does not have any pretense to the referential truth of its story or characters, yet its mise-en-scène might be heavily researched and detailed (or, alternatively, researched to include some historical indicators, but stylized, which is still a play on historical referentiality). But even for films with contemporary settings, a nodal point of the underlying principles bearing on the profilmic is 'research.'

A certain intrication of ideals of indexicality and of constructed resemblance is pervasive in mainstream film history. One indication of this intrication is the extensive use of photographs of distant locales and objects in classical studio research 'bibles' to provide models for the constructed profilmic of the studio; indexical documentation counts as a suitable source for conceiving of the form of a diegesis. This intrication meshes with other standard practices such as location shooting, sets coded as verisimilitudinous (often constructed not only on the basis of research, but to blend acceptably with locations), and a conventional minimum of plausible props and actions, whether they have to do with making coffee in a made-for-television romance movie or the settings and locations in a thriller.

This fluidity of boundaries between historiographic appeals and fictional genres on the level of the profilmic field suggests both the inevitability of film as documented and documenting, but also, always, its insufficiency as document. Because they are always hybridized with some degree of narrativized diegesis, details are also to be understood as components of a diegetic construction. The work of studio research departments participated in this overall process of converting document to diegesis in the narrative registers of mainstream film. This has made them a good emblem for the amount of effort and regulatory labor it requires.

A link between studio research departments, the normalization of narrative in the classical film as a film-historical development of signification, and broad expectations about spectatorship in mainstream cinema may be glossed by an analogy. It is as if the ontogeny of viewing an individual film recapitulates the historical phylogeny of classical cinema. Phylogenetically, commercial cinema passed through a brief period when its status as document was dominant, and then stabilized enough to make the status of the image as explicit diegesis the mark of dominant filmmaking. Ontogenetically, there is also a kind of passage or play between document and diegesis, but with a kind of residue, as if the diegeticized film attempts to retain something of the factual convincingness of the document. (It is here that some of the work and publicity around studio research departments makes its contribution.) The historical film is only that which pushes this passage to an extreme. In so doing, it can serve as one privileged site for understanding the stakes of the transition to classical cinema, as rationalization not only of production and exhibition, but of filmic textuality.

The spectacle of history

At this point it may still be objected that my account of the profilmic in mainstream textuality in relation to a postulated desire to apprehend the real underplays the artifices of mainstream cinema. The discussion of document and diegesis has been pegged to the disposition of a documentary or quasi-documentary force, which can be aligned with concerns proper to modern historiography. What about the range of stylizations one can find throughout the history of mainstream film? What of such seeming departures from indexicality as overt special effects, composite imagery, and the like? What about the effects on the profilmic of kinds of narrative worlds other than the doubly referential ones proper to the historical film, which include fantasy and the fantastic? In short, there is much more to deployments of the profilmic in mainstream cinema than reality effects.

Let me address this kind of objection through another filmic example, but one that belongs to one of the most stylized and artificial of classical genres, the studio musical. In the justly well known climactic title ballet from *An American in Paris* (1951), settings and costumes are modeled on Parisian scenes from famous impressionist paintings. The main character, Jerry (Gene Kelly), is at the center of an elaborate, heavily populated choreography, whose tone ranges from the comic to the ethereal to the sentimental. There is a deliberately 'unrealistic' use of Technicolor, and the particular stylization of mise-en-scène varies depending on the painting and particular dance format at that moment.

During this segment, spectatorial understanding is obviously not supposed to be that these are indexical registrations of Paris, nor that actual paintings are being used as backdrop. Nor is there supposed to be an understanding of the diegesis to the effect of 'That's what it [Paris] looks like.' It is rather that set and art designers created a showily artificial Paris as a background environment for a lengthy dance sequence. But if the sequence does not document Paris, nor provide an exacting reconstruction of what Paris looks like, it implicates spectatorial investment in a documentary fascination nevertheless – a document of Hollywood skills, of a show that is put on for the spectator. The preeminent objects in this document are probably the dance skills of Gene Kelly, Leslie Caron, and the troupe, but also include the artificial backgrounds and costumes. These actually existed for the making of this film and are themselves part of its display of virtuoso achievement.[6]

This suggests that spectatorial investment in the show does presume a certain documentary substructure based on assumptions circulating around the appeal of indexicality. This appeal is intertwined with other characteristics often attributed to the classical Hollywood musical. These include its emphasis on performance and performativity, which is associated with a certain foregrounding of artifice. In its turn, this is sometimes said to include the possibility of attenuating the saturation of narrative orderliness in the normalized feature-length film in favor of the insertion of musical performances.

Yet, one can still argue that a pretext framing all this indexically imprinted virtuosity with its documentary appeal is ultimately narrative order. In my example, the ballet itself has a general direction, which is to express and summarize the traumatic emotional progression that Jerry has experienced in the overall story that encloses the dance. Furthermore, within that story, this concluding ballet sequence serves as the culmination of Jerry's defeat before the quick dramatic reversal and happy ending that immediately follows it. During the ballet, the film may present itself as a document of performed virtuosity, but that virtuosity is still alibied by a certain administration of sense governed by narrative emplacement, which provides its rationale, or perhaps rationalization, depending on your viewpoint.

Furthermore, this documented performativity does not obviate an appeal to researched preexistents. Much as research for historical films commonly uses paintings originating in the depicted period as sources to model set and costume design, so does this classic musical sequence; however, it does textually foreground this genre of sources in a spectacular way, as part of its effects of virtuosity and 'style.' A spectator knowledgeable in the high (or commodity) culture of art history can have that knowledge confirmed by recognizing the virtuoso transformations involved in enacting those paintings.

In fact, research and appealing to a sense of the preexistent could be as common in the musical as in any other classical studio genre, though its intensity varied at different periods and among individual films; however, there is something suggestive about their mobilization in *An American in Paris.* A common thematic of classical studio musicals is an opposition between values attributed to subjectivity, such as lyrical freedom of expression, the realization of fantasy or desire, and interpersonal harmony on the one hand, and exigencies that obstruct their realization on the other. In show business musicals, for example, this could be narrativized as an opposition between performance itself and the blockage of performance. *An American in Paris* is representative of a type that narrativizes it as a division between subjectivity expressing itself through dream or daydream and a resistant everyday reality that is not subject to dream. (The ballet is not the only fantasy/dream sequence in the film.) The activation of a dream-reality dialectic requires, precisely, a 'reality' against which the lyricism of the dream can be defined. That 'reality' must be constructed as a profilmic field constituting a diegesis, and this usually involves the restoration of culturally recognizable preexistents; hence Parisian settings for non-oneiric scenes were fully 'authentic,' based (as usual) on research, including thousands of photographs of Paris. But the film uses the researched fantastic, painterly mises-en-scène of the ballet near the end of *An American in Paris* as a polar counterpart to the researched relative accuracy of Jerry's Paris apartment and neighborhood side street at the film's beginning. The representing of fantasy and free subjectivity as well as 'reality' is channeled through an order of knowledge, even at the level of the profilmic detail.

In general terms, this example is emblematic of some ways the musical – a classical genre one might reasonably postulate as significantly different in ambition from the historical film – shares some assumptions with the latter about the profilmic. The passage between preexistent detail and reality-effect must be negotiated even in the classical musical, which is to say that it even here remains necessary to organize and put in to play relations between document and diegesis. This is not to argue for an absolute equivalence; the emphasis on overt performance characteristic of so many musicals certainly makes for distinctions with respect to mise-en-scène. My point is that, whatever the range of options, these constructions partake of a broad textual rationality common within mainstream cinema. Reconfirming the ubiquity of appeals to an origin in the real as both documentable profilmic and/or researchable pre-text, the musical also takes us back to the regularizing sociocultural drive evident in the rationalization of the detail. This is the arena of the management of indexicality that, I have suggested through Barthes, has been a primary cultural assignment for cinema. And such constructions of indexicality, reference, and pastness in the present of the spectator connect mainstream cinema to historicity.

But an inverse point can be made. The direct appeal of the documented performance for the spectator that I have associated with the musical can also be activated in the mainstream historical film. Comolli suggests there is always some element of such overt, performed artifice in the historical film. There are cases where this element goes to an extreme. One such extreme is often called historical spectacle. In historical spectacle, a proliferation of detail seems to exceed the reality-effect, and in so doing becomes something like a virtuoso performance of the profilmic. From the perspective of the 'serious' historical film, historical spectacle unbalances the interplay between a 'true story' and a recognizably 'historical' mise-en-scène by emphasizing the underlying ambivalences of the latter with respect to referentiality. As we will see, it illustrates that the organization of socialized security – the management of indexicality – has more at its disposal than the construction of the profilmic as narrativized reality-effect, even if it never completely evades this level of significance.

Consider one more filmic fragment, the Tarsus sequence of DeMille's *Cleopatra* (1934). Made during the heyday of the classical studio period, this film draws on culturally prominent narrative-historical raw material. (It was neither the first nor the last film version of that material; it could draw on a long-standing iconographic tradition of representing it, as well as such illustrious theatrical predecessors as Shakespeare, Dryden, and Shaw.) The story events covered in the whole Tarsus sequence comprise the confrontation between a heretofore misogynist Antony, attempting to bring Egypt and Cleopatra under Rome's political and masculine discipline, and Cleopatra, who counters with a calculated, politically motivated, successful seduction of Antony. The Tarsus sequence as a whole manifests great narrative attenuation, taking approximately one-fifth of the film's running time (about eighteen minutes). As filmic performance and profilmic display, it is arguably the most sustained spectacular construction in a film that constitutes itself as historical spectacle.

This sequence demonstrates how concern with the detail in a historical film can go well beyond the goals of the reality-effect, and become transformed into a virtuosity of spectacle comparable to that of the musical.[7] Departing from the claims of accuracy, the detail has been liberated from background reality-effect to foregrounded, masterful address to the present that invites the spectatorial eye to exult in its apotheosis. This address to the present entails a certain release from referential claims, which is enacted throughout the film; for example, there are anachronistic patterns of design and costuming that go well beyond the usual compromise formations between past and present by appealing overwhelmingly to contemporary styles (e.g., the Art Deco inspirations obvious at many points), as well as indulgences in narrative and dialogue overtly addressed to the present (references to lines from Shakespeare, invented events, and so forth).

With respect to the detail, this liberation is so overwhelming, so extravagant, so playful, so performative as opposed to referential, that we call it spectacle. For what is spectacle in this sense other than the virtuosic textual organization of an impossibly large quantity of details, in a way that draws the spectator's attention to them as a construction for the spectator? Thus, Vivian Sobchack concludes that 'the phenomenological significance and discursive power of the Hollywood historical epic is not to be found in the specificity and accuracy of its historical detail.' Hence Steve Neale's remark that spectacle is concerned with 'the processes of rendering visible and of looking themselves.'[8]

And yet, perhaps astonishingly, none of this excludes a supporting discourse of research and the reality-effect. Whatever its excesses in this regard, *Cleopatra* does remain a species of the historical film, invoking actual historical personages, events, and settings, and this seems to provide an opening for a certain salesmanship of the detail in the usual terms. Here is Gordon Jennings, head of Paramount's Special Effects Department in 1934, discussing one element of the Tarsus sequence, Cleopatra's barge:

> This barge was painstakingly constructed from historical records of the ancient queen's actual barge: built to the scale of 100 feet to the foot, it was over twelve feet long and weighed several tons. The actual barge was propelled by 300 oars arranged in five banks, 150 to the side; this was not practical for our purposes, so the miniature was propelled by ropes attached below the water-line, and pulled by stagehands outside of the picture area. None the less, the oars must function, and this was achieved by . . .[9]

The conventional rationales of research are recognizable here. It is made clear that this is not the actual barge (it requires special effects to make images of it), but exactitude of reconstruction is said to be the rule and is confirmed quantitatively. We are again in the realm of 'what it [actually] looked like.'

How is it that such a rhetoric of referentiality can be applied to the profilmic elements of a film like *Cleopatra*? Conjunctural answers are conceivable (marketing rhetorics need not be logically coherent, research actually did occur in preproduction as it always does, and so forth), but this also points back toward a definitional principle: if spectacle is a form of excessive profilmic detail, excessiveness does not in itself radically separate it from the kind of reality-effect usually associated with more sober representations of history. Recall that Barthes's definition of the reality-effect as narrative rhetoric is the concrete detail elaborated over and above the necessities of any story functions. In that case, excessive detail is the common arena of both spectacle and the reality-effect. Of course, the transitional shots from *The Return of Martin Guerre* do seem significantly different than the finale of the Tarsus sequence in *Cleopatra*, but this only indicates that there are distinctive registers in the deployment and the regulation of excessive detail. From this perspective, such differences may be conceived as differences in degree rather than kind.

Note that the passage attributed to Gordon Jennings counters the impossibility of filming Cleopatra's actual barge with the miraculous exactitude enabled by special effects fakery, *which is being sold as such*. The construction of a scale-model barge based on research converges with a notion of Hollywood virtuosity. A virtuosity of the profilmic object is one of the attractions of the historical film as such. Consequently, this type of conflation underlies any film performance of the past for the present in the mainstream tradition. It amounts to a kind of hide-and-seek between referentiality with respect to the past and performance for the present, with both predicated on indexicality.

As a general proposition concerning mainstream cinema, it may be that neither reality-effect nor spectacle is ever completely absent; there are only different degrees of their import and intensities in relation to one another. That is, the opposition of reality-effect and spectacle, which superficially seems to be a division, is better treated as yet another dialectical polarity.

An auteur analysis of DeMille would reveal that the construction of this kind of diegetic spectacle in this kind of fictional setting is not limited to *Cleopatra*. From Araku's chamber in *The Cheat* (1915) to Dathan's tent in the second *Ten Commandments* (1956), analogous environments appear as places of seduction. They are hyperbolically designed reserves of the East, the Oriental. And they are most often places where foreign, Eastern men attempt to rape or seduce Western women, or places where (as in *Cleopatra*) Eastern women use Western men. The detail has indeed become spectacularized and performative. But that spectacle and performance is instantly understandable as a sensuous figuration of ideologically central otherness, a knotting of sexual and racial difference so typical that it can be called a cliché, although one that bears filmic elaboration far beyond the automatism that the term connotes.[10]

In one sense, the spectacle thus returns to narrative meaning after all. This spectacular apotheosis is in part an apotheosis of oppositions and hierarchies evoked in dialogue throughout the film: female/male, East/West, passivity/activity, private/public. It is surely not too surprising to find that such virtuosity of design in the display of historical knowledge of the detail can be described as conveying a threat and mastery of the Western male spectator. But of special interest here is that, as with the early film actualities, the distant in time and space is being brought to the vision of the spectator. But now, having been diegeticized, it is more efficiently tagged, identified (via gender and orientalism) with an ideological security informing and informed by narrative elements. The investment of the spectator in the indexical image has here been socially secured against the kind of privatized, radically disruptive fantasmatic diversion imagined by Barthes, and turned instead toward the socially requisite fantasies that ground DeMille's virtuosity. This socialized understanding of the other, of the distant in time and space, has been built in the very conversions between document and diegesis.

My argument is not that such ideological or ideational configurations are mechanically effective or untroubled 'messages.' (A more extensive analysis of *Cleopatra* could elaborate on contradictions, instabilities, and perversions of hierarchy around the conjunction of femininity, the East, and histories, as the character of Cleopatra, along with the term *love*, becomes a problematic confusion of public and private, male and female, West and East; this helps explain the perversions of the spectacle the film constructs.) But I am interested in them as clusters of associations and/or articulable descriptions or arguments that preexist the film and in which the film may participate in various explicit and implicit ways.

One characteristic of these representational-ideational configurations, considered as processes driving to secure socialized understandings, is their notional generality. As with logically formulated abstract ideas, concepts, and generalizations, they claim a wide applicability for themselves, one broader than any particular instance of the idea or the particular events being represented. That is, a generality is such because it can be reemployed in many particular cases and objects, regardless of referential or nonreferential context. This wide applicability with respect to referents and knowledge claims makes for repeatability, which helps a generality take on, as the classic accounts of ideology would have it, the appearance of the natural and/or the universal. To take an obvious example, it seems nearly impossible to avoid resolving mainstream narrative without coming to a conclusion about the status of a heterosexual couple, as evidenced by such different films as *The Return of Martin Guerre*, *An American in Paris*, and *Cleopatra*. This is not to deny differences in the status and treatment of the heterosexual couple. In these films alone, it is variously intricated with property and identity, romantic convention, love-death. It is simply to make the obvious point that the sheer repetition to which the routing of narrative problems through heterosexual coupling is subject bestows on the latter an ethos of the general. Not only narratives but spectacles, in order to remain within the bounds of social meanings, may call on such generalities. Performance as well as reference evinces the pull to *make sense*. Ideological generality thus provides an overdetermining justification or alibi for the detail.

In the present context, I would add that the temporal aspects of such generalities are responsive to, or at least reminiscent of, key elements of Western historicity. Once more one can find hints in some of the rhetoric surrounding research for the historical film. The statement of DeMille himself, cited as an epigraph to this chapter, moves from the promotion of research in the historical film to 'the eternal verity of the Law.'[11] The very generality asserted by such ideational configurations suggests that they tend to assert a force valid in other times than the present, outside of time; the strongest in this regard would be, precisely, 'eternal.' I have argued many times that the appeal of indexicality, including filmic indexicality, has been intertwined with the division between past and present characteristic of modern historical temporality. But such generalities serve precisely as a bridge over the gulf between past and present. They help the past 'live' because they apply then as now. More formally, to the extent that they are generalities, propositions and concepts known to be applicable in the present can also be applied to the past. The logic of employing currently acceptable general 'truths' to bridge the gap between past and present is also an aspect of disciplined historiography and is recognized as a necessity in many kinds of theories of history. The submission of the time-filled, researched particularities of the past to time-less truths provides a standpoint, a stability of positionality, on history and change. The reliance and/or evocation of such general 'truths' in mainstream film is one more indication of the importance of historical representation for mainstream cinematic textuality.

Notes

1 From a different theoretical tradition, see Oskar Negt and Alexander Kluge, *Public Sphere and Experience: Toward an Analysis of the Bourgeois and Proletarian Public Sphere*, trans. Peter Labanyi et al, Minneapolis, MN: University of Minnesota Press, 1993 for a work that foregrounds fantasy as a political terrain with special interest in media.

2 One canonical conceptualization of these processes is Pierre Bourdieu, with Luc Boltanski, Robert Castel, Jean-Claude Chamboredon, and Dominique Schnapper, *Photography: A Middle-Brow Art*, trans. Shawn Whiteside, Stanford, CA: Stanford University Press, 1990.

3 R. Barthes, *Camera Lucida: Reflections on Photography*, New York: Hill and Wang, 1972, 117. See 115–16, where Barthes finds some of the 'photographic' craziness he values in a scene from Fellini's *Casanova*, a narrative film. See also 111, but compare 89–90.

4 This recognizability is related to, but not as narrow as, the pioneering concept of 'reference period' in Pierre Sorlin, *The Film in History: Restaging the Past*, Totowa, NJ.: Barnes and Noble, 1980, chapter 2. C. S. Tashiro, *Pretty Pictures*, has much of importance to say about this (passim), but still attributes its force to perspective rather than indexicality (e.g., 58–59).

5 Jean-Louis Comolli, 'Historical Fiction: A Body Too Much,' 41–53 [reading 6].

6 And any spectatorial apprehension that the sets concretely existed as a profilmic field preserved on film is correct. See the comments and recollections of art, costume, and set designers in Hugh Fordin, *The Magic Factory: How MGM Made* An American in Paris, New York: Praeger, 1973, chapter 6.

7 In *The Epic Film: Myth and History*, Boston: Routledge and Kegan Paul, 1984, Derek Elley writes that in the 1930s, 'the costume picture took the side of the musical, with its glossy view of a privileged society at play . . . Claudette Colbert in DeMille's *The Sign of the Cross* (1933) and *Cleopatra* (1934) might just as well have been cavorting around a New York hotel suite as a palace or an imperial barge' (20). For Elley, this is a point of critique rather than the basis for an insight about the possible relatedness of the two genres around issues of referentiality and performance.

8 Vivian Sobchack, '"Surge and Splendor": A Phenomenology of the Hollywood Historical Epic,' *Representations*, 1990, no. 29, p. 28. See also S. Neale, 'Triumph of the Will: Notes on Documentary and Spectacle,' *Screen* 20, 1979, no. 1, p. 85.

9 G. Jennings, 'Special-Effects and Montage for *Cleopatra*,' *American Cinematographer*, 1934, no. 15, p. 350.

10 It is also a configuration with a cultural history and an important lineage in the function of the ornamental and spectacular in modem Western aesthetics. See N. Schor, *Reading in Detail: Aesthetics and the Feminine*, New York: Methuen, 1987, which also includes a perspicacious discussion of Barthes.

11 'Motion picture producers have sometimes been criticized for spending so much money on research – in the case of *The Ten Commandments* more than ever before. I do not agree with the criticism. I consider it money well spent to bring to the screen the results of the work of so many patient and selfless scholars whose labors, with spade and with pen, have helped us make the days of Moses live again. Research does not sell tickets at the box office, I may be told. But research does help bring out the majesty of the Lawgiver and the eternal verity of the Law.'

Roland Barthes

THE ROMANS IN FILMS

'The Romans in Films', in *Mythologies,* trans. A. Lavers, New York, 1972, pp. 26–8.

IN MANKIEWICZ'S *JULIUS CAESAR*, all the characters are wearing fringes. Some have them curly, some straggly, some tufted, some oily, all have them well combed, and the bald are not admitted, although there are plenty to be found in Roman history. Those who have little hair have not been let off for all that, and the hairdresser – the king-pin of the film – has still managed to produce one last lock which duly reaches the top of the forehead, one of those Roman foreheads, whose smallness has at all times indicated a specific mixture of self-righteousness, virtue and conquest.

What then is associated with these insistent fringes? Quite simply the label of Romanness. We therefore see here the mainspring of the Spectacle – the *sign* – operating in the open. The frontal lock overwhelms one with evidence, no one can doubt that he is in Ancient Rome. And this certainty is permanent: the actors speak, act, torment themselves, debate 'questions of universal import', without losing, thanks to this little flag displayed on their foreheads, any of their historical plausibility. Their general representativeness can even expand in complete safety, cross the ocean and the centuries, and merge into the Yankee mugs of Hollywood extras: no matter, everyone is reassured, installed in the quiet certainty of a universe without duplicity, where Romans are Romans thanks to the most legible of signs: hair on the forehead.

A Frenchman, to whose eyes American faces still have something exotic, finds comical the combination of the morphologies of these gangster-sheriffs with the little Roman fringe: it rather looks like an excellent music-hall gag. This is because for the French the sign in this case overshoots the target and discredits itself by letting its aim appear clearly. But this very fringe, when combed on the only naturally Latin forehead in the film, that of Marlon Brando, impresses us and does not make us laugh; and it is not impossible that part of the success of this actor in Europe is due to the perfect integration of Roman capillary habits with the general morphology of the characters he usually portrays. Conversely, one cannot believe in Julius Caesar, whose physiognomy is that of an Anglo-Saxon lawyer – a face with which one is already acquainted through a thousand bit parts in thrillers or comedies, and a compliant skull on which the hairdresser has raked, with great effort, a lock of hair.

In the category of capillary meanings, here is a sub-sign, that of nocturnal surprises: Portia and Calpurnia, woken up at dead of night, have conspicuously uncombed hair. The former, who is young, expresses disorder by flowing locks: her unreadiness is, so to speak, of the first degree. The latter, who is middle-aged, exhibits a more painstaking vulnerability: a plait winds round her neck and comes to rest on her right shoulder so as to impose the traditional sign of disorder, asymmetry. But these signs are at the same time excessive and ineffectual: they postulate a 'nature' which they have not even the courage to acknowledge fully: they are not 'fair and square'.

Yet another sign in this *Julius Caesar*: all the faces sweat constantly. Labourers, soldiers, conspirators, all have their austere and tense features streaming (with Vaseline). And close-ups are so frequent that evidently sweat here is an attribute with a purpose. Like the Roman fringe or the nocturnal plait, sweat is a sign. Of what? Of moral feeling. Everyone is sweating because everyone is debating something within himself; we are here supposed to be in the locus of a horribly tormented virtue, that is, in the very locus of tragedy, and it is sweat which has the function of conveying this. The populace, upset by the death of Caesar, then by the arguments of Mark Antony, is sweating, and combining economically, in this single sign, the intensity of its emotion and the simplicity of its condition. And the virtuous men, Brutus, Cassius, Casca, are ceaselessly perspiring too, testifying thereby to the enormous physiological labour produced in them by a virtue just about to give birth to a crime. To sweat is to think – which evidently rests on the postulate, appropriate to a nation of businessmen, that thought is a violent, cataclysmic operation, of which sweat is only the most benign symptom. In the whole film, there is but one man who does not sweat and who remains smooth-faced, unperturbed and watertight: Caesar. Of course Caesar, the *object* of the crime, remains dry since *he* does not know, *he does not think*, and so must keep the firm and polished texture of an exhibit standing isolated in the courtroom.

Here again, the sign is ambiguous: it remains on the surface, yet does not for all that give up the attempt to pass itself off as depth. It aims at making people understand (which is laudable) but at the same time suggests that it is spontaneous (which is cheating); it presents itself at once as intentional and irrepressible, artificial and natural, manufactured and discovered. This can lead us to an ethic of signs. Signs ought to present themselves only in two extreme forms: either openly intellectual and so remote that they are reduced to an algebra, as in the Chinese theatre, where a flag on its own signifies a regiment; or deeply rooted, invented, so to speak, on each occasion, revealing an internal, a hidden facet, and indicative of a moment in time, no longer of a concept (as in the art of Stanislavsky, for instance). But the intermediate sign, the fringe of Roman-ness or the sweating of thought, reveals a degraded spectacle, which is equally afraid of simple reality and of total artifice. For although it is a good thing if a spectacle is created to make the world more explicit, it is both reprehensible and deceitful to confuse the sign with what is signified. And it is a duplicity which is peculiar to bourgeois art: between the intellectual and the visceral sign is hypocritically inserted a hybrid, at once elliptical and pretentious, which is pompously christened '*nature*'.

Michelle Pierson

A PRODUCTION DESIGNER'S CINEMA

Historical authenticity in popular films set in the past

'A Production Designer's Cinema: Historical Authenticity in Popular Films Set in the Past', in *Spectacle and the Real*, ed. G. King, Bristol: Intellect, 2005, pp. 145–55.

THE AUSTRALIAN FILM CRITIC, Adrian Martin, put his finger on something when he suggested in a review of *Moulin Rouge!* (2001) that the film was 'all set design but no real mise-en-scène'.[1] Here we have one of those risky, 'what if' propositions whose very formativeness is their most productive quality. As is so often the case with this kind of writing (and not only film reviewing but academic writing too), there is less fun to be had in dismissing Martin's claim as obviously counter-intuitive than in asking: what *might* it mean? After the Academy of Motion Picture Arts and Sciences awarded Catherine Martin (Art Direction) and Brigitte Broch (Set Decoration) the award for best art direction at the 74th Academy Awards there would, of course, be those who would say that like the Academy, this remark merely registered the local and not so local gossip that *Moulin Rouge!* more strongly bears the imprimatur of its production designer than that of its director.

If production designers themselves are to have any say in the matter, however, it has to be said that there is not a production designer working today who does not insist that the role of the production designer is to realise the creative vision of the film's director. Or, as Vincent LoBrutto's description of the job would have it: 'the production designer researches the world in which the film takes place to capture a sense of authenticity and render the director's vision to celluloid reality'.[2] Adrian Martin himself would most certainly have resisted any attempt to be drawn on speculation about the nature of the collaborative partnership between Baz Luhrmann and his production designer wife. His comment on the absence of 'real mise-en-scène' in *Moulin Rouge!* is, in fact, more properly considered alongside the work of Siegfried Kracauer. For like Martin, Kracauer had also felt that some film-making choices inevitably place a strain on the relationship between production design and mise-en-scène. Kracauer, however, understood this tension to be less a product of any one film's unique circumstances of production, than of a more general condition of certain types of film-making.

The more general condition of film-making that I am interested in thinking about here is the condition of setting films in the past. This condition had also interested Kracauer in *Theory of Film: The Redemption of Physical Reality* (1960). My own approach to thinking about the way that popular films deal with the past engages in a critical interrogation of Kracauer's assumption that, because viewers of historical film are likely to remain 'conscious of the efforts going into [their] construction', the authenticity of these films' re-creations of the past will necessarily be in question.[3] I want to suggest that the 'staginess' that Kracauer associates with films set in the past does, indeed, condition the way that viewers engage with them: just not necessarily in the way he suggests. Other conditions that impact on how the authenticity of a film is determined by audiences – conditions that have a still more general applicability – might be suggested.

One way of understanding the tension between production design and mise-en-scène that Martin identifies in *Moulin Rouge!* might be to see it as arising out of circumstances in which, instead of being integrated into the actual staging and filming of the action, the realisation of a number of aspects of production design has been deferred until post-production. The contemporary production designer is not only responsible for choosing locations and overseeing set design and décor, but also for deciding whether a set should actually be built or whether it should be created in whole or in part with computer-generated imagery.[4] While these kinds of decisions are made in consultation with a director, any decision to delegate a substantial part of set construction to a visual effects supervisor will also have an impact on the kind of environment the director has to work with on-set. The extent to which the physical intangibility of this environment will mean that directors have less scope for control over the look of the film will depend, in part, on individual directors and their ability to make a not yet (fully) realised setting intellectually and emotionally tangible for actors and crew.

In cases where the nature of settings and/or the style of production design for a film is such that audiences too may be more or less aware of the conditions of their production – more or less aware of the physical intangibility of environments, objects, and even characters seen on-screen – some styles of performance may also be more effective than others at assuring audiences that these settings are still inhabited by and meaningful to characters played by actors. Martin was not the only viewer to complain that the acting in *Moulin Rouge!* 'comes in only two modes – star turns from Kidman and McGregor, and quirky, often tiresome eccentricities from everyone else'. Nor was he the only one to feel that, all things considered, McGregor also 'registers as the one completely convincing element in the movie'.[5]

Like other actors of his generation (but, perhaps, most notably Johnny Depp and Edward Norton), McGregor's performance style places less emphasis on virtuosity and craft (in the manner, say, of an actor like Kevin Spacey or the wonderfully histrionic Philip Seymour Hoffman), than on what can only be called 'sincerity'.

Lionel Trilling reminds us that the word 'sincerity' is typically taken to refer 'to a congruence between avowal and actual feeling'.[6] What remains suggestive about his account of the historical 'rise' and 'decline' of sincerity – its slide into anachronism and eclipse by the more morally strenuous term 'authenticity' – is the idea that sincerity was brought into disrepute by a creeping instrumentality. Far from implying an 'unmediated exhibition of self', it came to insinuate the intervention of performance: or, in Trilling's words, the 'fulfilment of a public role'.[7] In some sense, of course, all contemporary film actors are required to convey sincerity in their public role as actors. It is their job to convey the impression that public performance can still give expression to 'actual feeling'. Whereas an older generation of actors conveyed sincerity through a combination of learned technique and the refinement of individual gestures and mannerisms, today it is those actors whose performance styles are least clearly defined by a recognisable personal or 'emotional idiolect' that seem most sincere.[8] It is younger actors' less studied style of performance that today communicates sincerity to their younger audiences (consider, for instance, the warm response that Eminem's performance in *8 Mile* (2002) received from both audiences and critics).

Naturally, it is also those actors whose publicity most consistently reports on their ambivalence about Hollywood and its star system who are the most strongly identified with this performance style. Reports of Norton's privacy, Depp's move to France, and McGregor's London residence, all work to place them at some personal remove from Hollywood. The casting of McGregor and Liam Neeson in *Star Wars: Episode I: The Phantom Menace* (1999) provides one of the more obvious examples of the way performance sometimes gets called upon to address the potential for tension between production design and mise-en-scène under circumstances in which significant elements of the production design are disarticulated from the physical staging of the action. For much of the responsibility of convincing audiences of the emotional reality of the films' virtual sets and computer-generated characters falls on these actors' performances, and their ability to convey a sense of meaningful interaction between them. In allowing the actors in *Gladiator* (2000) to speak in their own accents, Ridley Scott also calculated that if there was a sacrifice to be made in terms of historical verisimilitude, it would be more than made up for by performances that would come across as less 'actorly' and therefore more sincere.

Moulin Rouge! and *Gladiator* are also both films set in the past: the first, a musical set in Paris in 1899, the latter an historical epic set in ancient Rome. Since films set in the past often require the re-creation of vistas, environments and material artefacts that no longer exist in the here and now, their settings have often been among the most recognisable as the work of design. As the example of *The Phantom Menace* makes clear, however, this is not a circumstance unique to period films. The settings in many science fiction and fantasy films, musicals, adventure and horror films also have the look of having been designed. Since the decision to leave the actual creation of sets or parts of sets to post-production is made as often (if not more often) by production designers and directors working within the genres of science fiction and fantasy, this is not a condition of filmmaking specific to films set in the past either. Kracauer's own grouping of historical with fantasy film is a reminder of this. It might still be argued, however, that both of these circumstances – the need to re-create the past for the present and the decision to re-create it in post-production – expand production designers' contributions to (if not exactly control over) mise-en-scène.

All films that have what Charles and Mirella Jona Affron call a high degree of 'design intensity' have to try to resolve the problem of how to make sets that exhibit degrees of invention ranging from studied whimsy to the highly stylised and even the pictorial *feel* authentic to audiences.[9] This is because audiences still want to experience films as authentic no matter how fantastic their settings and indeed their narratives might be. If, for the museum curator, determining the authenticity of an artefact involves verification of the circumstances in which it was produced, the term 'authenticity' means something quite different when it is used to describe a dimension of aesthetic experience. All films set in the past offer a number of solutions to the problem of providing audiences with a re-creation of the past that can be experienced as authentic, including (as I have already suggested) appealing to the sincerity of star performances. In a great variety of popular films set in the past – among them films such as *Moulin Rouge!*, *Gladiator*, *The Mummy* (Stephen Sommers, 1999) and *The Mummy Returns* (Stephen Sommers, 2001), *Sleepy Hollow* (Tim Burton, 1999), *Crouching Tiger, Hidden Dragon* (Ang Lee, 2000) or even something like *Kate and Leopold* (James Mangold, 2001) – the problem of how to make sets that have a high degree of design intensity look and feel authentic is one that is often addressed most powerfully and persuasively through production design.

With the possible exception of *Gladiator*, all of the films just listed are much more likely to be identified by audiences and critics according to genres such as the musical, fantasy-adventure, horror, sword-fight film or romantic comedy than as historical films. While scholarship on the historical film has long wrestled with the question of which types of films can or should be included in the category, the impulse of recent work in this area has been to recognise that all kinds of films, and not just bio-pics or films based on historical events, put history to use.[10] Some of this scholarship has been particularly concerned to stress the differences between the kinds of historical representations found in much popular cinema and those found both in scholarly historiography and in those forms of historical drama specifically concerned with re-creating past lives and events. In their introduction to a collection of essays on British historical cinema that includes discussion of costume dramas, *Carry On* films and examples such as *Zulu* (Cy Endfield, 1964) and Kenneth Branagh's *Henry V* (1989), Claire Monk and Amy Sargeant suggest, for instance, that their readers hardly 'need reminding that a "historical" film will often be a work of pure entertainment and pure fiction'.[11] With their mix of exotic historical settings, visual effects and fantasy narratives, films such as *Moulin Rouge!*, *Crouching Tiger* and *The Mummy* certainly make entertainment and, in particular, the enjoyment of their inventive settings and effects a high priority.

For all this blatant invention and patent artifice, these films nevertheless make history an important site of subjective investment for audiences. But the kind of historical remembering that they enact is not *only* the stuff of historical actuality. Much popular cinema is only selectively and unevenly concerned with staging the kinds of historical representations that ask audiences to believe that 'this really happened like this' or that 'things really looked like this in the past'. These kinds of concerns may not have been entirely absent from the minds of Luhrmann, Martin and Broch when they embarked on the making of *Moulin Rouge!*, or even from those of the team of artists and designers who worked with Stephen Sommers to re-create ancient Egypt or Cairo in the 1920s for the *Mummy* trilogy. But all of these films just as obviously present audiences with a whole other set of criteria for engaging with their re-creations of the past.

That it is through their own production histories that many popular films set in the past most strongly impress upon audiences a sense of their real historical significance, is something on which both Vivian Sobchack, and more recently Philip Rosen, have commented. In her insightful and acerbic account of the historical epics that came out of Hollywood in the 1950s and 1960s, Sobchack makes the point that this cinema offered the historical 'eventfulness' of its own production – announced through the monumental scope of its production design and through the widespread promotion of the monumental expenditure required to realise it for the cinema screen – as its guarantee of authenticity, assuring audiences that no amount of labour or expense had been spared in the making.[12] New releases of these old widescreen epics on DVD are, of course, being accompanied by extensive production notes that not only give details about the eventfulness of their original production, but also of their subsequent restoration. The production notes for a recent DVD release of *Spartacus* (Stanley Kubrick, 1960) take care, for instance, to point out that its restoration in the early nineties was the most extensive in history.

In his examination of the production history of historical epics such as Cecil B. DeMille's *Cleopatra* (1934), Rosen is particularly interested in the way research is used to authenticate the re-creation of the past. He argues that promotional assurances that producers have made every effort to make sure that sets, props, costumes – indeed every detail of the historical epic's elaborately rendered mise-en-scène – have been thoroughly researched by a team of advising experts, offer audiences a de facto guarantee that the artefacts of the past seen on-screen are historically accurate (or as accurate as cinematic, and especially genre, conventions will allow). Since this type of promotional material also foregrounds the process of actually making these films and, in particular, the labour that goes into realising mise-en-scène, this type of production discourse also makes an explicit appeal to audience appreciation of the real creative labour that has gone into their production.

Although Rosen's examination of popular films set in the past pays particular attention to the way in which the historical detail and production of their mise-en-scène grounds them in a researched and 'documentable profilmic', his discussion of the musical *An American in Paris* (Vincente Minnelli, 1951) also addresses the question of how a film's mise-en-scène can appear 'so overwhelming, so extravagant, so playful, so performative as opposed to referential that we call it spectacle', and still offer audiences an experience of the real [see reading 18]. One answer to this question has already been given. As is the case whenever special effects are foregrounded for audience attention, those elements of mise-en-scène that most strongly have the look of having been designed also most strongly invite appreciation of their creative realisation by production and visual effects designers. However, it is not only Rosen's argument that the 'showily artificial' settings in *An American in Paris* celebrate the virtuosity of their designers, but also that by grounding their origins in researched sources – in this case, impressionist paintings of the period in which the film is set – they still make history (in this case 'art history') the real site of their authentication.

Charles Tashiro, who along with the Affrons has written one of the few scholarly monographs on production design published in English, has also commented on the use of paintings in films set in the past. Tashiro's interest is more specific than Rosen's, focusing on those relatively rare occasions when films depicting a real historical event meticulously reproduce the mise-en-scène of a historical painting that is already well known for its depiction of the same event. For both of these writers, the self-conscious referencing of paintings in films performs two functions. On the one hand, the mise-en-scène of the past acquires greater authenticity for audiences because it accords with the understanding they have acquired of it through contact with other modes of historical representation. And, at the same time, individual viewers' exercise of the (art) 'historical capital' necessary for identifying the self-referential nature of this kind of aesthetic choice itself provides the feeling of engagement they associate with the experience of authenticity.[13]

Among the more popular films listed here, the production design for *Gladiator* is, perhaps, the least design-intensive. But even so, Ridley Scott and production designer Arthur Max have spoken at length about their sources of inspiration, citing not only the 'romantic vision of Rome' found in a number of nineteenth-century British and French paintings, but also films like Leni Riefenstahl's *Triumph of the Will*; recalling that '[w]e copied *them* [Nazi propaganda films] copying the Romans, which added an extra layer and another cultural interpretation'.[14] While discussion of the self-referential and even baroque nature of a popular cinema that consistently makes reference to its own history the most satisfying site of content for at least some of its viewers has certainly been taken up in other contexts, this aspect of popular cinema has less often been addressed within the context of the way these films depict the past.[15] Through the allusiveness of their production design and through promotion and discussion of their production in the popular and mass media – but perhaps most importantly through the commentary and bonus material that is increasingly packaged with DVD releases – many popular films also offer audiences identification of their detailed referencing of artworks, but especially other films and film styles, as one of their most satisfying sites of authentication.

Any one of the films listed here so far could be used to further illustrate this point. In an account of the making of *The Mummy Returns* in *Cinefex* – a publication that is neither a fan magazine nor a trade publication but is avidly read by both film fans and film professionals (but perhaps most significantly in this day and age, by film students) – every person contributing to the film describes their work in terms of the films that served as inspiration and model. If the direction for the film's matte paintings of London was to make it 'look like *Mary Poppins*' research for the film also included going back and looking at *Lawrence of Arabia*, at *Spartacus*, at 'all the great battle sequences from *Barry Lyndon*',[16] which are also such important references for *Gladiator*.

It is a detail about an early sketch for one of the more fanciful settings in *The Mummy Returns*, however, which has the most to say about the 'historicity' of production design in many popular films set in the past. The sketch – of the main characters sailing toward a mythical pyramid – is credited not only with being reminiscent of the work of Ray Harryhausen, but of being 'the first real design that captured the period romance and epic sweep of that part in the movie'.[17] The really telling part of this anecdote concerns, not the referencing of Harryhausen, but the detail that to achieve the right look, the sketch was 'scanned and tinted sepia in Photoshop'. Sepia has, of course, come to function as the colour of history in all sorts of popular cultural contexts. Think, for instance, of the photographs that visitors to many living history museums and theme parks can have taken of themselves as mementoes of their experience: their modern selves transported back into the past through the magic of mise-en-scène and sepia toning. As Robert Brent Toplin has also pointed out in his recent defence of Hollywood's treatment of history in the United States, 'the History Channel features this color icon in its brownish orange logo and in the background sets in its studio'.[18]

While research on the use of colour in early cinema suggests that in this period of experimentation colour tended not to be used to signify temporal shifts, so much as to mark its own, highly unregulated appearance as a temporal event in itself, conventions for using colour to evoke the past developed rather quickly after the 1920s.[19] In contrast to the use of Technicolor in the 1950s and 1960s to imbue epic cinema's spectacular mise-en-scène with a special vividness and intensity, the practice of using black and white to signal temporal shifts in narrative has, for instance, long been conventional for more serious and/or melodramatic films. More contemporary popular cinema has developed its own system of colour coding for capturing the period romance of 'olden times'. If the colour of the past in *The Mummy* and *The Mummy Returns* is not exactly sepia, these films' palette of sand, gold and brown nevertheless extends to every aspect of their production design – from buildings, costumes and lighting to the many digitally created sets – washing everything in a golden brown hue that is not so very far from it either. This use of colour is even more obvious in *Kate and Leopold*, which plucks its time-travelling romantic lead out of a brown nineteenth century and hurls him into the living colour of modern times. Toplin gives another, less obvious but more widely cited example of the use of a modified sepia palette to colour the past, reminding us of Steven Spielberg's desire to give the opening scenes of *Saving Private Ryan* (1998) 'the appearance of an old newsreel'.[20]

The association of sepia with history has its beginnings in the nineteenth century. When early photographs faded they lost their metallic lustre and took on a brown tinge. One way of thinking about the colour of the past in popular film, then, might be to suggest that to really give its settings historical authenticity, popular film not only remembers old films – through, for instance, the techniques of allusion, homage and pastiche – but also gives them something of the colour and grain of old techniques of photographic and cinematographic reproduction. In the opening sequence of *Moulin Rouge!*, it is not so much colour as the simulated flicker of early cinema that gives the film its period look. E. Elias Merhige's art-house film, *The Shadow of the Vampire* (2000), likewise insists that its film-within-a-film look like old film. *The Shadow of the Vampire* re-creates the making of F. W. Murnau's *Nosferatu* (1922), casting John Malkovich as Murnau and Willem Dafoe as the actor-vampire Max Schreck. For early scenes depicting the shooting of the film, the rolling of the camera motivates a transition from colour cinematography to grainy black and white.

But the 'real' *Nosferatu* (i.e. the version actually made by Murnau) has also been incorporated into the film: serving, at one moment, as an establishing shot of the ruined castle in which the film is being shot and, at another, as a glimpse of the film-in-progress. The latter occurs just after Schreck has sucked the living daylights out of one of the hapless crew under the cover of a momentary blackout during shooting. As Murnau sets about restoring order to the set, Schreck plays with a projector on which the film-in-progress is spooled. The film that Schreck glimpses – the film-within-the-film – is the real *Nosferatu*. For a brief moment, it fills the cinema frame, every scratch, every artefact of decades of wear and tear lovingly preserved.

Signs of the material deterioration of Murnau's film guarantees its authenticity for viewers in a way that no attempt to restore it to the time of the film's diegesis, when it was new, pristine, and still to be remembered, could have done. By inserting an old film where a new one should be, viewers of this arty, sometimes camp, and occasionally ponderous film, are invited to savour cinema's fragile materiality. But what of other films that re-create the past, not just through allusion to old paintings and films, but also by giving them something of the look of having been made at an earlier time: how might the terms in which these films lay claim to historical authenticity be understood? Even some of the films that appear to be the least concerned with whether or not their re-creations of the past accord with 'how things actually were' present audiences with a layered, multivalent imagining of the past that asks for their participation in making it *feel* authentic. To suggest that a wide range of popular films set in the past offer viewers the opportunity to participate in the exercise of a number of different modes of historical recognition and knowledge – in what might even be described as a form of popular historiography – is not to suggest that there might not also be reasons for being suspicious of a cinema that makes this exercise such a satisfying end in itself. It is, however, to again be reminded that under these conditions the authenticity of aesthetic experience is finally decided by audiences themselves.

Not even Eric Rohmer gets to circumvent audience desires to make these kinds of determinations without risking losing their interest. Earlier, I suggested that any time there is the possibility that audiences will become aware that significant elements of a film's mise-en-scène are not actually present for actors, production design becomes an especially important site for addressing their desire for the film to look and feel 'right' or authentic. While art cinema audiences bring a different set of criteria to their viewing of more experimental works, any historical film that stakes its claims to authenticity on a singular vision of the past nevertheless still takes a risk. For *L'Anglaise et le Duc* (*The Lady and the Duke*, 2001), a film set during the period of the French Revolution, Rohmer had the idea of using scenic backgrounds painted in the style of the period to re-create outdoor scenes of Paris in the late eighteenth century. Live action footage of actors filmed before a blue screen were keyed into these backgrounds in post-production. Asked to comment on this decision, he replied: 'Yes. I don't much care for photographic reality. In this film, I depict the Revolution as people would have seen it at the time'.[21] For viewers, though (and I mean viewers sympathetic to the spirit of creative experiment that this enterprise entails), the trouble with Jean-Baptiste Marot's paintings is that after the first few scenes, there is nothing more to discover in them: no surprise encounters with familiar but forgotten memories of other paintings, other films, await. Does the past recover in this gesture the quality of fundamental and unrecoverable difference from the present? Perhaps. But the film's conceit is to imagine that recourse to a 'highly visible artifice' is itself a sufficient condition for illuminating this truth. For all the obvious aesthetic and cultural conservatism of more popular, mass-market films, one of the things that they have going for them is that they long ago worked out that this kind of determination is not theirs alone to make.

Through the highly visible artifice of their own production design, many popular films create past worlds in which it is not so much the likeness of these worlds to historical actuality that is calculated to appeal to audiences, but the conventionality, familiarity and accessibility of their historical references. Not all viewers have the kind of (film) historical knowledge that might enable them to identify *The Mummy*'s debt to Harryhausen, and fewer still may actually have seen the early films that provided the inspiration for the opening sequence of *Moulin Rouge!* But by filtering the colour and texture of old photographs, newsreels and films through their production design, these films also give the past an historical authenticity that is more broadly, popularly, accessible.

Notes

1 A. Martin, Review of *Moulin Rouge!*, *The Age* [Melbourne, Australia], 24 May, 2001, p. A3 5.
2 V. LoBrutto, *By Design: Interviews with Film Production Designers*, Westport, CT: Praeger, 1992, p. ix.
3 S. Kracauer, *Theory of Film: The Redemption of Physical Reality*, London: Oxford University Press, 1978, p. 77.
4 P. Ettedgui, *Production Design and Art Direction*, Woburn, MA: Focal Press, 1999, p. 10.
5 A. Martin, 'Review of *Moulin Rouge!*', p. 5.
6 L. Trilling, *Sincerity and Authenticity*, London: Oxford University Press, 1972, p. 2.
7 Ibid., p. 9.
8 J. Naremore, *Acting in the Cinema*, Berkeley: University of California Press, 1988, p. 197.
9 C. Affron and M. J. Affron, *Sets in Motion: Art Direction and Film Narrative*, New Brunswick, NJ: Rutgers University Press, 1995, p. 116.
10 M. Landy, *Cinematic Uses of the Past*, Minneapolis, MN: University of Minnesota Press, 1996, pp. 1–29.
11 C. Monk and A. Sargeant (eds), *British Historical Cinema: The History, Heritage and Costume Film*, London: Routledge, 2002, p. 4.
12 V. Sobchack, '"Surge and Splendor": A Phenomenology of the Hollywood Historical Epic', *Representations*, 1990, vol. 29, p. 28.
13 Pierre Sorlin, as quoted in C. Tashiro, *Pretty Pictures: Production Design and the History Film*, Austin, TX: University of Texas Press, 2002, p. 20.
14 A. Max, as quoted in R. Magid, 'Rebuilding Ancient Rome', *American Cinematographer*, 2000, vol. 81(5), p. 55.
15 C. Tashiro, *Pretty Pictures*; and D. Cartmell, I. Q. Hunter and I. Whelehan (eds), *Retrovisions: Reinventing the Past in Film and Fiction*, London: Pluto Press, 2001.
16 J. Fordham, 'Warrior Kings', *Cinefex*, 2001, no. 86, p. 128.

17 Ibid., p. 14.
18 R. B. Toplin, *Reel History: In Defense of Hollywood*, Lawrence, KS: University Press of Kansas, 2002, p. 54.
19 D. Hertogs and N. de Klerk (eds), *Disorderly Order: Colours in Silent Film*, London: BFI, 1997.
20 R. B. Toplin, *Reel History*, p. 14.
21 A. Ferenzi, 'Interview with Eric Rohmer', *Senses of Cinema*, 2001, no. 16, available online at <www.sensesofcinema.com/contents/01/16/rhomer.html> [accessed 15 July 2008].

Linda Williams

MIRRORS WITHOUT MEMORIES

Truth, history, and the new documentary

'Mirrors without Memories: Truth, History, and the New Documentary', in B. Henderson and A. Martin with L. Amazonas (eds), *Film Quarterly: Forty Years, a Selection*, Berkeley: University of California Press, 1999, pp. 309–28.

THE AUGUST 12TH, 1990 ARTS AND LEISURE section of the *New York Times* carried a lead article with a rather arresting photograph of Franklin Roosevelt flanked by Winston Churchill and Groucho Marx. Standing behind them was a taut-faced Sylvester Stallone in his Rambo garb. The photo illustrated the major point of the accompanying article by Andy Grundberg: that the photograph – and by implication the moving picture as well – is no longer, as Oliver Wendell Holmes once put it, a 'mirror with a memory' illustrating the visual truth of objects, persons, and events but a manipulated construction. In an era of electronic and computer-generated images, the camera, the article sensationally proclaims, 'can lie.'

In this photo, the anachronistic flattening out of historical referents, the trivialization of history itself, with the popular culture icons of Groucho and Rambo rubbing up against Roosevelt and Churchill, serves almost as a caricature of the state of representation some critics have chosen to call postmodern. In a key statement, Fredric Jameson has described the 'cultural logic of postmodernism' as a 'new depthlessness, which finds its prolongation both in contemporary "theory" and in a whole new culture of the image or the simulacrum'.[1] To Jameson, the effect of this image culture is a weakening of historicity. Lamenting the loss of the grand narratives of modernity, which he believes once made possible the political actions of individuals representing the interests of social classes, Jameson argues that it no longer seems possible to represent the 'real' interests of a people or a class against the ultimate ground of social and economic determinations.

While not all theorists of postmodernity are as disturbed as Jameson by the apparent loss of the referent, by the undecidabilities of representation accompanied by an apparent paralysis of the will to change, many theorists do share a sense that the enlightenment projects of truth and reason are definitively over. And if representations, whether visual or verbal, no longer refer to a truth or referent 'out there,' as Trinh T. Minh-ha has put it, for us 'in here,'[2] then we seem to be plunged into a permanent state of the self-reflexive crisis of representation. What was once a 'mirror with a memory' can now only reflect another mirror.

Perhaps because so much faith was once placed in the ability of the camera to reflect objective truths of some fundamental social referent – often construed by the socially relevant documentary film as records of injustice or exploitation of powerless common people – the loss of faith in the objectivity of the image seems to point, nihilistically, like the impossible memory of the meeting of the fictional Rambo and the real Roosevelt, to the brute and cynical disregard of ultimate truths.

Yet at the very same time, as any television viewer and moviegoer knows, we also exist in an era in which there is a remarkable hunger for documentary images of the real. These images proliferate in the vérité of on-the-scene cops programs in which the camera eye merges with the eye of the law to observe the violence citizens do to one another. Violence becomes the very emblem of the real in these programs. Interestingly, violent trauma has become the emblem of the real in the new vérité genre of the independent amateur video, which, in the case of George Holliday's tape of the Rodney King beating by L.A. police, functioned to contradict the eye of the law and to intervene in the 'cops' official version of King's arrest. This home video might be taken to represent the other side of the postmodern distrust of the image: here the camera tells the truth in a remarkable moment of cinema vérité which then becomes valuable (though not conclusive) evidence in accusations against the L.A. Police Department's discriminatory violence against minority offenders.

The contradictions are rich: on the one hand the postmodern deluge of images seems to suggest that there can be no a priori truth of the referent to which the image refers; on the other hand, in this same deluge, it is still the moving image that has the power to move audiences to a new appreciation of previously unknown truth.

In a recent book on postwar West German cinema and its representations of that country's past, Anton Kaes has written that '[T]he sheer mass of historical images transmitted by today's media weakens the link between public memory and personal experience. The past is in danger of becoming a rapidly expanding collection of images, easily retrievable but isolated from time and space, available in an eternal present by pushing a button on the remote control. History thus returns forever – as film'.[3] Recently, the example of history that has been most insistently returning 'as film' to American viewers is the assassination of John F. Kennedy as simulated by film-maker Oliver Stone.

Stone's *JFK* might seem a good example of Jameson's and Kaes's worst-case scenarios of the ultimate loss of historical truth amid the postmodern hall of mirrors. While laudably obsessed with exposing the manifest contradictions of the Warren

Commission's official version of the Kennedy assassination, Stone's film has been severely criticized for constructing a 'countermyth' to the Warren Commission's explanation of what happened. Indeed, Stone's images offer a kind of tragic counterpart to the comic mélange of the *New York Times* photo of Groucho and Roosevelt. Integrating his own reconstruction of the assassination with the famous Zapruder film, whose 'objective' reflection of the event is offered as the narrative (if not the legal) clincher in Jim Garrison's argument against the lone assassin theory, Stone mixes Zapruder's real vérité with his own simulated vérité to construct a grandiose paranoid countermyth of a vast conspiracy by Lyndon Johnson, the C.I.A., and the Joint Chiefs of Staff to carry out a coup d'état. With little hard evidence to back him up, Stone would seem to be a perfect symptom of a postmodern negativity and nihilism toward truth, as if to say: 'We know the Warren Commission made up a story, well, here's another even more dramatic and entertaining story. Since we can't know the truth, let's make up a grand paranoid fiction'.

It is not my purpose here to attack Oliver Stone's remarkably effective deployment of paranoia and megalomania; the press has already done a thorough job of debunking his unlikely fiction of a Kennedy who was about to end the Cold War and withdraw from Vietnam.[4] What interests me however, is the positive side of this megalomania: Stone's belief that it is possible to intervene in the process by which truth is constructed; his very real accomplishment in shaking up public perception of an official truth that closed down, rather than opened up, investigation; his acute awareness of how images enter into the production of knowledge. However much Stone may finally betray the spirit of his own investigation into the multiple, contingent, and constructed nature of the representation of history by asking us to believe in too tidy a conspiracy, his *JFK* needs to be taken seriously for its renewal of interest in one of the major traumas of our country's past.

So rather than berate Stone, I would like to contrast this multimillion-dollar historical fiction film borrowing many aspects of the form of documentary to what we might call the low-budget postmodern documentary borrowing many features of the fiction film. My goal in what follows is to get beyond the much remarked self-reflexivity and flamboyant auteurism of these documentaries, which might seem, Rashomon-like, to abandon the pursuit of truth, to what seems to me their remarkable engagement with a newer, more contingent, relative, postmodern truth – a truth which, far from being abandoned, still operates powerfully as the receding horizon of the documentary tradition.

When we survey the field of recent documentary films two things stand out: first, their unprecedented popularity among general audiences, who now line up for documentaries as eagerly as for fiction films; second, their willingness to tackle often grim, historically complex subjects. Errol Morris's *The Thin Blue Line* (1987), about the murder of a police officer and the near execution of the 'wrong man,' Michael Moore's *Roger and Me* (1989), about the dire effects of General Motors' plant closings, and Ken Burns's 11-hour *The Civil War* (1990) (watched on PBS by 39 million Americans), were especially popular documentaries about uncommonly serious political and social realities. Even more difficult and challenging, though not quite as popular, were *Hitler, A Film from Germany* (Hans-Jürgen Syberberg, 1980), *Shoah* (Claude Lanzmann, 1985), *Hotel Terminus: The Life and Times of Klaus Barbie* (Marcel Ophuls, 1987) and *Who Killed Vincent Chin?* (Chris Choy and Renee Tajima,

1988). And in 1991 the list of both critically successful and popular documentary features *not* nominated for Academy Awards – *Paris Is Burning* (Jennie Livingston), *Hearts of Darkness: A Filmmaker's Apocalypse* (Fax Bahr and George Hickenlooper), *35 Up* (Michael Apted), *Madonna: Truth or Dare* (Alek Keshishian) – was viewed by many as an embarrassment to the Academy. *Village Voice* critic Amy Taubin notes that 1991 was a year in which four or five documentaries made it onto the *Variety* charts; documentaries now mattered in a new way.[5]

It is the paradox of the intrusive manipulation of documentary truth, combined with a serious quest to reveal some ultimate truths, that I would like to isolate within a subset of the above films. What interests me particularly is the way a special few of these documentaries handle the problem of figuring traumatic historical truths inaccessible to representation by any simple or single 'mirror with a memory,' and how this mirror nevertheless operates in complicated and indirect refractions. For while traumatic events of the past are not available for representation by any simple or single 'mirror with a memory' – in the vérité sense of capturing events as they happen – they do constitute a multifaceted receding horizon which these films powerfully evoke.

I would like to offer Errol Morris's *The Thin Blue Line* as a prime example of this postmodern documentary approach to the trauma of an inaccessible past because of its spectacular success in intervening in the truths known about this past. Morris's film was instrumental in exonerating a man wrongfully accused of murder. In 1976, Dallas police officer Robert Wood was murdered, apparently by a 28-year-old drifter named Randall Adams. Like Stone's *JFK*, *The Thin Blue Line* is a film about a November murder in Dallas. Like *JFK*, the film argues that the wrong man was set up by a state conspiracy with an interest in convicting an easy scapegoat rather than prosecuting the real murderer. The film – the 'true' story of Randall Adams, the man convicted of the murder of Officer Wood, and his accuser David Harris, the young hitchhiker whom Adams picked up the night of the murder – ends with Harris's cryptic but dramatic confession to the murder in a phone conversation with Errol Morris.

Stylistically, *The Thin Blue Line* has been most remarked for its film-noirish beauty, its apparent abandonment of cinema-vérité realism for studied, often slow-motion, and highly expressionistic reenactments of different witnesses' versions of the murder to the tune of Philip Glass's hypnotic score. Like a great many recent documentaries obsessed with traumatic events of the past, *The Thin Blue Line* is self-reflexive. Like many of these new documentaries, it is acutely aware that the individuals whose lives are caught up in events are not so much self-coherent and consistent identities as they are actors in competing narratives. As in *Roger and Me*, *Shoah*, and, to a certain extent, *Who Killed Vincent Chin?*, the documentarian's role in constructing and staging these competing narratives thus becomes paramount. In place of the self-obscuring voyeur of vérité realism, we encounter, in these and other films, a new presence in the persona of the documentarian.

Morris gives us some truths and withholds others. His approach to truth is altogether strategic. Truth exists for Morris because lies exist; if lies are to be exposed, truths must be strategically deployed against them. His strategy in the pursuit of this relative, hierarchized, and contingent truth is thus to find guilty those speakers whom he draws most deeply into the explorations of their past. Harris, the prosecutor Mulder, the false witness Emily Miller, all cozy up to the camera to remember incidents from their past which serve to indict them in the present. In contrast, the man found innocent by the film remains a cipher, we learn almost nothing of his past, and this lack of knowledge appears necessary to the investigation of the official lies. What Morris does, in effect, is partially close down the representation of Adams's own story, the accumulation of narratives from his past, in order to show how convenient a scapegoat he was to the overdetermining pasts of all the other false witnesses. Thus, instead of using fictionalizing techniques to show us the truth of what happened, Morris scrupulously sticks to stylized and silent docudrama reenactments that show only what each witness claims happened.

In contrast, we might consider Oliver Stone's very different use of docudrama reenactments to reveal the 'truth' of the existence of several assassins and the plot that orchestrated their activity, in the murder of JFK. Stone has Garrison introduce the Zapruder film in the trial of Clay Shaw as hallowed vérité evidence that there had to be more than one assassin. Garrison's examination of the magic bullet's trajectory does a fine dramatic job of challenging the official version of the lone assassin. But in his zealous pursuit of the truth of 'who dunnit,' Stone matches the vérité style of the Zapruder film with a vérité simulation which, although hypothesis, has none of the stylized, hypothetical visual marking of Morris's simulations and which therefore commands a greater component of belief. Morris, on the other hand, working in a documentary form that now eschews vérité as a style, stylizes his hypothetical reenactments and never offers any of them as an image of what actually happened.

In the discussions surrounding the truth claims of many contemporary documentaries, attention has centered upon the self-reflexive challenge to once hallowed techniques of vérité. It has become an axiom of the new documentary that films cannot reveal the truth of events, but only the ideologies and consciousness that construct competing truths – the fictional master narratives by which we make sense of events. Yet too often this way of thinking has led to a forgetting of the way in which these films still are, as Stone's film isn't, documentaries – films with a special interest in the relation to the real, the 'truths' which matter in people's lives but which cannot be transparently represented.

One reason for this forgetting has been the erection of a too simple dichotomy between, on the one hand, a naïve faith in the truth of what the documentary image reveals – vérité's discredited claim to capturing events while they happen – and on the other, the embrace of fictional manipulation. Of course, even in its heyday no one ever fully believed in an absolute truth of cinema vérité. There are, moreover, many gradations of fictionalized manipulation ranging from the controversial manipulation of temporal sequence in Michael Moore's *Roger and Me* to Errol Morris's scrupulous reconstructions of the subjective truths of events as viewed from many different points of view.

Truth is 'not guaranteed' and cannot be transparently reflected by a mirror with a memory, yet some kinds of partial and contingent truths are nevertheless the always receding goal of the documentary tradition. Instead of careening between idealistic faith in documentary truth and cynical recourse to fiction, we do better to define documentary not as an essence of truth but as a set of strategies designed to choose from among a horizon of relative and contingent truths. The advantage, and the difficulty, of the definition is that it holds on to the concept of the real – indeed of a 'real' at all – even in the face of tendencies to assimilate documentary entirely into the rules and norms of fiction.

As *The Thin Blue Line* shows, the recognition that documentary access to this real is strategic and contingent does not require a retreat to a Rashomon universe of undecidabilities. This recognition can lead, rather, to a remarkable awareness of the conditions under which it is possible to intervene in the political and cultural construction of truths which, while not guaranteed, nevertheless matter as the narratives by which we live. To better explain this point I would like to further consider the confessional, talking-cure strategy of *The Thin Blue Line* as it relates to Claude Lanzmann's *Shoah*. While I am aware of the incommensurability of a film about the state of Texas's near-execution of an innocent man with the German state's achieved extermination of six million, I want to pursue the comparison because both films are, in very different ways, striking examples of postmodern documentaries whose passionate desire is to intervene in the construction of truths whose totality is ultimately unfathomable.

In both of these films, the truth of the past is traumatic, violent, and unrepresentable in images. It is obscured by official lies masking the responsibility of individual agents in a gross miscarriage of justice. We may recall that Jameson's argument about the postmodern is that it is a loss of a sense of history, of a collective or individual past, and the knowledge of how the past determines the present: 'the past as "referent" finds itself gradually bracketed, and then effaced altogether, leaving us with nothing but texts'.[6] That so many well-known and popular documentary films have taken up the task of remembering the past – indeed that so much popular debate about the 'truth' of the past has been engendered by both fiction and documentary films about the past – could therefore be attributed to another of Jameson's points about the postmodern condition: the intensified nostalgia for a past that is already lost.

However, I would argue instead that, certainly in these two films and partially in a range of others, the postmodern suspicion of over-abundant images of an unfolding, present 'real' (vérité's commitment to film 'it' as 'it' happens) has contributed not to new fictionalizations but to paradoxically new historicizations. These historicizations are fascinated by an inaccessible, ever receding, yet newly important past which does have depth. History, in Jameson's sense of traces of the past, of an absent cause which 'hurts',[7] would seem, almost by definition, to be inaccessible to the vérité documentary form aimed at capturing action in its unfolding. The recourse to talking-heads interviews, to people remembering the past – whether the collective history of a nation or city, the personal history of individuals, or the criminal event which crucially determines the present – is, in these anti-vérité documentaries, an attempt to overturn this commitment to realistically record 'life as it is' in favor of a deeper investigation of how it became as it is.

Thus, while there is very little running after the action, there is considerable provocation of action. Even though Morris and Lanzmann have certainly done their legwork to pursue actors in the events they are concerned to represent, their preferred technique is to set up a situation in which the action will come to them. In these privileged moments of vérité (for there finally are moments of relative vérité) the past repeats. We thus see the power of the past not simply by dramatizing it, or reenacting it, or talking about it obsessively (though these films do all this), but finally by finding its traces, in repetitions and resistances, in the present. It is thus the contextualization of the present with the past that is the most effective representational strategy in these two remarkable films.

Each of these documentaries digs toward an impossible archeology, picking at the scabs of lies which have covered over the inaccessible originary event. The filmmakers ask questions, probe circumstances, draw maps, interview historians, witnesses, jurors, judges, police, bureaucrats, and survivors. These diverse investigatory processes augment the single method of the vérité camera. They seek to uncover a past the knowledge of which will produce new truths of guilt and innocence in the present. Randall Adams is now free at least partly because of the evidence of Morris's film; the Holocaust comes alive not as some alien horror foreign to all humanity but as something that is, perhaps for the first time on film, understandable as an absolutely banal incremental logic and logistics of train schedules and human silence. The past events examined in these films are not offered as complete, totalizable, apprehensible. They are fragments, pieces of the past invoked by memory, not unitary representable truths but, as Freud once referred to the psychic mechanism of memory, a palimpsest, described succinctly by Mary Ann Doane as 'the sum total of its rewritings through time.' The 'event' remembered is never whole, never fully represented, never isolated in the past alone but only accessible through a memory which resides, as Doane has put it, 'in the reverberations between events'.[8]

This image of the palimpsest of memory seems a particularly apt evocation of how these two films approach the problem of representing the inaccessible trauma of the past. When Errol Morris fictionally reenacts the murder of Officer Wood as differently remembered by David Harris, Randall Adams, the officer's partner, and the various witnesses who claimed to have seen the murder, he turns his film into a temporally elaborated palimpsest, discrediting some versions more than others but refusing to ever fix one as *the* truth. It is precisely Morris's refusal to fix the final truth, to go on seeking reverberations and repetitions that, I argue, gives this film its exceptional power of truth.

This strategic and relative truth is often a byproduct of other investigations into many stories of self-justification and reverberating memories told to the camera. For example, Morris never set out to tell the story of Randall Adams's innocence. He was interested initially in the story of 'Dr. Death,' the psychiatrist whose testimony about the sanity of numerous accused murderers had resulted in a remarkable number of death sentences. It would seem that the more directly and singlemindedly a film pursues a single truth, the less chance it has of producing the kind of 'reverberations between events' that will effect meaning in the present.

What animates Morris and Lanzmann is not the opposition between absolute truth and absolute fiction but the awareness of the final inaccessibility of a moment of crime, violence, trauma, irretrievably located in the past. Through the curiosity, ingenuity, irony, and obsessiveness of 'obtrusive' investigators, Morris and Lanzmann do not so much represent this past as they reactivate it in images of the present. This is their distinctive postmodern feature as documentarians. For in revealing the fabrications, the myths, the frequent moments of scapegoating when easy fictional explanations of trauma, violence, crime were substituted for more difficult ones, these documentaries do not simply play off truth against lie, nor do they play off one fabrication against another; rather, they show how lies function as partial truths to both the agents and witnesses of history's trauma. For example, in one of the most discussed moments of *Shoah*, Lanzmann stages a scene of homecoming in Chelmno, Poland, by Simon Srebnik, a Polish Jew who had, as a child, worked in the death camp near that town, running errands for the Nazis and forced to sing while doing so. Now, many years later, in the present tense of Lanzmann's film, the elderly yet still vigorous Srebnik is surrounded on the steps of the Catholic church by an even older, friendly group of Poles who remembered him as a child in chains who sang by the river. They are happy he has survived and returned to visit. But as Lanzmann asks them how much they knew and understood about the fate of the Jews who were carried away from the church in gas vans, the group engages in a kind of free association to explain the unexplainable.

> [Lanzmann] Why do they think all this happened to the Jews?
>
> [A Pole] Because they were the richest! Many Poles were also exterminated. Even priests.
>
> [Another Pole] Mr. Kantarowski will tell us what a friend told him. It happened in Myndjewyce, near Warsaw.
>
> [Lanzmann] Go on. [Mr. Kantarowski] The Jews there were gathered in a square. The rabbi asked an SS man: 'Can I talk to them?' The SS man said yes. So the rabbi said that around two thousand years ago the Jews condemned the innocent Christ to death. And when they did that, they cried out: 'Let his blood fall on our heads and on our sons' heads.' The rabbi told them: 'Perhaps the time has come for that, so let us do nothing, let us go, let us do as we're asked.'
>
> [Lanzmann] He thinks the Jews expiated the death of Christ?
>
> [The first? Pole] He doesn't think so, or even that Christ sought revenge. He didn't say that. The rabbi said it. It was God's will, that's all!
>
> [Lanzmann, referring to an untranslated comment] What'd she say?
>
> [A Polish woman] So Pilate washed his hands and said: 'Christ is innocent,' and he sent Barabbas. But the Jews cried out: 'Let his blood fall on our heads!'
>
> [Another Pole] That's all; now you know! (*Shoah*, 100).[9]

As critic Shoshana Felman has pointed out, this scene on the church steps in Chelmno shows the Poles replacing one memory of their own witness of the persecution of the Jews with another (false) memory, an auto-mystification, produced by Mr. Kantarowski, of the Jews' willing acceptance of their persecution as scapegoats for the death of Christ. This fantasy, meant to assuage the Poles' guilt for their complicity in the extermination of the Jews, actually repeats the Poles' crime of the past in the present.

Felman argues that the strategy of Lanzmann's film is not to challenge this false testimony but to dramatize its effects: we see Simon Srebnik suddenly silenced among the chatty Poles, whose victim he becomes all over again. Thus the film does not so much give us a memory as an action, here and now, of the Poles' silencing and crucifixion of Srebnik, whom they obliterate and forget even as he stands in their midst.[10]

It is this repetition in the present of the crime of the past that is key to the documentary process of Lanzmann's film. Success, in the film's terms, is the ability not only to assign guilt in the past, to reveal and fix a truth of the day-to-day operation of the machinery of extermination, but also to deepen the understanding of the many ways in which the Holocaust continues to live in the present. The truth of the Holocaust thus does not exist in any totalizing narrative, but only, as Felman notes and Lanzmann shows, as a collection of fragments. While the process of scapegoating, of achieving premature narrative closure by assigning guilt to convenient victims, is illuminated, the events of the past – in this case the totality of the Holocaust – register not in any fixed moment of past or present but rather, as in Freud's description of the palimpsest, as the sum total of its rewritings through time, not in a single event but in the 'reverberations' between.

It is important in the above example to note that while cinema vérité is deployed in this scene on the steps, as well as in the interviews throughout the film, this form of vérité no longer has a fetish function of demanding belief as the whole. In place of a truth that is 'guaranteed,' the vérité of catching events as they happen is here embedded in a history, placed in relation to the past, given a new power, not of absolute truth but of repetition.

Although it is a very different sort of documentary dealing with a trauma whose horror cannot be compared to the Holocaust, Errol Morris's *The Thin Blue Line* also offers its own rich palimpsest of reverberations between events. At the beginning of the film, convicted murderer Randall Adams mulls over the fateful events of the night of 1976 when he ran out of gas, was picked up by David Harris, went to a drive-in movie, refused to allow Harris to come home with him, and later found himself accused of killing a cop with a gun that Harris had stolen. He muses: 'Why did I meet this kid? Why did I run out of gas? But it happened, it happened.' The film probes this 'Why?' And its discovery 'out of the past' is not simply some fate-laden accident but, rather, a reverberation between events that reaches much further back into the past than that cold November night in Dallas.

Toward the end, after Morris has amassed a great deal of evidence attesting to the false witness born by three people who testified to seeing Randall Adams in the car with David Harris, but before playing the audio tape in which Harris all but confesses to the crime, the film takes a different turn – away from the events of November and into the childhood of David Harris. The film thus moves both forward and back in time: to events following and preceding the night of November, 1976, when the police officer was shot. Moving forward, we learn of a murder, in which David broke into the home of a man who had, he felt, stolen his girlfriend. When the man defended himself, David shot him. This repetition of wanton violence is the clincher in the film's 'case' against David. But instead of stopping there, the film goes back in time as well.

A kindly, baby-faced cop from David's home town, who has told us much of David's story already, searches for the cause of his behavior and hits upon a childhood trauma: a four-year-old brother who drowned when David was only three. Morris then cuts to David speaking of this incident: 'My Dad was supposed to be watching us . . . I guess that might have been some kind of traumatic experience for me . . . I guess I reminded him . . . it was hard for me to get any acceptance from him after that . . . A lot of the things I did as a young kid was an attempt to get back at him.'

In itself, this 'getting-back-at-the-father' motive is something of a cliché for explaining violent male behavior. But coupled as it is with the final 'confession' scene in which Harris repeats this getting-back-at-the-father motive in his relation to Adams, the explanation gains resonance, exposing another layer in the palimpsest of the past. As we watch the tape recording of this last unfilmed interview play, we hear Morris ask Harris if he thinks Adams is a 'pretty unlucky fellow?' Harris answers, 'Definitely,' specifying the nature of this bad luck: 'Like I told you a while ago about the guy who didn't have no place to stay . . . if he'd had a place to stay, he'd never had no place to go, right?' Morris decodes this question with his own rephrasing, continuing to speak of Harris in the third person: 'You mean if he'd stayed at the hotel that night this never would have happened?' (That is, if Adams had invited Harris into his hotel to stay with him as Harris had indicated earlier in the film he expected, then Harris would not have committed the murder he later pinned on Adams.) Harris: 'Good possibility, good possibility . . . You ever hear of the proverbial scapegoat? There probably been thousands of innocent people convicted . . .'

Morris presses: 'What do you think about whether he's innocent?' Harris: 'I'm sure he is.' Morris again: 'How can you be sure?' Harris: 'I'm the one who knows . . . After all was said and done it was pretty unbelievable. I've always thought if you could say why there's a reason that Randall Adams is in jail it might be because he didn't have a place for somebody to stay that helped him that night. It might be the only reason why he's at where he's at.'

What emerges forcefully in this near-confession is much more than the clinching evidence in Morris's portrait of a gross miscarriage of justice. For in not simply probing the 'wrong man' story, in probing the reverberations between events of David Harris's personal history, Morris's film discovers an underlying layer in the palimpsest of the past: how the older Randall Adams played an unwitting role in the psychic history of the 16-year-old David Harris, a role which repeated an earlier trauma in Harris's life: of the father who rejected him, whose approval he could not win, and upon whom David then revenged himself.

Harris's revealing comments do more than clinch his guilt. Like the Poles who surround Srebnik on the steps of the church and proclaim pity for the innocent child who suffered so much even as they repeat the crime of scapegoating Jews, so David Harris proclaims the innocence of the man he has personally condemned, patiently explaining the process of scapegoating that the Dallas county legal system has so obligingly helped him accomplish. Cinema vérité in both these films is an important vehicle of documentary truth. We witness in the present an event of simultaneous confession and condemnation on the part of historical actors who repeat their crimes from the past. Individual guilt is both palpably manifest and viewed in a larger context of personal and social history. For even as we catch David Harris and the Poles of Chelmno in the act of scapegoating innocent victims for crimes they have not committed, these acts are revealed as part of larger processes, reverberating with the past.

I think it is important to hold on to this idea of truth as a fragmentary shard, perhaps especially at the moment we as a culture have begun to realize, along with Morris, and along with the supposed depthlessness of our postmodern condition, that it is not guaranteed. For some form of truth is the always receding goal of documentary film. But the truth figured by documentary cannot be a simple unmasking or reflection. It is a careful construction, an intervention in the politics and the semiotics of representation.

An overly simplified dichotomy between truth and fiction is at the root of our difficulty in thinking about the truth in documentary. The choice is not between two entirely separate regimes of truth and fiction. The choice, rather, is in strategies of fiction for the approach to relative truths. Documentary is not fiction and should not be conflated with it. But documentary can and should use all the strategies of fictional construction to get at truths. What we see in *The Thin Blue Line* and *Shoah*, and to some degree in the other documentaries I have mentioned, is an interest in constructing truths to dispel pernicious fictions, even though these truths are only relative and contingent. While never absolute and never fixed, this under-construction, fragmented horizon of truth is one important means of combating the pernicious scapegoating fictions that can put the wrong man on death row and enable the extermination of a whole people.

The lesson that I would like to draw from [this] exemplary postmodern [documentary] is thus not at all that postmodern representation inevitably succumbs to a depthlessness of the simulacrum, or that it gives up on truth to wallow in the undecidabilities of representation. The lesson, rather, is that there can be historical depth to the notion of truth – not the depth of unearthing a coherent and unitary past, but the depth of the past's reverberation with the present. If the authoritative means to the truth of the past does not exist, if photographs and moving images are not mirrors with memories, if they are more, as Baudrillard has suggested, like a hall of mirrors, then our best response to this crisis of representation might be to do what Lanzmann and Morris do: to deploy the many facets of these mirrors to reveal the seduction of lies.

Notes

1 F. Jameson, 'Postmodernism or the Cultural Logic of Late Capitalism,' *New Left Review*, 1994, no. 146, p. 54.
2 M.-H. T. Trinh, 'Documentary Is/Not a Name,' October 1990, no. 52, p. 84.
3 A. Kaes, *From Hitler to Heimat: The Return of History as Film*, Cambridge, MA: Harvard University Press, 1989, p. 198.
4 See, for example: J. Maslin, 'Oliver Stone Manipulates His Puppet,' *New York Times*, January 5, 1992, p. 13; 'Twisted History,' *Newsweek*, December 23, 1991, pp. 46–54; A. Cockburn, 'J.F.K. and *J.F.K.*,' *The Nation*, January 6–13, 1992, pp. 6–8.
5 A. Taubin, 'Oscar's Docudrama,' *The Village Voice*, 13 March 1992, p. 62.
6 F. Jameson, 'Postmodernism or the Cultural Logic of Late Capitalism,' p. 64.
7 F. Jameson, *The Political Unconscious: Narrative as a Socially Symbolic Act*, Ithaca, NY: Cornell University Press, 1981, p. 164.
8 M. A. Doane, 'Remembering Women: Physical and Historical Constructions in Film Theory,' in E. A Kaplan, (ed.), *Psychoanalysis and Cinema*, New York: Routledge, 1990, p. 58.
9 I have quoted this dialogue from the published version of the *Shoah* script but I have added the attribution of who is speaking in brackets.
10 S. Felman, 'A L'Age du temoignage: *Shoah* de Claude Lanzmann,' in *Au sujet de* Shoah: *le film de Claude Lanzmann*, Paris: Editions Belin, 1990, pp. 120–8.

H. A. Giroux

MEMORY AND PEDAGOGY IN THE 'WONDERFUL WORLD OF DISNEY'

Beyond the politics of innocence

'Memory and Pedagogy in the "Wonderful World of Disney": Beyond the Politics of Innocence', in E. Bell, L. Haas and L. Sells (eds), *From Mouse to Mermaid: The Politics of Film, Gender and Culture*, Bloomington, IN: University of Indiana Press, 1995, pp. 43–61.

THERE ARE FEW CULTURAL ICONS in the United States that can match the signifying power of the Disney Company. Relentless in its efforts to promote a happy, kindly, paternal image of its founder, Walt Disney, and an endless regime of representations and commodities that conjure up a nostalgic view of America as the 'magic kingdom,' the Disney Company has become synonymous with a notion of innocence that aggressively rewrites the historical and collective identity of the American past. Behind the ideological appeal to nostalgia, wholesome times, and the land that is 'the happiest place on earth,' there is the institutional and ideological power of a $4.7 billion multinational conglomerate that wields enormous influence pedagogically and politically in a variety of public spheres.

When corporate politics is cloaked in the image of innocence, there is more at stake than the danger of simple deception. There is the issue of cultural power and how it works to make claims on our understanding of the past, national coherence, and popular memory as a site of injustice, criticism, and renewal.[1] Innocence in Disney's world becomes the ideological vehicle through which history is both rewritten and purged of its seamy side. In this case, innocence becomes important as an ideological construct less through its appeal to nostalgia, stylised consumption, or a unified notion of national identity than as a marker for recognising the past as a terrain of pedagogical and ideological struggle. The Disney Company is not ignorant of history, it reinvents it as a pedagogical and political tool to secure its own interests, authority, and power.

Innocence is not only about the discursive face of domination, it also points to important pedagogical issues regarding how people as subjects learn to place themselves in particular historical narratives. As a pedagogical construct that promotes a particular view of history in Disney's diverse public cultures, innocence, when coupled with a mythic rendering of the past, offers people the opportunity to envision themselves as agents of history, as part of a community longing for security and redemption in a world that often seems hostile to such desires.

Through its ordering and structuring of popular representations, Disney mobilises a notion of memory that parades under the longing for childlike innocence, wholesome adventure, and frontier courage. Organised through affective and ideological forms of address, such representations make particular claims upon the present and serve to define how we 'come to know how we are constituted and who we are'.[2] What is so important about the 'wonderful world of Disney' as an 'historical-cultural theatre of memory'[3] is that it powerfully represents the degree to which

> popular culture has historically become the dominant form of global culture . . . the scene, par excellence, of commodification, of the industries where culture enters directly into the circuits of . . . power and capital. It is the space of homogenisation where stereotyping and the formulaic mercilessly process the material and experiences it draws into its web, where control over narratives and representations passes into the hands of established cultural bureaucracies, sometimes without a murmur.[4]

The 'Wonderful World of Disney' is more than a logo; it signifies how the terrain of popular culture has become central to commodifying memory and rewriting narratives of national identity and global expansion. Disney's power and reach into popular culture combine an insouciant playfulness and the fantastic possibility of making childhood dreams come true with strict gender roles, an unexamined nationalism, and a notion of choice that is attached to the proliferation of commodities.

The strategies of entertaining escapism, historical forgetting, and repressive pedagogy in Disney's books, records, theme parks, movies, and TV programs produce a series of identifications that relentlessly define America as white and middle class. Pedagogy in Disney's texts functions as a history lesson that excludes the subversive elements of memory. Reduced to vignettes of childhood innocence, adventure, and chivalry, memory is removed from the historical, social, and political context that defines it as a process of cultural production that opens rather than closes down history. It is precisely this pedagogical policing of memory that undercuts its possibility as a form of critical remembrance that positions human agency against the restrictions and boundaries set by the historical past. For Disney, memory has nothing to do with remembering differently, nor is it a compelling force for arousing 'dormant emancipatory energies . . . [and] intellectually satisfying and emotionally compelling political images'.[5] On the contrary, narrating the past becomes a vehicle for rationalising the authoritarian, normalising tendencies of the dominant culture that carry through to the present. Hence, Disney's pretence to innocence is shattered under the weight of a promotional culture predicated on the virtues of fun, innocence, and, most importantly, consumption.[6] In the past year, with the bankruptcy of EuroDisney and the appearance of a number of unflattering revelations concerning Walt's life, the mythology of a clean consumerism and an unproblematic innocence has been gradually demystified. According to Herbert Mitgang of the *New York Times*, 'from 1940 until his death in 1966 . . . [Disney served] as a secret informer for the Los Angeles office of the Federal Bureau of Investigation'. It seems that Walt Disney was not only an agent dedicated to rooting out communist agitators in the film industry, but he also allowed the FBI access to the Disneyland facilities for 'use in connection with official matters and for recreational purposes'.[7] Most disturbingly, Disney allowed J. Edgar Hoover, then Director of the FBI, to censor and modify the scripts of Disney films such as *That Darn Cat* (1965) and *Moon Pilot* (1962) so as to portray Bureau agents in a favourable light.

Behind the pretence to innocence and its appeal to a childlike state in which forgetting the past becomes more important than engaging it, the policing function of memory erases its emancipatory possibilities. This is illuminated, in part, through recent public revelations indicating that the Disney Company has, on occasion, exceeded the moral bounds of its promotional enthusiasm by preventing the publication of books critical of Walt Disney and the Disney Company's image.[8] It appears that beneath the promotion of the magical name of Disney and the public spaces it represents as 'the happiest place on earth' lurks the power of a multinational conglomerate that has little regard for free speech and public criticism.

As an ideological construct that mobilises particular cultural practices in diverse regimes of representations, whether they be theme parks, comics, or movies, Disney's appeal to pristine innocence and high adventure is profoundly pedagogical in its attempt to produce specific knowledge, values, and desires. It is precisely this intersection of the political and pedagogical as a hegemonic practice that necessitates making Disney's world of representations the object of critical analysis. Moreover, such an analysis is not warranted simply through its claim to welding deconstructive skills; it is also important because it offers possibilities for educators and other cultural workers to understand more clearly how politics and pedagogy intersect in the production, circulation, and reception of popular culture and the formation of national identity.

Notes

1 For example, Jane Kuenz and Susan Willis have analysed how in Disney's theme parks intimacy, imagination, and spontaneity are replaced by the expertise of the well-placed park attendants, the picture perfect photo sites, and the endless spectacles in which fun becomes consumption and memory is reduced to the purchase of souvenirs. Similarly, theorists such as Dorfman and Matellart have indicated how Disney's comics serve to reproduce sexist, racist, and colonial ideologies. See J. Kuenz, 'It's a Small World After All: Disney and the Pleasures of Identification', *South Atlantic Quarterly* 1993, vol. 92(1), pp. 63–88; S. Willis, 'Disney World: Public Use/Private Space,'

South Atlantic Quarterly 1993, vol. 92(1), pp. 119–37; and A. Dorfman and A. Mattelart, *How to Read Donald Duck: Imperialist Ideology in the Disney Comic*, New York: International General Editions, 1975.

2 S. Hall, 'What Is This "Black" in Popular Culture?' In *Black Popular Culture*, ed. G. Dent, Seattle, WA: Bay Press, 1992, p. 30.

3 J. Clifford, 'On Collecting Art and Culture' in *Out There: Marginalization and Contemporary Cultures*, eds. R. Ferguson, M. Gever, T. T. Minh-ha, and C. West, Cambridge, MA: MIT Press, 1990, p. 164.

4 S. Hall, 'What Is This "Black" in Popular Culture?', p. 22.

5 W. Adamson, *Marx and the Disillusionment of Marxism*, Berkeley, CA: University of California Press, 1984, p. 238.

6 On the issue of memory and politics, I am indebted to R. Simon, 'Forms of Insurgency in the Production of Popular Memories: The Columbus Quincentenary and the Pedagogy of Counter-Commemoration', *Cultural Studies* 1993, vol. 7(l), pp. 73–88; H. Kaye, *The Powers of the Past*, Minneapolis, MN: University of Minnesota Press, 1991; W. Adamson, *Marx and the Disillusionment of Marxism*; R. Tiderman, *Discourse/Counter-Discourse*, Ithaca, NY: Cornell University Press, 1985; and J. E. Young, *Writing and Rewriting the Holocaust: Narrative and the Consequences of Interpretation*, Bloomington, IN: Indiana University Press, 1990.

7 H. Mitgang, 'Disney Link to the FBI and Hoover Is Disclosed', *New York Times*, 6 May 1993, p. B4.

8 For example, see Weiner's comments on the Disney Company's involvement in preventing Marc Eliot's book, *Walt Disney: Hollywood's Dark Prince*, from being published by Bantam in 1991, in I. Weiner, 'Murdered Ink', *The Nation*, 1993, vol. 256(21), pp. 743–50.

PART 5

Marketing and receiving historical film

HISTORIOGRAPHERS HAVE LONG BEEN INTERESTED in the readers of histories. The mid-twentieth-century theorist Paul Ricoeur, for instance, looked to nineteenth-century theological and philosophical writings to formulate his argument that the writers and readers of histories meet and negotiate meaning in a 'hermeneutic arc'. More recently, Greg Dening has proposed that the 'forms and structures' of histories vary according to different social contexts and Keith Jenkins has suggested that reading a history is like eating a piece of cake in different ways and places.[1] Jenkins has also argued, however, that some readings of particular histories dominate because they affirm the needs and aspirations of certain social groups. In Jenkins's view, historiography thus entails the study of relations of power manifested in the construction of textual meaning by all groups who engage with histories.

As Jerome de Groot has observed, many forms of histories are 'consumed'.[2] Whether 'consuming' histories renders audiences politically inactive or susceptible to particular forms of ideology, however, is something yet to be established by historians of all kinds of texts. Many of the writings we encountered in the last two parts of the *Reader* positioned film audiences as passive or open to political suggestion. Further, it was argued that 'writerly' films – the kinds of films favoured by a range of writers, from Rosenstone to Williams – encourage viewers to action by making them aware of conventional 'reality effects'. Film history, though, allows for the possibility of what Stuart Hall calls 'oppositional' or 'aberrant' reception, in which viewers depart from what authors or conventions expect.[3]

As was argued in the introduction to this *Reader*, undertaking film reception research is not easy. Film viewers often leave little trace of their experiences, and the evidence that we have might be far from representative. Box office or DVD sales figures do not allow us to conclude that films impute political views to viewers. Nor, conversely, do all viewers poach, appropriate and refashion historical films to suit their own ends. Further, it is currently unclear how often the regulatory activities of 'connoisseur' or 'fan' viewers coincide with the commercial imperatives of film promotion and merchandise companies. The extracts in this final Part of the *Reader* offer us intimations of the complex relationship between the makers, promoters and audiences of histories that future research might fill out. The first reading in this section is part of the introduction to Roy Rosenzweig and David Thelen's study of how people in the US think about their past. After conducting telephone interviews with just over 1000 people in 1994, Rosenzweig and Thelen discovered something that was later affirmed in both an Australian study and Annette Kuhn's research on cinema goers: that when people are asked about the past, they are more likely to talk about their own experiences and those of friends and family than national or international events such as wars. Further, their accounts of national and international events are almost always anchored to privatised or parochial experiences.[4]

Cinema ranked second only to photographs in Rosenzweig and Thelen's study as the chief means by which people come into contact with, or indeed feel connected with, the past. By contrast, very few participants reported that they had read histories or participated in the formal study of history in the preceding year. Findings like these suggest that visual histories are perhaps worthy of more attention than they have been granted in the past. Further, they highlight the need for more research on film viewers' experiences. Linda Hutcheon, for instance, wonders whether Jameson's clear division between 'historical' and 'nostalgia' films, and a further suggestion that the latter is connected with a flight from both politics and history, is tenable. Historical films, she reminds us, can be made or watched ironically, and irony allows us to see the uses of the past in the present.

Hutcheon's idea of ironic readings of films perhaps runs counter to the conclusions that might be drawn from Charles Eckert's and Jeff Smith's studies of fashion, music and cross-promotion for films in the 1930s and *Titanic* (1997). Eckert's article, first published in the 1970s, shows how commercial tie-ins transformed stars' clothes and cosmetics into consumer products within the price range of working women. His observations continue to be borne out by the cosmetic, clothing and jewellery products sold in association with films such as *Chicago* (2002) and *Marie Antoinette* (2006). Further, Smith's article reveals how important music is in promoting films prior to their release, and in encouraging repeat viewings. That film companies are now part of conglomerates that connect food, radio, clothing, cosmetic and magazine companies is reflected in the variety of media and products that are used to promote cinematic and DVD releases. As Annette Kuhn and I have argued, however, the activities of film promoters do not always prevent viewers from making their own merchandise or adapting it, or from rewriting film stories to suit their own ends.[5]

No studies have conclusively shown that either viewer agency or viewer subordination to commercial and ideological imperatives dominates film reception. This is because, as Richard Maltby shows in the final reading, film history, and by extension historical film studies, is still at a nascent stage. Looking at his suggestions for a history of 'cinema from below' – a history of cinema that both reflects and adds to the insights of cultural historians who have recovered the experiences of ordinary people – it seems that we have only just begun to chart the depths of viewer experiences. Maltby's reading encourages us to think not only about an expanded history of cinema, but also about the relationship between reflections on written and filmic histories. His work shows us that much is to be gained from thinking about histories as films as well as books, and from drawing the reflections of both historiographers and 'historiophotists' – as Hayden White would call them – together. When we do so, a richer and more complex understanding of history will emerge, one that might lead us to rethink the idea of having separate book and film reviews in journals. The answer to Robert Schneider's concerns about the adequate treatment of films in *American Historical Review* – outlined in the introduction to this *Reader* – lies not with separate bodies of theorists, but with the realisation that 'history' refers to a much wider variety of texts than historiography has traditionally considered.

Notes

1 G. Dening, *Performances*, Melbourne: Melbourne University Press, 1996, p. 49; and K. Jenkins, *Re-thinking History*, London: Routledge, 1991, p. 24.

2 J. de Groot, *Consuming History: Historians and Heritage in Contemporary Popular Culture*, London: Routledge, 2008.

3 S. Hall, 'Encoding/decoding', *Culture, Media, Language*, London: Hutchinson, 1980, pp. 128–38.

4 P. Ashton and P. Hamilton, 'At Home with the Past: Background and Initial Findings from the National Survey', *Australian Cultural History*, 2003, no. 23, pp. 5–30; and A. Kuhn, *An Everyday Magic: Cinema and Cultural Memory*, London: I. B. Tauris, 2002. Published in the USA as *Dreaming of Fred and Ginger: Cinema and Cultural Memory*, New York: New York University Press, 2002.

5 A. Kuhn, *Dreaming of Fred and Ginger*; and M. Hughes-Warrington, *History Goes to the Movies: Studying History on Film*, London: Routledge, 2007, ch. 8.

Roy Rosenzweig and David Thelen

THE PRESENCE OF THE PAST

Popular uses of history in American life

The Presence of the Past: Popular Uses of History in American Life, New York: Columbia University Press, 1998, Introduction.

ON MONDAY MORNING, May 15, 1989, ten people crowded around the dining-room table at the Chateau Delaware, a nineteenth-century stone mansion in Indianapolis. The mansion – recently converted into a bed-and-breakfast – seemed an appropriate setting for a retreat devoted to mapping previously uncharted intersections between present and past. We looked out on a historic block – Benjamin Harrison's house was down Delaware Street – in a neighborhood just north of the city's thoroughly modern downtown. Next door, another mansion housed the Indiana Humanities Council.

The retreat itself was the brainchild of Allie Stuart, a program officer with the Council. A few months earlier, she had invited David Thelen to lunch at a Cajun cafe in Bloomington to talk about better ways of connecting academic historians with larger audiences. Dave had said that he knew several professionals at universities and museums who shared the same dream, and mused that it would be great to get them together. He remembers choking on his Diet Coke when Allie replied that the Indiana Humanities Council would provide the funding for such a conference if Dave would invite participants and report their ideas.

The defining moment of the weekend . . . occurred that first morning as we went around the table, sharing our concerns about the practice of professional history. Person after person described struggles to imagine or build alternatives that might break down barriers between professionals and wider audiences. As we talked, it became clear that we shared the conviction that professional historians were painfully unaware of how people outside their own circles understood and used the past. We discussed books we'd read and experiments we'd tried, and as these began to mount, we felt a sense of excitement – a sense that we, the individuals in that room, might actually be able to make a difference in narrowing the gap.

John Gillis, who was leading a project on the historical construction of identities at Rutgers University, said his research had led him to see the history that families create as a rich alternative to academic history. D. D. Hilke, director of audience research at the National Museum of American History, described her ethnographic studies of how museum visitors turned exhibits into things they recognized from their own experience. Philip Scarpino, John Bodnar, and Michael Frisch, leaders in the fields of oral history and public history, discussed oral historians' attempts to share authority – to create history jointly with the people they interviewed. The historians around the table reported on studies and theories from many fields that investigated the ways Americans use the past in their everyday lives, screening professional 'texts' (museum exhibits, books, movies) through these everyday uses.

We spent the rest of the weekend trying to design ways of improving exchanges between professional and popular historians. Someone would grab a Magic Marker, write four or five themes on a piece of paper, and drape it over the back of a chair. Then someone else would impose a second dimension and turn the list into a grid. On grids and maps we constructed models that compared professional historymaking with that done by individuals in their daily lives, by television producers, by advertisers, by leaders of ethnic and religious groups, and by collectors.

How should we proceed? Each of us had brought along favorite ideas for projects, and we dreamed up more on the spot: ethnographic observation of people in natural settings; in-depth interviews with people who pursue history as a hobby; participant observation of the uses of history in family conversations; textual analyses of diaries or memoirs; experiments that ask people to visualize the past by having them draw a picture of what history looks like to them. While this group of humanists had ingrained scepticism about the scientific claims of survey research, some of us were enthusiastic about surveying a cross section of Americans. We believed that this would allow us to listen to people as they used the past in their daily lives, to map out patterns, and to define starting points for deeper investigations.

As we tried to define the questions to investigate, we used terms like 'historical consciousness' and 'historical memory.' At one point somebody threw out the phrase 'popular historymaking.' Many of us liked its implication that Americans take an active role in using and understanding the past – that they're not just passive consumers of histories constructed by others.

The intensity and urgency of our conversation that weekend grew out of the conjunction of two historical circumstances. Writing a few months later in one of the dozens of internal documents generated by the group, Michael Frisch captured this intellectual and political moment: 'The study and understanding of history occupies a paradoxical and problematic place in contemporary American culture. On the one hand, it is widely believed that we face a general crisis of historical amnesia; on the other hand, there is clearly enormous and growing public interest in history, manifest in museum attendance, historically oriented tourism, participation in festivals, and even the media-driven excesses of nostalgia and commemoration of recent historical periods.'[1]

We met in an atmosphere of both crisis and excitement, Roy recalls, about the state of historymaking in America. In the late 1980s, much-publicized jeremiads warned ominously of historical amnesia and historical illiteracy suffocating the nation. Shortly before Dave began to plan the Indianapolis meeting, Lynne Cheney, then chairman of the National Endowment for the Humanities, had issued a pamphlet called *American Memory*, which began with the declaration: 'A refusal to remember . . . is a primary characteristic of our nation.'[2]

The historians gathered in Indianapolis thought that the real issue was not, as pundits were declaring, what Americans did not know about the past but what they *did* know and think. Incredibly, since many commentators had surveyed American ignorance, no one had actually investigated how Americans understood and used the past. And we believed that we needed to seek out and listen to the voices of the people who were being denounced for their ignorance.

Our motivations were more complex than a desire to offer a different perspective on what would become known as the culture wars and the history wars. We also approached the question of 'how Americans understand the past' from the opposite direction – from excitement rather than worry, from our perception of deep public fascination with the past. Here, the historical context was not the conservative assault on historical illiteracy but the emergence, starting in the late 1960s, of what was called 'public history' or 'people's history.'

Carried along by the social movements of the 1960s and 1970s, many advocates of people's history and public history saw the past as a source of empowerment and political mobilization. They wanted to democratize not just the content of history (adding the stories of African Americans, industrial workers, immigrants, women, and gays) but also its practice; they wanted to turn audiences into collaborators. In the 1970s and 1980s some of us had begun collaborating with new audiences through museums and state humanities councils, historical films, community oral history programs, and trade union historical classes. These successes inspired us at the Chateau Delaware.

But our failures also goaded us. While we and others of our generation had widened the topics, voices, methods, and viewpoints that scholars called 'history' – indeed, this success had provoked the conservative counterattack – we had been less successful in turning audiences into partners. In a paper he presented that weekend, Dave argued that the major barrier to such collaboration came not from conservatives but from scholars who had failed to overcome habits of professionalization. Reporting responses from a thousand readers to a *Journal of American History* survey, he noted that an increasingly voluminous, fragmented, and specialized scholarship – though wonderfully rich and diverse – seemed 'narrow, overspecialized, and boring' even to many *Journal* subscribers.[3]

As we contemplated reaching outside our professional circles, we realized how little we knew about the values and perspectives Americans were bringing from their personal experiences to these historical dialogues. To help create a history that would extend beyond the content and practice of elites, we needed to hear a much wider range of people tell us about how (or even whether) the past mattered to them.

Because many of us in Indianapolis had contributed to an emerging body of scholarship on popular historical consciousness and historical memory,[4] we were particularly aware of the limitations of this scholarship. It told much more about how the past had been popularly presented than about how it had been popularly understood. Historians had begun to look at the presentations of the past in textbooks, children's books, movies, museums, and magazines, but we often fell back on speculation when it came time to talk about what people made of those sources. We had been influenced by the movement to write 'history from the bottom up,' but we had done little to uncover popular historical consciousness at its most obvious source – the perspectives of a cross section of Americans.

By the late 1980s, scholars from many fields were decrying this omission and developing theories and methods to study popular reception, reader response, and visitor behavior. The studies in these new fields suggested that Americans engaged historical texts (and all cultural forms) in ways molded by their own personalities, experiences, and traditions and that their engagements were often quite different from what producers of those texts had hoped for.[5]

These overlapping practical, political, and scholarly agendas heated up our conversations in Indianapolis and propelled us forward. As we circulated position papers and met once again, we evolved a concrete plan and sketched out a number of ambitious projects.

One of them was a national survey . . . On October 19, 1990, we walked through the Smithsonian's National Museum of American History, acutely aware of the presence of the past. Time frames shifted and merged; the air seemed saturated with their fluidity. Hundreds of visitors streamed by exhibits of eighteenth-century chairs and nineteenth-century guns and twentieth-century cars, intently scrutinizing these artifacts or chatting with their companions about what they'd observed.

That afternoon four of us (D. D. Hilke, Roy Rosenzweig, Dave Thelen, and Lois Silverman, who had recently come to work at Indiana University on history projects) met in one of the museum's conference rooms to brainstorm about the popular historymakers outside the door. What did they make of what they were seeing? What questions would allow them, and Americans like them, to open up to us – to speak candidly about how they used and understood the past?

D. D. and Lois had both studied the responses of museum visitors; they pointed us in useful directions, helping to hone and refine questions for a survey of popular historymaking. By the end of the meeting, we'd come up with an eclectic list that covered both historical activities (How often do you visit history museums? Have you done any research – formal or informal – into your family's history?) and attitudes (What do you think of when you hear, the word history/past/heritage/tradition? Where do you go for trustworthy information on the Civil War, the Vietnam War, and your family's history? Do you use a knowledge of the past in everyday life?). It was time to take the questions on the road for their first tryout.

In January 1991 fifteen graduate students in the Public History Program at Arizona State University joined Dave for a week-long course designed to test and refine the questions we had come up with. For him, Dave recalls, the challenge of turning vision into reality took concrete form in Tempe. The first morning began with some rough questions we hoped might lead people to talk about their uses of the past. Each afternoon students would conduct two- or three-hour-long open-ended interviews with people of all ages and educational backgrounds from the rich ethnic mix of people in Phoenix. (All together, they interviewed 135 people that week.) The next morning the class would compare results, trying to find wording that had elicited the richest responses. At the end of the week, students wrote essays about the questions that had worked best and the themes that had emerged during the interviews.

The conversations reported by these students convinced us that we needed to pay attention to how we introduced our topic. *History* is the word that scholars privilege to describe how they approach the past. But in Phoenix *history* conjured up something done by famous people that others studied in school; respondents said history was formal, analytical, official, or distant. Words like *heritage* and *tradition* conjured up warm and fuzzy feelings but not very rich experience or sharp observation. *The past* was the term that best invited people to talk about family, race, and nation, about where they had come from and what they had learned along the way. *Trust* was the concept that best captured how people viewed sources of information about the past. And the metaphor that best captured what mattered to them in the past could be elicited by the concept of *connection*. To which pasts did they feel most connected?

A few months later, graduate students at the University of Toledo took our questions into the field. These and other trials convinced us that it was time to carry out the project in a systematic, nationwide manner. But that required money – around $200,000. Our best bet, the National Endowment for the Humanities, turned us down initially. In the summer of 1993, we hatched a last-ditch funding scheme that sought money from a consortium of state humanities councils.

As we worked on that complicated series of proposals, we received unexpected good news: we had received a $25,000 chairman's discretionary grant from the Spencer Foundation and the NEH had reconsidered its rejection of our proposal. In the winter of 1993–94, we suddenly had money to carry out the survey we had conceived in Indianapolis three and a half years before.

On March 7, 1994, we crowded around the desk in the office of John Kennedy, director of the Center for Survey Research at Indiana University, listening to amplified snatches of telephone conversations. With some trepidation, we had just begun a week of what survey professionals call pretesting. Having thought and talked about this survey for almost five years, we were finally getting a chance to try out our questions through random telephone calling. The pretesting might be less politely and more accurately called eavesdropping. John Kennedy would push a button, and his office would be filled with voices from an interview in progress. Next door, in a large room segmented into small cubicles, half a dozen Indiana University students talked on the telephone. As these young interviewers conversed, they stared at computer screens that generated questions for them to ask and space for them to type in answers. The process was mechanistic, but the conversations themselves were intensely human.

Person after person was willing – even eager – to talk. We felt a rush of excitement and relief. Anyone who has been interrupted at dinner by phone calls from salespeople and solicitors (and who in the 1990s has not?) knows the strong temptation to slam down the phone. But that week more than forty people spent half an hour talking with a stranger from Indiana. For many of them, the past was clearly part of the rhythm of everyday life. We listened as a government office clerk told an interviewer: 'When you think about the past, you feel comfortable, like you belong, and that is the way I feel with my family.'

We had feared that a telephone survey would evoke vague or abstract responses. But people took the past personally: many of their answers were vivid, candid, creative, passionate. We had fretted that people might not reveal their deepest feelings. On the contrary, emotions often ran high in the conversations we overheard. Several people shared intimate details about their past and their present. One woman described being sexually abused. Another started to cry when asked to talk about the person from the past – her, mother – who had particularly affected her.

That week we were often moved by the powerful presence of the past. But we had work to do. We were trying to refine the survey – to decide which questions gave us the richest answers, to come up with final wording for those questions. We wanted to feel that we had taken full advantage of every phone call, that the interviewer had given the person at the other end of the telephone line the most compelling invitation to talk.

Every evening at ten or eleven o'clock, when the students had finished their interviews, they met with us to discuss which prompts and follow-ups had worked and which hadn't. We learned, for example, that we got next to nothing when we asked historians' favorite question – Why did you do something? – but we got wonderful answers when we asked how or when or with whom, when we asked respondents to elaborate on an experience. The interviewers were our collaborators. We'd all sit around a table and toss out alternative wordings.

By the time the week was over, we had confirmed some of the hunches we had had at the Chateau Delaware – about both the depth and variety of popular history-making and the value of surveying a cross section of Americans. We felt exhilarated, but also a little worried. Nothing in our professional training had prepared us to interpret what we were hearing. With the help of these terrific student interviewers, we were getting transcripts of rich conversations, but how would we find general patterns to make sense of these individual encounters?

On June 5, 1994, the past lay piled up on the porch of Roy's house in Arlington, Virginia. It lay on our laps in thick spiral-bound volumes and printouts of computer-generated tables as we tried to get a hold on what we had learned since March. How *do* Americans understand their pasts?

The data in front of us were somewhat overwhelming. Between March and June, John Kennedy's survey team had called almost all the 808 people who would make up the 'national sample.' The calls had taken about thirty minutes each. Interviewers had devoted about ten minutes of each call to asking closed-ended (and hence readily quantifiable) questions like: 'During the past twelve months, have you read any books about the past?' They used the rest of the time for follow-up questions like 'What were the reasons you looked into the history of your family or worked on your family tree?' In an innovation in standard survey practice, the interviewers had been allowed to use humor, interjections, and more probing questions ('Can you recall any of the history books you read?') to get people to open up. Typing as rapidly as possible, the interviewers transcribed respondents' answers. Those transcripts filled the formidable spiral volumes stacked before us.

Although the national survey was not quite done and we were still planning three 'minority' samples that would eventually reach more than six hundred African Americans, Mexican Americans, and American Indians, we decided that this was a good moment to compare notes on what we had gathered so far and describe to each other the headlines that leaped out at us from the data.

From the start we saw that the interviews were filled with intimate talk about the past. Families and their stories dominated the numbers as well as the words. For the people we called, the past was pervasive, a natural part of everyday life, central to any effort to live in the present. By June, our quick impressions from listening to the pretest interviews could be confirmed by the statistical evidence. Looking at the tables, we found overwhelming evidence that Americans participated regularly in a wide range of past-related 'activities,' from taking photos to preserve memories, to watching historical films and television programs, to taking part in groups involved in preserving or presenting the past. We also found that people said they felt particularly connected to the past in a range of different settings, from museums and historical sites to gatherings with their families.

If the past was omnipresent in these interviews, 'history' as it is usually defined in textbooks was not. This absence of conventional historical narratives and frameworks surprised us. Roy recalls that he had assumed we would hear people talking about how the defeat of the South in the Civil War, the struggle to settle Montana, or the victory of the auto workers in the 1937 sit-down strikes shaped their identities or their current political views. He had expected to gather stories about how grandparents had faced 'No Irish Need Apply' signs or had been barred from neighborhoods because they were Jewish. But these stories weren't there. Neither, were the narratives of American national progress – the landing of the Pilgrims, the winning of the American Revolution, the writing of the Constitution, the settling of the West – that have been told for generations in grade school classes and high school textbooks.

Dave remembers our excitement as we discovered that each of us had separately identified the same social traits as consistently important to respondents and others as strangely unimportant – strange because the absent traits were ones that scholars presumed to be essential in determining values and behavior. We had independently concluded that social class, regional identity, political conviction, and ethnicity among whites were much less important in shaping respondents' understanding of the past than race (particularly for blacks and Indians) and religion (particularly for evangelicals of all kinds).

Black respondents started out sounding like white respondents as they talked about the importance of the family. But most of them quickly moved beyond their families to talk of African Americans. In extending out from the family to broader historical narratives, black respondents shared a common set of references – slavery, the civil rights movement, and Martin Luther King Jr. – that we couldn't find in the interviews with European Americans. Black respondents not only constructed group narratives and drew on materials from the conventional canon of American history (like the story of slavery), they also presented stories that fit the standard narrative of group progress. A 42-year-old African American from Milwaukee said he was born in Mississippi, where 'you always got to say yes ma'am and no ma'am,' but that thanks to the civil rights movement, 'we don't have to be on the back of the bus.'

Sitting on the porch that afternoon, we got an inkling that Native Americans also tended to move from family stories to group stories and connect to larger national narratives. Asked why he rated the history of his 'racial or ethnic group' as most important to him, one man said, 'I'm an Indian. We got screwed out of everything that was ours, pushed aside.' The national sample – which reached 76 African Americans, 33 Latinos, 20 American Indians, and 13 Asian Americans – did not include enough minority voices for us to be sure about these conclusions. But we couldn't ignore what we saw.

Since the transcripts were reported by case number and not by demographic characteristic, we had to refer to a separate record when we wanted to know about the social characteristics of a respondent. As we read transcripts without reference to demographic features, we thought we could almost always tell whether a respondent was black or Indian. Since we hadn't asked about religion, we both were struck by how important religion was for evangelicals in ordering their perspectives on family and nation alike. We, two secular scholars, were so puzzled by this finding that at dinner that night we kept talking about it with Deborah Kaplan, Roy's very patient wife, who shared our attempts to understand the implications of a society in which the only things that seemed really to unite some blacks and some whites in their uses of the past were their commitments to family and evangelical religion.

On May 16, 1995, six years after our meeting in Indianapolis, we sat around another dining-room table, this time at Roy's house in Arlington. We'd moved beyond 'data' to our interpretation of the data, organized into rough drafts of chapters. Our training as historians did not equip us to handle the rich and messy responses we heard. (During the nine months of the survey, interviewers spent a thousand hours talking to 1,500 Americans. The transcripts of those conversations totaled about 850,000 words and the statistical summary of the answers that could be tabulated covered several hundred pages.)

More than one third had investigated the history of their family in the previous year; two fifths had worked on a hobby or collection related to the past. For most of the people who talked with us, the familial and intimate past, along with intimate uses of other pasts, matters most. They prefer the personal and firsthand because they feel at home with that past: they live with it, relive it, interpret and reinterpret it; they use it to define themselves, their place in their families, and their families' place in the world . . . Individuals turn to their personal experiences to grapple with questions about where they come from and where they are heading, who they are and how they want to be remembered. Again and again, the Americans we interviewed said they want to make a difference, to take responsibility for themselves and others. And so they assemble their experiences into patterns, narratives that allow them to make sense of the past, set priorities, project what might happen next, and try to shape the future. By using these narratives to mark change and continuity, they chart the course of their lives.

The people who told us they want to get as close to experience as possible – to use the past on their own terms – also recognize the need to reach toward people who have lived in other times and other places . . . Many respondents said they fear being manipulated by people who distort the past to meet their own needs – whether commercial greed, political ambition, or cultural prejudice. In their desire to strip away layers of mediation, respondents trust eyewitnesses more than television or movies. They feel connected to the past in museums because authentic artefacts seem to transport them straight back to the times when history was being made. They feel unconnected to the past in history classrooms because they don't recognize themselves in the version of the past presented there. When asked to describe studying history in school, they most often use the words *dull* and *irrelevant*.

The Americans we surveyed do not reject all aspects of national history; they simply reject nation-centered accounts they were forced to memorize and regurgitate in school . . . As they build bridges between personal pasts and larger historical stories, Americans – especially white Americans – tend to personalize the public past. African Americans, American Indians, and evangelical Christians sometimes construct a wider set of usable pasts, building ties to their communities as well as their families. Mexican Americans occupy a figurative – as well as geographical – borderland. Like white European Americans, they rely on family pasts as they work through multiple allegiances and sort out fundamental issues of identity, but they also draw on their ethnic and national roots. Unlike white European Americans, Mexican Americans tell a version of the traditional national narrative of progress: they talk about getting closer to owning a piece of the American dream.

In [a] counternarrative, the arrival of Columbus, the westward movement of European settlers, slavery and emancipation, wars and treaties at home and abroad add up to an American history in which blacks and Indians have been oppressed and betrayed by whites, who then depict their actions in movies and textbooks that lie about Indians and exclude African Americans. A collective voice comes easily to these two groups. African Americans speak of 'our race,' 'our roots,' 'our people'; American Indians speak of 'our history,' 'our heritage,' 'our culture,' 'our tribe.' The 'we' they invoke stands in sharp opposition to the triumphal American 'we': the narrative of the American nation-state – the story often told by professional historians – is most alive for those who feel most alienated from it. This departure from conventional wisdom, like so many other insights that emerged during survey interviews, eloquently supports the hunch we discussed that weekend in Indianapolis: professional history practitioners have much to learn from listening to Americans talk about how they use and understand the past.

Notes

1 Michael Frisch, 'Cracking the Nutshell: Making History-Making,' unpublished document, 20 September 1989, in possession of authors.

2 Lynne V. Cheney, *American Memory: A Report on Humanities in the Nation's Public Schools*, National Endowment for the Humanities, undated but published in September 1987, p. 5. See also, C. Finn Jr. and D. Ravitch, 'Survey Results: U.S. 17-Year-Olds Know Shockingly Little About History and Literature,' *The American School Board Journal*, 1987, no. 174, pp. 31–33, as quoted in D. Whittington, 'What Have 17-Year-Olds Known in the Past?' *American Educational Research Journal*, 1991, vol. 28, p. 763. There is a large literature debating the work of Ravitch and Finn. For one brief critique, see W. Ayers, 'What Do 17-Year-Olds Know? A Critique of Recent Research,' *Education Digest*, 1988, vol. 53, pp. 37–39.

3 D. Thelen, 'How Do Americans Understand Their Pasts? A Second Working Draft,' unpublished paper, April 1989, in possession of authors.

4 See, for example, the essays in *Journal of American History*, 1989, vol. 75(4) and in S. Porter Benson, S. Brier, and R. Rosenzweig, *Presenting the Past: Essays on History and the Public*, Philadelphia, PA: Temple University Press, 1986.

5 See, for example, J. Radway, *Reading the Romance: Women, Patriarchy, and Popular Literature*, Chapel Hill, NC: University of North Carolina Press, 1984. See also R. Merton, *Mass Persuasion: The Social Psychology of a War Bond Drive*, New York: Harper Brothers, 1946; D. Morley, *The Nationwide Audience: Structure and Decoding*, London: British Film Institute, 1980; Doris A. Graber, *Processing the News: How People Tame the Information Tide*, New York: Longman, 1984; P. Palmer, *The Lively Audience: A Study of Children Around the TV Set*, Sydney: Allen and Unwin, 1986; and J. Fiske, *Television Culture*, London: Methuen, 1986, chapter 6.

Linda Hutcheon

IRONY, NOSTALGIA, AND THE POSTMODERN

'Irony, Nostalgia, and the Postmodern', *Iowa Journal of Cultural Studies*, 2005, no. 5, pp. 1–15.

WHAT IS 'NOSTALGIA'? Or perhaps the first question really should be: what WAS nostalgia? With its Greek roots – *nostos*, meaning 'to return home' and *algos*, meaning 'pain' – this word sounds so familiar to us that we may forget that it is a relatively new word, as words go. It was coined in 1688 by a 19-year-old Swiss student in his medical dissertation as a sophisticated (or perhaps pedantic) way to talk about a literally lethal kind of severe homesickness (of Swiss mercenaries far from their mountainous home).[1] This medical-pathological definition of nostalgia allowed for a remedy: the return home, or sometimes merely the promise of it. The experiencing and the attributing of a nostalgic response appeared well before this, of course. Think of the psalmist's remembering of Zion while weeping by the waters of Babylon. But the term itself seems to be culturally and historically specific.

This physical and emotional 'upheaval . . . related to the workings of memory' – an upheaval that could and did kill, according to seventeenth- and eighteenth-century physicians – was seen as a 'disorder of the imagination' from the start.[2] But by the nineteenth century, a considerable semantic slippage had occurred, and the word began to lose its purely medical meaning,[3] in part because the rise of pathologic anatomy and bacteriology had simply made it less medically credible. Nostalgia then became generalized,[4] and by the twentieth century, it had begun to attract the interest of psychiatrists.[5] But curious things happened in that generalizing process: nostalgia became less a *physical* than a *psychological* condition; in other words, it became psychically internalized. It also went from being a *curable* medical illness to an *incurable* (indeed unassuageable) condition of the spirit or psyche.[6] What made that transition possible was a shift in site from the spatial to the temporal. Nostalgia was no longer simply a yearning to return home. As early as 1798, Immanuel Kant had noted that people who did return home were usually disappointed because, in fact, they did not want to return to a *place*, but to a *time*, a time of youth.[7] Time, unlike space, cannot be returned to – ever; time is irreversible. And nostalgia becomes the reaction to that sad fact.[8] As one critic has succinctly put this change: 'Odysseus longs for home; Proust is in search of lost time.'[9]

Nostalgia, in fact, may depend precisely on the *irrecoverable* nature of the past for its emotional impact and appeal. It is the very pastness of the past, its inaccessibility, that likely accounts for a large part of nostalgia's power – for both conservatives and radicals alike. This is rarely the past as actually experienced, of course; it is the past as imagined, as idealized through memory and desire. In this sense, however, nostalgia is less about the past than about the present. It operates through what Mikhail Bakhtin called an 'historical inversion': the ideal that is *not* being lived now is projected into the past.[10] It is 'memorialized' as past, crystallized into precious moments selected by memory, but also by forgetting, and by desire's distortions and reorganizations.[11] Simultaneously distancing and proximating, nostalgia exiles us from the present as it brings the imagined past near. The simple, pure, ordered, easy, beautiful, or harmonious past is constructed (and then experienced emotionally) in conjunction with the present – which, in turn, is constructed as complicated, contaminated, anarchic, difficult, ugly, and confrontational. Nostalgic distancing sanitizes as it selects, making the past feel complete, stable, coherent, safe from 'the unexpected and the untoward, from accident or betrayal'[12] – in other words, making it so very unlike the present. The aesthetics of nostalgia might, therefore, be less a matter of simple memory than of complex projection; the invocation of a partial, idealized history merges with a dissatisfaction with the present. And it can do so with great force. Think of how visceral, how physically 'present' nostalgia's promptings are: it is not just Proust for whom tastes, smells, sounds, and sights conjure up an idealized past. If you are not like me (that is, if you are capable of nostalgia), you can think of your own experience – or, if need be, do as I have to do and think of the power of the taste of Proust's madeleine or the scent of violets in Tennyson's 'A dream of fair women' or of a geranium leaf in *David Copperfield*.[13]

There are, of course, many ways to look backward. You can look and reject. Or you can look and linger longingly. In its looking backward in this yearning way, nostalgia may be more of an attempt to defy the end, to evade teleology. As we approach the millennium, nostalgia may be particularly appealing as a possible escape from what Lee Quinby calls 'technological apocalypse.'[14] If the future is cyberspace, then what better way to soothe techno-peasant anxieties than to yearn for a Mont Blanc fountain pen? But there is a rather obvious contradiction here: nostalgia requires the availability of evidence of the past,[15] and it is precisely the electronic and mechanical reproduction of images of the past that plays such an important role in the structuring of the nostalgic imagination today, furnishing it with the possibility of 'compelling vitality.'[16] Thanks to CD ROM technology and, before that, audio and video reproduction, nostalgia no longer has to rely on individual memory or desire: it can be fed forever by quick access to an infinitely recyclable past.

That original theory of nostalgia as a medical condition was developed in Europe 'at the time of the rise of the great cities when greatly improved means of transportation made movements of the population much easier';[17] in other words, you would be more likely to be away from home and thus yearn for it. The postmodern version of nostalgia may have been developed (in the West, at least) at the time when the rise of information technology made us question not only (as Jean-François Lyotard told us we must[18]) what would count as knowledge, but what would count as 'the past' in relation to the present. We have not lacked for critics who lament the decline of historical memory in our postmodern times, often blaming the storage of memory in data banks for our cultural amnesia, our inability to engage in active remembrance. But, as Andreas Huyssen has convincingly argued, the contrary is just as likely to be true. In his words: 'The more memory we store on data banks, the more the past is sucked into the orbit of the present, ready to be called up on the screen,' making the past simultaneous with the present in a new way.[19]

Nostalgia, however, does not simply repeat or duplicate memory. Susan Stewart's provocative study, *On Longing*, suggestively calls nostalgia a 'social disease,' defining it as 'the repetition that mourns the inauthenticity of all repetition.'[20] The argument is that, denying or at least degrading the present as it is lived, nostalgia makes the idealized (and therefore always absent) past into the site of immediacy, presence, and authenticity. And here she approaches one of the major differences between nostalgia and irony. Unlike the knowingness of irony – a mark of the fall from innocence, if ever there was one – nostalgia is, in this way, 'prelapsarian' and indeed utopian, says Stewart.[21] Few have ever accused irony (even satiric irony) of successfully reinstating the authentic and the ideal.

Nostalgia has certainly not lacked for defenders, most of whom are psychoanalytically-oriented.[22] This is not surprising if you think of the significant relationship psychoanalysis posits between identity and the personal psychic past unearthed by memory. This relationship becomes the model for the link between collective identity and memory for those who see a move to nostalgic transcendence and authenticity as a positive move. As one person in this camp has put it: 'Longing is what makes art possible.'[23] By 'longing,' he means the emotional response to deprivation, loss, and mourning. Nostalgia has, in this way, been deemed the necessary inspirational 'creative sorrow' for artists.[24] This position draws on the original seventeenth-century meaning of the word; it sees nostalgia in our century as the positive response to the homelessness and exile of both private 'nervous disorder and [public] persecution of actual enslavement and barbaric cruelty.'[25] When I think of the displaced homeless peoples of Rwanda or Bosnia, however, the more trivialized, commercialized connotations of the word 'nostalgia' do stand in the way for me. My feelings when experiencing those lushly nostalgic Merchant/Ivory film versions of earlier novels must be different (in kind and not only in degree) from the experience of political refugees yearning for their homeland. But perhaps not.

In other words, despite very strong reservations (based in part on personality limitations), I do know that I should never underestimate the power of nostalgia, especially its visceral physicality and emotional impact. But that power comes in part from its structural doubling-up of two different times, an inadequate present and an idealized past.[26] But this is where I must return to that other obsession of mine – irony – for irony too is doubled: two meanings, the 'said' and the 'unsaid,' rub together to create irony – and it too packs considerable punch. People do not usually get upset about metaphor or synecdoche, but they certainly do get worked up about irony, as they did a few years ago in Toronto, where I live and work, when the aptly named Royal Ontario Museum put on an exhibition that used irony to deal with the relationship of Canadian missionaries and military to Empire in Africa. Sometimes, as we all know well, people get upset because they are the targets or victims of irony. Sometimes, though, anger erupts at the seeming inappropriateness of irony in certain situations. Witness the remarks of the Curriculum Advisor on Race Relations and Multiculturalism for the Toronto Board of Education at the time: 'The implied criticism of colonial intrusion and the bigotry of the white missionaries and soldiers relies heavily on the use of irony, a subtle and frequently misunderstood technique. In dealing with issues as sensitive as cultural imperialism and racism, the use of irony is a highly inappropriate luxury' – especially, I might add, when condemnation is what is expected and desired.[27]

What irony and nostalgia share, therefore, is a perhaps unexpected twin evocation of both affect and agency – or, emotion and politics. I suspect that one of the reasons they do so is that they share something else – a secret hermeneutic affinity that might well account for some of the interpretive confusion with which I began, the confusion that saw postmodern artifacts, in particular, deemed simultaneously ironic and nostalgic. I want to argue that to call something ironic or nostalgic is, in fact, less a *description* of the ENTITY ITSELF than an *attribution* of a quality of RESPONSE. Irony is not something *in* an object that you either 'get' or fail to 'get': irony 'happens' for you (or, better, you *make* it 'happen') when two meanings, one said and the other unsaid, come together, usually with a certain critical edge. Likewise, nostalgia is not something you 'perceive' *in* an object; it is what you 'feel' when two different temporal moments, past and present, come together for you and, often, carry considerable emotional weight. In both cases, it is the element of response – of active participation, both intellectual and affective – that makes for the power.

Because people do not talk about this element of *active attribution*, the politics of both irony and nostalgia are often written off as quietistic at best. But irony is what Hayden White calls 'transideological': it can be made to 'happen' by (and to) anyone of any political persuasion. And nostalgia too is transideological, despite the fact that many would argue that, whether used by the right or the left, nostalgia is fundamentally conservative in its praxis, for it wants to keep things as they were – or, more accurately, as they are imagined to have been.[28] But, the nostalgia for an idealized community in the past has been articulated by the ecology movement as often as by fascism,[29] by what Jean Baudrillard calls '[m]elancholy for societies without power.'[30] From the seventeenth century on, nostalgia seems to have been connected to the desire to return specifically to the *homeland*. In nineteenth-century Europe, that homeland became articulated in terms of the nation state, and nostalgia began to take on its associations with nationalism – and chauvinism.[31] Even its more innocent-seeming forms – such as the preparing and eating of familiar foods by immigrant groups – can be seen as a nostalgic enactment of ethnic group identity, a collective disregarding, at least temporarily, of generational and other divisions.[32]

One brave anthropologist has claimed that, unlike such searches for ethnicity, *feminism* has 'no tendency toward nostalgia, no illusion of a golden age in the past.'[33] It has been suggested that this lack of nostalgic response is because the *narratives* of nostalgia – from the Bible onward – are *male* stories, Oedipal stories which are alienating to women (who usually remain at home like Penelope, while men wander the world and risk getting homesick).[34] And, in support of such a theory, literary and film critics alike have located strains of a current antifeminist, nostalgic retreat to the past in the face of the changes in culture brought about by the rise of feminism.[35] Humankind has not infrequently responded with a nostalgic defensive retreat into the past when feeling threatened: for example, despite its forward-looking ideology, the late nineteenth-century United States gave great new value to its Colonial past – as an 'exclusive WASP [White Anglo-Saxon Protestant] heritage' – in part to combat the mass immigration that was accompanying industrialization and that felt so new and so un-'American.'[36]

The politics of nostalgia are not only national or gender politics, of course. Think of the popularity in the 1980s of the David Lean film of Forster's *A Passage to India* or of *The Jewel in the Crown*, the television adaptation of Paul Scott's *The Raj Quartet*. The intended anti-nostalgic exposé of the corruption and exploitation of empire in India may have been less the cause of their success than either a nostalgic liberal-utopian hope that two races might have been able to live as equals – despite history – or a nostalgic memory of the time when Britain was not a minor world power but, rather, ruler of an empire upon which the sun never set.[37] This is what Renato Rosaldo calls 'imperial nostalgia,' the kind that makes racial domination appear innocent through elegance of manners.[38] But, this nostalgia puts us, as viewers, into the same position as the very agents of empire, for they too have documented at length their paradoxical nostalgia for the cultures they had colonized – in other words, the ones they had intentionally and forcefully altered. This is the nostalgia of those who believe in 'progress' and innovation, a nostalgia (again, paradoxically) for more simple, stable worlds – such as those of the putatively static societies they destroyed.

Post-colonial critics have pointed to nostalgic moments in the history of the colonized, too, however. To some, the 'négritude' move in African cultural theory, with its focus on the pre-capitalist, pre-imperial past, was the sign of a nostalgic search for a lost coherence.[39] Many oppressed people – Holocaust survivors and North American First Nations peoples among them – have had a strong and understandable nostalgia for what is perceived as their once unified identity. But most often, the post-colonial focus of attention has been on the nostalgia of the (usually) European colonizers, on their sense of loss and mourning for the cultural unity and centrality they once had.[40] But, as Fredric Jameson has said, 'a history lesson is the best cure for nostalgic pathos.'[41]

Jameson's own attack on the postmodern is in itself worth examining in this context because it is an attack on both its regressive nostalgia and its trivializing irony. One of Jameson's main targets is what he calls the postmodern 'nostalgia film' – a term that he has used to refer to anything from George Lucas's *American Graffiti* to Lawrence Kasdan's *Body Heat*. These are what he calls 'fashion-plate, historicist films' that reveal 'the desperate attempt to appropriate a missing past.'[42] To him, these are the inauthentic, nostalgic 'celebrations of the imaginary style of a real past' which he sees as 'something of a substitute for that older system of historical representation, indeed as a virtual symptom-formation, a formal compensation for the enfeeblement of historicity in our own time.'[43] This medicalized psychoanalytic language – 'symptom-formation', 'compensation' – is used quite deliberately by Jameson because he feels that the postmodern taste for such films corresponds to certain needs in what he calls 'our present economic-psychic constitution.'[44]

But film theorist Anne Friedberg has pointed out that what Jameson is really protesting here is the distanced relation of *every* film from its historical referent. In other words, it is the medium and not postmodernism that gives the illusion of a 'perpetual present interminably recycled.'[45] Or, as Derek Jarman put it when rewriting Marlowe in his postmodern film version of *Edward II*, '[f]ilmed history is always a misinterpretation. The past is the past, as you try to make material out of it, things slip even further away.'[46] But, even if Jameson is wrong in where he puts the blame for the nostalgia, what interests me is that, when he finds something nostalgic – be it in the theorizing of the Frankfurt School or the novels of J. G. Ballard – nostalgia is meant to be taken negatively as 'regressive.'[47] Yet his *own* rhetoric and position can themselves at times sound strangely nostalgic: in article after article in the 1980s, he repeatedly yearned for what he called 'genuine historicity' in the face of a postmodernism which, in his words, was 'an elaborated symptom of the waning of our historicity, of our lived possibility of experiencing history in some active way.'[48] And yet, it is precisely nostalgia for this kind of 'lost authenticity' that has proved time and time again to be paralyzing in terms of historical thinking.[49] Indeed Jameson's position has been called both regressive and defeatist.[50] Is Jameson's implicit mythologizing and idealizing of a more stable, pre-*late*-capitalist (that is, modernist) world not in itself perhaps part of an aesthetics (or even politics) of nostalgia? If so, it is one he shares with his Marxist predecessor, Georg Lukács, for whom it was not modernism but realism that constituted that implied 'moment of plenitude'[51] in the past around which literary historical nostalgia revolved.

Michael Bérubé has, in fact, suggested that the Left, in America at least, has at times recently seemed paralyzed 'by dreams of days when things were better.' As he puts it: 'it was only the repeated interventions of women, ethnic minorities and variously queer theorists that finally shattered the pernicious sense of nostalgia to which so many *men* on the antipostmodern left fell victim.'[52] Nostalgia can certainly be, in Tim Reiss's strong terms, 'functionally crippling.'[53] Jameson's preference for science fiction over these period-recreation 'nostalgia' films is a bit deceptive, for it simply points to his orientation toward the very common *futuristic* dimension of an equally nostalgic utopian drive.[54] If the present is considered irredeemable, you can look either back or forward. The nostalgic and utopian impulses share a common rejection of the here and now.

It is not that the here and now, the present, does not have its problems, however. All 'presents' have always had their problems, but there is little doubt that there has been, in the last few decades, a commercialization of nostalgia, especially in the mass media, a commercialization that many have seen as a real evasion of contemporary issues and problems.[55] Ralph Lauren's 'Safari' fashion and perfume line a few years ago allowed us to experience the nostalgic style of an era without bearing any of its historical costs; it also offered us, as one writer put it, 'a chance to relive the days of the tragically doomed upper class engaging in their white mischief on the plains of the Serengeti' – 'living without boundaries', as the ads said. This is a combination of commercial nostalgia – that teaches us to miss things we have never lost – and 'armchair nostalgia' – that exists without any lived experience of the yearned-for time.[56]

Is this part of the 'postmodern'? Since it is part of late-capitalist culture, Jameson would say it is. But, to generalize the term 'postmodern' into a synonym for the contemporary is to abandon its historical and cultural specificity – an abandonment Jameson would never condone for modernism, for example. To illustrate what I mean about the need to make distinctions, think of the difference between contemporary postmodern architecture and contemporary *revivalist* (nostalgic) architecture; the *postmodern* architecture does indeed recall the past, but always with the kind of ironic double vision that acknowledges the final impossibility of indulging in nostalgia, even as it consciously evokes nostalgia's affective power. In the postmodern, in other words, (and here is the source of the tension) nostalgia itself gets both called up, exploited, *and* ironized.[57] This is a complicated (and postmodernly paradoxical) move that is both an ironizing of nostalgia itself, of the very urge to look backward for authenticity, and, at the same moment, a sometimes shameless invoking of the visceral power that attends the fulfilment of that urge.[58]

Perhaps the history of the wider cultural entity called postmodern*ity* would help explain this paradox. If, as it has been argued often, nostalgia is a by-product of cultural *modernity* (with its alienation, its much lamented loss of tradition and community),[59] then *post*modernity's complex relationship with modernity – a relationship of both rupture and continuity – might help us understand the necessary addition of irony to this nostalgic inheritance. It has become a commonplace to compare the end of the nineteenth century to the end of our own, to acknowledge their common doubts about progress, their shared worries over political instability and social inequality, their comparable fears about disruptive change.[60] But if nostalgia was an obvious consequence of the *last* fin-de-siècle panic – 'manifest in idealizations of rural life, in vernacular-revival architecture, in arts-and-crafts movements, and in a surge of preservation activity'[61] – then some, not all (not the commercial variety, usually), but *some* nostalgia we are seeing today (what I want to call postmodern) is of a different order, an ironized order. If the nineteenth century turned nostalgically to the historical novels of Walter Scott and familiar Gothic Revival architecture, the twentieth has combined nostalgia with irony to produce the historiographic metafictions of Salman Rushdie and historically suggestive, parodic architectural ideas of Charles Moore's once splendid Piazza d'Italia in New Orleans. Gone is the sense of belatedness of the present vis-à-vis the past; the act of ironizing (while still implicitly invoking) nostalgia undermines modernist assertions of originality, authenticity, and the burden of the past, even as it acknowledges their continuing (but not paralyzing) validity as aesthetic concerns.

Our contemporary culture is indeed nostalgic; some parts of it – postmodern parts – are aware of the risks and lures of nostalgia, and seek to expose those through irony. Given irony's conjunction of the said and the unsaid – in other words, its inability to free itself from the discourse it contests – there is no way for these cultural modes to escape a certain complicity, to separate themselves artificially from the culture of which they are a part. If our culture really is obsessed with remembering – and forgetting – as is suggested by the astounding growth of what

Huyssen calls our 'memorial culture' with its 'relentless museummania,'[62] then perhaps irony is one (though only one) of the means by which to create the necessary distance and perspective on that anti-amnesiac drive. Admittedly, there is little irony in most memorials, and next to none in most truly nostalgic re-constructions of the past – from Disney World's Main Street, USA to those elaborate dramatized re-enactments of everything from the American Civil War to medieval jousts restaged in contemporary England. But there is much ironized nostalgia too – in Angela Carter's meditation on gender and the dawn of the twentieth century in *Nights at the Circus* or in the wonderful generic paradox of a new work commissioned by the Metropolitan Opera of New York: William Hofman and John Corigliano's *The Ghosts of Versailles*. It is ironically and paradoxically called a 'grand opera buffa' – for 'grand' is the only kind of 'intimate' opera buffa you can put on at that particular opera house, with its more than 3000 seats and its penchant for spectacle and indeed for 'grand opera.' From a postmodern point of view, the knowingness of this kind of irony may be not so much a defense against the power of nostalgia as the way in which nostalgia is made palatable today: invoked but, at the same time, undercut, put into perspective, seen for exactly what it is – a comment on the present as much as on the past.

Seen from that angle, though, not only have irony and nostalgia gone hand in hand in the postmodern, but perhaps they have done so for a long time (as those who work in earlier periods may know only too well): Don Quijote gave us those wonderful ironies of incongruity and inappropriateness precisely through his nostalgia for a chivalric past. In like vein, the all too ready attribution of irony to someone like Madonna in her Marilyn (and maybe even in her Evita) phase cannot really be separated from nostalgia. This may in part be because irony and nostalgia are not qualities of *objects*; they are responses of *subjects* – active, emotionally- and intellectually-engaged subjects. The ironizing of nostalgia, in the very act of its invoking, may be one way the postmodern has of taking responsibility for such responses by creating a small part of the distance necessary for reflective thought about the present as well as the past.

Notes

1 J. Hofer, *Dissertatio medica de nostalgia, oder Heimwehe*, Basel, 1688, translated in *The Bulletin of the Institute of the History of Medicine*, 1934, vol. 7, pp. 379–91.

2 See J. Starobinski, 'The Idea of Nostalgia,' *Diogenes*, 1966 vol. 54, pp. 81–103. The citations are from pages 90 and 87 respectively.

3 The medical meaning did see a revival, evidently, during the American Civil War. See J. T. Calhoun, 'Nostalgia as a Disease of Field Service,' *Medical and Surgical Reporter* 11 (27 February 1864); D. C. Peters, 'Remarks on the Evils of Youthful Enlistments and Nostalgia,' *American Medical Times*, 14 February 1863.

4 See A. Prete, 'L'assedio della lontananza,' in Antonio Prete, ed., *Nostalgia: storia di un sentimento* (Milan: Raffaello Cortina, 1992), 17.

5 See the discussion of, among others, Karl Jaspers' *Heimweh und Verbrechen* (1909) in J. Starobinski 'The Idea of Nostalgia,' 99–101.

6 For more on the medical and psychological angle on nostalgia, see W. H. McCann, 'Nostalgia – A Review of the Literature,' *Psychological Bulletin*, 1941, vol. 38, pp. 165–82; and 'Nostalgia: A Descriptive and Comparative Study,' *Journal of Genetic*

Psychology, 1943, vol. 62, pp. 97–104; G. Rosen, 'Nostalgia: A "Forgotten" Psychological Disorder,' *Clio Medica*, 1975, vol. 10(1), pp. 28–51.

7 I. Kant, *Anthropologie in pragmatischer Hinsicht* (1798). More recently, it has been argued that the appeal of the comic strip in French culture today is nostalgia for childhood. See Irène Pennacchioni, *La Nostalgie en images: une sociologie du récit dessiné*, Paris: Librairie des Méridiens, 1982.

8 See V. Jankélévitch's meditation on this in *L'Irreversible et la nostalgie*, Paris: Flammarion, 1974.

9 J. Phillips, 'Distance, Absence, and Nostalgia,' in D. Ihde and H. J. Silverman, eds., *Descriptions*, Albany, NY: SUNY P, 1985, p. 65.

10 M. M. Bakhtin, *The Dialogic Imagination: Four Essays*, ed. Michael Holquist, trans. C. Emerson and M. Holquist, Austin, TX: University of Texas Press, 1881, p. 147. Thanks to Russell Kilbourn for calling this to my attention.

11 See J. Phillips, 'Distance, Absence, and Nostalgia,' p. 65.

12 L. Lowenthal, *Literature, Popular Culture and Society*, New York: Prentice Hall, 1961, p. 62; Douglas T. Miller and Marion Nowak, *The Fifties: The Way We Really Were*, New York: Doubleday, 1977.

13 But is this perhaps how nostalgia only 'masquerades as memory,' as one theorist puts it? See E. B. Daniels, 'Nostalgia: Experiencing the Elusive,' in D. Ihde and H. J. Silverman, eds., *Descriptions*, p. 84.

14 L. Quinby, *Anti-Apocalypse: Exercises in Genealogical Criticism*, Minneapolis, MN: University of Minnesota Press, 1994, p. xvi.

15 M. Chase and C. Shaw, 'The Dimensions of Nostalgia,' in C. Shaw and M. Cross, eds., *The Imagined Past: History and Nostalgia*, Manchester: Manchester University Press, 1989, p. 4. Chase and Shaw also point out that the photograph is the 'paradigm case of the moment of nostalgia', p. 9.

16 L. Lowenthal, *Literature, Popular Culture and Society*, p. 30.

17 J. Starobinski, 'The Idea of Nostalgia,' pp. 101–2.

18 See J.-F. Lyotard, *The Postmodern Condition: A Report on Knowledge*, trans. G. Bennington and B. Massumi, Minneapolis, MN: University of Minnesota Press, 1984.

19 Andreas Huyssen, *Twilight Memories: Marking Time in a Culture of Amnesia*, London: Routledge, 1995, p. 253.

20 S. Stewart, *On Longing: Narrative of the Miniature, the Gigantic, the Souvenir, the Collection*, Baltimore, MD: Johns Hopkins University Press, 1984, p. 23.

21 S. Stewart, *On Longing*, p. 23.

22 See, for instance, R. Peters, 'Reflections on the Origin and Aim of Nostalgia,' *Journal of Analytic Psychology*, 1985, vol. 30, pp. 135–48; or N. Fodor, 'Varieties of Nostalgia,' *Psychoanalytic Review*, 1950, vol. 37, pp. 25–38.

23 L. Lerner, *The Uses of Nostalgia: Studies in Pastoral Poetry*, London: Chatto and Windus, 1972, p. 52.

24 M. M. Mason, 'The Cultivation of the Senses for Creative Nostalgia in the Essays of W. H. Hudson,' *Ariel*, 1989, vol. 20(1), p. 23. It has also been called our 'moral conscience' for it is said to let us know what values we hold most dear and help us fight 'the sickness of despair.' See R. Harper, *Nostalgia: An Existential Exploration of Longing and Fulfilment in the Modern Age*, Cleveland, OH: Western Reserve University Press, 1966, p. 28.

25 R. Harper, *Nostalgia*, p. 21.

26 All nostalgia, then, would be what Fred Davis calls 'interpreted nostalgia' wherein an analysis of an experience, however brief or mistaken, comes to be fused with that primary experience and thus alters it. See *Yearning for Yesterday: A Sociology of Nostalgia*, New York: Free Press, 1979, p. 25.

27 The Curriculum Advisor on Race Relations and Multiculturalism for the Toronto Board of Education, cited in 'Analyzing Racism at ROM' in *The Varsity*, June 1990, p. 4.

28 See S. Bennett, *Performing Nostalgia: Shifting Shakespeare and the Contemporary Past*, London: Routledge, 1996, pp. 5; 161, n.4.
29 See A. Arblaster, *Viva la libertà: Politics in Opera*, London: Verso, 1992, p. 180.
30 J. Baudrillard, 'The Precession of Simulacra,' in J. P. Natoli and L. Hutcheon, eds., *A Postmodern Reader*, New York: State University of New York Press, 1993, p. 361. He goes on to call nostalgia 'the phastasmal parodic rehabilitation of all lost referentials,' p. 372.
31 See Jankélévitch, *L'Irreversible et la nostalgie*; K. Parthé, 'Village Prose: Chauvinism, Nationalism, or Nostalgia?' in S. D. Graham, ed., *New Directions in Soviet Literature*, London: Macmillan, 1992, pp. 106–21.
32 See R. Raspa, 'Exotic Foods among Italian-Americans in Mormon Utah: Food as Nostalgic Enactment of Identity,' in L. K. Brown and K. Mussell, eds., *Ethnic and Regional Foodways in the United States: The Performance of Group Identity*, Knoxville, TN: University of Tennessee Press, 1984, pp. 185–94.
33 M. M. J. Fischer, 'Autobiographical Voices (1, 2, 3) and Mosaic Memory,' in K. Ashley, L. Gilmore, and G. Peters, eds., *Autobiography and Postmodernism*, Amherst, MA: University of Massachusetts Press, 1994, p. 92.
34 T. M. Brown, 'Rewriting the Nostalgic Story: Woman, Desire, Narrative,' Ph.D. dissertation, University of Florida, 1989.
35 See J. Doane and D. Hodges, *Nostalgia and Sexual Difference: The Resistance to Contemporary Feminism*, London: Methuen, 1987, p. xiii. See also B. Creed, 'From Here to Modernity: Feminism and Postmodernism,' *Screen*, 1987, vol. 28(2), pp. 47–67 on film nostalgia and issues of gender which Fredric Jameson does NOT deal with. For a discussion of the condemnation of utopian 'future nostalgia' by feminist writers, see K. D. Finney, 'The Days of Future Past or Utopians Lessing and LeGuin Fight Future Nostalgia,' in D. M. Hassler, ed., *Patterns of the Fantastic*, Mercer Island, WA: Starmont House, 1983, pp. 31–40. For a general critique of various kinds of utopian thinking, including nostalgic ones, see V. P. Pecora, *Households of the Soul*, Baltimore, MD: Johns Hopkins University Press, 1996.
36 L. Lowenthal, *Literature, Popular Culture and Society*, p. 121.
37 On Shakespeare's role in this kind of nostalgia, see S. Bennett, *Performing Nostalgia*, p. 145.
38 R. Rosando, *Culture and Truth: The Remaking of Social Analysis*, Boston, MA: Beacon Press, 1989, p. 68. Thanks to Monika Kaup for calling this to my attention.
39 S. Simonse, 'African Literature between Nostalgia and Utopia: African Novels since 1953 in the Light of the Modes-of-Production Approach,' *Research in African Literatures*, 1982, vol. 13(4), pp. 451–87.
40 See I. Ang, 'Hegemony-in-Trouble: Nostalgia and the Ideology of the Impossible in European Cinema,' in D. Petrie, ed., *Screening Europe: Image and Identity in Contemporary European Cinema*, London: British Film Institute, 1992, pp. 21–31.
41 F. Jameson, *Postmodernism, or the Cultural Logic of Late Capitalism*, Durham, NC: Duke University Press, 1991, p. 156.
42 F. Jameson, *Postmodernism*, pp. xvii and 19, respectively.
43 F. Jameson, *Signatures of the Visible*, London: Routledge, 1990, pp. 85 and 130 respectively.
44 F. Jameson, 'Nostalgia for the Present,' *The South Atlantic Quarterly*, 1989, vol. 88(2), p. 527.
45 A. Friedberg, '*Les Flaneurs du Mal(l)*: Cinema and the Postmodern Condition,' *PMLA*, 1991, vol. 106(3), pp 419–31.
46 D. Jarman, *Queer Edward II*, London: British Film Institute, 1991, p. 86.
47 See, respectively, F. Jameson, *The Ideologies of Theory: Essays 1971–1986, Volume I: Situations of Theory*, Minneapolis, MN: University of Minnesota Press, 1988, p. 110 and *Postmodernism*, p. 156.

48 F. Jameson, *Postmodernism*, pp. 19, 21.
49 J. Frow, 'Tourism and the Semiotics of Nostalgia,' *October*, 1991, vol. 57, p. 135.
50 S. During, 'Postmodernism or Post-colonialism Today,' *Textual Practice*, 1987, vol. 1(1), pp. 32–47.
51 See F. Jameson, *Marxism and Form: Twentieth-Century Dialectical Theories of Literature*, Princeton, NJ: Princeton University Press, 1971, p. 38. The phrase is used to describe Adorno's critique of theories of history organized around the covert hypothesis of such a 'moment of plenitude' in the past or future.
52 M. Bérubé, 'Just the Fax, Ma'am, Or, Postmodernism's Journey to Decenter,' *Village Voice*, October 1991, p. 14.
53 T. J. Reiss, 'Critical Environments: Cultural Wilderness or Cultural History?' *Canadian Review of Comparative Literature*, 1983, vol. 10(2), p. 193.
54 But it does so at a time when, as Andreas Huyssen has argued, Western culture's utopian imagination 'is shifting from its futuristic pole toward the pole of remembrance.' See A. Huyssen, *Twilight Memories*, p. 88.
55 See A. Graham, 'History, Nostalgia, and the Criminality of Popular Culture,' *Georgia Review*, 1984, vol. 38(2), pp. 348–64. See also E. Wilson, *Adorned in Dreams: Fashion and Modernity*, London: Virago, 1985, p. 172.
56 These are the terms of A. Appadurai, in his *Modernity at Large: Cultural Dimensions of Globalization*, Minneapolis, MN: University of Minnesota Press, 1996, pp. 77–8.
57 This is one step beyond what has been called the ironic nostalgia of, say, post-Soviet artists who, according to Svetlana Boym, 'reconfigure and preserve various kinds of imagined community and offer interesting cultural hybrids – of Soviet kitsch and memories of totalitarian childhood.' See S. Boym, 'From the Russian Soul to Post-Communist Nostalgia,' *Representations*, 1995, vol. 49, p. 151.
58 There may be analogies here with what Bennett calls 'queer nostalgia' wherein 'identity-forming discourses of the past are both confirmed and fractured at the moment of performance', S. Bennett, *Performing Nostalgia*, p. 159.
59 See M. Chase and C. Shaw, 'The Dimensions of Nostalgia,' p. 7.
60 See L. Lowenthal, *Literature, Popular Culture and Society*, pp. 394–6.
61 Ibid., p. 396.
62 A. Huyssen, *Twilight Memories*, p. 5.

Charles Eckert

THE CAROLE LOMBARD IN MACY'S WINDOW

'The Carole Lombard in Macy's Window', in J. Gaines and C. Herzog (eds), *Fabrications: Costume and the Female Body*, London: Routledge, 1990.

WHEN THE FIRST MOVIE CAMERAMAN shot the first street scene that included a shop sign or a labeled product (Lumiere? 1895?) all of the elements of a new advertising form were implicit: a captive audience unlikely to ignore what was placed before it, a manufacturer, and a filmmaker. The short dramas and comedies of the first decade of this century, especially those that pictured the contemporary lifestyles of the middle and upper classes, presented innumerable opportunities for product and brand name tie-ins. But more than this, they functioned as living display windows for all that they contained; windows that were occupied by marvelous mannequins and swathed in a fetish-inducing ambiance of music and emotion.

These films merely had to be shown to Americans who lived away from big cities, or to audiences in foreign countries, to generate a desire for the cornucopia of material goods they proffered. Around 1912, according to Benjamin Hampton, English and German manufacturers became alarmed at the decline in demand for their goods and an attendant rise in American imports. An investigation disclosed that American movies were responsible: 'They began to complain to their governments that audiences saw American sewing machines, typewriters, furniture, clothing, shoes, steam shovels, saddles, automobiles and all sorts of things in the cinema shows, and soon began to want these things . . .'

From this discovery, a complex chapter of film history arose. The periods immediately preceding and following World War I saw attempts at the establishment of quotas for both American products and films, and at shoring up national film industries (especially in England and Germany). This history is tangential to our interests, but the struggle attending it served to alert Hollywood and American industry to the full potential of film as a merchandiser of goods.

When Joseph Kennedy brought executives of the film industry to Harvard in 1927 for a series of lectures, the topic of film and foreign trade came up again and again. Kennedy had just returned from England where diplomats had told him that American films exerted a 'formidable' influence. Kent, Paramount's head of sales, ingenuously informed Harvard's undergraduates: 'If you investigate the automobile situation you will find that the American automobiles are making terrific inroads on foreign makes of cars and that the greatest agency for selling American automobiles abroad is the American motion picture. Its influence is working insidiously all the time and even though all this is done without any conscious intent, the effect is that of a direct sales agency.'

The demurral on conscious intent was undoubtedly directed at Kent's academic audience. Film executives spoke with another voice before government or industrial groups. William Fox told Upton Sinclair, 'I tried to bring government officials to realize that American trade follows American pictures, and not the American flag . . .' The most prominent spokesman for celluloid imperialism, however, was Will Hays. In a 1930 radio speech sponsored by *Nation's Business* he repeated a theme that he turned to many times:

> Motion pictures perform a service to American business which is greater than the millions in our direct purchases, greater than our buildings . . . The industry is a new factor in American economic life and gives us a solid basis of hope for the future by creating an increase in demand for our products. The motion picture carries to every American at home, and to millions of potential purchasers abroad, the visual, vivid perception of American manufactured products.

As if to underscore Hays's remarks, a government study published in 1929 revealed that foreign sales of bedroom and bathroom furnishings had increased 100 percent because of movies.

The mid- and late-1920s were also marked by an industrywide attempt to vitiate foreign film industries by hiring away their best stars, directors, and technicians. The logic of this development was very complex: A von Sternberg film made in Hollywood could be expected to stimulate Paramount's film rentals in Europe, to defeat foreign, chauvinist critics and quota setters, to undercut foreign competitors, and to keep the doors open for American films and products they showcased. By the early 1930s the European struggle against Americanization through films had lessened trade barriers and a worldwide Depression combined to diminish the effects of the process – for a time. From 1931 on one finds more concern among Hollywood executives with the film industry's relation to the domestic economy. Although I shall concentrate on this economy exclusively for the rest of this essay, we should bear in mind that the foreign market did not drop from Hollywood's consciousness, even though it was seldom publicly discussed.

The story of Hollywood's plunge into the American marketplace involves two separate histories: that of the showcasing of fashions, furnishings, accessories, cosmetics, and other manufactured items, and that of the establishment of 'tie-ups' with brand name manufacturers, corporations, and industries. The two histories are interpenetrating, but they were distinctive enough to give rise to specialists who worked independently within and without the studio.

The scope of the first history can be set forth in a sentence: At the turn of the century Hollywood possessed one clothing manufacturer (of shirts) and none of furniture; by 1937 the Associated Apparel Manufacturers of Los Angeles listed 130 members, and the Los Angeles Furniture Manufacturers Association listed 150, with an additional 330 exhibitors. Furthermore, 250 of the largest American department stores kept buyers permanently in Los Angeles.

When those intimately associated with this development reminisced about its origins, they spoke first of Cecil B. DeMille. In his autobiography DeMille maintained that the form of cinema he pioneered in the late teens and twenties was a response to pressures he received from the publicity and sales people in New York. They wanted few (preferably no) historical 'costume' dramas, but much 'modern stuff with plenty of clothes, rich sets, and action.' DeMille brought to Paramount's studios talented architects, designers, artists, costumers, and hairdressers who both drew upon the latest styles in fashions and furnishings and created hallmarks of their own. DeMille's 'modern photoplays' – films like *For Better, For Worse* and *Why Change Your Wife?* – guaranteed audiences a display of all that was chic and avant-garde. They also pioneered a cinematic style, the 'DeMille style,' perfectly tailored to the audience's desire to see the rich detail of furnishings and clothes.

While DeMille perfected a film display aimed at the fashion-conscious, fan magazines and studio publicity photos helped spread an indigenous Hollywood 'outdoors' style made up of backless bathing suits, pedal-pushers, slacks, toppers, and skirts. By the early 1930s these styles had penetrated the smallest of American small towns and had revolutionized recreational and sport dress.

The years 1927 through 1929 saw an explosive expansion of fashion manufacture and wholesaling in Los Angeles. Some of DeMille's designers opened shops which catered to a well-heeled public. The Country Club Manufacturing Company inaugurated copyrighted styles modeled by individual stars and employing their names. It was followed by 'Miss Hollywood Junior' which attached to each garment a label bearing the star's name and picture. This line was sold exclusively to one store in each major city, with the proviso that a special floor-space be set aside for display. Soon, twelve cloak and suit manufacturers banded together to form Hollywood Fashion Associates. In addition, the Associated Apparel Manufacturers began to coordinate and give national promotion to dozens of style lines. The latter association took the lead in a form of publicity that became commonplace through the 1930s: it shot thousands of photographs of stars serving as mannequins in such news-editor-pleasing locales as the Santa Anita race track, the Rose Bowl, Hollywood swimming pools, and formal film receptions. The photos were distributed free, with appropriate text, to thousands of newspapers and magazines. In a more absurd vein, the Association organized bus and airplane style shows, which ferried stars, designers and buyers to resorts and famous restaurants amid flashbulbs and a contrived sense of occasion.

If one walked into New York's largest department stores toward the end of 1929 one could find abundant evidence of the penetration of Hollywood fashions, as well as a virulent form of moviemania. One store employed uniformed Roxy ushers as its floor managers. Another advertised for sales girls that looked like Janet Gaynor and information clerks that looked like Buddy Rogers. At Saks, Mrs. Pemberton would inform you that she was receiving five orders a day for pajamas identical with the pair that Miriam Hopkins wore in *Camel Thru a Needle's Eye*. She also had received orders for gowns and suits worn by Pauline Lord, Lynne Fontaine, Frieda Innescourt, Sylvia Fields, and Murial Kirkland.

The New York scene became organized, however, only with the advent in 1930 of Bernard Waldman and his Modern Merchandising Bureau. Waldman's concern soon played the role of fashion middleman for all the major studios except Warner Brothers (Warners, always a loner, established its own Studio Styles in 1934). By the mid-1930s Waldman's system generally operated as follows: sketches and/or photographs of styles to be worn by specific actresses in specific films were sent from the studios to the Bureau (often a year in advance of the film's release). The staff first evaluated these styles and calculated new trends. They then contracted with manufacturers to have the styles produced in time for the film's release. They next secured advertising photos and other materials which would be sent to retail shops. This ad material mentioned the film, stars, and studio as well as the theaters where the film would appear. Waldman's cut of the profits was five percent. The studios at first asked for one percent, but before 1937 provided their designs free in exchange for abundant advertising.

Waldman's concern also established the best-known chain of fashion shops, Cinema Fashions. Macy's contracted for the first of these shops in 1930 and remained a leader in the Hollywood fashion field. By 1934 there were 298 official Cinema Fashions Shops (only one permitted in each city). By 1937 there were 400, with about 1,400 other shops willing to handle some of the dozens of the Bureau's star-endorsed style lines. Cinema Fashions catered only to women capable of spending thirty dollars and more for a gown. It agreed with the studios that cheaper fashions, even though they would be eagerly received, would destroy the aura and exclusivity that surrounded a Norma Shearer or Loretta Young style. Cheaper lines might also cheapen the stars themselves, imperiling both box-office receipts and the Hollywood fashion industry.

Inevitably, competitors and cheaper lines did appear. Copyrighted styles that had had their run in the Waldman-affiliated shops were passed on to mass production (though seldom if the style was associated with a currently major star). By the later 1930s Waldman had added a line of Cinema Shops that sold informal styles at popular prices. The sale of these fashions was tremendously aided by the release of photos to newspapers (they saturated Sunday supplements), major magazines, and the dozens of fan magazines – *Hollywood*, *Picture Play*, *Photoplay*, *Shadowplay*, *Modern Movies*, *Screenbook*, *Movieland*, *Movie Story*, *Movies Stories*, *Modern Movies*, *Modern Screen*, *Motion Pictures*, and the rest. In monthly issues of each of these magazines, millions of readers saw Bette Davis, Joan Crawford, Claudette Colbert, and Norma Shearer in a series of roles unique to this period: as mannequins modeling clothes, furs, hats, and accessories that they would wear in forthcoming films. The intent behind these thousands of style photos is epitomized in a 1934 *Shadowplay* caption for a dress modeled by Anita Louise: 'You will see the dress in action in Warner's *First Lady*.' Occasionally one was informed that the fashions were 'on display in leading department and ready-to-wear stores this month.' The names of the leading studio designers, Adrian of MGM, Orry-Kelly of Warners, Royer of 20th Century-Fox, Edward Stevenson of RKO, Edith Head of Paramount, Walter Plunkett of Selznick, became as familiar to readers as the stars themselves.

From July 30th to August 4, 1934, Los Angeles presented the first of a twice annual series of trade fairs called, inelegantly, the Combined Market Week. More than 400 local firms displayed women's apparel, millinery, children's and men's wear, dry goods, furniture, flooring, housewares, pottery, machinery, and other lines. More than 7,000 buyers attended. By 1936 the fair attracted over 10,000 buyers and included 185 women's clothing manufacturers and 260 furniture manufacturers. In less than a decade Los Angeles had become indisputably first in the fields of sport clothes, street dress, and modern and outdoor furniture, and arguably second to New York and Pan's in high fashion.

To all of this we must add Hollywood's influence upon the cosmetics industry. In a field dominated by eastern houses like Helena Rubenstein, Elizabeth Arden, and Richard Hudnut, Hollywood's Max Factor and Perc Westmore were merely two large concerns. But Hollywood seemed to dominate the cosmetics industry because its stars appeared in the hundreds of thousands of ads that saturated the media. In the mid-1930s cosmetics ranked only second to food products in amount spent on advertising. The cycle of influence made up of films, fashion articles, 'beauty hints,' columns featuring stars, ads which dutifully mentioned the star's current film, and tie-in advertising in stores, made cosmetics synonymous with Hollywood. The same was true for many brands of soap, deodorants, toothpastes, hair preparations, and other toiletries. No more potent endorsements were possible than those of the women who manifestly possessed the most 'radiant' and 'scintillant' eyes, teeth, complexions, and hair.

Almost as significant for films as the scope of this merchandising revolution was the conception of the consumer that underpinned it. As one reads the captions beneath the style photos, the columns of beauty advice, and the articles on the coordination of wardrobes and furnishings, one senses that those who bought these things were not varied as to age, marital status, ethnicity, or any other characteristic. Out there, working as a clerk in a store and living in an apartment with a friend, was *one* girl – single, nineteen years old, Anglo-Saxon, somewhat favoring Janet Gaynor. The thousands of Hollywood-associated designers, publicity men, sales heads, beauty consultants, and merchandisers had internalized her so long ago that her psychic life had become their psychic life. They empathized with her shyness, her social awkwardness, her fear of offending. They understood her slight weight problem and her chagrin at being a trifle too tall. They could tell you what sort of man she hoped to marry and how she spent her leisure time.

They could imagine her, for instance, awakening on a Saturday, realizing that it was her day off, and excitedly preparing to do shopping. After a long soak in a bubble bath (Lux), she prepared herself to meet the critical stares of Fifth Avenue. She first applied successive coats of cleansing (Ponds), lubricating (Jergens), and foundation creams (Richard Hudnut). She then chose a coordinated group of cosmetics keyed to daylight wear and the current fashions of natural flesh tone and heavy lip color. Over a coat of light pink pancake makeup she applied a light orange rouge high and back upon the cheek-bones, accentuating the oval effect (Princess Pat). A brown eyebrow pencil, employed to extend the line back along the cheeks, and brown mascara (Lucille Young) was combined with a gray-blue eyeshadow flecked with metallic sheen, appropriate for day wear (Elizabeth Arden). A bright red-orange lipstick, richly applied (Max Factor) and a light dusting of true skin tone face powder (Lady Esther) completed her facial. From her several perfumes she chose a refreshing, outdoor type (Lentheric). She then added a 'fingertip-full' of deodorant to each armpit (Mum), massaged her hands (Hinds), and applied a fresh coat of nail enamel (Revlon).

Stepping out of her dressing gown she lightly dusted herself with a body powder (Luxor), then, following a hint from Edith Head, taped her ever-so-slightly too large breasts so that they were separated as widely as possible. A Formfit bra, Undikins, a Bonnie Bright Frock (the Frances Dee model from *Of Human Bondage*, RKO, 1934), silk stockings (Humming Bird) and a pair of Nada White Buck shoes (Enna Jettick) completed her outfit. Donning her Wittnauer watch ('Watches of the Stars') and a simple necklace (the Tecla worn by Barbara Stanwyck in *Gambling Lady*, Warners, 1934), she picked up her metallic-sheen purse and left.

After several lovely hours of window-shopping she happened to pass Macy's and was thunderstruck at the sight of the original Travis Banton gown worn by Carole Lombard in her just-released film *Rumba* (also starring – in smaller print – George Raft). Rushing up to Macy's Cinema Fashions Shop she discovered a $40 copy of the gown, almost as careful in its detail as the original. Her imagination heated by this encounter, she immediately left to catch the early matinee of the film. Three dresses and a fur coat later, the gown entered. Back-lit, descending a stair, vivified by motion and music, it whispered and sighed its way into George Raft's roguish arms. Through the alchemy of his caresses it became libidinous, haunted. It slipped from Carole Lombard's shoulder and had to be lifted back again. It snaked its way across one knee, cascaded from the stairs to the floor like liquid light.

From the rear of one theater two slight moans could be heard. The first small sound, tinged with ecstasy and fulfillment, issued from the girl. The second, somewhat grosser but still redolent with satisfaction, came from Bernard Waldman.

Now for our second history, that of the tie-up. In mid-May 1931, a Mr. Tielhet, reporter for the *Outlook and Independent*, sat with a stopwatch in hand viewing a fifteen minute 'screen-playlet' which a theater was offering as a bonus to its audiences. The next day, he published this report.

> The news reel was run off first. Then the caption, which will be called, for the purpose of this article, 'Seduction – featuring Blanche la Belle,' was flashed upon the screen. The scene opened in the boudoir of la Belle, and the brassy voice of the dialogue blared forth. The plot was of little importance. I was interested in counting the length in seconds that a bottle of 'Seduction Fleur Parfum' was displayed before the audience. The story with unobtrusive cunning brought out the irresistible attracting powers of a seductive perfume. It showed how a comparatively plain

> woman, deserted by her fiance, suddenly developed an almost overwhelming charm by the lure of this perfume. Ten times was the square bottle of 'Seduction Fleur' displayed before us, for a total of seventy-eight seconds . . . Then a seven second title was flashed, 'This film is sponsored for your entertainment by the Parfum de Fleurs Company, Paris and London, Levy and Grosstein, New York, sole importers for United States and Canada.'
>
> In the lobby the two advertising men from the production company were busy interviewing as many of the audience as possible in order to determine whether the sponsored film had been successful. Next day one of the interviewers gave me his figures. He had talked with 191 men and women. So cunning was the advertising that 54 out of the 191, did not even realize that they had witnessed a sponsored film!

This was but one of a series of advertising shorts shown in early 1931, the first year of catastrophic downturn in box-office receipts. On May 13, *Variety* reported that 50 percent of the theaters were showing advertising films of some sort. Two of the hardest-pressed studios, Paramount and Warners, were seriously committed to these films. In the same month, Paramount revealed that it would produce 50 shorts in response to the favorable receptions accorded to just released *Movie Memories* (Liggett and Myers), *In My Merrie Oldsmobile* and *Jolt for General Germ* (Lysol). Warners projected a dozen or more to follow its *On the Slopes of The Andes* (A & P), *Graduation Day in Bugland* (Listerine), a Chesterfield series, and others. Both studios had many signed contracts in hand. MGM was fearful of exhibitor reactions to this development and was a silent spectator. RKO was said to be 'on the fence.'

If a moviegoer was extremely unlucky he might encounter a Paramount advertising short on the same program with its feature film, *It Pays To Advertise*, starring Carole Lombard and Norman Foster (1931). This comedy, set in an advertising agency, aroused the anger of P. S. Harrison, editor of *Harrison's Reports*, a reviewing service directed at independent exhibitors:

> The Paramount picture, 'It Pays to Advertise,' is nothing but a billboard of immense size. I have not been able to count all the nationally advertised articles that are spoken of by the characters, but some of them are the following: Boston Garters, Arrow Collars, Manhattan Shirts, Colgate Cream, Gillette Razors, B.V.D.'s, Hart, Schaeffner & Marx clothes, Listerine, Victor phonographs, Murad cigarettes, Florsheim shoes, Dobbs hats, Forhans toothpaste, and others. But the most subtle thing is the brand, '13 Soap, Unlucky for Dirt.' A trade mark such as this does not, of course, exist; but I understand that Paramount has made the picture for the purpose of making a trade mark out of it. My information is to the effect that Colgate has offered $250,000 for it, and that Paramount is asking $500,000. I understand, in fact, that Paramount has decided to make a regular business out of creating trade marks and then selling them.

Harrison went on in this and subsequent articles to enumerate the brand names he had seen in recent feature films, including ones made by MGM, RKO, and United

Artists. The response he generated from exhibitors was as angry as his own. Dozens of them supplied his articles to newspapers that were already alert to the threat to their advertising income posed by sponsored shorts.

The offers this man received were part of a reciprocal business between studio publicity people and their counterparts in business advertising agencies. *The New York Times* described the agencies' side of the operation in a 1929 editorial:

> Articles to be advertised are offered as props for films in the making. Automobile manufacturers graciously offer the free use of high-priced cars to studios. Expensive furnishings for a set are willingly supplied by the makers, and even donated as permanent studio property. For kitchen scenes the manufacturers of nationally advertised food products fill cupboard shelves.
>
> *Variety* reports in a Hollywood dispatch that agents eager for publicity for jewelry or wearing apparel approach movie stars directly. If they will agree to wear a certain article in their picture, it is given to them. In cases where an object is 'hard to plant,' the agency will even offer monetary consideration.

Given the long history behind brand name props and tie-ups, and the deepening of the Depression through 1932, it was inevitable that the restraint brought on by the excesses of 1931 would not last. By early 1933 Columbia, a studio not burned by Harrison, had moved aggressively into solicited tie-ups. Prior to the production of *Ann Carver's Profession*, a scene-by-scene breakdown was prepared and mailed to agents for manufacturers of the products that would appear in the film. The intent was not merely to solicit props, but to promote on-going tie-ups that would reduce studio overhead and gain advertising for films.

Through the first half of 1931 so much pressure was brought to bear upon the major studios that executives were compelled to make public statements. Carl Laemmle of Universal was unequivocally on the exhibitors' side: 'I appeal to every producer not to release "sponsored" moving pictures . . . Believe me, if you jam advertising down their throats and pack their eyes and ears with it, you will build up a resentment that will in time damn your business.' Nicholas Schenck, head of MGM, pledged his studio to the crusade. He stated that although Lowe's had been the first to be offered huge sums to produce 'subsidized motion pictures,' it has always refused to run commercials in its theaters.

When Harrison subsequently revealed that Paramount had threatened to run him out of business, the general reaction was one of shock. By the end of May both Paramount and Warners were compelled to apologetically disavow their practices and their future plans. Harrison announced Paramount's capitulation coldly, but commended Warners for 'taking it on the chin.'

This early Depression development had its antecedents in practices as old as the industry. Product display in films had become common prior to World War I. Occasionally the studios solicited props in exchange for the free advertising they could provide, or they accepted or solicited fees for foregrounding brand names or recognizable articles.

By 1934 enough brand names had returned to films to arouse critics – and the interest of manufacturer's agents. 'What has particularly heated the industrialists lately,' *Variety* said in June 1934, 'are the great plug insertions in recent films. A particular bubble in the pot is the reference in that "Three Little Pigs" cartoon to the Fuller Brush Man, while the three pictures centering around Greyhound buses in the past two months is another thing eating at the hearts of industrial rivals.' By 1935 one could see a package of Lucky Strikes flashed in RKO's *Strangers All*, Chesterfields and Wonder Bread in a Laurel and Hardy film, and Donald Cook asking a bartender for a 'Clicquot' in RKO's *Gigolette.* And if one attended RKO's *The Rainmakers* (aka *Silver Streak*) one spent eighty minutes on the Burlington's streamlined 'Zephyr,' accompanied by Western Union, the company that timed its record run.

All this was small potatoes, however, compared to tie-up schemes fabricated at the two most powerful studios, Warners and MGM. Determined not to rekindle the controversies of 1931, these two studios evolved a form of tie-up that revolutionized sales and publicity – and permanently affected the character of films. The keystone of the method was a contractual agreement with a large established manufacturer. If the product would seem blatantly displayed if shown in a film – a bottle of Coca-Cola, for instance – the contract provided merely for a magazine and newspaper campaign that would employ pictures and endorsements of stars, and notice of recent studio releases. MGM signed a $500,000 contract with Coca-Cola in March 1933, providing that company with the vaunted 'star-power' of the most star-laden studio.

There were other products, however, that could be prominently displayed in films without arousing criticism, except from the most knowledgeable. Warner's tie-up with General Electric and General Motors provided both for the use of Warner's stars in magazine ads and for the display of appliances and autos in films. Anyone familiar with the GE Monitor-top refrigerator will recognize it in a number of Warner films of this period. A tie-up with Buick (GM) provided for the display of autos in films and for a national advertising campaign that tied Buick to ten Warner films, among them *Gold Diggers of 1933*, *Go Into Your Dance*, *The Goose And The Gander*, *A Night At The Ritz*, and *In Caliente.*

At the end of the campaign, in May 1935, *Variety* reported, 'Automobile manufacturers have gone daffy over picture names following the campaign just completed by Buick and Warners. Latter company has tied up to stars on the last 10 pictures with Buick buggies.' Among the manufacturers said to be 'wild on commercial tie-ups' and anxious to make deals were Auburn, Packard, Dodge, Armour Co., Jantzen Knitting Co., Walkover Shoes, Pure Oil, and Helena Rubenstein.

General Motors itself was so euphoric that it contemplated raiding the studios for stars, producing its own commercial films, and offering them free to exhibitors. It did, in fact, produce at least five of these, employing such tertiary stars as John Mack Brown, Sheila Manners, and Hedda Hopper. In April 1935, Will Hays spoke out against the return of commercial pictures, scotching General Motors' plans before they got out of hand. Only twenty exhibitors were actually offered the GM commercials.

In September 1934, Charles Einfeld explained the Warner's system to *Sales Management*: 'Our idea is to prepare with an advertiser a scheme that works just as much to his advantage as it does to ours. Our company has prepared a special department of such tie-ups. It has pursued a definite policy of working with important nationally advertised products. We have religiously avoided the mass of small advertisers who for years have capitalized on the endorsements of movie stars with ultimate injury to both stars and the motion picture industry.'

In 1934 Warners also made deals with Quaker Oats ($91,000 worth of cereal and bicycle advertising for a Joe E. Brown film, *6 Day Bike Rider*) and Farrar and Rinehart, publishers of the best-selling *Anthony Adverse*. The book was made into a major film, one that inaugurated a cycle of Warner historical films tied to highly advertised novels. To further promote *Anthony Adverse*, a $10,000 contest was announced in *Photoplay* with tie-in prizes of five Ford automobiles, a United Air Lines trip to the World's Fair, a Tecla necklace, six Orry-Kelly gowns, and Mojud stockings. *Sales Management* reported that the merchandise connected with *Anthony Adverse* was expected to develop nearly as great a dollar sales as the picture.

While Warners probably secured more major tie-ups than any other studio, MGM ran it a close race. We can illustrate its exploitational technique by examining the pressbook for *Dinner At Eight*, the studio's most ambitiously promoted film of 1934. A page of photos of department store displays arranged in many cities was captioned, 'The merchandising value of Jean Harlow's name was never better demonstrated than by the dozens of *Dinner At Eight* fashion and show windows.' The next page was headed, 'Tie-ups A Million Dollars Worth of Promotion' and included this text: '250,000 Coca-Cola dealers will exploit *Dinner at Eight*. First visible evidence of the extensiveness of this national arrangement between the largest selling soft drink in America and MGM, which has individually and collectively the greatest star power names in the industry, appears in September 1933 issues of *Saturday Evening Post*, *Colliers*, *Liberty*, and the *Country Gentleman* – full color pages advertising the rare entertainment qualities of *Dinner at Eight*.' In addition, Coca-Cola delivery trucks would carry side billboards advertising the film. Other tie-ups, accompanied by relevant stills from the film, included Max Factor cosmetics, Lux Soap (full page newspaper ads), Gillette Safety Razor Co., Lord and Taylor Hats, *Modern Screen*, A. S. Beck Shoes (four-column ads in New York newspapers) and Marconigrams. Dozens of opportunities for local tie-ups were provided by other products appearing in the film: furniture, dinner settings, chocolates, shaving brushes, watches, clocks, and so forth. The dress worn by Madge Evans had been shown in Macy's window and was available in Cinema Shops.

Both studios must have monitored audience reactions carefully and half expected the epiphany of another P. S. Harrison. But the new formula worked. The audience, after all, was not assailed with brand names, merely by the products themselves. The exhibitor did not feel that his screen was obviously usurped. Perhaps most importantly, the tie-ups increased the advertising revenues of magazines and newspapers, the most effective critics of the sponsored shorts of 1931. Through the rest of the thirties, all of the major studios adopted and helped to perfect this system. In its classic – or perhaps Hellenistic – form, the head of exploitation supervised an effort that coordinated the creation of the script (tie-ups were often formative influences), the breakdown of the script into categories of products and services, and the search for sponsors. Wilma Freeman of Warners told *Nation's Business* in 1940 that she asked first to design 'a product that conforms with the picture.'

In return Ms. Freeman offered the sponsor 12,000 theaters and an audience of 80,000,000 each week. When the product came through, a star was posed with it and the pressbook was made up. The formula, as a mathematician would say, had achieved elegance.

Because this system won wide acceptance in the late 1930s it became possible to insert some brand names into films again. They were inserted sparingly and as realistically as possible. Examples are: Kay Francis in *First Lady* (Warners, 1937) stating that 'Ford always makes good cars'; Spencer Tracy in *Test Pilot* (MGM, 1938) asking for 'two Coca-Colas, please'; and Barbara Stanwyck in *Always Goodbye* (20th Century-Fox, 1938), asking for a ticket 'on the Normandie.' The offering of props for films also became highly organized. Two of the largest agencies, the Walter E. Kline Agency and the Stanley-Murphy Service Agency, solicited properties and placed them for a small fee. Certain manufacturers sent their latest models to these agencies as a matter of course.

We can gain considerable insight into Hollywood's role in the evolution of consumerism, and into many of the characteristics of films of the 1930s and later, by combining this history with all the elements we have so far discussed in isolation. First we have an economy suddenly aware of the importance of the consumer and of the dominant role of women in the purchasing of most consumer items. (Consumer statistics widely disseminated in the late 1920s and early 1930s show that women made 80 to 90 percent of all purchases for family use. They bought 48 percent of drugs, 96 percent of dry goods, 87 percent of raw products, 98 percent of automobiles.) Second we have a film industry committed to schemes for product display and tie-ins, schemes that brought some direct revenue to the studios but more importantly reduced prop and art department and advertising overheads. Add to all this a star system dominated by women – at MGM Shearer, Loy, Harlow, Garbo, Russell, Crawford, Goddard, Lombard, Turner, Lamarr; at Warners Davis, Francis, Stanwyck, Young, Chatterton, and so on – hundreds of women stars and starlets available to the studio publicity, sales tie-in departments as – to use the favored phrase – merchandising assets.

On one, more local, level, the combination of all these factors had some obvious and immediate effects on the kinds of films that were made. There appeared a steady output of films dominated by starlets – those hundreds of 'women's films,' which are of such interest to feminist critics like Molly Haskell and Marjorie Rosen. In addition, Hollywood developed a preference for 'modern films,' because of the opportunities they offered for product display and tie-ins. In many instances storylines were reshaped, to provide more shooting in locales suitable for tie-ins. Movies were made in fashion salons, department stores, beauty parlors, middle- and upper-class homes with modern kitchens and bathrooms, large living rooms, and so forth.

On another level, the studio tie-ins became important far beyond the influence they exerted on the kinds of films made. It is to this more comprehensive level that I would move as I draw back from the cluttered summary I have led you through, to make some larger suggestions, not just about merchandising's contribution to Hollywood but about Hollywood's contributions to the form and character of consumerism itself. By the early 1930s, market analyses were talking about the sovereignty of the consumer, the importance of women as purchasers, and the necessity of learning more about their tastes and predilections. By the early 1940s, market research had been invented, with its studies of the hidden needs and desires of consumers and its discovery that many products were bought for their images, their associations, or the psychological gratifications they provided. Between these two movements Hollywood had cooperated in a massive effort to sell products employing a sales method that was essentially covert, associational, and linked to the deeply gratifying and habituating experiences that films provided. Furthermore, the many fine sensibilities of Hollywood's designers, artists, cameramen, lighting men, directors, and composers had lent themselves, even if coincidentally, to the establishment of powerful bonds between the emotional fantasy-generating substance of films and the material objects those films contained.

One can argue only from inference that Hollywood gave consumerism a distinctive bent, but what a massive base this inference can claim. Tens of millions of Americans provided the captive audience for the unique experiments in consumer manipulation, that the showcasing of products in films and through star endorsements constituted. And this audience reacted so predictably that every large manufacturer in America would have bought its own small MGM had this been possible. Instead they were forced to await the advent of television with its socially acceptable juxtaposition of commercials and entertainment. The form television commercials have taken, their fusion of images augmented by editing and camera techniques, with music, lyrics, and charismatic personalities, is obviously an extension of the techniques pioneered by Hollywood.

But is it equally obvious, as market researchers have claimed, that consumerism is grounded in psychological universals? What should we ascribe to the potent acculturation provided by Hollywood for several decades? Were we, as consumers, such skilled and habituated perceivers of libidinal cues, such receptive audiences for associational complexes, such romanticizers of homes, stores, and highways before Hollywood gave us *Dinner At Eight*, *The Big Store*, and *The Pace That Kills?* I would suggest that we were not, that Hollywood, drawing upon the resources of literature, art, and music, did as much or more than any other force in capitalist culture to smooth the operation of the production-consumption cycle by fetishizing products and putting the libido in libidinally invested advertising.

Reading 26

Jeff Smith

SELLING MY HEART

Music and cross-promotion in *Titanic*

'Selling My Heart: Music and Cross-Promotion in *Titanic*', in K. S. Sandler and G. Studlar (eds), *Titanic: Anatomy of a Blockbuster*, New Brunswick, NJ: Rutgers University Press, 1999, pp. 46–60.

THROUGHOUT ITS HISTORY, Hollywood has long used music to sell films and vice versa.[1] During the silent era, for example, several exhibitors included song slides and singers as special attractions in their programs. The singers were frequently employed by music publishers for the express purpose of 'plugging' a particular tune. In exchange for the plug, the exhibitor typically sold copies of sheet music in the theater and retained a small percentage of the monies from such sales.[2] This period also witnessed the rise of the 'musical illustration' as a specific film genre. According to Charles Merrell Berg, these films were a variation of the song slide principle since they were created not only to accompany a specific song but also to illustrate that song dramatically. Interest in this genre culminated in the late teens with two series of song illustrations produced by Harry Cohn and Carl Laemmle respectively. By featuring song slides and filmed 'illustrations' of music, movie theaters joined department stores, music shops, and vaudeville as important venues for song-plugging and as hubs of a multimillion-dollar industry.[3]

The practice of using song slides gradually died out in the 1920s when composers began writing specific theme songs for films. Although sheet music sales for film themes were generally modest in the early years of that decade, the music industry took note of the promotional possibilities proffered by a specially composed or compiled film score. Early sound films reversed this trend, however, with the estimable success of 'Charmaine' from *What Price Glory?* (1926) and 'Diane' from *Seventh Heaven* (1927). In the wake of these successful theme scores, which were typically organized around a single prominent tune, record companies advised their retailers that 'each week the tune studded talking picture leaves customers of yours with impressively presented theme songs echoing in their ears.'[4]

With the coming of sound, several studios began buying music publishing houses in order to gain copyright control of the songs that appeared in their films. Although Paramount and Loew's were the first to buy their own publishing houses, Warner Bros. proved to be the most aggressive in its acquisitions. In January of 1929, Warners purchased the original Tin Pan Alley house, M. Witmark & Sons, and shortly thereafter acquired interests in the Harms Music Publishing Company, the Remick Music Corporation, and a host of smaller music houses. By mid-1929, Warners' newly formed music division commanded a major share of the music publishers' vote in the American Society of Composers, Authors, and Publishers (ASCAP), the major performance rights organization in the United States.[5] By 1939, the thirteen music houses affiliated with Hollywood earned about two-thirds of the total monies distributed to publishers by ASCAP.[6]

When sheet music sales declined in the 1950s, due in part to competition from the burgeoning market for recorded music, Hollywood turned to new forms of cross-promotion, such as the soundtrack album and theme song single. Between 1957 and 1958, several film distributors, among them Paramount, Twentieth Century Fox, and United Artists, followed the lead of MGM and Universal by either buying or starting up their own record subsidiaries. Hollywood's sudden interest in recorded music was at least partly spurred by the resurgence of the theme score in the mid-1950s. The success of musical tie-ins for films like *High Noon* (1952), *Love Is a Many Splendored Thing* (1955), and *A Summer Place* (1959) led to a rash of imitators, and soon producers were commissioning pop songs to serve as the basis of theme scores.[7]

Generally speaking, however, Hollywood was less interested in the outright sale of records than it was in using records and radio as promotional vehicles for film scores and theme songs. Consequently, most studios approached their cross-promotional campaigns much as a publisher or song plugger would. Rather than seek sales and exposure of a particular version of a theme song, film companies simply sought as much repetition of the tune as possible and often commissioned several recordings of the song, each released by a different label. By authorizing multiple versions of the song, studios not only enhanced the tune's overall licensing revenues but also increased its chances for heavy radio play.[8]

When a film theme clicked, the benefits of this multiple exposure became obvious. During a single week in 1961, Ernest Gold's theme for *Exodus* (1960) was featured on four different albums in *Billboard's Top Fifty*. In addition, *Exodus*'s soundtrack spent fourteen weeks at the top of the charts, a record for score albums that was only recently broken by *Titanic*. Similarly, Manos Hadjidakis's theme from *Never on Sunday* (1960) was recorded more than thirty times in the United States, and more than four hundred times worldwide. Together these different versions of the song accounted for sales of approximately 14 million singles. Through its sales and airplay, a hit song or album could easily supply as much as $1 million's worth of 'cuffo promotion.'[9]

Although the record industry's climate of 'profitless prosperity' encouraged some studios to sell off their record interests during the 1970s, the soundtrack album remained a key component of film promotion, its position sustained by several notable hits, including *The Graduate* (1967), *Easy Rider* (1969), *American Graffiti* (1973), *Saturday Night Fever* (1977), and *Grease* (1978). By 1979, the role of film and music cross-promotions had become so standardized that there was a general industry awareness of what was necessary to create a hit soundtrack: '[C]ommercially viable music. Timing. Film cooperation on advance planning and tie-ins. Music that's integral to the movie. A hit movie. A hit single. A big-name recording star. A big-name composer.'[10] While not all of these ingredients were absolutely essential, the absence of one or two could spell the difference between a soundtrack's overall success or failure. The 1980s saw minor changes in this formula following music video's emergence as an additional ancillary market for film music. By 1985, the typical film and music cross-promotion operated according to a concise formula that R. Serge Denisoff and George Plasketes express as 'movie + soundtrack + video = $$$.'[11]

Of these ingredients, timing is perhaps the most critical element. Since 1960, the conventional wisdom about soundtracks is that they should be released about four to six weeks before the film's general release in order to give the music an opportunity to work its way up the charts and circulate the film's title in radio and retail markets.[12] The same generally holds true for theme songs and music videos. In theory, a so-called scout single generates positive buzz for the film, which in turn creates consumer interest in the film's theme song and soundtrack album. As record executive Danny Goldberg explained in coining the term 'synergy' to describe such cross-promotions, interest in one component synergistically feeds off interest in the other until both film and soundtrack album reign supreme over box offices and record charts.[13] To illustrate the effect of such tie-ins, industry analysts conservatively estimate that a successful theme song can add as much as $20 million to a film's box office take.

Yet most cross-promotional campaigns work better in theory than in actual practice. As Denisoff and Plasketes point out, several films succeed despite the lack of consumer interest in their music ancillaries.[14] Similarly, soundtrack albums like *Above the Rim* (1994) and *The Crow* (1994) sometimes outpace their counterparts by attracting record buyers who have never seen the films they accompany. In still other instances, both film and soundtrack fail in their respective markets. When problems occur, they can often be traced to difficulties coordinating the release schedules of album and film. After all, although film companies, music publishers, and record labels all exploit soundtracks through a kind of joint venture, one company's short-term economic interests may impinge on its cooperation with the other two points of the cross-promotional triangle. Because they are primarily interested in the soundtrack's promotional function, film companies generally want to coordinate the album's release with the film's release. Record labels, on the other hand, realize most of their profits in album sales and are thus more inclined to schedule releases that are favorable to the album itself or to the recording artists who participate in the soundtrack. (Executives often view soundtrack cuts as stopgap measures designed to keep artists in the public eye between major releases.) Publishers, however, derive their revenues from licensing fees. As such, they show comparatively greater interest in pushing the film's theme song in the hope that it will become an 'evergreen,' an oft-recorded standard like 'Moon River' that will generate revenues for many years to come.

Not only did the *Titanic* soundtrack pose fewer scheduling problems than a multiartist pop compilation usually does, but it benefited from the careful coordination of music and film interests. Yet the success of *Titanic*'s soundtrack might never have occurred if composer James Horner had strictly adhered to the instructions given to him by director James Cameron. Horner and Cameron had previously collaborated on *Aliens* (1986), but their experience working together on that film was one of mutual frustration. According to Horner, 'It was a very difficult experience for both of us, because there was so little time for such a mammoth job. I wasn't able to give him everything he wanted.'[15] After receiving several Oscar nominations for such scores as *Apollo 13* (1995) and *Braveheart* (1995), Horner reunited with Cameron on *Titanic*. The two met in February 1997 during the final two months of filming, and Cameron reportedly gave Horner two simple instructions: no standard orchestration and no pop songs.[16]

After starting work on *Titanic*, however, Horner soon decided that the best way to capture Rose's feelings at film's end and the best way to give the film a timeless, yet contemporary appeal was to compose a song for the closing credits. To that end, Horner secretly hired lyricist Will Jennings to write words for the tune and got longtime friend Celine Dion to surreptitiously record a demo in May of 1997 at New York's Hit Factory. Knowing the problems with their previous collaboration, Horner withheld the tape from Cameron for about three weeks until he was sure he had established a good rapport with the director. Then after what Horner describes as a 'good long streak of positive vibes,' the composer played the tape for Cameron in his study. After hearing it two or three times, the director was sold.[17]

Horner's decision to use Jennings and Dion proved wise from a commercial standpoint because each had well-established track records for film. In fact, all three of them had worked together once before on the song 'Dreams to Dream' for the film *An American Tail: Fievel Goes West* (1991). More important, though, Jennings had penned lyrics for six previous chart-topping singles, most notably Joe Cocker and Jennifer Warnes's recording of 'Up Where We Belong' for the film *An Officer and a Gentleman* (1982). Films had played an equally important role in Celine Dion's buildup as a recording artist. According to her husband and manager, Rene Angelil, her organization made a decision in 1991 to use movie work as 'a way for her to get known quickly.'[18] Dion's team then pursued several plum film assignments and succeeded in placing her on the soundtracks for *Beauty and the Beast* (1991), *Sleepless in Seattle* (1993), and *Up Close and Personal* (1996). After the latter spawned a huge hit with 'Because You Loved Me,' Dion became widely regarded as an artist who specialized in romantic movie themes. Not surprisingly, she is pitched to some twenty films each year.[19] More than that, however, Dion's soundtrack participation helped her become one of the top-five recording artists in the industry with sales of her 1995 album, *Falling Into You*, tallying more than 25 million units worldwide.

Even before Dion's involvement, however, Horner and Cameron began peddling the soundtrack rights to the *Titanic* score. Citing the soundtrack's estimated $1-million price tag, several labels turned them down, including Polygram, which had previously released Horner's score for *Braveheart* in 1995. The soundtrack finally found a home at Sony Classical, which bought the rights as part of a broader plan to use film scores as a way of sustaining the label's fortunes.[20] In October 1997, Sony Classical announced that *Titanic* would be released as part of a long-term, exclusive deal with Horner. Under the terms of this contract, Sony Classical secured the rights to several of Horner's future projects, including a ballet score as well as a symphonic work based on his themes for *Titanic*.[21]

Meanwhile, Horner frantically worked to ready his score for *Titanic*'s initial release date of 4 July. Although composers work under great duress in the best of circumstances, Horner's problems were exacerbated by *Titanic*'s three-hour running time and by the production's late reshoots, which threatened to cut even further into the composer's work schedule. When Cameron's rough cut was finally ready, Horner had approximately six weeks to write and record *Titanic*'s 138-minute score. Horner's furious work pace, however, suddenly slackened when *Titanic*'s release was pushed back to 19 December. The score continued to evolve throughout the fall of 1997 as Horner refined and polished his work to accommodate the various editing changes made by Cameron.[22]

On 1 November 1997, *Titanic* received its world premiere at the Tokyo International Film Festival. There were several reasons for choosing Tokyo as the site of the film's premiere, chief among them being the popularity of Cameron, Dion, and Leonardo DiCaprio within the Japanese entertainment market. The decision proved to be a shrewd one on the part of *Titanic*'s production and marketing team for the film's screening sold out within a matter of minutes. The clamor for tickets undoubtedly helped create a positive buzz for the film, as did reports that the festival's office was 'inundated with requests from domestic and international media for press passes as well as from scores of U.S. movie execs.'[23] The Tokyo premiere's combination of intense curiosity, high expectations, and a largely receptive local audience helped give *Titanic* the 'must-see' aura it so desperately needed some six weeks before its U.S. release. Perhaps more important, the laudatory notices sent back by trade reviewers established a welcome precedent for the largely favorable critical reception *Titanic* received in the United States.

About two weeks after the film's premiere, Sony began its campaign on behalf of Horner's score. On 18 November, the company's music group issued two albums featuring *Titanic*'s theme song, 'My Heart Will Go On.' The first, of course, was the *Titanic* soundtrack, and the second was Dion's *Let's Talk About Love*, the much anticipated follow-up to *Falling Into You*. Noting the unusual nature of this simultaneous release, some industry observers questioned the wisdom of Sony's marketing strategy by arguing that the new Dion album could potentially siphon off prospective buyers of the soundtrack.

In retrospect, such fears proved to be quite unfounded. For one thing, it is rather unlikely that Sony saw these two albums as competing products in the first place. After all, the respective targets for each album – a small, largely male, niche market of film score connoisseurs for the *Titanic* soundtrack; a massive, largely female, adult contemporary audience for Dion – are rather different indeed, and the expectation of sales for each album would be calculated accordingly. Sony undoubtedly anticipated the multiplatinum success of Dion's album but probably only hoped to top about 100,000 in sales of the *Titanic* soundtrack. Moreover, Sony executives must have recognized that each album would have a rather different sales pattern. To use a film analogy, Dion's album is the record industry equivalent of a blockbuster receiving a saturation booking. Released for the crucial holiday sales period, *Let's Talk About Love* was virtually guaranteed a significant number of sales and extensive airplay. In contrast, the *Titanic* soundtrack is closer to a 'sleeper' film that requires a platform release pattern in order to build strong word of mouth. As such, Sony executives would expect sales of the soundtrack to be sluggish until the film was released in theaters. Once the film was out, the album, which is almost entirely instrumental, would depend heavily on the film for whatever financial success it could muster.

Viewed from this perspective, the simultaneous release not only reveals the interdependent logics behind the *Titanic* campaign but also offers a textbook example of film and record industry synergies at work. On the one hand, the release of Dion's album in November accords with industry wisdom that the Christmas season is a peak period of buying. In fact, it has become axiomatic for record labels to hold back greatest hits packages or major new releases until the holidays in order to take advantage of those occasional consumers who purchase compact discs as gifts and stocking stuffers. In 1997, several companies hoped that new releases by Dion, Garth Brooks, and the Spice Girls would help boost overall sales figures and salvage a somewhat moribund year. On the other hand, both the soundtrack and the Dion album would help promote *Titanic* during the crucial month-long period before the film's release. The immediate hoopla surrounding Dion's album would help garner airplay for 'My Heart Will Go On,' while the use of the song in trailers would highlight the film's romantic story line by taking advantage of 'Queen Celine's' previous track record with melodramatic ballads. The month-long window would also give Dion's album a chance to ascend to the Top Ten at the time *Titanic* was released to theaters. In return, *Titanic*'s opening weekend would help give Dion's album one final push in the week before Christmas and, at least in theory, would help sustain sales of both albums during the early part of 1998.

The plan's success is evident in the chart action achieved by both the two albums and the theme song. Although it did not reach number one on *Billboard*'s charts until January of 1998, *Let's Talk About Love* became the fastest-selling album of Dion's career. Within two months, it had sold more than 3 million copies domestically and more than 12 million worldwide. Attesting to her popularity abroad, the album achieved platinum status in twenty-four sales territories, including Norway, France, Hong Kong, and Japan.[24] According to its most recent tally, *Let's Talk About Love* showed sales of more than 8 million units in the United States and a comparable number abroad.

If anything, the chart performance of the *Titanic* soundtrack was even more astonishing. As expected, sales of the soundtrack were slow at first, but before the year was out, the album debuted at number 154 on *Billboard*'s Top 200. The following week it leaped to 72, and the week after that it hit 31. By 17 January, some two months after the album's release, the soundtrack neared the Top Ten with overall sales in the neighborhood of 1 million units. Describing the soundtrack's initial sales pattern, Eric Vaughan, a major label buyer for the retailer Disc Jockey, said, 'We really didn't see anything happening with the album until the movie opened. Then it just snowballed.'[25] To the surprise of nearly everyone, the album reached number one on 24 January and stayed there for a record-breaking sixteen weeks.

Even more impressively, weekly sales of both albums increased throughout the month of February. During the week of 14 February, the *Titanic* soundtrack sold more than 580,000 units, while Dion's album tallied a sum of 236,000.[26] Buoyed by sales from Valentine's Day shopping, both albums posted huge gains during the next two weeks. By the end of February, the soundtrack was selling a whopping 850,000 copies a week, while Dion's album experienced a slightly smaller sales bulge to 339,000 units. As the two top-selling albums of that week, *Titanic* and *Let's Talk About Love* together tallied more than the combined sales of the eight remaining albums in the Top Ten. As Geoff Mayfield put it, 'So large was the growth that, if an album sold only what *Titanic* gained – 259,000 units – it would have ranked No. 3 for the week.'[27] By the start of March, worldwide sales of the *Titanic* soundtrack reached more than 10 million as the album leaped to number one in some twenty-one countries.

More significant from a promotional perspective, the film's theme song, 'My Heart Will Go On,' broke broadcasting records by racking up the largest number of radio performances measured in one week. According to data provided by *Billboard*'s Broadcast Data Systems (BDS), Dion's single logged nearly 9,500 spins from some 223 different radio stations during the first week of February. Some stations were playing the song as many as seventy-three times a week or approximately once every two hours. Not surprisingly, with the song reaching some 105 million listeners, 'My Heart Will Go On' also broke the record for the largest radio audience ever monitored by BDS.[28]

While Dion's single was largely played within Top Forty formats, the song garnered additional performances in Adult Contemporary and Dance formats through cover versions recorded by Kenny G and Deja Vu respectively. The Kenny G recording was initially intended to serve only as a promotional item, a behind-the-counter premium given away to consumers who purchased Kenny G's *Greatest Hits* package.[29] In addition, radio also began circulating a version of the song that spliced five audio clips from the film. The ploy, which had first succeeded with Bruce Springsteen's recording of 'Secret Garden' from *Jerry McGuire* (1996), used sound bites to illustrate the dramatic arc of Rose and Jack's relationship in the film, and it enabled listeners to 'relive the three-hour plus film in 4:40 minutes.'[30] VH1 also used this 'audio drop-in' technique to create a special video for 'Southampton,' the second single off the *Titanic* soundtrack.

Like the sales of the *Titanic* soundtrack, the song's airplay was significantly boosted by the popularity of the film. John Ivey, program director at Boston's WXKS, noted that although the song got a great response even before *Titanic* was released to theaters, the mania surrounding the film cemented its popularity among the radio station's largely female listeners. Moreover, Dion's record distributor reported that radio stations were being deluged with listener requests that coincided with the times the film was being let out. According to Hilary Shaev, 550 Music's senior vice president of promotion, moviegoers who had just left the theater were calling to request the song from their car phones.[31] If this is true, it means that spectators were hearing the song as they made their way out of the theater and were calling to hear it again almost as soon as they reached the parking lot.

As of this writing, the *Titanic* soundtrack has chalked up sales of 10 million albums in the United States. A bonanza for all concerned, the album's success has been especially important to Horner and Sony Classical. According to *Variety*, Horner is expected to receive more than $20 million in royalties from sales of the soundtrack, a figure that is comparable to the asking price of major stars like John Travolta and Jim Carrey.[32] The album has also been a major boon to its record company, which on the average sells about five hundred copies a week of works from the canon of Western classical music. Not surprisingly, the *Titanic* soundtrack is expected to bring in more revenues than Sony Classical's entire catalogue did in 1997.[33] Moreover, both Horner and Sony Classical expect to receive additional revenues from something we won't see from the film: a sequel. A second album, *Return to Titanic*, was issued in the fall of 1998, its release timed to coincide with the release of the film as a sell-through home video. The album features some cues from Horner's score that were not included on the first album, some of the Irish dance music, and 'Nearer My God to Thee,' which is played in the film by a string quartet as the *Titanic* sinks.[34] Although sales of *Return to Titanic* will not match that of the first album, it quickly leaped to number two on *Billboard*'s album charts and is expected to become the industry's best-selling soundtrack sequel.

Few people could have predicted the soundtrack's amazing chart run, but then again few people anticipated the film's $1.8-billion gross. Most of the album's fortunes can be traced to the film itself. As Sony Music's president, Tommy Mottola, puts it, 'The success of the film was the greatest marketing advantage that any company could have.'[35] Yet the album's success should not have been entirely unexpected. After all, the marketing of the album relied on a cross-promotional formula that has been conventional wisdom in the industry for decades. Returning for a moment to the 1979 *Billboard* article that enumerated the ingredients necessary for a hit soundtrack, the *Titanic* campaign had most if not all of them: a big-name composer in Horner, a big-name recording star in Dion, a hit single, a hit movie, and music that is integral to the film. More than that, however, the campaign was also impeccably timed. The tandem release of *Let's Talk About Love* and the *Titanic* soundtrack enabled 'My Heart Will Go On' to garner moderate radio play during the crucial period leading up to the film's release. Once *Titanic* was in theaters, both the single and the soundtrack album rode on the film's coattails to the top of the charts. The sales performance of the *Titanic* soundtrack was unprecedented for a film score; the campaign it used to achieve that success most certainly was not.

The commercial fortunes of the *Titanic* soundtrack are only part of the story, however. As I noted earlier, an important aspect of the public's consumption of Dion's recording derived from the film score's ability to elicit recall of one's emotional responses to the film.[36] As any number of industry analysts point out, spectators are more likely to purchase the film's score in its commodity form if the music is 'married' to strong dramatic material. For this reason, one must examine a film song's dramatic functions alongside its commodity functions insofar as one cannot be completely understood without the other. In this section, I will take a closer look at the score's four major musical themes in order to highlight the ways in which each serves the film's narrative. In doing so, I intend to show how Horner uses the popular song's form to cleverly intertwine elements from two of the score's main themes. Through this musical gesture, 'My Heart Will Go On' brings together several of *Titanic*'s thematic concerns to provide an aural correlative of the film's synthesis of historical spectacle, class politics, and romantic sacrifice.

To begin with, though, a few comments about the score's overall concept and musical style are in order. According to Horner, both he and Cameron wanted to avoid doing a 'Hollywood 1940s type big-drama score.'[37] On its face, Horner's assertion would appear to be patently absurd insofar as his score shares several compositional and stylistic elements with Hollywood scores of the studio era. First, Horner's music is structured around several distinct themes and leitmotifs. Second, by using music to reinforce the film's approach to character, setting, and action, Horner's score also adheres to classical conceptions of dramatic appropriateness. Third, although it achieves its effects through slightly different means, Horner's score also strives for and achieves the range of orchestral color and emotional sweep that is generally associated with Hollywood music. *Titanic*'s adherence to Hollywood convention is perhaps most evident in the cues that underscore the film's moments of suspense, especially those involving the crew's reaction to the iceberg sighting, the efforts to turn the ship to avoid the iceberg, and in several sequences depicting Rose and Jack's attempts to escape the rising waters below deck. Here, Horner relies on several compositional devices that are the film composer's stock-in-trade: agitato string passages, pedal tones, repeated melodic motifs, and chromatically ascending harmonies.

Having said that, a closer examination of *Titanic*'s score reveals a certain substance to Horner's comments. While it does not reject a conception of 'Hollywood music' in toto, the score nonetheless deviates from certain aspects of classical tradition. The most important of these deviations is evident in *Titanic*'s orchestrations. In order to get away from the string-dominated sound of the classical Hollywood era, Horner relies rather heavily on synthesizer and vocal textures, sometimes combining them with the resources of a more conventional orchestra. In doing so, the composer attempted to create a sound that was at once contemporary and elegiac, symphonic in its emotional sweep, but lilting, melancholy, and ethereal in its more intimate moments.[38] A key component of this sound was provided by the wordless vocalizing of Norwegian singing star Sissel. Horner reports that he became enamored with her voice after hearing her albums, which mix native folk elements with New Age music in a manner that has earned Sissel comparisons with the Gaelic superstar Enya. Not surprisingly, Sissel's involvement in *Titanic* has brought accusations that Horner merely aped the sound of Enya, a charge which has a certain merit when one considers the fact that Cameron used the latter's 'Book of Days' in an early trailer.[39] But even if it was true, the similarities between *Titanic*'s music and Enya are more or less beside the point. Horner himself admits that such comparisons are pretty much unavoidable for anyone using Gaelic idioms. More important, Horner's mix of synthesizers and vocals neatly positioned *Titanic*'s soundtrack to straddle several niche markets, namely, Worldbeat and New Age. In fact, although it is difficult to prove, one might speculate that Sissel's participation played a vital role in the soundtrack's performance in international markets.

In addition to its orchestrations, *Titanic*'s music differs from the classical Hollywood score in its handling of leitmotifs and themes. In contrast to something like John Barry's 'James Bond Theme,' which serves as a kind of aural tag for the series's central character, Horner's leitmotifs tend to develop a looser association between musical ideas and cinematic elements. *Titanic*'s major musical themes are rarely tied to specific characters or settings, but rather are linked more generally to a cluster of related motifs and concepts. A good example of this is the twinkly piano motif used to accompany Rose's reminiscence of her experience on *Titanic.* This musical motif, the first of four major themes I will discuss, is introduced in the film's prologue during the scene in which Brock Lovett's crew examines the contents recovered from Cal's safe. Although they have failed to find the diamond, Le Coeur de la mer (the Heart of the Ocean), we see the nude sketch of Rose being cleaned, a drawing which at least offers some proof of the diamond's existence. The tinkling piano motif mentioned above first appears under the shot of this sketch and returns shortly thereafter as the older Rose overhears a television report on the exploration of the sunken ship. At least initially, this piano melody appears to be a leitmotif for Rose herself. Subsequent appearances of the motif, however, link it more specifically to Rose as an old woman as well as to the ideas of memory and lost love. This is especially evident in the scene in which Jack shows Rose the sketch he made of Madame Bijou, an elderly Parisian woman who would sit at a bar every night, wearing all of her jewelry and waiting for her long lost love. The tinkly piano motif returns under the insert of Jack's drawing of Madame Bijou, a musical gesture which links her to the elderly Rose. In doing so, Horner's score offers an eerie foreshadowing of what Rose might have become if she had not heeded Jack's urgent plea to survive, marry, and have children.

The second major theme is one that is largely associated with the sea. Although it appears on the soundtrack in several guises, it first appears under the film's opening credits played in unison by a flute and human voice (Sissel). The tune itself is reminiscent of a Celtic sea chantey, a compositional choice which not only highlights the film's British and North Atlantic locales but also serves to musically underline the social divisions depicted in *Titanic* . . . Horner's score contributes to this characterization by yoking musical signifiers of 'Irishness' to the film's representation of laborers and passengers in steerage. This is especially true of the film's source music (i.e., music that occurs within the world of the story), which reinforces this linkage by contrasting the lively drinking and dancing that occurs in steerage with the stultifying conversation and social gamesmanship that occurs during Jack's dinner with the social elite. The former is accompanied by the folk music of an Irish band; the latter, by the ship orchestra's performance of light classics. Moreover, Celtic folk music also accompanies the sequences in which Jack and his friend Fabrizio make their mad dash to board the ship, and during Jack and Rose's journey through the ship's 'lower depths' in an effort to elude Spicer Lovejoy, the henchman of Cal Hockley, Rose's fiancé.

While class difference in the film is signaled by the spatial divisions of the ship, especially the differences between those above and below deck, *Titanic*'s music slightly refines those divisions by ascribing cultural values to each side. More specifically, the Celtic touches in Horner's score associate the working class with nature rather than culture, with eroticism and physical pleasure rather than intellectual or commercial pursuits, and with romantic love rather than social propriety. Viewed in this light, the opening cue develops associations with two different but interrelated thematic clusters in the film: one identified with the sea, the mysteries of nature, and the cruelties of fate; the other identified with *Titanic*'s dead, many of whom were poor Irish laborers and passengers. Later appearances of the theme serve to reinforce this elegiac function through a more general association with death.

The theme underscores the scenes in which Rose contemplates suicide as she hangs on the railing of the ship's stern; her gradual realization toward the end of the film that Jack has frozen to death beside her; and the montage of the survivors waiting for 'an absolution that would never come.'

The third major musical theme of *Titanic* is associated with the ship itself, especially those moments that highlight its power and majesty. Elements of this 'ship' theme first appear in a couple of brief cues showing Lovett's recovery mission, but the theme gets its most vivid exposition in 'Southampton,' which plays under the sequences showing Titanic's boarding and departure. It returns shortly after, cued by Captain Smith's order to 'Take Her to Sea, Mr. Murdoch.' The montage that accompanies this latter version of the theme illustrates the various workings of the ship and culminates in the shots of Jack perched at the ship's prow, arms outstretched, yelling, 'I'm the King of the World.' Horner's use of synthesized textures is most evident in these two cues, which alternate chordal passages with a soaring, heroic melody. To suggest this sense of triumph, Horner structures the first two bars of his melody around the outline of a D major chord, then follows that with a dramatic octave leap on the tonic. While such wide leaps are a rather conventional device for suggesting heroism, Horner adds a bit of tonal color to the theme by using a low D as a pedal tone. As a result, the metric accents of the melody thus appear to fall on the passing tones rather than on the notes of the tonic triad suggested by the pedal tone. With its synthesized textures and heroic melody, several critics and industry analysts have compared this 'ship' theme to Vangelis's popular theme for *Chariots of Fire* (1981).

By far the most important of the four themes, however, is *Titanic*'s love theme, 'My Heart Will Go On.' As a leitmotif representing the relationship between Rose and Jack, the theme underscores several of the film's most memorable moments, among them the scene in which Rose poses for Jack's drawing; Rose and Jack's first kiss on the prow of the ship, the couple's steamy encounter in the back of a Renault; Rose's tearful good-bye to Jack after climbing aboard a lifeboat; Rose's rescue; and her final dream vision of being reunited with Jack on the ship's grand staircase. As I noted earlier, the emotional intensity of these scenes and their role in furthering the romantic plotline of the film were important factors in coaxing film audiences to seek out the soundtrack. Yet the emotional impact of these scenes was also enhanced by the restraint with which the music is used. Horner's orchestrations for these scenes tend toward smaller ensembles that frequently pit solo instruments against synthesized and orchestral backgrounds. These lighter textures nicely underplay the emotional elements of the love story's most dramatic moments. Instead of the sweeping, melodramatic, and sentimental sounds that we typically associate with Hollywood, Cameron and Horner opt for a quieter, more lyrical, more subdued approach to the orchestration and dynamics of *Titanic*'s love theme.

Yet while Cameron's skillful handling of these scenes brought the necessary emotional connection between music and audience, the theme's commercial prospects were enhanced by certain structural features of the song itself. All of these structural features serve two important functions within the song insofar as they not only furnish it with memorable hooks but also communicate a requisite sense of drama and romantic passion.[40] As was true of the 'ship' theme, *Titanic*'s love theme also features a dramatic octave leap in the third bar of the song's chorus. The rising and falling shape of the melody here endows the theme with a certain emotive significance, one fraught with feelings of heroism, tragedy, and desire. Moreover, as the tune moves from verse to chorus, the shift from major to minor sonorities serves a somewhat similar function. As Robert Walser points out in his analysis of Bon Jovi's 'Livin' on a Prayer,' such shifts in modality create a contrast and corresponding tension between two affective states. The octave leap in 'My Heart Will Go On' – its 'moment of transcendence,' to use Walser's phrase – thus coincides with a return to an A major chord, the subdominant in the song's home key of E major. Thus, like the Bon Jovi song, 'My Heart Will Go On' uses the modal contrasts between verse and chorus to musically signify the rapturous dimension of romantic union.[41] Finally, a second moment of transcendence occurs with the dramatic key change from E to A flat major that occurs before the last chorus. On Celine Dion's single, this moment is reinforced by a thickening of musical textures and an increase in dynamic intensity. When combined with the rise in pitch, these structural features create one last emotional surge that is ultimately resolved by the song's cadence and the final diminution of its coda.

More important, perhaps, Horner uses a harmonic motif common to all three themes – the 'sea' theme, the 'ship' theme, and the love theme – to create a thematically and motivically integrated score. The musical figure to which I am referring here is a series of descending chords that move from the submediant to the dominant and back again. This harmonic pattern is used both in the chorus of 'My Heart Will Go On' and in the opening phrase of the score's 'sea' theme. In addition, a slightly more developed variation of it appears in the chordal passages of the 'ship' theme. From a dramatic perspective, such thematic integration offers several advantages to a film composer. For one thing, it endows the score with an overarching sense of musical unity and organicity. For another, it enables the composer to move smoothly from one theme to another and to interweave different themes or leitmotifs throughout the score. By integrating these harmonic and melodic elements, Horner was able to create a score that seems deceptively simple, but in fact contains several kinds of musical and semiotic complexity.

Yet Horner's synthesis of musical themes was also important from a commercial perspective. In Dion's recording of 'My Heart Will Go On' and in several cues in the film, Horner rather cleverly incorporates elements of the 'sea' theme into the song's introduction and into the transitional passages that move from the song's chorus back to its verse. Through this technique of thematic integration, 'My Heart Will Go On' proves to be more than a simple love song. By yoking together musical signifiers of death, nature, fate, and transcendent love, Horner's tune effectively summons up many of the elements that made *Titanic* a commercial success as a film. Through this system of shared musical associations, 'My Heart Will Go On' not only reminds us of Jack and Rose's undying love but also brings back *Titanic*'s depiction of class struggle, historical spectacle, epic tragedy, and technological folly.

The commercial success of *Titanic*, both as a film and a soundtrack album, was undoubtedly the major story in the entertainment industry last year. As a score album, *Titanic* generally lacked the commercially savvy sound exhibited by many hit soundtracks, but nonetheless featured a highly regarded composer in James Horner, a bankable recording star in Celine Dion, the promotional backing of Sony Music, and a film that beautifully showcased the score's main musical themes.

Moreover, the campaign for *Titanic*'s soundtrack was carefully timed to make the most of its various elements. Through its immediate exposure on radio, 'My Heart Will Go On' was able to build positive buzz for *Titanic*, which would later translate to positive buzz for the soundtrack album once the film had topped box offices around the world. In addition, Dion's popularity as a romantic balladeer helped to foreground the film's love story in a way that revised early speculation about *Titanic*'s generic predecessors. Once audiences had heard 'My Heart Will Go On,' *Titanic* suddenly seemed less like a disaster film (*The Poseidon Adventure*, 1972 or *Earthquake*, 1974) and more like a film that places romance against the backdrop of historically momentous events (*Gone With the Wind*, 1939, or *Doctor Zhivago*, 1965).

Still, 'My Heart Will Go On' would have had little impact if it were not so effective within its dramatic context. To paraphrase *Variety* columnist Theda Sandiford-Waller, audiences had a much greater appreciation for the song once they had seen the film.[42] In fact, in communities around the country, radio stations were flooded with requests for the song just after screenings of *Titanic* were let out. Much of this emotional attachment to the song came from Horner's skillful use of it during the film's memorable love scenes, but it also derived from the way in which Dion's recording summoned up many of *Titanic*'s narrative elements. Through Horner's techniques of thematic integration, 'My Heart Will Go On' became a complex and multivalent signifier of the film's representations of death, fate, and love.

Yet for all of their dramatic effectiveness, both 'My Heart Will Go On' and the *Titanic* soundtrack will best be remembered in their commodity forms. Through the emotional bonds it built with the film's audience, the score came to function as one of *Titanic*'s many souvenirs. As the elderly Rose says in the film's epilogue, 'A woman's heart is a deep ocean of secrets.' Ultimately, *Titanic* would have no better object to symbolize Rose's heart than Le Coeur de la mer and no better aural object than Horner's 'My Heart Will Go On.' Like the blue diamond, the song serves as a nostalgic memento of lost love, one that quavers with a sense of mystery and eternity.

Notes

1. See D. Gomery, *The Hollywood Studio System*, New York: St. Martin's Press, 1986 and A. Doty, 'Music Sells Movies: (Re) New (ed) Conservatism in Film Marketing,' *Wide Angle*, 1988, vol. 10(2), pp. 70–79. For a more complete overview of the history of film and music cross-promotions, see my recent book, *The Sounds of Commerce: Marketing Popular Film Music*, New York: Columbia University Press, 1998.
2. Charles Merrell Berg, *An Investigation into the Motives for and the Realization of Music to Accompany the American Silent Film*, New York: Arno Press, 1976, p. 254.
3. Ibid., 255.
4. Quoted in A. Millard, *America on Record: A History of Recorded Sound*, New York: Cambridge University Press, 1995, p. 160. For more on the theme score, see K. Kalinak, *Settling the Score: Music in the Classical Hollywood Film*, Madison, WI: University of Wisconsin Press, 1992, pp. 185–187.
5. See R. Sanjek, *American Popular Music and Its Business from 1900 to 1984*, New York: Oxford University Press, 1988, pp. 91–114; and D. Gomery, *The Hollywood Studio System*, pp. 106–110.

6 See R. Sanjek, *From Print to Plastic: Publishing and Promoting America's Popular Music (1900–1980)*, Brooklyn: Institute for Studies in American Music, 1983, p. 19.

7 The composers and lyricists for these songs are as follows: 'Do Not Forsake Me, Oh My Darlin'' from *High Noon* by Dimitri Tiomkin and Ned Washington; 'Love Is a Many Splendored Thing' by Sammy Fain and Paul Francis Webster; 'Theme from *A Summer Place*' by Max Steiner.

8 For a more complete discussion of the way in which these multiple versions help to maintain the record industry's profitability, see T. Anderson, 'Which Voice Becomes the Property?: Tie-Ups, Intertexts, and Versioning in the Production of *My Fair Lady*,' *Spectator*, 1997, vol. 17, pp. 74–91.

9 M. Gross, 'Pix Promotion's Cuffo Ride,' *Variety*, 6 September 1961, pp. 45–46. According to Robert Allen and Douglas Gomery, 'cuffo promotion' lies somewhere between publicity and promotion. It is not 'free' in the same sense as publicity since studios have to pour a certain amount of money into album pressings, rerecording costs, arranging fees, and so forth. However, it is 'free' in the sense that studios do not pay radio stations for airplay or record stores for display space. This contrasts 'cuffo promotion' with things like premiere parties, promotional tours, or even press junkets – all of which entail costs above and beyond production costs and do not offer any kind of financial return. See *Film History: Theory and Practice*, New York: McGraw-Hill, 1985.

10 S. Peterson, 'Selling a Hit Soundtrack,' *Billboard*, 6 October 1979, ST-2.

11 R. S. Denisoff and G. Plasketes, 'Synergy in 1980s Film and Music: Formula for Success or Industry Mythology,' *Film History*, 1990, vol. 4(3), pp. 257–276.

12 The need for a four- to six-week window became most obvious in those situations where this strategy was not used. Problems with the cover art for the *Let's Make Love* soundtrack delayed the album's release until three weeks after the film's premiere. Consequently, the album failed to help the film in key first-run markets. See 'This Is "Love?"' *Variety*, 14 September 1960, p. 43.

13 For a more detailed explication of this theory, see R. S. Denisoff and G. Plasketes, 'Synergy in 1980s Film and Music,' pp. 257–276.

14 In the 1980s, there were several films that succeeded without strong cross-promotional support from a soundtrack. All of the following made over $100 million but had only modest sales for their accompanying albums: *Gremlins* (1984), *Platoon* (1986), *Fatal Attraction* (1987), *Rainman* (1988), and *Lethal Weapon 2* (1989). In 1986, the soundtrack for *Back to the Future* sold barely 500,000 copies despite the fact that the film made more than $200 million and that the album contained a chart-topping single by Huey Lewis and the News ('The Power of Love'). In the 1990s, there were several blockbusters that succeeded without huge albums: *Home Alone* (1990), *Jurassic Park* (1993), *Schindler's List* (1993), and *Independence Day* (1996).

15 Quoted in R. Bennett, 'James Horner,' *Hollywood Reporter*, 13 January 1998, pp. 19–20.

16 D. Browne, 'Star-Ship Enterprise,' *Entertainment Weekly*, online at: <www.ew.com/ew/article/0,,282209,00.html> [accessed 15 July 2008].

17 R. Bennett, 'James Horner,' p. 22; and D. Browne, 'Star-Ship Enterprise,' p. 28.

18 Quoted in D. Browne, 'Star-Ship Enterprise,' p. 33.

19 Ibid.

20 According to Peter Gelb, the president of Sony Classical, 'New Music in the form of soundtracks and other avenues is what the classical record industry is relying upon for a successful future.' Quoted in C. A. Olson, 'Soundtracks and Film Score News,' *Billboard*, 22 November 1997, p. 19.

21 C. A. Olson, 'The Reel Thing,' *Billboard*, 11 October 1997, p. 24; and H. Waleson, 'Classical: Keeping Score,' *Billboard*, 18 November 1997, p. 42.

22 R. Bennett, 'James Horner,' p. 20.

23 J. Herskovitz and C. Petrikin, '*Titanic* Preem a Sellout,' *Variety*, 3 November 1997, p. 7.
24 Anon, 'The Unsinkable Celine Dion,' *Billboard*, 7 February 1998, p. 89.
25 Quoted in E. Fitzpatrick, '*Titanic* Makes Big Splash for Sony Classical,' *Billboard*, 24 January 1997, p. 92.
26 G. Mayfield, 'Between the Bullets,' *Billboard*, 14 February 1998, p. 104.
27 G. Mayfield, 'Between the Bullets,' *Billboard*, 28 February 1998, p. 90. See also 'Shipping the Ship,' *Hollywood Reporter*, 2 March 1998, p. 90.
28 C. Taylor, 'Dion's "Heart" Goes On, and On, and On,' *Billboard*, 7 February 1998, p. 5.
29 M. Newman, 'Sony Classical Enjoying Titanic Success of Hit Film's Soundtrack,' *Billboard*, 21 February 1998, p. 76.
30 T. Sandiford-Waller, 'Hot 100 Singles Spotlight,' *Billboard*, 24 January 1998, p. 94.
31 C. Taylor, 'Dion's "Heart" Goes On,' 89.
32 M. Fleming, 'Fox, Par in Choppy Waters over Cameron's Cash,' *Variety*, 5 April 1998, p. 4.
33 D. Browne, 'Star-Ship Enterprise,' p. 28.
34 M. Newman, 'Sony Classical Enjoying Titanic Success,' 76; and E. Fitzpatrick, '*Titanic* Makes Big Splash,' 92.
35 Quoted in M. Newman, 'Sony Classical Enjoying Titanic Success,' p. 76.
36 For more on this aspect of film music reception, see my forthcoming essay, 'Movie Music as Moving Music: Emotion, Cognition, and the Film Score,' in *Passionate Views*, ed. C. Plantinga and G. Smith, Baltimore, MD: Johns Hopkins University Press, 1999.
37 R. Bennett, 'James Horner,' p. 20.
38 Ibid.
39 D. Browne, 'Star-Ship Enterprise,' p. 31.
40 For more on the role of hooks in popular film songs, see my *The Sounds of Commerce*, pp. 15–21.
41 See R. Walser, *Running with the Devil: Power, Gender, and Madness in Heavy Metal Music*, Hanover, NH: Wesleyan University Press, 1993, pp. 121–123.
42 See T. Sandiford-Waller, 'Hot 100 Singles Spotlight,' *Variety*, 17 January 1998, p. 83.

Richard Maltby

ON THE PROSPECT OF WRITING CINEMA HISTORY FROM BELOW

'On the Prospect of Writing Cinema History from Below', *Tijdschrift voor Mediagescheidenis*, 2006, vol. 9(2), pp. 74–96.

BEGINNING WITH A CONSIDERATION of recent discussions of the state of film history, this essay explores some aspects of the relationship between the historiography of cinema and broader currents in contemporary historiography, including the poststructuralist critique of history as a realist fiction. It engages with what one 1970s theorist has recently called 'the weaknesses and insularity' of contemporary film studies by advocating the development of histories of cinema that place audiences, rather than films, at their centre, and integrate the quantitative methods of social history with the concrete and particular conditions of experience that are the predominant concern of microhistory.[1]

Film historiography: a modest critique

In her contribution to a 2004 *Cinema Journal* forum on the state of film history, Sumiko Higashi questions the extent to which cinema studies has seen a turn toward history based on empirical research in the past two decades. Citing statistics on recent submissions to *Cinema Journal* and papers given at the Society of Cinema and Media Studies conference, she argues that 'the bypass onto the "historical turn" is far from crowded', a phenomenon she ascribes in part to the proposition that 'most academics who train students in film studies have not themselves been trained to do empirical research'.[2] Seeking to differentiate between what she calls 'history proper' and work that she identifies as 'social and cultural media history', Higashi offers a critique of those 'film historians who began academic life as theoreticians' and remain deductive in their methodology.[3] 'Proper' historians, by contrast, 'assume human agency; privilege empirical data . . . write with specificity and in great detail; eschew jargon; and make contingent, even contradictory generalisations.'[4]

What is perhaps most striking about the essays in the *Cinema Journal* forum, including Higashi's, is the extent to which their debates over the nature of film history appear to be largely untouched by the central preoccupations of contemporary historiography, engendered by the fervent uncertainties of postmodern thought. Beyond the narrow confines of film studies, structuralist and post-structuralist critiques have deconstructed the conventionalised authorial voice of the history text, questioning its implicit rhetorical claim to authoritative knowledge of the past.[5] Maintaining that the construction of history is a discursive act of narration unattached to the reality of the past, some theorists have gone further to argue that we can know nothing genuinely truthful about the past, both because the past is accessible to us only through its discursive traces and because 'historical narratives are verbal fictions, the contents of which are as much invented as found and the forms of which have more in common with their counterparts in literature than they have with those in the sciences'.[6] Cinema historians' relative lack of engagement with poststructuralist theory's denial of the intellectual foundation of historical practice is both notable and, given the influence of poststructuralist thought on the development of film studies, somewhat surprising.[7] Higashi's description of historical practice, for example, would rest comfortably alongside the account provided by a reflective but unreconstructed professional practitioner such as Arthur Marwick, who dismisses 'the postmodernist case' as a construct of 'a priori attitudes . . . rigid conventions . . . specialist language [and] lack of practical experience', and as a consequence 'irrelevant to the aims of working historians'.[8]

In her contribution to the *Cinema Journal* forum, Jane Gaines suggests that film scholars' disengagement from questions of metahistory and the 'linguistic turn' in contemporary historiography is an indication of their relative sophistication. For Gaines, reading contemporary critiques of historical writing induces a sense of *déjà vu*, since the alleged defects of historical narrative – that readers are given 'the illusion of a privileged relation to the historical real' – echo those charges levelled in the 1970s against 'the classic realist text'.[9] While I share Gaines' sense of displaced familiarity, I suspect that a more substantial explanation for the relatively unreflective nature of film history's 'archive fever' lies elsewhere in the intellectual history of film studies as a field of enquiry, in the mutual antipathy between history and theory.

Writing about the 1970s in their anthology of historical writing from *Screen*, editors Annette Kuhn and Jackie Stacey observe that 'the current of heroic theory then coursing with fervent energy through the pages of *Screen*' resulted in the journal's regarding an engagement with 'the new film history' as being 'tangential to its preoccupations with film language and with the ideological practices of cinema'.[10] The 'new film historians' then publishing revisionist histories of American cinema were themselves more concerned with winning some nineteenth-century historiographic battles than with engaging with poststructuralism.[11] As Barbara Klinger described it, the most urgent task for film history in the late 1970s was to 'displace secondary and anecdotal forms of history with primary documentation, archival research and other historiographical tools of evidence and verification'.[12] In his 1976 *Screen* article on Warner Bros. and sound, for example, Douglas Gomery complained that earlier historians of the American film industry 'have not even followed the most basic practices of the field' in explaining their methodologies or citing their sources: 'no other brand of history is so casual in violating this basic attribute of scholarship'.[13] The critique of existing survey histories offered by Gomery and Robert Allen in their 1985 book *Film History: Theory and Practice*, that their omission of footnotes or bibliographies made it 'impossible to trace conclusions back to their evidentiary sources', might not have seemed out of place to Leopold von Ranke in 1824.[14] Beginning from such a position, academic film history, which scarcely existed before the mid-1970s, spent most of its early years untroubled by external requirements that it address the uncertainties of contemporary historiography as they affected its more established relatives in other subject areas. As Allen and Gomery emphasised, its concerns were with the practical and organisational issues involved in undertaking the 'tremendous amount of film historical scholarship' that remained to be done – with what Jeffrey Klenotic has called '"rolling up their sleeves" in the face of the archive'.[15] 'To do film history today', wrote Thomas Elsaesser in 1986,

> one has to become an economic historian, a legal expert, a sociologist, an architectural historian, know about censorship and fiscal policy, read trade papers and fan magazines, even study Lloyd Lists of ships sunk in World War One to calculate how much of the film footage exported to Europe actually reached its destination.[16]

The 'new film historians' were thus sufficiently engaged with problems of source and skills acquisition to add too many branches of poststructuralist theory to their list of responsibilities.

The tasks of the 'new film history' of the 1970s and 1980s were threefold: to revise and correct the existing, under-researched histories that represented the available overviews of the period; to develop a film history that adhered more closely to the established protocols of academic historiography; and to provide an alternative mode of study to the dominant practices of textual interpretation, borrowed in the main from literary criticism and inflected with the concerns of semiotic, structuralist and psychoanalytic theories. As Klenotic commented, the methodological debates within film history remained 'centred over what should constitute "proper" or "valid" historical explanation' and were concerned to correct the historical record 'by re-examining the primary historical archive rather than relying on the secondary resources provided by prior histories'.[17] To take, perhaps, the most obvious example, Douglas Gomery's revisionist account of the innovation of sound technology corrected previous entertaining but inaccurate versions through its use of a much wider range of primary sources and its self-conscious adherence to what Philip Rosen has called the 'conventional kinds of protocols and venues of academic historiography', or what Higashi calls 'proper history'.[18] By comparison to previous accounts, no-one could seriously question the superior accuracy of Gomery's account, based on its broader evidentiary base and higher standards of critical evaluation and analysis. As Allen and Gomery pointed out in *Film History*, however, works of comparable scholarship and rigor were few and far between in the field, and it has simply taken time to build a sufficient body of consensual historical knowledge around which to stage a debate about historical method. Cinema history is still subject to the kinds of revelatory discovery – exemplified by Richard Abel's *The Red Rooster Scare* or Ruth Vasey's *The World According to Hollywood* – that seldom occur in the historiography of more established historical terrain, simply because the body of available primary source material pertaining to cinema has been far less thoroughly examined.[19] There remains, to paraphrase Thomas Kuhn, a great deal of ordinary cinema history yet to be written.[20]

Except for occasional low-level skirmishes in pieces of academic journalism, the two camps of Theory and History largely ignored each other. Relatively few works of 'new film history' were – or indeed are – either published or reviewed in the most prominent theoretically-inflected journals, while the historians' suspicions of abstract theorising has reproduced what Rosen calls 'the most traditional of modern disciplinary debates', first articulated in 'the rivalry between students of Hegel and Ranke at the foundations of the modern discipline of "History"'.[21] Rather than being conducted over the grounds of historical practice, however, the debate has largely taken place at a simplified level, in which 'History' and 'Theory' are placed in mutually uncomprehending opposition to each other. Discursive complexity continues to be taken as a sure sign of the presence of 'theory' while a plethora of footnotes, even if they are all to *Variety*, continues on the one hand to pass as a claim to historical veracity and on the other to lead to accusations of simple-minded 'empiricism'.

In his 2001 book *Change Mummified: Cinema, Historicity, Theory* Philip Rosen provides the most fully elaborated account of the central propositions of the postmodern critique of history-writing as it pertains to the history of cinema. Rosen describes what he considers to be the basic uncertainty 'about the very possibility of making secure referential truth claims in historiography' as resulting from two fundamental problems.[22] The first relates to the fragmentary and indexical nature of historical evidence, the second to the position and referential authority of the historian. In common with many empirical historians, Rosen questions the extent to which the late twentieth-century critiques of modern historical practice have raised new epistemological and methodological issues, rather than merely rephrasing a set of concerns that have been repeatedly confronted by historians and philosophers of history. Few professional historians make claims for the absolute truth of their account; and whatever equivocation is involved in the maintenance of an ideal of more thoroughly reliable, less fragmentary knowledge of the past than is currently available, such pragmatic equivocation clearly also marks a recognition of the limits of the certainty with which any given account is produced. Ironically, however, there remains an apparently unbridgeable divide between the pragmatic equivocation expressed in E.H. Carr's answer to his own question *What Is History?*, that it is 'a continuous process of interaction between the historian and his facts, an unending dialogue between the present and the past', and the deconstructionist certainty that 'epistemology shows we can never really know the past; that the gap between the past and history (historiography) is an ontological one, that is, is in the very nature of things such that no amount of epistemological effort can bridge it'.[23]

Practicing historians have found themselves obliged to reject the poststructuralist critique – sometimes perhaps too vehemently – because in its assertion that the past is inherently unknowable it is so disabling to their practice. As Georg G. Iggers has observed, 'were one to accept the premises of this critique, meaningful historical writing would be impossible'.[24] However salutary might be the critical reminders that every historical account is a discursive construct and every encounter with a source text an act of mediation, historians cannot practice their trade – the 'dirty and tedious archival work' of digging evidence out of sources – unless they regard the resulting account as bearing a plausible relation to an historical reality.[25] As historian Carlo Ginzburg has argued, however, asserting this view does not, as the critique often asserts, involve naively assuming that the relationship between evidence and reality is transparent or unmediated.[26] On the contrary, the recognition that

> all phases through which research unfolds are *constructed* and not *given*: the identification of the object and its importance; the elaboration of the categories through which it is analyzed; the criteria of proof; the stylistic and narrative forms by which the results are transmitted to the reader [requires that] the obstacles interfering with re-search in the form of lacunae or misrepresentations in the sources must become part of the account.[27]

In his commentary on Hayden White's *Metahistory*, Rosen observes that White and many subsequent rhetorical theorisations of historiography, have 'continued the long-standing tendency among theorists of modern historiography to concentrate on the philosophical, ideological, metaphysical, and/or formal-aesthetic' aspects of the problem, and as a result have underplayed 'the implications of normative disciplinary procedures with respect to sources and evidence stemming from the heritage of the critical method'.[28]

The problems of writing film history under such constraints are exemplified by Vivian Sobchack's 'What is Film History?, or, the Riddle of the Sphinxes', in Christine Gledhill and Linda Williams' anthology, *Reinventing Film Studies.* The editors introduce Sobchack's essay as setting the stage for 'the new film history's theoretically informed historicizing of its objectives. No longer a simple matter of "excavating" original documents and material traces and causes of an objectively existing past, film history has taken on a self-reflective awareness of its own discursive processes of writing and mediation.'[29] Sobchack certainly talks the talk of the historical deconstructionists, describing a dichotomy between an 'old' and a 'new' history, in which

> Grand, coherent, and evolutionary narratives have given way to local and micro histories – and the gaps and ruptures in our knowledge of the past are foregrounded rather than smoothed over . . . history has lost its stability as the grounded site upon which knowledge of the past is accumulated, coherently ordered, and legitimated; rather, it has become an unstable site in which fragments of past representations do not necessarily 'add up' or cohere but, instead, are subject to 'undisciplined' (and often 'undisciplining') contestation and use.[30]

Exactly where this new self-reflective history has displayed its self-awareness is, however, more difficult to discern either in Sobchack's essay or in the references it lists. Instead, Sobchack elevates a somewhat quirky but otherwise unremarkable project in historical archaeology – the excavation of the remains of the sets for Cecil B. DeMille's 1923 movie *The Ten Commandments* in the Guadalupe Dunes near Santa Barbara, California – into 'a symbol of the destabilised grounds of contemporary historical theory and practice', a 'revelatory allegory' of 'our increased estrangement from and desire to recuperate a history we know we never knew'.[31] Asserting that 'a traditionalist empiricist [*sic*] film history whose temporal trajectory, causations, and meanings can be excavated, represented and understood in terms of some linear, unidirectional, and progressive notion of "original" events and chronological "order" based upon the "coherence", "consistency", and "reliability" of an accumulation of "authentic" trace "evidence" left by the past' is no more than a 'crazy dream', Sobchack argues that the buried set represents 'a fabricated version of yet another lost Egyptian city whose "authenticity" and "origins" are irrecoverable, unknowable and hence historically "fabulous"'.[32] What she fails to do, however, is to demonstrate what the destabilised and undisciplined 'historical nomadism' she advocates would tell us. Remaining true to her theoretical premises by declining to confront a concrete (or even a plaster-of-Paris) historical subject matter, Sobchack's essay envisions historical journeys that she might embark on, but goes nowhere.[33]

The grand, coherent, evolutionary narratives of cinema history to which Sobchack alludes have been more imagined than actually written.[34] In 1973, Jean Mitry proposed an ideal of film history as

> simultaneously, a history of its industry, its technologies, its systems of expression (or, more precisely, its systems of signification), and aesthetic structures, all bound together by the forces of the economic, psychosocial and cultural order.[35]

This version of film history as simultaneously medium-specific and totalising remains common to much contemporary film historiography, although its intellectual origins in the *Annales* School of French history are less often acknowledged. French film historian Michèle Lagny follows Mitry in describing her version of a preferred film history as 'a part of a larger ensemble, the sociocultural history . . . conceived as an articulation among three types of analysis, dealing with cultural objects, with the framework of their creation, making and circulation, and finally with their consumption'. She sees the desirable condition of film history as being that of 'an open field where different forces (economic, social, political, technical, cultural or aesthetic) come into being and confront each other'. She insists, however, that films are central to film history: 'the core is the film text, because only the film is the sign that cinema does exist (or doesn't exist any longer). Working from the cinema or on the cinema means starting from the film, and going back to it'.[36]

In her 1997 *Screen* essay, 'Film History Terminable and Interminable', Barbara Klinger invokes Fernand Braudel's unattainable ambition 'if not to see everything, at least to locate everything, and on the requisite grand scale' before describing 'a cinematic *histoire totale*' that places 'a film within multifarious intertextual and historical frames', to produce a 'Rashomon-like effect where the researcher uncovers different historical "truths" about a film as she/he analyses how it has been deployed within past social relations' and 'the film's variable, even contradictory, ideological meanings come into focus'.[37] The 'totalised perspective' that Klinger proposes 'provides a sense of what the historical prospects were for viewing at a given time by illuminating the meanings made available within that moment'.[38] In keeping with Lagny's prescription, however, Klinger places the individual film text at the centre of the multifarious intersections she describes.

A consequence of the expectation that the film text must be the central object of film history surfaces in Richard Abel's argument, in his essay in the *Cinema Journal* forum, that Robert Allen's recent work on audiences in the American South

> generally succeeds as social or cultural history more than as cinema history; that is, its chief interest lies in describing and analyzing the social conditions and cultural practices within which moving pictures could be as important for their relative absence as for their presence.[39]

In common with the other historians I have cited, Abel remains reluctant to abandon the medium-specificity of film history in order to integrate it into what Charles Musser describes warily as 'a broader and more amorphous cultural and social history'. Musser declares that 'I have found it productive to imagine cinema as an element (typically a crucial element) of other histories', but the problem that film historians face is that relatively few writers of 'other histories' have shared Musser's sense of film history's productivity or importance.[40] Despite the extensive historical analysis of early cinema, a recently-published 976-page history of late Victorian and Edwardian England, for example, devotes only one paragraph to cinema, providing a telling instance of the extent to which social and cultural historians have not yet found it necessary to address the historical work on early cinema.[41] In his 2004 introductory survey, *What is Cultural History?*, Peter Burke makes no mention of any work on cinema.[42]

In the second edition of *Global Hollywood*, published in 2004, Toby Miller and his colleagues come to bleak conclusions about the condition of screen studies, which they see as being irrelevant to both popular and policy-driven discussions of films and failing 'to engage political and social history and social theory on the human subject, the nation, cultural policy, the law and the economy'.[43] 'What would it take', they ask, 'for screen studies to matter more?' Part of their answer is to avoid the 'reproduction of "screen studies" in favour of work that studies the screen, regardless of its intellectual provenance'.[44] One aspect of such a project may be to recognise the limited intellectual value in trying to maintain the coherence of a medium-specific academic discipline, and acknowledging, instead, that the study of the economics of distribution has little in common with the study of the aesthetics of lighting. More specifically, cinema's historians might question both the practicality and the ideal of an *histoire totale*, and consider the possibility of a history of cinema that is not centrally about films.

In a 1997 essay, James Hay argues that most film history has been written under the assumption of the centrality of the film text, producing a 'self-contained, self-perpetuating' aesthetic history of film as a distinct, '"language" or set of formal conventions . . . without a clear sense of cinema's relation to other social sites'.[45] While historical studies of cinema 'classicism' have examined the relationship between film form and mode of production, Hay suggests that they have seldom examined other determinations for the history of 'the cinematic', implying that cinema perpetuated itself as 'an aesthetic and an ideological effect regulated by a mode of production . . . In these studies, cinema is never understood overtly as a relation among sites and in terms of the relation of cinematic sites to other sites.'[46]

Lee Grieveson, similarly, proposes that in an historical poetics which maintains 'the primacy of style' in the last instance, 'the possibility of the social affecting textuality is never simply denied but rather is bracketed off, giving priority to the examination of formal norms and industrial formations as "proximate" contexts'.[47] Seeking a history that tracks 'the complex traffic between aesthetic and cultural spheres, making judicious interpretations of the connections that can be made and of the ways culture functions in texts, just as texts function in culture', Grieveson's project turns out to be similar to Klinger's, in aiming to 'situate cinema in relation to social, political, and cultural histories and at the confluence of questions about aesthetics, commerce, and power'.[48]

In response to Grieveson, David Bordwell has criticised the presupposition that while 'One can legitimately *ask questions* concerning aesthetic resources or strategies, . . . the *answers* will ultimately rest upon broader social, political, or cultural processes (law, economics, identity politics, etc.)':

> Does regulation, or response to 'reform anxieties' . . . tell us why we have dialogue hooks, montage sequences, goal-oriented protagonists, and a switch from orthochromatic to panchromatic film stock? It seems unlikely . . . I suspect that many of the norms we trace [in *The Classical Hollywood Cinema*], at various levels of generality, are satisfactorily explained without invoking modernity, reform anxieties, moral discourse, or other factors – simply because every explanation must stop somewhere, and it's impossible to spell out all the preconditions for any historical event.[49]

Stylistic and technological histories of cinema can, obviously, be constructed from more tightly circumscribed evidentiary sources than cultural histories pursuing relationships of correspondence or congruence among contingent circumstances, but the sources an historian needs are determined by the question he or she is asking. Certainly, we can make more fine-grained distinctions among historical agencies than Bordwell allows. The files of the Production Code Administration are replete with specific examples of regulatory involvement with the production process, and the analysis of a broad sample of these records can establish both the specific stylistic effects of regulation and the specific influence of 'reform anxiety' on the content and appearance of movies at particular historical moments. 'Reform anxieties' in the early 1930s, for example, challenged the industry's frequently-expressed view that if a movie told a properly moral narrative, in which good and evil were clearly distinguished and good seen to triumph, then the audience's moral principles would be reaffirmed. Arguing that young viewers failed to construct an 'organised interpretation' of a movie's narrative, Payne Fund researchers Herbert Blumer and Philip Hauser maintained that they were, instead, 'particularly responsive to incidents which are dramatic, exciting, and tempting'. As a result, they were likely to find 'details or elements of the picture' more significant than the moral contained in the movie's resolution.[50] This question became a central point at issue in the increasingly strident debate over movie censorship in the early 1930s, and led to classical Hollywood's formulation of strategies of indeterminacy, elision, enigma and suggestion, which achieved the contradictory goal of presenting a predetermined narrative that simultaneously accommodated the viewer's imaginative agency.[51]

Pursuing a much less direct causal chain, what has become known as the 'modernity thesis' argues that the forms of early cinema 'engaged the experience of modernity', exemplifying a particularly modern form of aesthetics and responding to the specifics of modern and especially urban life.[52] Whether any of the advocates of modernity's influence on cinema insist that the relationship between modernity and cinematic style is a causal one is a point in dispute; its critics, however, maintain that the relationship is of consequence only if a causal linkage can be established, since otherwise the relationship is no more than an uninteresting generalisation, 'a commonplace that offers us nothing to investigate'.[53]

Modernity's advocates and their critics are engaging in quite different forms of enquiry, with separate aims and methodologies. One is a fine-grained examination of proximate forces that may provide causal explanations of particular stylistic decisions, the other a much broader consideration of the complex and elusive connections between a society and its cultural-aesthetic expressions.[54] Addressing different questions by different methods at different levels of generality and detail, they are not necessarily in competition or in conflict with each other, yet each wishes the problems of an *histoire totale* upon the other, at the same time as they suggest that the other's view of historical determination is overly simplistic. Neither can meet the other's explanatory requirements.[55] The history of textual relations and stylistic influence borrows its methods and rationale from the practices of art and literary history. It is predominantly a history of production and producers, concerned with issues of intention and agency underpinning the process of cultural production, usually at the level of the individual, and relatively little interested in anything – other than influence – that happens after the point of production. If the form of classical Hollywood cinema can, indeed, be sufficiently explained by the 'proximate forces' of 'industrial maturation and attempts at standardizing production practices' with little engagement with the history of cinema as a social or cultural institution, there is little reason for historians in other fields to be much concerned with the topic.[56]

Broader cultural histories of cinema are, however, methodologically much more problematic, particularly in their capacity to demonstrate a sufficient degree of correspondence between an historical condition (for instance, the social conditions of the early Depression) and a cultural object (for instance, *I Am a Fugitive from a Chain Gang*) to argue for any causal relationship. As Bordwell observes, 'why would we search for congruences unless they led us toward some explanatory hypotheses?'[57] Too often, explanation takes the form of textual interpretation, allowing the writer to juxtapose a movie and 'an array of social facts . . . about the concurrent social environment as though media texts have some obvious direct relation to their social context', in a *Zeitgeist* account of film as cultural history.[58] To argue, as Michèle Lagny does, that films should be seen 'socially and historically . . . as symptoms', advances us no further than the questionable methodology of ideological inference by allusion elaborated by Siegfried Kracauer in the late 1940s.[59] Borrowing such methodologies, social and political historians have incorporated back into their accounts of broader historical phenomena the genre-based, mythological and ahistorical assumptions about the relationship of movies to the culture of which they are a part. Even as they are incorporated into a larger version of social history, the movies remain under the obligation to entertain: accounts of *I Am a Fugitive from a Chain Gang* or *Scarface*, for example, appear as diverting boxed features on 'social realism in the movies' to alleviate the statistical tedium of histories of the early Depression. Lagny's declaration of cinema's historical inconsequentiality – '[films] never are a consequence (of economic, social, cultural or political determining factors . . .), nor the cause of anything (a political action, a social reaction, or the production of other films)' – goes beyond Bordwell's circumscription and consigns cinema to the historical irrelevance it occupies in most accounts of twentieth-century history.[60]

Cinema history: a modest proposal

I am arguing for the desirability of distinguishing more emphatically between an aesthetic history of textual relations among individuals or individual objects, and the socio-cultural history of the economic institution of cinema. This distinction engages with the project advocated by Bordwell and Noël Carroll for 'piecemeal theorising' and 'middle-level research' that resists the hope that a Grand Interpretation will provide for 'a master reconciliation of all research programs'.[61] The history of the American cinema is not exclusively the history of its products any more than the history of railroads is the history of locomotives. The development of locomotive design forms part of the history of railroads, but so, far more substantially, do government land policies and patterns of agricultural settlement. A history of cinema that will address the proposition 'that films, by improving the general quality and availability of entertainment at a low admission cost, contributed positively to the stock of social well-being, in the same way that low cost electric street lighting did by markedly improving the quality of illumination', will have significantly different concerns from film studies' preoccupation with the textuality of films, acts of interpretation of textual meaning and theoretical approaches to these acts of interpretation.[62]

A history of cinema, that is not a history of textual relations among films must, however, be concerned with the history of reception, which must itself include histories of distribution and exhibition. One crucial feature of the history of the reception of American cinema is that for most audiences for most of the history of cinema, their primary relationship with 'the cinema' has not been with individual movies-as-artefacts or as texts, but with the social experience of cinema.[63] An historical examination of the ways in which the cinema has provided a site and an occasion for particular forms of social behaviour, or of the ways in which individual movies have specified the nature of the site, the occasion, and the behaviour, is an enquiry into the production of meaning, but that meaning is social, not textual.

What would it take for cinema history to matter more? We can, perhaps, imagine some counter-factual historical circumstances. What if the Payne Fund Studies researchers had been right? What if the basic claims of effects, researchers since 1910 about the direct deleterious effects of movie consumption on youth, had any substance? What if the anti-American jeremiads of bourgeois cultural nationalists, that Hollywood movies 'literally poison the souls of our children, young people, young girls, who are to be turned into the docile slaves of the American multi-millionaires', accurately depicted the impact of American consumer products on other cultures?[64] Were any of these propositions, with which so much commentary on the media remains preoccupied, demonstrable, we would find it much easier to raise grant money to study the history of cinema reception. We would also find it easier to persuade other historians of the significance of our research. So long as cinema history remains solipsistically committed to medium-specificity, starting and ending with the film text, then the history of entertainment will remain no more than an entertaining diversion occupying the illustrative margins of other histories. For cinema history to matter more, it must engage with the social history of which it is a part, not through the practices of textual interpretation, but by attempting to write cinema history from below; that is, to write histories that are concerned not with the kings and queens of Hollywood but with their audiences and with the roles that these performances of celebrity played in the ordinary imaginations of those audiences.

In part, I am advocating an historical return to the prevailing concerns of the earliest studies of cinema as an object of sociological and psychological enquiry, rather than the object of aesthetic, critical and interpretive enquiry that has ensued from the construction of film studies as an academic discipline in the humanities. These earlier studies, from Hugo Münsterberg to the Payne Fund research, concerned themselves with what Frankfurt School theorist Leo Lowenthal called 'the underlying social and psychological function' of cinema as a component in the modern urban environment; their methods were those of the 'human sciences', and their objects of enquiry were people, rather than artefacts.[65] A return to such concerns in the history-writing that I am advocating invites an engagement by cinema historians with a different and far more productive series of dialogues in social and cultural historiography since 1970 than that provided by poststructuralism.

In the third quarter of the twentieth century, quantitative research methods permeated historical studies, underpinning claims that history was, like other social sciences, a scientific discipline. Demographic and economic histories, reliant on statistical data compiled from censuses or parish records, constructed a 'history without people', arguing that historians could examine those groups placed at the bottom of the social ladder only through the anonymity of quantitative data, in which, as E. P. Thompson wrote, 'working people are seen as a labour force, as migrants, or as the data for a statistical series'.[66] In his quest to 'rescue the poor stockinger, the Luddite cropper . . . and even the deluded follower of Joanna Southcott, from the enormous condescension of posterity', Thompson sought to restore 'the agency of working people, the degree to which they contributed by conscious efforts to the making of history'.[67] This aim was shared by several groups of historians concerned at the elimination of the particular in the grand narratives of social scientific history, who sought 'to reconstruct the lives of individual men and women from the popular classes of the past', with the specific purpose of reconstructing 'the *relationship* (about which we know so little) between individual lives and the contexts in which they unfold'.[68]

A history concerned with the conditions of everyday life as they are experienced by ordinary people requires, as George Iggers has argued, a new conceptual and methodological approach that sees history

> no longer as . . . a grand narrative in which the many individuals are submerged, but as a multifaceted flow with many individual centers . . . And if we are dealing with the individual lives of the many, we need an epistemology geared to the experiences of these many that permits knowledge of the concrete rather than the abstract.[69]

Such histories of individual existence and experience are not, however, incompatible with those of broad social process. Ideally, the microhistories of Carlo Ginzburg and Giovanni Levy, extend, complement and qualify the broader generalisations provided by quantitative methods, and their dialogue provides models for the histories of cinema from below that I am advocating.[70] To paraphrase Thompson, the aim of such histories would be to rescue the membership of cinema's audiences from the condescension of a posterity more concerned to contemplate 'its own desires, criteria, and representational structures for achieving historical coherence and meaning' than it is to construct a meaningful account of the past.[71] Like Barbara Klinger's *histoire totale*, such accounts would necessarily be contextual; the task is not so much a matter of trying to reconstruct the experiences of a particular cinema audience, largely unknown to each other, in a particular cinema at a particular screening on a particular day, as it is of seeking to understand the elements from which those experiences were constructed, on as specific a level of generalisation as the evidence may make available to us. For a history of cinema that is not centrally about films, however, the contexts to be invoked are quite different, as are the adjacent fields of knowledge that may be illuminated by a more fully-elaborated socio-cultural history of the economic institution of cinema. In the remainder of this paper, I briefly sketch three examples of the broader issues to which a history of cinema might be connected: demographics, Americanisation, and consumption.

As Robert Allen has argued, cinema history, and particularly the history of its audiences, is demographic history.[72] A more exact sense of who made up cinema's audiences, and when, provides us with an alternative means of understanding cinema's cultural function as well as its product, but as yet relatively little work has been done in correlating broad demographic shifts against changing patterns of cinema attendance, or in mapping cinema provision against demographic data. In combination with other sources, such quantitative information has much to tell us about the changing composition of cinema's audiences over time, as well as about those sectors of the population largely excluded from attendance. I would, for example, argue that Richard Abel's recent investigations of 'how moving pictures circulated in medium- and small-sized cities' in the North-eastern United States in the 1910s are methodologically entirely compatible with Allen's studies of cinema-attendance and non-attendance in the American South. Abel's aim of using data from those areas to interrogate cinema's role in either fostering 'a more or less homogeneous American mass public' or sustaining an 'ethnically and culturally heterogeneous society' forms part of the same broad about the place and function of cinema for its audiences that Allen is addressing.[73]

If, as Abel suggests, cinema played a significant role in the Americanisation of its urban population, its role in a more global process of Americanisation – that of 'sell[ing] America to the world with American motion pictures', as Will H. Hays proselytised in 1923 – has long been asserted by both enthusiasts and detractors alike. Whether 'every film that goes from America abroad', has correctly portrayed 'the purposes, the ideals, the accomplishments, the opportunities, and the life of America', as Hays claimed it would, has been a subject of contention ever since.[74] In April 2001, State Department spokesman Richard Boucher celebrated the accelerating expansion of the global market for American-sourced popular culture as a functional substitute for his department's disengagement from cultural diplomacy, by declaring to the *Advertising Age* that his department had now 'taken the view that to know us is to love us'.[75] As early as 1924, on the other hand, Secretary of State Charles Evans Hughes was complaining that the movies' 'false distortion of American life' had produced 'a pernicious distortion among other people with respect to the way in which our people live'.[76]

The shock following September 11 was not merely President Bush's amazement 'that there is such misunderstanding of what our country is about, that people would hate us'.[77] It was also the shocked and apparently sudden recognition that the abandonment of cultural diplomacy to corporate commerce had not resulted in 'the triumph of American ideas'.[78] Instead, suggested House International Relations Committee Chairman Henry Hyde, 'the country that invented Hollywood and Madison Avenue has allowed . . . a destructive and parodied image of itself to become the intellectual coin of the realm overseas'.[79] Viewed from abroad, where the concept of Americanisation has long carried fewer positive connotations and has more frequently been a term hovering somewhere between critique and abuse, the catastrophic failure of the ideological project encapsulated by Hays seems much less surprising. If the imaginary 'American' culture of the movies became, in Richard Kuisel's phrase, 'everyone's second culture', it did so far more successfully as an agent of commerce than as an instrument of ideology.[80] As Victoria de Grazia has argued,

> it is not at all clear how as elusive a force as consumer culture, being the sum of myriads of marketing strategies, second-order decisions of government, and mundane choices about getting and spending, was converted into great power. Nor is it clear how the United States exercised this great power to promote democracies of consumption elsewhere, much less to advance global concord.[81]

Some of the histories of cinema I am proposing might reconsider Hollywood's role in 'the Americanisation of the world' by exploring the dissonance between the commercial and political effects of American cultural hegemony.[82]

In the decade after World War I, Hollywood became the most visible signifier of an unparalleled American economic expansionism, as the United States 'flooded the world with products, branch plants, and investment capital', while American radio and cable companies, wire services and airlines built the foundations of the American communications empire in what Owen D. Young, head of the Radio Corporation of America, described as the 'economic integration of the world'.[83]

To proponents such as Young and Hays, America's expansion was inherently benign, since it was based 'not on military force or government design but on the wonders of its private industry, the skill of its experts, the goodness of its philanthropists', and the ubiquity of its communications technologies.[84] 'Film America', as the German trade press called Hollywood, was a powerful agent of this policy, as both a sales apparatus for American goods and as a demonstration of what de Grazia has characterised as 'the enduring capacity of the American "empire without frontiers" to discover, process, and redistribute techniques, styles, and tastes of global provenance'.[85]

In 1929, economist Christine Frederick described this commercial version of Americanisation as 'Consumptionism . . . the greatest idea that America has to give to the world; the idea that workmen and masses be looked upon not simply as workers and producers, but as consumers . . . Pay them more, sell them more, prosper more is the equation.'[86] In *An All-Consuming Century*, Gary Cross has argued that: 'Consumerism, the belief that goods give meaning to individuals and their roles in society', was the 'ism' that won the political and ideological engagements of the twentieth century 'even though it had no formal philosophy, no parties, and no obvious leaders'.[87] Reflecting and often fulfilling real social needs, consumerism challenged class, religion, and ethnicity as principles of political solidarity, and 'succeeded where other ideologies failed because it *concretely* expressed the cardinal political ideals of the century – liberty and democracy – and with relatively little self-destructive behavior or personal humiliation'.[88] Cross's uncommonly optimistic account of consumerism emphasises that the 'essential ambiguity of consumer goods was and is fundamental to their meaning and continued appeal'. The semantic malleability and complexity of consumer products have, in his analysis, been the source of their power to divert great social disharmonies into small, individualised disharmonies, to help 'individuals contend with social conflict and ambiguity, evade clear-cut choices, and even hold contradictory desires'.[89]

Textual indeterminacy is a structural property of Hollywood movies, resulting from the economic conditions of their circulation: their distribution to a multiplicity of venues for a multiplicity of audiences, and the requirement that the single object serve multiple audience pleasures. Cross's arguments suggest that in this indeterminacy the movies both represented and embodied the semantic fluidity of consumerism itself. They were teaching their audiences the possibilities of pleasure in the democratisation of meaning, and of the power to interpret.

In her history of the spread of Americanised consumer culture in Europe from 1900 to 1970, de Grazia repeatedly demonstrates that different countries – and within each country different classes and groups – acquired the material capacity to participate in consumption at significantly different times. Undoubtedly, the movies, like advertising, reinforced a new economy of desire. But the public directly addressed by advertising – the public possessed of discretionary spending capacity – varied considerably from around 70% of the US population in the late 1920s to 30% of the population of Britain and Northwest Europe, to less than 10% of the population of Italy and Spain. Studies of the standards of living among American and European workers in Ford factories in 1929, for example, indicated such great differences in purchases of clothing, home conveniences and transport as to make comparison almost meaningless.[90]

Writing about the differential spread of consumer durables in different parts of Europe in the 1970s and 1980s, de Grazia argues that the 'narrative of how household goods came to be possessed . . . was in large measure indifferent to variations in class, local cultures, and history'. At any given historical moment, however, what these goods meant, socially and culturally, varied from nation to nation and region to region depending on how far the particular nation or region had progressed through the reiterated narrative of 'technological change, rise in family incomes, and revolution in outlooks, all sanctioned and pushed by a new cross-Atlantic standard of living'.[91]

Our present understanding of how cinema functioned as an agent of consumerism in both the US and abroad might stand some interrogation when considered in relation to the experience of consumption in different places at different times in the last century. If movies and movie attendance were classless, in the sense that it was a habit of all people of all classes, then in Europe, they behaved differently from other, comparable consumer goods, which acted as sources of social fragmentation, producing 'new sources of differentiation and exclusion rather than making standards more homogeneous and accessible'.[92] But because movie attendance was geographically specific – attendance at this cinema in this neighbourhood with these people and these detailed local understandings of social distinction, attendance – and therefore exhibition – it could, clearly, not be separated from the patterns of social distinction in practical operation at the time. Indeed, as Christopher McKenna's work on the 'tripartheid' practices of segregation in Lumberton, North Carolina, shows, these patterns of social distinction had to be constructed into the architecture of the cinemas themselves.[93]

To what extent did cinema, as a social agent in the promulgation of 'consumptionism', require pre-existing economic conditions, including a level of discretionary spending among its potential audience? Where these conditions did not exist, did cinema exhibition remain a marginal activity not simply because people were too poor to attend frequently, but also because the pleasures of cinema – the aspirational pleasures of viewing consumption and viewing-as-consumption that were part of what economist Simon Pattern had called the surplus or pleasure economy – were insufficiently engaged with or integrated into their daily lives?[94] Can we correlate patterns of cinema exhibition to the markedly variant patterns of retail sales in the US and Europe for much of the century? And if we can – or, for that matter, if we cannot – what will that tell us about the social function of cinema? Did cinema represent a sort of half-way house between access to 'Americanised' consumer culture and the practicalities of economic possibility, both for poorer communities in the US and for much of Europe in the first half of the 20th century and beyond? To what extent, where, and when, did the cinema provide a substitute for consumption – a placebo – rather than an aspiration to consume and a guidebook or practical manual in the development of the practice of consumption?

If the answers to these questions are not yet clear, what are somewhat clearer is that such explanations as we may be able to offer will require different historical methods and tools from those that have so far predominated in film history. Instead, these tools are likely to be drawn from the methodological dialogues of social and cultural historians. To begin with, we will need detailed historical maps of cinema exhibition, telling us what cinemas were where and when, amplified by whatever detailed evidence we can recover about the nature and frequency of attendance – precisely the kind of scholarly work pioneered by Karel Dibbets and the Cinema Context Collections project.[95] This data then needs to be combined with broader statistical information derived from census data and other surveys to amplify our understanding of cinema's audiences – of the extent, for example, to which the geography of cinema produced new forms of social differentiation at the same time that the images its audiences consumed, projected a dissolution of 'the sumptuary lines between classes'.[96]

Such detailed quantitative information is vital if we are to progress beyond our current broad-brush knowledge based on trade figures, diplomatic accounts and grand theories of classical cinema as vernacular modernism. As vital, however, is the inclusion of experience that will ground quantitative generalisations in the concrete particulars of microhistorical studies of local situations, effects and infrastructure, based perhaps around the records of individual cinemas or small chains. The heroes of these microhistories – the Menocchios of the cinema – will be the small businessmen who acted as cultural brokers, navigators and translators of the middle ground constructing a creolised culture out of their community's encounters with the mediated external world.[97] One of these microhistories may become the *Montaillou* of cinema history, through what it may reveal about how its citizen consumers explained themselves and their place in the world through their encounters with the forces of global and globalising culture.[98] Such histories, self-consciously acknowledging their own constructions and mediations, may also form part of comparative local histories, and, finally, may underpin attempts to consider the cultural function and performance of individual movies in more secure social and cultural detail than we can presently achieve.

Notes

1 C. MacCabe, 'Preface' to Slavoj Žižek, *The Fright of Real Tears: Krzysztof Kieslowski between Theory and Post-Theory,* London 2001, p. vii. Quoted in D. Bordwell, 'Slavoj Žižek: Say Anything', April 2005. <www.davidbordwell.net/zizek-say-anything.htm> accessed 26 August 2006.

2 S. Higashi, 'In Focus: Film History, or a Baedeker Guide to the Historical Turn', *Cinema Journal*, 2004, vol. 44(1), p. 94.

3 Ibid., p. 95.

4 Ibid., p. 96.

5 H. White, *Metahistory: The Historical Imagination in Nineteenth-Century Europe,* Baltimore, MD: Johns Hopkins University Press, 1975; D. LaCapra, *History and Criticism*, Ithaca, NY: Cornell University Press, 1985. See also A. Munslow, *Deconstructing History,* London: Routledge, 1997; C. Behan McCullagh, *The Truth of History,* London: Routledge, 1998.

6 H. White, 'Historical Texts as Literary Artifact', in: *Tropics of Discourse: Essays in Cultural Criticism*, Baltimore, MD: Johns Hopkins University Press, 1978, p. 82.

7 R. Berkhofer, 'The Challenge of Poetics to (Normal) Historical Practice', *Poetics Today*, 1988, vol. 9, pp. 435–452; J. F. Klenotic, 'The Place of Rhetoric in "New" Film Historiography: The Discourse of Corrective Revisionism', *Film History*, 1994, vol. 6, p. 45.

8 A. Marwick, 'Author's Response to a Review by Alan Munslow [of Arthur Marwick, *The New Nature of History: Knowledge, Evidence, Language*, London 2001]', <www.history.ac.uk/discourse/marwick2.html> accessed 27 August 2006.

9 J. Gaines, 'Film History and the Two Presents of Feminist Film Theory', *Cinema Journal*, 2004, vol. 44(1) p. 116; C. MacCabe, 'Realism and the Cinema: Notes on Some Brechtian Theses', *Screen*, 1974, vol. 15(2), pp. 7–22.

10 A. Kuhn and J. Stacey, 'Screen Histories: An Introduction', in: A. Kuhn and J. Stacey (ed.), *Screen Histories: A Screen Reader*, Oxford: Oxford University Press, 1998, p. 3. The most striking example of the subsumption of historical analysis to what Kuhn and Stacey call *Screen*'s 'theoretical-political agenda', which has lost none of its power to register the mutual incomprehension between competing discourses, is Christopher Williams's addendum, 'The Deep Focus Question: Some Comments on Patrick Ogle's Article', *Screen*, 1971, vol. 13(1), reprinted in: John Ellis (ed.), *Screen Reader 1*, London: SEFT, 1977, pp. 109–112.

11 In addition to the work of Douglas Gomery cited below, examples would include T. Balio, *United Artists: The Company Built by the Stars*, Madison, WI: Johns Hopkins University Press, 1976; T. Balio (ed.), *The American Film Industry*, Madison, WI: Johns Hopkins University Press, 1976; R. Allen, *Vaudeville and Film 1895–1915: A Study in Media Interaction*, New York: Ayer, 1980.

12 B. Klinger, 'Film History Terminable and Interminable: Recovering the Past in Reception Studies', *Screen*, 1997, vol. 38(2), p. 111. Haden Guest provides a valuable account of the work of an earlier generation of American film historians to establish more rigorous standards of evidence in the compilation of filmographies. H. Guest, 'Experimentation and Innovation in Three American Film Journals of the 1950s', in: L. Grieveson and H. Wasson (ed.), *Inventing Cinema Studies*, Durham, NC: University of North Carolina Press, forthcoming.

13 D. Gomery, 'Writing the History of the American Film Industry: Warner Bros. and Sound', *Screen*, 1976, vol. 17(1), p. 41.

14 R. Allen and D. Gomery, *Film History: Theory and Practice*, New York: Knopf, 1985, p. 46. 'The basis of the present work, the sources of its material, are memoirs, diaries, letters, diplomatic reports, and original narratives of eyewitnesses; other writings were used only if they were immediately derived from the above mentioned or seemed to equal them because of some original information. These sources will be identified on every page.' L. von Ranke, 'Preface: Histories of the Latin and German Nations from 1494–1514' (1824), in: F. Stern (ed.), *The Varieties of History, from Voltaire to the Present*, New York: Meridian, 1972, p. 56.

15 R. Allen and D. Gomery, *Film History: Theory and Practice*, p. 41; and J. Klenotic, 'The Place of Rhetoric in "New" Film Historiography', p. 51.

16 T. Elsaesser, 'The New Film History', *Sight and Sound*, 1986, vol. 55(4), p. 248.

17 J. Klenotic, 'The Place of Rhetoric in "New" Film Historiography', p. 46.

18 P. Rosen, *Change Mummified: Cinema, Historicity, Theory*, Minneapolis, MN: University of Minnesota Press, 2003, p. xxi.

19 R. Abel, *The Red Rooster Scare: Making Cinema American, 1900–1910*, Berkeley, CA: University of California Press, 1999; R. Vasey, *The World According to Hollywood, 1919–1939*, Exeter, WI: University of Wisconsin Press, 1997.

20 T. Kuhn, *The Structure of Scientific Revolutions*, Chicago, IL: University of Chicago Press, 1962. David Bordwell describes 'ordinary criticism' as being, like Kuhn's 'normal Science', 'the ongoing program of a group of researchers using approved problem/solution routines to expand and fill out the realm of the known'. D. Bordwell, *Making Meaning: Inference and Rhetoric in the Interpretation of Cinema*, Cambridge, MA: Harvard University Press, 1989, p. 25.

21 P. Rosen, *Change Mummified*, pp. xxi–xxii.

22 Ibid., p. 127.

23 E. H. Carr, *What Is History?*, London: Penguin, 1961, p. 29; K. Jenkins, *Rethinking History*, London: Routledge, 1991, p. 19.

24 G. G. Iggers, *Historiography in the Twentieth Century*, Middletown, CT: Wesleyan University Press, 1997, p. 11.

25 L. Stone, 'History and Postmodernism', *Past and Present*, 1992, vol. 135, p. 194; G. G. Iggers, *Historiography in the Twentieth Century*, p. 145.

26 C. Ginzburg, 'Checking the Evidence: The Judge and the Historian', *Critical Inquiry*, 1991, vol. 18(1), pp. 83–84.

27 C. Ginzburg, 'Microhistory: Two or Three Things that I Know About It', *Critical Inquiry*, 1993, vol. 20(1), pp. 32, 28.

28 P. Rosen, *Change Mummified*, p. 388, n. 28.

29 C. Gledhill and L. Williams, 'The Return to History', in: C. Gledhill and L. Williams (eds), *Reinventing Film Studies*, Oxford: Oxford University Press, 2000, pp. 297–298.

30 V. Sobchack, 'What is Film History?, or, the Riddle of the Sphinxes', in: C. Gledhill and L. Williams (ed.), *Reinventing Film Studies*, p. 301.

31 Ibid., p. 308.

32 Ibid., pp. 310, 308.

33 In his 1977 essay, 'On the Writing of the History of the Cinema', Geoffrey Nowell-Smith wrote that 'no one now accepts accounts of film history . . . which pass blandly from one "fact" to another . . . And yet no one knows how to do better, except at a cost of a sceptical unwillingness to do anything.' G. Nowell-Smith, 'On the Writing of the History of the Cinema: Some Problems', in: *Edinburgh '77 Magazine: History/ Production/ Memory*, 1977, p. 10.

34 In their introduction to *Film History: An Introduction*, Kristin Thompson and David Bordwell articulate their ambition as being 'to sum up the history of film as it is presently conceived, written, and taught by its most accomplished scholars', but they also qualify the scale of their project by insisting that 'there is no single narrative of film history that accounts for all events, causes and consequences. And the variety of historical approaches guarantees that historians will draw diverse and dissenting conclusions . . . When historians focus on different questions, turn up different evidence, and formulate different arguments, we have not a single history but a diverse set of historical arguments.' K. Thompson and D. Bordwell, *Film History: An Introduction*, New York: Prentice Hall, 1994, pp. xxvi–xxvii.

35 J. Mitry, 'De quelques problèmes d'histoire et d'esthétique de cinema', *Cahiers de la cinémathèque*,1973, vols 10–11, p. 115. Trans and quoted in R. Abel, '"Don't Know Much about History", or the (In)vested Interests of Doing Cinema History', *Film History*, 1994, vol. 6(1), p. 111.

36 M. Lagny, 'Film History: or History Expropriated', *Film History*, 1994, vol. 6(1), pp. 27, 41.

37 B. Klinger, 'Film History Terminable and Interminable: Recovering the Past in Reception Studies', *Screen*, 1997, vol. 38(2), p. 110; F. Braudel, *Capitalism and Material Life, 1400–1800*, London: Harper 1967, pp. 441–442.

38 B. Klinger, 'Film History Terminable and Interminable', p. 114.

39 R. Abel, 'History Can Work for You, You Know How to Use It', *Cinema Journal*, 2004, vol. 44(1), pp. 108–109.

40 C. Musser, 'Historiographic Method and the Study of Early Cinema', *Cinema Journal*, 2004, vol. 44(1), p. 105.

41 G. R. Searle, *A New England? Peace and War 1886–1918*, Oxford: Oxford University Press, 2004. My thanks to Luke McKernan for this reference.

42 P. Burke, *What is Cultural History?*, Cambridge: Polity, 2004.

43 T. Miller, N. Govil, J. McMurria, R. Maxwell and T. Wang, *Global Hollywood 2*, London: BFI, 2004, p. 31.

44 Ibid., p. 45.

45 J. Hay, 'Piecing Together What Remains of the Cinematic City', in: D. B. Clarke (ed.), *The Cinematic City*, London: Routledge, 1997, pp. 210–212.

46 Ibid., pp. 213–214, 223.

47 L. Grieveson, 'Woof, Warp, History', *Cinema Journal*, 2004, vol. 44(1), pp. 121–122.

48 Ibid., p. 124; 'In a total history, the analyst studies complex interactive environments or levels of society involved in the production of a particular event, effecting a historical synthesis, an integrated picture of synchronic as well as diachronic change.' B. Klinger, 'Film History Terminable and Interminable', pp. 108–109.

49 D. Bordwell, 'Film and the Historical Return' (March 2005). <www.davidbordwell.net/film-historical-return.htm> accessed 26 August 2006.

50 H. Blumer and P. Hauser, *Movies, Delinquency and Crime*, New York: Ayer, 1933, pp. 134–135.

51 For a more elaborated version of this argument, see R. Maltby, '"A Brief Romantic Interlude": Dick and Jane Go to Three-and-a-Half Seconds of the Classical Hollywood Cinema', in: D. Bordwell and N. Carroll, *Post-Theory: Reconstructing Film Studies*, Madison, WI: University of Wisconsin Press, 1996, pp. 434–459; R. Maltby, 'Why Boys Go Wrong: Gangsters, Hoodlums and the Natural History of Delinquent. Careers', in: L. Grieveson, E. Sonnett and P. Stanfield (eds), *Mob Culture: The American Gangster Film*, New Brunswick, NJ: Berg, 2005, pp. 41–66.

52 T. Gunning, 'Systematizing the Electric Message: Narrative Form, Gender, and Modernity in The Lonedale Operator', in: C. Keil and S. Stamp (eds), *American Cinema's Transitional Era: Audiences, Institutions, Practices*, Berkeley, CA: University of California Press, 2004, p. 44; T. Gunning, 'The Whole Town's Gawking: Early Cinema and the Visual Experience of Modernity', *Yale Journal of Criticism*, 1994, vol. 7(2), pp. 189–201.

53 T. Gunning, 'Systematizing the Electric Message', p. 44; D. Bordwell, *On the History of Film Style*, Cambridge, MA: Harvard University Press, 1997, pp. 139–146, 301–302, n. 100; C. Keil, '"To Here from Modernity": Style, Historiography, and Transitional Cinema', in: C. Keil and S. Stamp (ed.), *American Cinema's Transitional Era: Audiences, Institutions, Practices*, Berkeley, CA: University of California Press, 2004, pp. 53–54.

54 B. Singer, *Melodrama and Modernity: Early Sensational Cinema and Its Contexts*, New York: Columbia University Press, 2001, pp. 104, 128. Lee Grieveson explores the relationship between early twentieth-century studies of cinema and contemporaneous work in sociology and psychology on subjectivity and social control in his chapter, 'Mimesis at the Movies: Cinema Studies and the conduct of Conduct', in: L. Grieveson and H. Wasson (eds), *Inventing Cinema Studies*.

55 B. Singer, *Melodrama and Modernity*, pp. 118, 127.

56 C. Keil, 'To Here from Modernity', p. 52.

57 D. Bordwell, *On the History of Film Style*, p. 302, n. 100.

58 J. Staiger, 'The Future of the Past', *Cinema Journal*, 2004, vol. 44(1), pp. 128–129.

59 M. Lagny, 'Film History: or History Expropriated', p. 41; S. Kracauer, *From Caligari to Hitler: A Psychological History of the German Film*, Princeton, NJ: Princeton University Press, 1947, pp. 6, 8; R. Maltby, 'The Politics of the Maladjusted Text', in: I. Cameron (ed.), *The Movie Book of Film Noir*, London: Cassell, 1992, pp. 39–48.

60 M. Lagny, 'Film History: or History Expropriated', p. 41.

61 D. Bordwell, 'Film and the Historical Return'. See also D. Bordwell, 'Contemporary Film Studies and the Vicissitudes of Grand Theory' and N. Carroll, 'Prospects for Film Theory: A Personal Assessment', both in: D. Bordwell and N. Carroll (eds), *Post Theory: Reconstructing Film Studies*, Madison, WI: University of Wisconsin Press, 1996, pp. 27ff, 37–70.

62 J. Sedgwick *et al*, 'Proposal for a COST Action on the History of Film Exhibition and Reception', unpublished paper, September 2004.

63 K. Bowles and N. Huggett, 'Cowboys, Jaffas and Pies: Researching Cinemagoing in the Illawarra', in: R. Maltby and M. Stokes (eds), *Hollywood Abroad: Audiences and Cultural Exchange*, London: BFI, 2004, pp. 64–77.

64 Maurice Thorez, 18 April 1948, quoted in J.P. Jeancolas, 'From the Blum-Byrnes Agreement to the GATT Affair', in: G. Nowell-Smith and S. Ricci (eds), *Hollywood and Europe: Economics, Culture, National Identity, 1945–95*, London: BFI, 1998, p. 51.

65 Leo Lowenthal, quoted in Grieveson, 'Mimesis at the Movies.' The history of the 'disciplinarisation' of film studies, and in particular its establishment as a critically-based humanities subject and its divorce from earlier connections to the social sciences and communication studies, is traced in several essays in *Inventing Cinema Studies*, and in particular in Lee Grieveson and Haidee Wasson's 'Introduction: on the Histories of Studying Cinema'.

66 E. Le Roy Ladurie, *The Territory of the Historian*, Chicago, IL: University of Chicago Press, 1979, p. 285; E. P. Thompson, *The Making of the English Working Class*, London: Vintage, 1963, p. 12. See also F. Furet, 'Quantitative History', in: F. Gilbert and S. R. Grubard (eds), *Historical Studies Today*, New York: W. W. Norton, 1972.

67 E. P. Thompson, *The Making of the English Working Class*, p. 13.

68 C. Ginzburg, 'Checking the Evidence', pp. 89–90.

69 G. G. Iggers, *Historiography in the Twentieth Century*, p. 103.

70 G. Levi, 'On Microhistory', in: Peter Burke (ed.), *New Perspectives on Historical Writing*, University Park, PA: Berghahn 1992, pp. 91–113; G. Levi, *Inheriting Power: The Story of an Exorcist*, Chicago, IL: University of Chicago Press, 1988; C. Ginzburg, *The Cheese and the Worms: The Cosmos of* a *Sixteenth-Century Miller*, Baltimore, MD: Johns Hopkins University Press, 1980.

71 V. Sobchack, 'What is Film History?', p. 303.

72 R. Allen, 'Home Alone Together: Hollywood and the Family Film', in: M. Stokes and R. Maltby (eds), *Identifying Hollywood's Audiences: Cultural Identity and the Movies*, London: BFI, 1999, pp. 109–131.

73 R. Abel, 'History Can Work for You', p. 109.

74 'What is Being Done for Motion Pictures', statement by Will H. Hays, London, 5 October 1923, p. 8, in: D. Gomery (ed.), *The Will Hays Papers* (microfilm, Frederick MD 1986), part 1, reel 12, frame 813.

75 Quoted in S. Dumenco, 'Stopping Spin Laden', *New York Magazine*, 12 November 2001. Accessed from www.newyorkmetro.com/nymetro/news/media/features/5379/index2.html.

76 Charles Evans Hughes, 1924, quoted in J. Trumpbour, *Selling Hollywood to the World*, Cambridge: Cambridge University Press, 2002, p. 29.

77 Quoted in S. Dumenco, 'Stopping Spin Laden'.

78 F. Foer, quoted in 'Background Briefing: Culture Bombs', *Australian Broadcasting Corporation National Radio Broadcast*, 7 July 2002. Accessed at www.abc.net.au/m/talks/bbing/docs/bb_020707_culture.rtf.

79 Quoted in 'Background Briefing: Culture Bombs'.

80 R. Kuisel, *Seducing the French: The Dilemma of Americanization*, Berkeley, CA: University of California Press, 1993, p. 237.

81 V. de Grazia, *Irresistible Empire: America's Advance Through 20th-Century Europe*, Cambridge, MA: Harvard University Press, 2005, p. 3.

82 R. Maltby, 'Introduction: The Americanization of the World', in: R. Maltby and M. Stokes (eds), *Hollywood Abroad*, pp. 1–20.

83 E. S. Rosenberg, *Spreading the American Dream: American Economic* and *Cultural Expansion, 1890–1945*, New York: Hill and Wang, 1982, pp. 87–107, 122; Owen D. Young, speech, July 1930, quoted in F. Costigliola, *Awkward Dominion: American Political, Economic, and Cultural Relations with Europe, 1919–1933*, Ithaca, NY: Cornell University Press, 1984, p. 140.

84 O. D. Young, quoted in Costigliola, *Awkward Dominion*, p. 153.
85 V. de Grazia, 'Mass Culture and Sovereignty: The American Challenge to European Cinema, 1920–1960', *Journal of Modern History*, 1989, vol. 61, p. 60.
86 C. Frederick, *Selling Mrs. Consumer*, New York: University of Georgia Press, 1929, p. 5.
87 G. Cross, *An All-Consuming Century: Why Commercialism Won in Modern America*, New York: Columbia University Press, 2000, p. 1.
88 Ibid., p. 2.
89 Ibid., p. 21.
90 V. de Grazia, *Irresistible Empire*, pp. 78–95.
91 Ibid., p. 446.
92 Ibid., p. 107.
93 C. J. McKenna, 'Tripartheidism in Early American Movie-Going: Tracing the Development of Tri-racial Theaters in Robeson County, North Carolina (1896–1940)', in: R. Maltby, M. Stokes and R. Allen (eds), *Going to the Movies: Hollywood and the Social Experience of Moviegoing*, Exeter: University of Exeter Press, 2007.
94 S. Patten, *The New Basis of Civilization*, New York: Harvard University Press, 1907, p. 9.
95 www.cinemacontext.nl/.
96 V. De Grazia, *Irresistible Empire*, p. 100. An exemplary model for such a project can be found in J. Klenotic, 'Moviegoing and Everyday Life Outside the Movie Palace', in: R. Maltby, M. Stokes and R. Allen (eds), *Going to the Movies: Hollywood and the Social Experience of Moviegoing*.
97 C. Ginzburg, *The Cheese and the Worms*.
98 E. Le Roy Ladurie, *Montaillou: The Promised Land of Error*, New York, Vintage, 1978.

Filmography

Readers will note that there are in some cases discrepancies in the dates listed for particular films. This arises more often than not from the multiple release dates of films in different global localities. Where possible, the dates in this filmography derive from the database Film Index International, which is supported by the British Film Institute.

Above the Rim (1994)
directed by Jeff Pollack, New Line Cinema

Ace Ventura Pet Detective (1994)
directed by Tom Shadyac, Morgan Creek Productions

Aliens (1986)
directed by James Cameron, Twentieth-Century Fox

All that Heaven Allows (1955)
directed by Douglas Sirk, Universal International Pictures

All the President's Men (1976)
directed by Alan J. Pakula, Warner Bros.

Alphaville (1965)
directed by Jean-Luc Godard, Athos Films

Always Goodbye (1938)
directed by Sidney Lanfield, Twentieth-Century Fox

Amarcord (1973)
directed by Federico Fellini, FC Produzioni

American Graffiti (1973)
directed by George Lucas, Lucasfilm

An American in Paris (1951)
directed by Vincente Minnelli, MGM

An American Tail: Fievel Goes West (1991)
directed by Phil Nibbelink and Simon Wells, Universal Pictures

Amistad (1997)
directed by Steven Spielberg, DreamWorks SKG

And the Ship Sails On (1983)
directed by Federico Fellini, Vides Cinematografica

L'Anglaise et le Duc (*The Lady and the Duke*, 2001)
directed by Eric Rohmer, Compagnie Eric Rohmer (CER)

Ann Carver's Profession (1933)
directed by Edward Buzzell, Columbia Pictures

Another Country (1984)
directed by Marek Kanievska, Castlezone

Anthony Adverse (1936)
directed by Mervyn LeRoy, Warner Bros.

Apollo 13 (1995)
directed by Ron Howard, Universal Pictures

Aren't We Wonderful (*Wir Wunderkinder*) (1958)
directed by Kurt Hoffmann, Filmaufbau

Atonement (2007)
directed by Joe Wright, Working Title Films

Au revoir les enfants (1987)
directed by Louis Malle, MK2 Productions

Back to the Future (1985)
directed by Robert Zemeckis, Universal City Studios

Band of Brothers (2001)
directed by David Frankel and Tom Hanks, DreamWorks SKG

Barry Lyndon (1975)
directed by Stanley Kubrick, Warner Bros.

Battle of San Pietro (1945)
directed by John Huston, US Army Pictorial Services

Battleship Potemkin (*Bronenosets Potemkin*) (1925)
directed by Sergei Eisenstein, First Studio Goskino

Beauty and the Beast (1991)
directed by Gary Trousdale, Silver Screen Partners IV

Betrayal (1983)
directed by David Hugh Jones, Horizon Pictures

The Bicycle Thief (1948)
directed by Vittoria de Sica, Produzioni de Sica

The Big Store (1941)
directed by Charles Reisner, MGM

Black Hawk Down (2001)
directed by Ridley Scott, Revolution Studios Distribution LLC

Blow-up (1966)
directed by Michelangelo Antonioni, Bridge Films

Body Heat (1981)
directed by Lawrence Kasdan, The Ladd Company

Born on the Fourth of July (1989)
directed by Oliver Stone, Ixtlan

Braveheart (1995)
directed by Mel Gibson, B.H. Finance CV

Breathless (1960)
directed by Jean-Luc Godard, Les Productions des Georges de Beauregard

The Butcher Boy (1997)
directed by Neil Jordon, Butcher Boy Film

Camelot (1967)
directed by Joshua Logan, Warner Bros/Seven Arts

Camel Thru a Needle's Eye (1929)
directed by Martin Beck, Martin Beck Theatre

Les Camisards (1972)
directed by René Allio, Office de Radiodiffusion Télévision Française (ORTF)

Camp at Thiaroye (1988)
directed by Ousmane Sembène, Enaproc

Carrington (1995)
directed by Christopher Hampton, Canal Films

Carry On series (1958–76)
directed by Gerald Thomas, Peter Rogers Productions

Il Casanova di Federico Fellini (1976)
directed by Federico Fellini, Kapustan Industries N.V.

Casualties of War (1989)
directed by Brian de Palma, Columbia

Ceddo (1976)
directed by Sembène Ousmane, Filmi Doomireev

Chariots of Fire (1981)
directed by Hugh Hudson, Enigma Productions

The Cheat (1915)
directed by Cecil B. DeMille, Jesse L. Lasky Feature Play Company

Chicago (2002)
directed by Rob Marshall, KALIS Productions GmbH & Co. KG

Chinatown (1974)
directed by Roman Polanski, Long Road Productions

Cinema Paradiso (1988)
directed by Giuseppe Tornatore, Cristaldifilm

Citizen Kane (1941)
directed by Orson Welles, RKO Radio Pictures

The Civil War (1990)
directed by Ken Burns, American Documentaries Inc.

Cleopatra (1934)
directed by Cecil B. DeMille, Paramount Pictures

Collateral Damage (2002)
directed by Andrew Davis, Warner Bros.

Coming Home (1978)
directed by Hal Ashby, United Artists

Courage Under Fire (1996)
directed by Edward Zwick, Twentieth-Century Fox Film Corporation

Crimes and Misdemeanors (1989)
directed by Woody Allen, MGM

Crouching Tiger, Hidden Dragon (*Wo Hu Zang Long*) (2000)
directed by Ang Lee, United China Vision Incorporated

The Crow (1994)
directed by Alex Proyas, Crowvision

Dance with a Stranger (1985)
directed by Mike Newell, Channel Four Films

The Day the Clown Cried (*Le jour ou le clown pleura*) (1972)
directed by Jerry Lewis, Capitole Films (Paris)

Day of Wrath (1943)
directed by Carl Dreyer, Palladium Productions

Deconstructing Harry (1997)
directed by Woody Allen, Jean Doumanian

The Deer Hunter (1978)
directed by Michael Cimino, EMI

Dinner at Eight (1933)
directed by George Cukor, MGM

Distant Voices, Still Lives (1988)
directed by Terence Davies, British Film Institute Production Board

Doctor Zhivago (1965)
directed by David Lean, MGM

Down by Law (1986)
directed by Jim Jarmusch, Black Snake

Earthquake (1974)
directed by Mark Robson, The Filmmakers Group

Easy Rider (1969)
directed by Dennis Hopper, Columbia Pictures

Edward II (1991)
directed by Derek Jarman, British Broadcasting Corporation

8 Mile (2002)
directed by Curtis Hanson, Imagine Entertainment

84 Charlie Mopic (1989)
directed by Patrick Sheane Duncan, Charlie Mopic

Eijanaika (1981)
directed by Shohei Imamura, Imamura Productions, Shochiku Co. Ltd

Everybody Go Home (*Tutti a casa*) (1960)
directed by Luigi Comencini, Dino de Laurentis Cinematografica

Excalibur (1981)
directed by John Boorman, Orion Pictures

Exodus (1960)
directed by Otto Preminger, Otto Preminger Films

Fahrenheit 9/11 (2004)
directed by Michael Moore, Lions Gate

The Fall of the Roman Empire (1964)
directed by Anthony Moore, Rank

Farewell My Concubine (1993)
directed by Kaige Chen, Beijing Film Studio

Far from Heaven (2002)
directed by Todd Haynes, Vulcan Productions

Far from Poland (1984)
directed by Jill Godmilow, Beach Street Films

Fatal Attraction (1987)
directed by Adrian Lyne, Paramount

Fiddler on the Roof (1971)
directed by Norman Jewison, Cartier Productions

First Knight (1995)
directed by Jerry Zucker, Columbia

First Lady (1937)
directed by Stanley Logan, Warner Bros.

First Name Carmen (*Prénom Carmen*) (1984)
directed by Jean-Luc Godard, JLG Films

The Fisher King (1991)
directed by Terry Gilliam, Columbia

For Better, For Worse (1919)
directed by Cecil B. DeMille, Famous-Players Lasky Corporation

Forrest Gump (1994)
directed by Robert Zemeckis, Paramount Pictures

Four Days in July (1985)
directed by Mike Leigh, British Broadcasting Corporation

The French Lieutenant's Woman (1981)
directed by Karel Reisz, Juniper Films

Friday the 13th (1980)
directed by Sean S. Cunningham, Georgetown Productions

Full Metal Jacket (1987)
directed by Stanley Kubrick, Natant

Gambling Lady (1934)
directed by Archie Mayo, Warner Bros.

Gandhi (1982)
directed by Richard Attenborough, Carolina Bank Ltd.

Il Gattopardo (*Le guépard; The Leopard*) (1963)
directed by Luchino Visconti, Titanus

Genghis Cohn (1993)
directed by Elijah Moshinsky, A&E

Ghare Baire (*The Home and the World*) (1984)
directed by Satyajit Ray, National Film Development Corporation of India

The Ghost and Mrs Muir (1947)
directed by Joseph L. Mankiewicz, Twentieth-Century Fox

Gigolette (1935)
directed by Charles Lamont, Select Productions Inc.

Girl of My Dreams (*La niña de tus ojos*) (1998)
directed by Fernando Trueba, Cartel

Gladiator (2000)
directed by Ridley Scott, DreamWorks LLC

Glory (1989)
directed by Edward Zwick, TriStar

Go Into Your Dance (1935)
directed by Archie Mayo, Warner Bros.

Gold Diggers of 1933 (1933)
directed by Mervyn LeRoy, Warner Bros.

Gone with the Wind (1939)
directed by Victor Fleming, Selznick International Pictures

The Good Fight (1984)
directed by Noel Buckner, Abraham Lincoln Brigade Film Project

Good Morning, Vietnam (1987)
directed by Barry Levinson, Touchstone Pictures

The Goose and the Gander (1935)
directed by Alfred L. Green, Warner Bros.

The Graduate (1967)
directed by Mike Nichols, Embassy Pictures

Graduation Day in Baghdad (1930)
RKO

The Grand Illusion (*La grande illusion*) (1937)
directed by Jean Renoir, RAC

Grease (1978)
directed by Randal Kleiser, Paramount

The Great Dictator (1940)
directed by Charles Chaplin, Charles Chaplin Corporation

Gremlins (1984)
directed by Joe Dante, Warner Bros.

Hamburger Hill (1987)
directed by John Irvin, RKO

Harold and Maude (1971)
directed by Hal Ashby, Paramount

Hearts of Darkness (1991)
directed by Fax Bahr, Showtime

Henry V (1989)
directed by Kenneth Branagh, British Broadcasting Corporation

Heritage Africa (1988)
directed by Kwaw Ansah, Film Africa

High Noon (1952)
directed by Frank Zinnemann, Stanley Kramer Productions

Hiroshima, mon amour (1959)
directed by Alain Resnais, Argos Films

History of the World: Part I (1981)
directed by Mel Brooks, Brooksfilms Ltd

Hitler, a Film from Germany (1977)
directed by Hans-Jürgen Syberberg, Westdeutscher Rundfunk (WDR)

Hogan's Heroes (1965–71)
Bing Crosby Productions

Holocaust (1978)
directed by Marvin J. Chomsky, Titus Productions

Home Alone (1990)
directed by Chris Columbus, Hughes Entertainment

Hotel Terminus (1988)
directed by Marcel Ophuls, Samuel Goldwyn

The Human Beast (*La bête humaine*) (1938)
directed by Jean Renoir, Paris Film Production

I am a Fugitive from a Chain Gang (1932)
directed by Mervyn LeRoy, Warner Bros.

Imitation of Life (1959)
directed by Douglas Sirk, Universal International Pictures

I'm Not There (2007)
directed by Todd Haynes, Killer Films

In Caliente (1935)
directed by Lloyd Bacon, Warner Bros.

Independence Day (1996)
directed by Roland Emmerich, Twentieth-Century Fox

In My Merrie Oldsmobile (1931)
directed by Davie Fleischer, Fleischer Studios

In the Name of the Father (1993)
directed by Jim Sheridan, Hell's Kitchen Films

Intolerance (1916)
directed by D. W. Griffith, Wark Producing Corporation

It Pays to Advertise (1931)
directed by Frank Tuttle, Paramount Pictures

Ivan and Abraham (*Moi Ivan, toi Abraham*) (1993)
directed by Yolande Zauberman, Belarus Film

Ivan the Terrible (*Ivan Grozni*) (1945)
directed by Sergei M. Eisenstein, Mosfilm

Jacob the Liar (*Jakob, der Lügner*) (1974)
directed by Frank Breyer, DEFA-Studio für Spielfilme, Deutscher Fernsehfunk, Filmové Studio Barrandov, Westdeutscher Rundfunk

Jefferson in Paris (1995)
directed by James Ivory, Touchstone

Jerry McGuire (1996)
directed by Cameron Crowe, Gracie Films

Je t'aime je t'aime (1968)
directed by Alain Resnais, Parc Film

The Jewel in the Crown (1984)
directed by Christopher Morahan and Jim O'Brien, Granada Television

JFK (1991)
directed by Oliver Stone, Warner Bros.

A Jolt for General Germ (1930)
Paramount Pictures

The Joy Luck Club (1993)
directed by Wayne Wang, Hollywood Pictures

Julius Caesar (1953)
directed by Joseph L. Mankiewicz, Loew's Incorporated

Jurassic Park (1993)
directed by Steven Spielberg, Universal City Studios

Kate and Leopold (2001)
directed by James Mangold, Konrad Pictures

La Kermess héroique (1935)
directed by Jacques Feyder, Films Sonores Tobis

King Arthur (2004)
directed by Antoine Fuqua, Touchstone Pictures

Knights of the Round Table (1953)
directed by Richard Thorpe, MGM

The Knights of the Square Table (1917)
directed by Alan Crosland, Thomas Edison

The Last Butterfly (*Posledni motyl*) (1991)
directed by Karol Kachyna, Atlantique Productions

The Last Picture Show (1971)
directed by Peter Bogdanovich, BBS Productions

Last Year at Marienbad (1961)
directed by Alain Resnais, Argos Films

Lawrence of Arabia (1962)
directed by David Lean, Ace Films Productions

Lethal Weapon 2 (1989)
directed by Richard Donner, Warner Bros.

Let's Make Love (1960)
directed by George Cukor, Company of Artists

Life is Beautiful (*La vita è bella*) (1997)
directed by Roberto Benigni, Melampo Cinematografica srl (Rome)

The Lord of the Rings: The Fellowship of the Ring (2001)
directed by Peter Jackson, New Line Cinema

The Lord of the Rings: The Return of the King (2003)
directed by Peter Jackson, New Line Cinema

The Lord of the Rings: The Two Towers (2002)
directed by Peter Jackson, New Line Cinema

Love is a Many-Splendoured Thing (1955)
directed by Henry King, Twentieth-Century Fox

Madame Bovary (1933)
directed by Jean Renoir, NSF-Gaston Gallimard

Madonna: Truth or Dare (1991)
directed by Alek Keshishian, Boy Toy

Malcolm X (1992)
directed by Spike Lee, 40 Acres and a Mule Filmworks

Marie Antoinette (2006)
directed by Sofia Coppola, Columbia Pictures

La Marseillaise (1937)
directed by Jean Renoir, Société de Production et d'Exploitation du Film

Mary Poppins (1964)
directed by Robert Stevenson, Walt Disney Productions

The Matrix (1999)
directed by Andy Wachowski and Larry Wachowski, Warner Bros.

Maurice (1987)
directed by James Ivory, Merchant Ivory Productions

Me and the Colonel (1958)
directed by Peter Glenville, Court Enterprises

Mediterraneo (1991)
directed by Gabriele Salvatores, AMA Film

Medium (1995–)
CBS

Michael Collins (1996)
directed by Neil Jordon, Warner Bros.

Missing in Action (1984)
directed by Joseph Zito, Cannon Films

The Mission (1986)
directed by Roland Joffé, Warner Bros.

Mississippi Masala (1991)
directed by Mira Nair, Black River Productions

Moi, Pierre Rivière (1976)
directed by René Allio, Arquebuse

Monty Python and the Holy Grail (1975)
directed by Terry Gilliam and Terry Jones, Michael White

Moon Pilot (1962)
directed by James Neilson, Walt Disney Pictures

Mother's Courage (*Mutters Courage*) (1995)
directed by Michael Verhoeven, Sentana Filmproduktion

Moulin Rouge! (2001)
directed by Baz Luhrmann, Twentieth-Century Fox Film Corporation

Movie Memories (1935)
Paramount

Mueda, Memoria e Massacre (1980)
directed by Ruy Guerra

The Mummy (1999)
directed by Stephen Sommers, Universal Pictures

The Mummy Returns (2001)
directed by Stephen Sommers, Universal Pictures

Naked Among Wolves (*Nackt unter Wölfen*) (1963)
directed by Frank Beyer, Deutsche Film (DEFA)

The Nasty Girl (*Das Schreckliche Mädchen*) (1990)
directed by Michael Verhoeven, Film Verlag der Autoren

Never on Sunday (1960)
directed by Jules Dassin, Lopert Pictures

Night and Fog (*Nuit et brouillard*) (1955)
directed by Alain Resnais, Argos-Films

A Night at the Ritz (1935)
directed by William C. McGann, Warner Bros.

Night on Earth (1991)
directed by Jim Jarmusch, Victor Company of Japan (JVC)

1900 (1976)
directed by Bernardo Bertolucci, Produzioni Europee Associati

Nixon (1995)
directed by Oliver Stone, Cinergi Productions N.V. Inc.

Nosferatu (1922)
directed by F. W. Murnau, Jofa-Atelier Berlin-Johannisthal

La nuit de Varennes (1982)
directed by Ettore Scola, France 3 (FR3)

October (*Oktiabr*) (1928)
directed by Sergei M. Eisenstein, Sovkino

Of Human Bondage (1934)
directed by John Cromwell, RKO Radio Pictures

An Officer and a Gentleman (1982)
directed by Taylor Hackford, Capital Equipment Leasing

On the Slopes of the Andes (1930)
RKO

The Pace that Kills (1935)
directed by William O'Connor, Willis Kent Pictures

Paisan (1946)
directed by Roberto Rossellini, Organizzazione Film Internazionali

Pan's Labyrinth (2006)
directed by Guillermo del Toro, Tequila Gang

Panther (1995)
directed by Mario Van Peebles, Gramercy

Paris is Burning (1990)
directed by Jeanie Livingston, Off White Productions Inc.

A Passage to India (1984)
directed by David Lean, EMI Films

Passion (*Passion amour/travail*) (1982)
directed by Jean-Luc Godard, Sonimage

La passion de Jeanne d'Arc (1928)
directed by Carl Theodor Dreyer, Société générale des films

Pearl Harbor (2001)
directed by Michael Bay, Touchstone Pictures

Platoon (1986)
directed by Oliver Stone, Cinema 86

The Poseidon Adventure (1972)
directed by Ronald Neame, Irwin Allen Productions

Possessed (1947)
directed by Curtis Bernhardt, Warner Bros.

The Private Life of Henry VIII (1933)
directed by Alexander Korda, London Film Productions and United Artists

The Producers (1968)
directed by Mel Brooks, Embassy Pictures Corporation

Punch Me in the Stomach (1994)
directed by Francine Zuckerman, Punch Me in the Stomach Films

Queen Christina (1933)
directed by Rouben Mamoulian, MGM

Que la fête commence (*Let Joy Reign Supreme*) (1975)
directed by Bernard Tavernier, Fildebroc

Quilombo (1984)
directed by Carlos Diegues, CDK

Radio Bikini (1987)
directed by Robert Stone, Crossroads

The Rainmakers (aka *Silver Streak*) (1935)
directed by Frank Gioul, RKO Radio Pictures

Rain Man (1988)
directed by Barry Levinson, United Artists

Raise the Red Lantern (1991)
directed by Yimou Zhang, Century Communications

Rambo: First Blood Part II (1985)
directed by George P. Cosmatos, Carolco Pictures Inc.

Rashomon (1950)
directed by Akira Kurosawa, Daiei

Reds (1981)
directed by Warren Beatty, Barclays Mercantile Industrial Finance

Rembrandt (1936)
directed by Alexander Korda, London Film Productions

The Return of Martin Guerre (*Le retour de Martin Guerre*) (1982)
directed by Daniel Vigne, Société Française de Production de Cinéma

Roger and Me (1989)
directed by Michael Moore, Dog Eat Dog Films

Rome, Open City (*Roma, città aperta*) (1945)
directed by Roberto Rossellini, Excelsa

Roots (1977)
directed by Marvin J. Chomsky and others, David L. Wolper Productions

The Rules of the Game (*La règle du jeu*) (1939)
directed by Jean Renoir, Nouvelle Edition Française

Rumba (1935)
directed by Marion Gering, Paramount

Sans Soleil (1982)
directed by Chris Marker, Argos Films

Saturday Night Fever (1977)
directed by John Badham, Robert Stigwood Organization (RSO)

Saving Private Ryan (1998)
directed by Steven Spielberg, DreamWorks SKG

Scandal (1988)
directed by Michael Caton-Jones, British Screen Productions

Scarface (1983)
directed by Brian de Palma, Universal Pictures

The Scarlet Empress (1934)
directed by Josef von Sternberg, Paramount Productions

Schindler's List (1993)
directed by Steven Spielberg, Universal Pictures

The Searchers (1956)
directed by John Ford, C. V. Whitney Pictures Company

Secrets of a Soul (*Geheimnisse eine Seele*) (1926)
directed by Georg Wilhelm Pabst, Neumann FilmProduktion

Senso (1954)
directed by Luchino Visconti, Lux Film (Rome)

Sergeant York (1941)
directed by Howard Hawks, Warner Bros.

Seven Beauties (*Pascaline settebellezze*) (1975)
directed by Lina Wertmüller, Medusa Produzione

Seventh Heaven (1927)
directed by Frank Borzage, Fox Film Corporation

The Shadow of the Vampire (2000)
directed by E. Elias Merhige, British Broadcasting Corporation

Shakespeare in Love (1998)
directed by John Madden, Universal

Shoah (1985)
directed by Claude Lanzmann, Films Aleph

The Shop on Main Street (*Obchod na Korze*) (1965)
directed by Ján Kádár, Filmmové Studio Barrandov

The Sign of the Cross (1932)
directed by Cecil B. DeMille, Paramount Publix Corporation

6 Day Bike Rider (1934)
directed by Lloyd Bacon, First National Pictures

Six Feet Under (1996–2001)
Home Box Office (HBO)

The Sixth Sense (1999)
directed by M. Night Shyamalan, Barry Mendel

Sleepless in Seattle (1993)
directed by Nora Ephron, TriStar Pictures

Sleepy Hollow (1999)
directed by Tim Burton, Paramount Pictures

Slow Motion (*Sauve qui peut (la vie)*) (1980)
directed by Jean-Luc Godard, Centre National de la Cinématographie

Solaris (2002)
directed by Steven Soderbergh, Twentieth Century Fox

Son of the Pink Panther (1993)
directed by Blake Edwards, Filmauro

Spartacus (1960)
directed by Stanley Kubrick, Universal Pictures Company

Stalag 17 (1953)
directed by Billy Wilder, Paramount

Star Wars (1977)
directed by George Lucas, Lucasfilm

Star Wars: Episode I – The Phantom Menace (1999)
directed by George Lucas, Lucasfilm

The Story of Adèle H. (1975)
directed by François Truffaut, Les Films du Carrosse

Strangers All (1935)
directed by Charles Vidor, RKO

A Summer Place (1959)
directed by Delmer Daves, Warner Bros.

Swimming to Cambodia (1987)
directed by Jonathan Demme, The Swimming Customer

Sword of Lancelot (1963)
directed by Cornel Wilde, Emblem

The Ten Commandments (1923)
directed by Cecil B. DeMille, Paramount Pictures

The Ten Commandments (1956)
directed by Cecil B. DeMille, Paramount Pictures

Tess (1979)
directed by Roman Polanski, Renn Productions

Test Pilot (1938)
directed by Victor Fleming, MGM

That Darn Cat (1965)
directed by Robert Stevenson, Walt Disney Pictures

The Thin Blue Line (1987)
directed by Errol Morris, American Playhouse

The Thin Red Line (1998)
directed by Terrence Malick, Fox 2000

35 Up (1991)
directed by Michael Apted, Granada Television

Three Days of the Condor (1975)
directed by Sydney Pollack, Dino de Laurentiis

300 (2006)
directed by Zack Snyder, Warner Bros.

Three Kings (1999)
directed by David O. Russell, Warner Bros.

Thunderheart (1992)
directed by Michael Apted, Tribeca

Titanic (1997)
directed by James Cameron, Twentieth-Century Fox Film Corporation

To Be or Not to Be (1942)
directed by Ernst Lubitsch, Romaine Film Corporation

To Be or Not to Be (1983)
directed by Alan Johnson, Brooksfilm

Train of Life (*Train de vie*) (1998)
directed by Radu Mihaileanu, Noe Productions

Tree of Wooden Clogs (*L'albero degli zoccoli*) (1978)
directed by Ermanno Olmi, Rai

Triumph of the Will (*Triumph des Willens: Das Dokument vom Reichsparteitag 1934*) (1936)
directed by Leni Riefenstahl, Nazionalsozialistische Deutsche Arbeiterpartei

The Two of Us (*Le vieil homme et l'enfant*) (1966)
directed by Claude Berri, PAC

Uncle Tom's Cabin (1903)
directed by Edwin S. Porter, Edison

Uncommon Valor (1983)
directed by Ted Kotcheff, Milius Feitschans

Underground (1995)
directed by Emir Kusturica, CiBy 2000

Up Close and Personal (1996)
directed by Jon Avnet, Avnet/Kerner Productions

La vie est à nous (1936)
directed by Jean Renoir, Parti Communiste Français

We Were Soldiers (2002)
directed by Randall Wallace, Motion Picture Production GmbH & C Erste KG

What Price Glory? (1926)
directed by Raoul Walsh, Fox Film Corporation

Who Killed Vincent Chin? (1988)
directed by Chris Choy and Renee Tajima, WVTA Detroit

Why Change Your Wife? (1920)
directed by Cecil B. DeMille, Artcraft Pictures

Wild Strawberries (*Smultronstället*) (1957)
directed by Ingmar Bergman, Svensk Filmindustri

You Natzy Spy! (1940)
directed by Jules White, Columbia Pictures

Young Mr Lincoln (1939)
directed by John Ford, Cosmopolitan Films

Young Mr Pitt (1942)
directed by Carol Reed, Twentieth-Century Fox

Zulu (1964)
directed by Cy Endfield, Diamond Films

Index